Lecture Notes in Computer Science 14738

Founding Editors

Gerhard Goos
Juris Hartmanis

The series Lecture Notes in Computer Science (LNCS), including its subseries Lecture Notes in Artificial Intelligence (LNAI) and Lecture Notes in Bioinformatics (LNBI), has established itself as a medium for the publication of new developments in computer science and information technology research, teaching, and education.

LNCS enjoys close cooperation with the computer science R & D community, the series counts many renowned academics among its volume editors and paper authors, and collaborates with prestigious societies. Its mission is to serve this international community by providing an invaluable service, mainly focused on the publication of conference and workshop proceedings and postproceedings. LNCS commenced publication in 1973.

June Wei · George Margetis

Editors

Human-Centered Design, Operation and Evaluation of Mobile Communications

5th International Conference, MOBILE 2024
Held as Part of the 26th HCI International Conference, HCII 2024
Washington, DC, USA, June 29 – July 4, 2024
Proceedings, Part II

 Springer

Editors
June Wei
University of West Florida
Pensacola, FL, USA

George Margetis
Foundation for Research
and Technology – Hellas (FORTH)
Heraklion, Crete, Greece

ISSN 0302-9743 ISSN 1611-3349 (electronic)
Lecture Notes in Computer Science
ISBN 978-3-031-60486-7 ISBN 978-3-031-60487-4 (eBook)
https://doi.org/10.1007/978-3-031-60487-4

Foreword

This year we celebrate 40 years since the establishment of the HCI International (HCII) Conference, which has been a hub for presenting groundbreaking research and novel ideas and collaboration for people from all over the world.

The HCII conference was founded in 1984 by Prof. Gavriel Salvendy (Purdue University, USA, Tsinghua University, P.R. China, and University of Central Florida, USA) and the first event of the series, "1st USA-Japan Conference on Human-Computer Interaction", was held in Honolulu, Hawaii, USA, 18–20 August. Since then, HCI International is held jointly with several Thematic Areas and Affiliated Conferences, with each one under the auspices of a distinguished international Program Board and under one management and one registration. Twenty-six HCI International Conferences have been organized so far (every two years until 2013, and annually thereafter).

Over the years, this conference has served as a platform for scholars, researchers, industry experts and students to exchange ideas, connect, and address challenges in the ever-evolving HCI field. Throughout these 40 years, the conference has evolved itself, adapting to new technologies and emerging trends, while staying committed to its core mission of advancing knowledge and driving change.

As we celebrate this milestone anniversary, we reflect on the contributions of its founding members and appreciate the commitment of its current and past Affiliated Conference Program Board Chairs and members. We are also thankful to all past conference attendees who have shaped this community into what it is today.

The 26th International Conference on Human-Computer Interaction, HCI International 2024 (HCII 2024), was held as a 'hybrid' event at the Washington Hilton Hotel, Washington, DC, USA, during 29 June – 4 July 2024. It incorporated the 21 thematic areas and affiliated conferences listed below.

A total of 5108 individuals from academia, research institutes, industry, and government agencies from 85 countries submitted contributions, and 1271 papers and 309 posters were included in the volumes of the proceedings that were published just before the start of the conference, these are listed below. The contributions thoroughly cover the entire field of human-computer interaction, addressing major advances in knowledge and effective use of computers in a variety of application areas. These papers provide academics, researchers, engineers, scientists, practitioners and students with state-of-the-art information on the most recent advances in HCI.

The HCI International (HCII) conference also offers the option of presenting 'Late Breaking Work', and this applies both for papers and posters, with corresponding volumes of proceedings that will be published after the conference. Full papers will be included in the 'HCII 2024 - Late Breaking Papers' volumes of the proceedings to be published in the Springer LNCS series, while 'Poster Extended Abstracts' will be included as short research papers in the 'HCII 2024 - Late Breaking Posters' volumes to be published in the Springer CCIS series.

I would like to thank the Program Board Chairs and the members of the Program Boards of all thematic areas and affiliated conferences for their contribution towards the high scientific quality and overall success of the HCI International 2024 conference. Their manifold support in terms of paper reviewing (single-blind review process, with a minimum of two reviews per submission), session organization and their willingness to act as goodwill ambassadors for the conference is most highly appreciated.

This conference would not have been possible without the continuous and unwavering support and advice of Gavriel Salvendy, founder, General Chair Emeritus, and Scientific Advisor. For his outstanding efforts, I would like to express my sincere appreciation to Abbas Moallem, Communications Chair and Editor of HCI International News.

July 2024   Constantine Stephanidis

HCI International 2024 Thematic Areas
and Affiliated Conferences

- HCI: Human-Computer Interaction Thematic Area
- HIMI: Human Interface and the Management of Information Thematic Area
- EPCE: 21st International Conference on Engineering Psychology and Cognitive Ergonomics
- AC: 18th International Conference on Augmented Cognition
- UAHCI: 18th International Conference on Universal Access in Human-Computer Interaction
- CCD: 16th International Conference on Cross-Cultural Design
- SCSM: 16th International Conference on Social Computing and Social Media
- VAMR: 16th International Conference on Virtual, Augmented and Mixed Reality
- DHM: 15th International Conference on Digital Human Modeling & Applications in Health, Safety, Ergonomics & Risk Management
- DUXU: 13th International Conference on Design, User Experience and Usability
- C&C: 12th International Conference on Culture and Computing
- DAPI: 12th International Conference on Distributed, Ambient and Pervasive Interactions
- HCIBGO: 11th International Conference on HCI in Business, Government and Organizations
- LCT: 11th International Conference on Learning and Collaboration Technologies
- ITAP: 10th International Conference on Human Aspects of IT for the Aged Population
- AIS: 6th International Conference on Adaptive Instructional Systems
- HCI-CPT: 6th International Conference on HCI for Cybersecurity, Privacy and Trust
- HCI-Games: 6th International Conference on HCI in Games
- MobiTAS: 6th International Conference on HCI in Mobility, Transport and Automotive Systems
- AI-HCI: 5th International Conference on Artificial Intelligence in HCI
- MOBILE: 5th International Conference on Human-Centered Design, Operation and Evaluation of Mobile Communications

List of Conference Proceedings Volumes Appearing Before the Conference

1. LNCS 14684, Human-Computer Interaction: Part I, edited by Masaaki Kurosu and Ayako Hashizume
2. LNCS 14685, Human-Computer Interaction: Part II, edited by Masaaki Kurosu and Ayako Hashizume
3. LNCS 14686, Human-Computer Interaction: Part III, edited by Masaaki Kurosu and Ayako Hashizume
4. LNCS 14687, Human-Computer Interaction: Part IV, edited by Masaaki Kurosu and Ayako Hashizume
5. LNCS 14688, Human-Computer Interaction: Part V, edited by Masaaki Kurosu and Ayako Hashizume
6. LNCS 14689, Human Interface and the Management of Information: Part I, edited by Hirohiko Mori and Yumi Asahi
7. LNCS 14690, Human Interface and the Management of Information: Part II, edited by Hirohiko Mori and Yumi Asahi
8. LNCS 14691, Human Interface and the Management of Information: Part III, edited by Hirohiko Mori and Yumi Asahi
9. LNAI 14692, Engineering Psychology and Cognitive Ergonomics: Part I, edited by Don Harris and Wen-Chin Li
10. LNAI 14693, Engineering Psychology and Cognitive Ergonomics: Part II, edited by Don Harris and Wen-Chin Li
11. LNAI 14694, Augmented Cognition, Part I, edited by Dylan D. Schmorrow and Cali M. Fidopiastis
12. LNAI 14695, Augmented Cognition, Part II, edited by Dylan D. Schmorrow and Cali M. Fidopiastis
13. LNCS 14696, Universal Access in Human-Computer Interaction: Part I, edited by Margherita Antona and Constantine Stephanidis
14. LNCS 14697, Universal Access in Human-Computer Interaction: Part II, edited by Margherita Antona and Constantine Stephanidis
15. LNCS 14698, Universal Access in Human-Computer Interaction: Part III, edited by Margherita Antona and Constantine Stephanidis
16. LNCS 14699, Cross-Cultural Design: Part I, edited by Pei-Luen Patrick Rau
17. LNCS 14700, Cross-Cultural Design: Part II, edited by Pei-Luen Patrick Rau
18. LNCS 14701, Cross-Cultural Design: Part III, edited by Pei-Luen Patrick Rau
19. LNCS 14702, Cross-Cultural Design: Part IV, edited by Pei-Luen Patrick Rau
20. LNCS 14703, Social Computing and Social Media: Part I, edited by Adela Coman and Simona Vasilache
21. LNCS 14704, Social Computing and Social Media: Part II, edited by Adela Coman and Simona Vasilache
22. LNCS 14705, Social Computing and Social Media: Part III, edited by Adela Coman and Simona Vasilache

47. LNCS 14730, HCI in Games: Part I, edited by Xiaowen Fang
48. LNCS 14731, HCI in Games: Part II, edited by Xiaowen Fang
49. LNCS 14732, HCI in Mobility, Transport and Automotive Systems: Part I, edited by Heidi Krömker
50. LNCS 14733, HCI in Mobility, Transport and Automotive Systems: Part II, edited by Heidi Krömker
51. LNAI 14734, Artificial Intelligence in HCI: Part I, edited by Helmut Degen and Stavroula Ntoa
52. LNAI 14735, Artificial Intelligence in HCI: Part II, edited by Helmut Degen and Stavroula Ntoa
53. LNAI 14736, Artificial Intelligence in HCI: Part III, edited by Helmut Degen and Stavroula Ntoa
54. LNCS 14737, Design, Operation and Evaluation of Mobile Communications: Part I, edited by June Wei and George Margetis
55. LNCS 14738, Design, Operation and Evaluation of Mobile Communications: Part II, edited by June Wei and George Margetis
56. CCIS 2114, HCI International 2024 Posters - Part I, edited by Constantine Stephanidis, Margherita Antona, Stavroula Ntoa and Gavriel Salvendy
57. CCIS 2115, HCI International 2024 Posters - Part II, edited by Constantine Stephanidis, Margherita Antona, Stavroula Ntoa and Gavriel Salvendy
58. CCIS 2116, HCI International 2024 Posters - Part III, edited by Constantine Stephanidis, Margherita Antona, Stavroula Ntoa and Gavriel Salvendy
59. CCIS 2117, HCI International 2024 Posters - Part IV, edited by Constantine Stephanidis, Margherita Antona, Stavroula Ntoa and Gavriel Salvendy
60. CCIS 2118, HCI International 2024 Posters - Part V, edited by Constantine Stephanidis, Margherita Antona, Stavroula Ntoa and Gavriel Salvendy
61. CCIS 2119, HCI International 2024 Posters - Part VI, edited by Constantine Stephanidis, Margherita Antona, Stavroula Ntoa and Gavriel Salvendy
62. CCIS 2120, HCI International 2024 Posters - Part VII, edited by Constantine Stephanidis, Margherita Antona, Stavroula Ntoa and Gavriel Salvendy

https://2024.hci.international/proceedings

Preface

With the rapid technological advances of mobile communications, mobile applications are not only changing people's living style but also changing operation, management, and innovation in organizations, industries, and governments in a new way, which further impacts the economy, society, and culture all over the world. Human-computer interaction plays an important role in this transition.

The 5th International Conference on Human-Centered Design, Operation and Evaluation of Mobile Communications (MOBILE 2024), an affiliated conference of the HCI International conference, addressed the design, operation, evaluation, and adoption of mobile technologies and applications for consumers, industries, organizations, and governments. The purpose of this conference is to provide a platform for researchers and practitioners from academia, industry, and government to discuss challenging ideas, novel research contributions, and the current theory and practice of related mobile communications research topics and applications.

The papers accepted for publication this year offer a comprehensive overview of the prevalent themes and subjects in the field of mobile communications. In particular, in the domain of mobile user experience and interaction design the accepted papers explore a diverse range of topics related to user requirements, design research and evaluation across a wide variety of contexts, and delve into preferences and behavior analysis for different target groups. Motivated by the proliferation of smartphones and mobile devices and their potential to revolutionize healthcare, promote healthier lifestyles, and improve overall well-being, a considerable number of submissions have explored the role of intuitive interfaces, personalized experiences, and seamless integration of sensors and wearables to empower users' health and support behavior change. Furthermore, exploring the limitless possibilities of Augmented Reality and mobile technologies, submissions showcased how we can reshape our interactions with the world around us, offering insights into a future of boundless innovation and progress. Finally, articles in this volume introduce examples of mobile applications, detailing their design and overall user experience. Emphasis is placed on application domains where mobile apps have made significant strides, including education, commerce, marketing, but also privacy, and security. We invite readers to delve into this collection of papers, which offers valuable insights and state-of-the-art methods, procedures, and applications to researchers, designers, developers, or simply anyone interested in the transformative potential of mobile technologies toward technology for a better world.

Two volumes of the HCII 2024 proceedings are dedicated to this year's edition of the MOBILE conference. The first focuses on topics related to Mobile Health and Well-being, Mobile Applications, Serious Games, and Advanced interfaces, while the second focuses on topics related to Mobile Commerce, Marketing and Retail, Mobile Security, Privacy and Safety, and Mobile User Experience and Design.

The papers of this volume were accepted for publication after a minimum of two single-blind reviews from the members of the MOBILE Program Board or, in some cases, from members of the Program Boards of other affiliated conferences. We would like to thank all of them for their invaluable contribution, support, and efforts.

July 2024   June Wei
                                                                            George Margetis

5th International Conference on Human-Centered Design, Operation and Evaluation of Mobile Communications (MOBILE 2024)

The full list with the Program Board Chairs and the members of the Program Boards of all thematic areas and affiliated conferences of HCII 2024 is available online at:

http://www.hci.international/board-members-2024.php

HCI International 2025 Conference

The 27th International Conference on Human-Computer Interaction, HCI International 2025, will be held jointly with the affiliated conferences at the Swedish Exhibition & Congress Centre and Gothia Towers Hotel, Gothenburg, Sweden, June 22–27, 2025. It will cover a broad spectrum of themes related to Human-Computer Interaction, including theoretical issues, methods, tools, processes, and case studies in HCI design, as well as novel interaction techniques, interfaces, and applications. The proceedings will be published by Springer. More information will become available on the conference website: https://2025.hci.international/.

General Chair
Prof. Constantine Stephanidis
University of Crete and ICS-FORTH
Heraklion, Crete, Greece
Email: general_chair@2025.hci.international

https://2025.hci.international/

Contents – Part II

Mobile Security, Privacy and Safety

Mobile User Experience and Design

Contents – Part I

Mobile Applications, Serious Games and Advanced Interfaces

Mobile Commerce, Marketing and Retail

Online Commerce and Beehive Adoption Services Through User-Centred Design: The MyHive Platform for Direct Beekeeper-Consumer Interaction

Charalambos Alifieris[1], Theodora Chamaidi[1] , Katerina Malisova[1] ,
Nikolaos Politopoulos[1] , Chrysostomos Rigakis[1], Sofia Gounari[2],
and Modestos Stavrakis[1]([⊠])

[1] Department of Product and Systems Design Engineering, University of the Aegean,
84100 Syros, Greece
{babis,theodora.chamaidi,katemalisova,npol,chr.rigakis,
modestos}@aegean.gr
[2] Lab. of Apiculture, Inst. of Mediterranean Forest Ecosystems, Hellenic Agricultural
Organization, DEMETER, Terma Alkmanos Str., 11528 Ilisia, Athens Hellas, Greece
sgounari@fria.gr

Abstract. The paper presents the design and implications of the MyHive e-commerce platform, a system that promotes direct interaction between beekeepers and consumers. It addresses the challenges faced by beekeepers in traditional commerce and demonstrates how the Beehive Adoption Marketing Strategy, supported by a user-centered design approach, can potentially mitigate these issues. The research presented in this paper outlines the user experience (UX)/Interaction Design processes used in MyHive's development and proposes a design approach that integrates User-Centred Design in E-commerce, the Beehive Adoption Marketing Strategy, and the application of technology in apiculture. The study proposes a design and marketing strategy of beehive adoption as a service and through this underscores the importance of direct beekeeper-consumer engagement for environmental conservation and sustainable beekeeping practices, offering insights for designers of similar platforms and services.

Keywords: beehive adoption · user-centered design · e-commerce

1 Introduction

Mobile technologies, devices and applications are revolutionising service engagement in various industries, including apiculture. Through these digital platforms, consumers and beekeepers can interact directly, creating a novel space for commerce, education, and environmental conservation. Technology has the potential to bridge the gap between the often-overlooked world of beekeeping and its commercial character and a new generation of environmentally conscious consumers who seek an active role in preserving bee populations and supporting sustainable practices.

J. Wei and G. Margetis (Eds.): HCII 2024, LNCS 14738, pp. 3–19, 2024.
https://doi.org/10.1007/978-3-031-60487-4_1

The introduction of "MyHive", part of the IOHIVE Project [1–3], is an example of this evolution in online (desktop e-commerce and mobile commerce / m-commerce), where it's not just about purchasing bee products, but also embracing services that resonate with consumers' values and interests towards apiculture, both in terms of preserving biodiversity and cultural heritage. Central to the marketing approach of MyHive is the strategy of beehive adoption [4].

The objective of this paper is twofold and is significantly informed by the insights and experiences derived from the development of the MyHive and IOHIVE projects. Firstly, it aims to identify the challenges that beekeepers face within traditional commerce models and explores the potential role of technology in tackling these issues. This section will include an overview of MyHive's business model, and its *Beehive Adoption Marketing Strategy* used to inform the design of the actual service for the beekeeping community. Secondly, the paper focuses on the User Experience (UX)/Interaction Design and user engagement mechanisms that were followed through its methodology, design, and prototyping practices. Building on this ground, the paper proposes a design approach and language to assist designers of similar products in producing and evaluating services and applications tailored to these specific user groups. The proposed approach is connected with three fundamental pillars: a) User-Centred Design (UCD) in E-commerce, b) Beehive Adoption Marketing Strategy (proposed and analysed later in this paper), and c) Apiculture and Technology, with emphasis on smart beekeeping technologies.

The paper is structured as follows: Sect. 2 reviews similar projects, identifying their objectives, strategies, and technologies utilised. Section 3 presents the Beehive Adoption Marketing Strategy employed in this project. Section 4 offers a concise overview of the MyHive platform, focusing on its core functionality. Section 5 describes the methodology and analyses the phases involved in completing this project, including research, design, and evaluation. Finally, Sect. 6 provides a discussion on the process and its results.

2 Related Work

Undoubtedly, apiculture, or beekeeping, plays a crucial role in biodiversity and holds significant cultural importance across various societies. Bees, through pollination, facilitate the reproduction of numerous plants, including those vital for food crops, thus sustaining a cyclical condition essential for the maintenance of biodiversity [5]. The cultural significance of beekeeping extends back thousands of years, reflecting in ancient traditions, religious practices, and folklore, symbolising community, diligence, and harmony with nature, reflecting the deep-rooted respect societies have held for bees and their role in the natural world [6]. However, beekeepers, the actual producers of bee products of today, face challenges in traditional commerce models [7]. These challenges include market access difficulties, price volatility, and competition with large-scale commercial operations [8, 9]. Moreover, environmental threats such as climate change, habitat loss, and pesticide use worsen the struggles for beekeepers, impacting bee health and their productivity. The potential role of technology in addressing these challenges is significant and can contribute through many channels including precision apiculture [10], supply chain management [11], climate modelling and forecasting tools [12], digital education and networking [13], other digital beekeeping technologies [14, 15] and market access and digital platforms [16–18]. For instance, several studies highlight the use of smart technologies, IoT and wireless sensor network-based infrastructure for precision apiculture [10, 19–21]. These technologies allow for the gathering of data by monitoring the productivity of beehive colonies, with sensors deployed to capture various parameters such as temperature, humidity, and weight of the combs. This approach can significantly inform and thus help beekeepers optimise hive conditions, improve health and productivity of bees, and ultimately enhance their commercial viability. Incorporating such technologies into apiculture offers an alternative route to overcome traditional challenges by enabling better monitoring and management of bee health, enhancing productivity, and opening new paths for market access and integration into digital commerce platforms. On top of these, this technological integration could potentially support sustainable practices, ensuring the preservation of biodiversity and the continuation of cultural traditions associated with beekeeping.

There are several commercial services and online products offering apicultural adoption services. During the research phase we identified more than fifteen e-commerce websites and online services with similar purposes. In the following Table 1 we summarise most of them and then provide a discussion on their purpose, methods and strategies used for promoting their products, services, and scope.

Table 1. Available commercial services and online products for beehive adoption.

No	Service Name/country	Purpose	Strategy Used	Ref.
1	Adoptabeehive - UK	Supporting beekeeping and bee conservation	Adopt beehives by paying a fee	[22]
2	SW Honey Farms - UK	Educational programs, community involvement, and environmental conservation	Sponsor a beehive	[23]
3	Sponsor-A-Hive - US/CA	Support urban beekeeping and pollinaor habitats in cities. Promote biodiversity	Sponsor a beehive	[24]
4	3bee - IT	Support beekeeping and honey production	Adopt beehives by subscription model	[25]
5	Adoptabeehive - AU	Honeybee conservation	Adopt beehives, Receive progress updates	[26]
6	Grant Boys Honey - US	Support beekeeping and honey production	Sponsor a beehive and receive honey	[27]
7	BEE1 - UK	Support beekeeping and pollination activities	Sponsor a beehive and receive honey	[28]
8	MOB Honey - US	Support beekeeping and honey production	Sponsor a beehive and receive honey	[29]
9	IntoTheBlue - UK	Gifts or for personal enjoyment	Adopt beehives, receiving updates and honey	[30]

(continued)

Table 1. (*continued*)

No	Service Name/country	Purpose	Strategy Used	Ref.
10	Hunajalahde - FI	Support beekeeping and honey production	Sponsor a beehive and receive honey	[31]
11	CrowdFarming - UK	Support bee populations and honey production	Adopt beehives	[32]
12	Staunton-Park - UK	Support bee populations. Corporate Social Responsibility	Sponsor a beehive	[33]
13	l'Abeille de Ré - FR	Support beekeeping and honey production	Sponsor a beehive and receive honey	[34]
14	Backedbybees - US	Support beekeeping and honey production	Sponsor a beehive and receive honey	[35]
15	The-hive - UK	Support beekeeping and honey production	Sponsor a beehive and receive honey	[36]

It appears that many of these sites and services are aligned with campaigns such as "Bring Back the Bees" that took place in the United States, Canada, and the United Kingdom. These campaigns aimed to raise awareness about the declining bee populations and promote actions to support bee conservation and habitat restoration. The British Beekeepers Association supported wildflower planting and pollinator habitats through this campaign allowing customers to symbolically adopt a beehive [37]. The SW Honey Farms is a UK-based company that offers beehive adoption with various customisable packages for individuals and businesses, including honey deliveries and personalised updates on the adopted hive [23]. The Bee Conservancy, a non-profit organisation, offers a 'Sponsor-a-Hive' program directly funding new hives for beekeepers, creating more habitat for bees [24]. More recently the 3Bee project uses IoT, AI, and machine learning to monitor bee colonies in real time. It provides beekeepers with actionable insights, alerts, and data-driven strategies to improve hive management and bee health. The project also contributes to ecological research, addressing the global decline in bee populations and offers a beehive adoption agenda that allows individuals, companies, and other entities to adopt a beehive, contributing financially to the care and monitoring of the bees. The adoption program serves multiple purposes: it provides a direct revenue stream to support the technological and ecological efforts of the umbrella project, raises awareness about the importance of bees to ecosystems and agriculture, and engages the public in conservation efforts [25].

Finally, an interesting case is the Crowdfarming platform which enables individuals to support farmers by pre-ordering or sponsoring agricultural products directly from the source of production [32]. This platform aims to promote transparency in food production, support sustainable farming practices, and provide consumers with access to high-quality, locally produced goods. Through crowdfarming, consumers can establish a direct relationship with the farmers who grow their food, fostering a sense of community and supporting small-scale agriculture. The platform operates on a *direct-to-consumer marketing model*, facilitating direct sales between farmers and consumers without intermediaries [38]. It also employs a *crowdfunding approach*, allowing consumers to pre-order or sponsor agricultural products directly from farmers, fostering a sense of community and support for sustainable agriculture [39]. Utilising a *subscription-based service*, consumers can opt for regular deliveries of fresh produce, ensuring a steady income for farmers while providing convenience to consumers. The platform embodies the principles of *community-supported agriculture (CSA)*, where consumers invest in a farm's harvest in advance and receive a share of the produce, promoting local agriculture and strengthening relationships between farmers and consumers [40]. Through *social commerce* and *relationship marketing strategies*, the platform encourages engagement and transparency, empowering consumers to support farmers and make informed choices about their food purchases.

In reviewing the aforementioned projects, it appears that the effectiveness of the *Beehive Adoption/Sponsorship* strategy stems from its ability to forge emotional connections, tell positive stories, and generate direct impact. Adopting a beehive enables consumers to establish a personal link with nature, fostering a sense of involvement in conservation efforts. This emotional connection, coupled with narratives of sustainability and ecological commitment, enhances brand perception and cultivates consumer loyalty. Moreover, the proceeds from such initiatives directly support critical beekeeping infrastructure and conservation projects, allowing consumers to tangibly contribute to biodiversity preservation and ecosystem protection.

The marketing strategies related to beehive adoption incorporate elements from various established marketing theories and approaches. *Cause-Related Marketing* aligns the product with the decline of bee populations and environmental conservation, fostering emotional connections and brand loyalty. *Experiential Marketing* offers more than the mere purchase of honey, providing regular updates about hives and bee progress to engage consumers over time. In certain models, a *Subscription Model* introduces recurring subscriptions, generating predictable revenue streams and lasting customer-brand relationships. *Storytelling* crafts a compelling narrative about saving bees, supporting research, and receiving personalised products. *Direct-to-Consumer (DTC)* marketing eliminates intermediaries to sell directly to the consumer, highlighting the fundamental strategy behind beehive adoption. Personalized Relationship Marketing underscores the importance of the personal connection fostered through direct communication and ownership of a specific hive, prioritising relationships beyond mere transactions.

3   The Beehive Adoption Marketing Strategy

The MyHive project is built upon on a "Beehive Adoption Marketing Strategy," which combines technological innovations, commercial models, bee conservation efforts, and current marketing strategies to support beekeepers. This section provides a detailed analysis of this strategy by examining its components.

The Beehive Adoption Marketing Strategy combines a set of concepts which include Technological Innovations, Commercial Models, Conservation Efforts, Marketing Strategies. This strategy is deliberately broad in its thematic range to ensure inclusivity and a holistic approach.

The first concept deals with technological innovations. The technologies used are based on the IOHIVE ecosystem and its infrastructure, incorporating the Internet of Things (IoT) and wireless sensor networks for real-time beehive monitoring and data-driven management. The second category of concepts is about the commercial models. The commercial aspect is led by an e-commerce platform, providing direct-to-consumer marketing, potential crowdfunding for agricultural products, and a subscription-based service delivering bee products from the adopted hives. This model enables direct funding for new hives and supports ongoing ecological research and conservation efforts through the innovative use of IoT and monitoring technologies.

The third concept focuses on marketing strategies. The marketing strategies employed are diverse, focusing on cause-related marketing that emphasises the project's role in addressing bee population decline and promoting environmental conservation. Experiential marketing is crucial, offering adopters regular updates on their hive's progress and the health of its bee population, fostering a deeper connection with the cause. The direct-to-consumer (DTC) approach eliminates intermediaries, enhancing transparency and trust, while personalised relationship marketing builds connections with each adopter. A subscription model ensures predictable revenue streams, vital for the project's sustainability. Finally, storytelling is used to weave narratives that provide cultural context, share the journey of saving bees, supporting research, and delivering personalised products to the adopters, creating a rich, engaging experience that resonates on a personal and community level.

The following Table 2 summarises into general categories the methods and strategies used in the examples given and provides the context for the Beehive Adoption Strategy used in for this project.

3.1   Benefits for Local Beekeepers

Beehive adoption programs, grounded in marketing strategies like cause-related marketing, experiential marketing, direct-to-consumer sales, personalised relationship marketing, subscription models, and storytelling, offer local beekeepers and bee product producers a variety of benefits. These programs not only raise public awareness about the vital role bees play in biodiversity and the challenges they face, thereby increasing interest and demand for bee products, but also help producers improve their brand image by associating with conservation and sustainable practices. This is crucial as consumers are increasingly drawn to products from companies that are socially and environmentally responsible. Additionally, some programs provide direct financial support to cover beekeeping costs, further enhancing the sustainability of local operations. They also offer educational opportunities that can boost consumer appreciation and willingness to pay for local bee products, build a supportive community of consumers, producers, and conservationists, and ensure the long-term availability of essential pollination services. Finally, by participating in these programs, producers can differentiate their products in the market, appealing to niche markets and potentially commanding premium prices.

Table 2. Methods and Strategies Overview

Category	Methods/Strategies Used
Technological Innovations	1. Precision Apiculture (Smart technologies, IoT, wireless sensor networks) 2. Supply Chain Management 3. Climate Modelling and Forecasting Tools 4. Digital Education and Networking 5. Market Access and Digital Platforms
Commercial Models	1. E-commerce Websites and Online Services for Apicultural Adoption 2. Crowdfarming Platform (Direct-to-consumer marketing, crowdfunding for agricultural products, subscription-based service for fresh produce)
Conservation Effort	1. "Bring Back the Bees" Campaign (Wildflower planting, pollinator habitats) 2. Beehive Adoption Programs (Direct funding for new hives, real-time monitoring with IoT and AI, ecological research contributions)
Marketing Strategies	1. Cause-Related Marketing (Aligning products with bee population decline and environmental conservation) 2. Experiential Marketing (Providing updates about hive and bee progress) 3. Direct-to-Consumer (DTC) Marketing (direct to the consumer, eliminating intermediaries) 4. Personalised Relationship Marketing (personal connections) 5. Subscription Model (Recurring subscriptions for predictable revenue streams) 6. Storytelling (Narratives on saving bees, supporting research, and receiving personalised products, provide cultural context)

4   MyHive

As already mentioned, the introduction of "MyHive" is an example of this evolution in online (desktop e-commerce and mobile commerce / m-commerce), where it's not just about purchasing bee products, but also embracing services that resonate with consumers' values and interests towards apiculture, both in terms of biodiversity and cultural heritage.

Through "MyHive," beekeepers can utilise the platform to promote their bee products, present various activities related to their profession such as educational sessions, informational content, and also organise actual apiary tours, thereby engaging users. This multifaceted approach allows beekeepers not only to sell their products but also to share their expertise and passion for beekeeping, thus creating a more engaged and informed community of consumers. The platform also affords the presentation of informational content, such as articles, videos, and infographics, a functionality that further supplements their efforts to promote their work. Moreover, by organising tours at their apiaries, beekeepers can offer a hands-on learning experience that immerses consumers in the world of beekeeping. These tours can serve as a powerful tool for fostering a deeper connection between consumers and the source of the bee products they purchase, enhancing their appreciation for the labour and knowledge involved in this profession.

On the other hand, customer users can utilise either their smartphones, tablets, or desktop devices to buy products or discover beekeeping practices and to participate in beehive adoption services designed to support ecological and pro-environmental behaviour, conservation of the environment and the bee populations. The platform allows its users to directly support apiculture sustainability initiatives by adopting an actual beehive. Through this functionality user are provided with regular updates, detailed reports on the health and productivity of their adopted bees and can even order actual bee products produced from these specific beehives. Integration of m-commerce functionality into "MyHive" brings a dual benefit: it provides beekeepers with a direct channel to engage with and educate the public about the importance of bees in our ecosystem, and also offers to the consumers a hands-on approach to environmental stewardship through their mobile or desktop devices (Fig. 1).

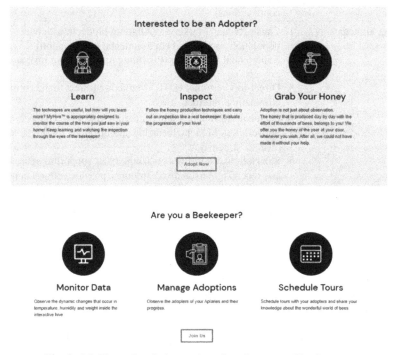

Fig. 1. MyHive subscription options for adopters and beekeepers.

The MyHive platform aims to enhance the availability and visibility of bee products and beekeeping services, as described in the strategies discussed in Sect. 2. Fundamentally, it utilises web technologies to transform the interaction between consumers and agricultural services. It allows producers to engage directly with consumers through its e-commerce model that aims to eliminate intermediaries and middlemen who often act as barriers (increase cost, reduce transparency and communication, limited control over marketing and branding etc.) between producers and customers. The platform operates as an online marketplace enabling beekeepers to establish online e-shops where they can market beehive adoption subscription services and sell products and services directly to their customers. This *Direct-to-Consumer* approach gives beekeepers greater control over their offerings (Fig. 2).

Fig. 2. MyHive Adopters' mobile dashboard

Through its *Subscription Model*, customers can adopt a specific beehive from a beekeeper and pay ongoing subscription fees depending on the services they select. In return, the adopting customer receives regular shipments of raw honey, beeswax, propolis and other bee products harvested directly from their adopted hive. MyHive handles payment processing, order fulfilment, subscription management and other e-commerce functions on behalf of the beekeeper. This gives beekeepers greater control over pricing, distribution, branding and customer relationships. By selling directly to customers, beekeepers can potentially earn higher profit margins (Fig. 3).

The platform enables consumers to virtually adopt actual beehives, thus directly linking them to the origin of honey and various bee-related products and services. This connection not only promotes bee conservation awareness but also allows users to observe

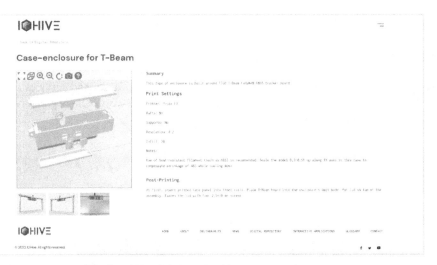

Fig. 3. IOHIVE & MyHive 3D assets repository.

the production process via smart beekeeping monitoring technologies. In addition to the bee products, MyHive, through its *Experiential Marketing* and *Storytelling* strategies, provides customers access to educational materials about beekeeping, apiculture practices, cultural heritage of beekeeping, the booking of field visits to apiaries as well as 3D digital repositories of assets of bee related souvenir products and equipment that users can download, and 3D print on their own. Moreover, the MyHive platform provides users with immediate access to real-time data from their adopted beehives, captured through sensor technologies used also for other purposes of precision or smart beekeeping by the IOHIVE ecosystem. It also enables direct interactions with beekeepers, offering insights into their daily practices. These features foster a deeper user involvement and a personal connection to the beekeeping journey, enhancing engagement and instilling a sense of responsibility towards the production process. Furthermore, it provides an educational experience by offering users insights into the local cultural heritage of beekeeping, thereby enriching their understanding and appreciation of traditional beekeeping practices. In addition to its role as a commercial hub, MyHive acts as an educational platform and CRM online channel, focusing on supporting beekeepers in alignment with global concerns regarding declining bee populations, but also in new ways of preserving beekeeping heritage, and promoting related practices (Fig. 4).

The platform prioritised user experience (UX) design, a design practice that supports conventional marketing approaches by focusing on user needs throughout its development lifecycle which includes phases such as research, design and prototyping and evaluation. As we will discuss in the following sections, the UX and interaction design processes followed throughout its development were iterative, encompassing research, ideation, conceptual design, low to high-fidelity prototypes, and evaluation.

Fig. 4. Process of recording and documenting informational and educational content.

5   Methodology: Research, Design and Evaluation

The methodology is structured into three main phases: Research, Design, and Evaluation, each phase building upon the insights and outcomes of the preceding one to ensure a consistent and user-centred development process.

5.1   Research Phase

During the research phase of this methodology, a design research approach was adopted, combining Interaction Design and User Experience (UX) methods with the Beehive Adoption Marketing Strategy. The aim was to understand user needs, behaviours, and motivations as well as their marketing needs. This phase was grounded in the principles of User-Centred Design (UCD), focusing on gathering extensive user insights to instruct the development of the MyHive e-commerce platform. Techniques such as contextual inquiry, user interviews, focus groups and usability testing were employed to research the ways actual users interact with similar digital platforms. The research phase was extensive and given emphasis on user involvement and observation. Emphasis was placed on user involvement and observation, particularly regarding services, applications, and platforms that facilitate beehive adoption, bee conservation, and the adoption of other agricultural products. This qualitative research session helped the design team in identifying key user requirements, which were essential in designing an intuitive and engaging user interface both for beekeepers, customers, content creators and other stakeholders. Additionally, by incorporating the Beehive Adoption Marketing Strategy into this phase, the research aimed to identify specific attitudes and perceptions towards bee conservation and the context they inhabit. It aimed to a better understanding of how cause-related marketing, experiential marketing, and personalised content could enhance user engagement and support for the cause (Fig. 5).

The thorough integration of Interaction Design and UX methods with the Beehive Adoption Strategy, within the expansive scope of the IOHIVE ecosystem [1–3], offered

Fig. 5. Field visits and interviews with stakeholders.

insights about the diverse user base, which spans from environmentally conscious individuals to typical consumers interested in bee-related products like honey and propolis. This dual focus not only highlighted the potential to utilise IOHIVE's beehive monitoring and networking capabilities but also underscored the wide-ranging consumer interest in buying bee products following a conventional consumer model.

The research phase thus served a dual purpose: it enlightened the design team about the actual user preferences for direct-to-consumer interactions and subscription models, and it also revealed a significant interest among users in supporting bee conservation efforts through their product purchasing or beehive adoption choices. This comprehensive understanding allowed for the development of a user experience that not only resonates with the audience's desire to contribute to environmental sustainability but also caters to their consumer needs. The integration of compelling storytelling and updates about bee conservation efforts with the opportunity to purchase authentic bee products created a versatile platform that adapts to user needs and requirements. By ensuring that the design phase addressed both the functional needs and the conservation goals of users, the research laid a foundation for a platform that not only engages users with a cause but also provides them with tangible value, aligning perfectly with the Beehive Adoption Marketing Strategy's aim to offer a holistic user experience that maintains user involvement over extended periods. This analysis of user interactions and preferences was pivotal in developing a design language that combines smart apiculture technologies with an immersive e-commerce experience, promising a blend of conservation support and consumer satisfaction.

5.2 Design Phase

During the design phase, the design team followed an iterative design methodology. This approach was central to refining and realising the vision for an e-commerce platform dedicated to beehive adoption with focus on bee conservation and the sale of bee-related products and services. This phase began with ideation and concept development, where a range of creative brainstorming techniques and designers' team collaborative sessions were employed to generate a broad spectrum of ideas (idea pool). These initial concepts were grounded in the insights gathered during the research phase, ensuring that the proposed solutions were rooted in user needs and preferences as well as the ideas behind the Adopt Beehive Marketing Strategy. Following the ideation process, the design team moved towards a conceptual phase of creating low-fidelity prototypes. These early prototypes, which included sketches and wireframes, allowed for rapid experimentation with different interaction designs and user experience flows. The iterative nature of this process enabled the design team to quickly gather feedback from potential users and stakeholders, ensuring that the evolving designs were aligned with user expectations and the overarching goals of the project. This approach facilitated a collaborative environment where ideas could be shared and refined, laying a foundation for the development of more detailed mockups and high-fidelity prototypes that later expressed the actual functionality of the MyHive platform.

As the design phase progressed, the focus shifted towards refining these low-fidelity prototypes into detailed mockups and high-fidelity prototypes of the web interfaces. This step involved a focus on the visual and interactive aspects of the platform, including the integration of the IOHIVE ecosystem's functionalities (visualisation tools, widgets etc.). The design team utilised online collaborative prototyping tools to create interactive models that closely mimicked the final product, allowing for an in-depth evaluation of user interactions, interface aesthetics, and the overall user experience. Through successive iterations, feedback from user testing sessions was systematically incorporated into the design, refining both the usability and the appeal of the interfaces and the flow of interactions. This iterative cycle of prototyping and testing was crucial for the development of the platform. The commitment to an iterative design methodology from the initial stages of ideation to the final high-fidelity prototypes ensured that the final product was comprehensively designed with a user-centric focus (Fig. 6).

5.3 Evaluation

In the evaluation phase of the project, a comprehensive approach to usability testing and user experience evaluation was employed, spanning both formative and summative stages to ensure the platform's design met the highest standards of user satisfaction and usability. During the iterative design phase, formative evaluation played a crucial role, with methods such as think-aloud protocols, heuristic evaluation, and usability testing being employed to gather real-time feedback on the usability and user experience of prototypes. Online tools like Useberry were utilised to facilitate remote testing and heat mapping, allowing for a broad analysis of user interactions and engagement patterns. These formative evaluations informed ongoing design refinements, ensuring that each iteration of the platform was progressively aligned with user needs and expectations. Upon the completion of the final working prototype, a summative evaluation was conducted to assess the comprehensive user experience and usability of the platform. The

Fig. 6. IOHIVE & MyHive functionality, widgets and other screen design of the high-fidelity prototypes

summative evaluation provided a holistic view of the platform's performance, identifying both its strengths and areas for further improvement, and confirming its readiness for public deployment.

6   Discussion and Results

The combination of the Beehive Adoption Marketing Strategy with the User-Centered Design (UCD) approach offers a model for the design of e-commerce / m-commerce applications. The proposed research and design model provides actionable insights into designing platforms that prioritize user engagement, environmental sustainability, and community building with hybrid online and actual professional groups like the beekeepers. This design approach demonstrates how e-commerce platforms can leverage UCD principles to align business objectives with social causes, particularly in promoting connections between consumers and beekeepers/producers while dealing with causes that promote sustainable futures for the human and the other species on the planet. This approach presents a valuable framework for designers aiming to create impactful, user-friendly, and sustainable digital commerce experiences.

Summative user experience evaluations of the MyHive platform revealed substantial levels of user satisfaction, indicating that the platform effectively meets the needs and expectations of its users (both for the beekeepers and the adopters). Engagement metrics showed significant interaction with the platform's features, such as bee adoption and direct purchases, highlighting its success in supporting active participation. Moreover, there was a noticeable increase in bee conservation awareness among users, demonstrating the platform's ability in educating its audience about the importance of bees to the environment. These findings underscore the impact of user-centred design in creating meaningful and engaging user experiences.

Beekeepers using the MyHive platform have provided positive feedback, particularly highlighting the benefits of direct market access, which allows them to reach consumers more efficiently than through traditional channels. They appreciate the increased control over their product offerings, enabling them to tailor their products to meet consumer demand more effectively. Furthermore, the platform has facilitated enhanced consumer relationships, allowing beekeepers to build trust and loyalty with their customer base by engaging directly and educating them about the importance of bee conservation as well as the beekeeping practices and how do they perform them. This feedback underscores the platform's success in creating a mutually beneficial ecosystem for beekeepers and consumers alike.

While the study presents promising results, it acknowledges limitations such as the focus on a specific agricultural sector and a confined geographical scope, specifically the Aegean archipelago's island complex of Cyclades. Future research could explore scaling the MyHive model to other agricultural sectors, assessing its applicability and impact across diverse contexts. Investigating additional features, like gamification or social sharing, could further enhance user engagement and participation. Moreover, longitudinal studies on the platform's impact on bee populations and broader environmental outcomes would provide valuable insights into its long-term efficacy and sustainability.

Acknowledgments. This research has been co-financed by the European Union and Greek national funds through the Operational Program 'Research Innovation Strategies for Smart Specialisation in South Aegean ΟΠΣ 3437', under the call South Aegean Operational Plan 2014 - 2020 (project code: ΝΑΙΓ 1-0043435). Parts of this work was done in collaboration with our project partners: The Institute of Mediterranean Forest Ecosystems and Forest Products Technology (Dr. Sofia Gounari) and Kudzu P.C (Dimitrios Mamalis).

References

1. IOHIVE Project Website and Services. https://iohive.aegean.gr. Accessed 11 Apr 2023
2. Chamaidi, T., et al.: IOHIVE: design requirements for a system that supports interactive journaling for beekeepers during apiary inspections. In: Soares, M.M., Rosenzweig, E., and Marcus, A. (eds.) Design, User Experience, and Usability: UX Research, Design, and Assessment. pp. 157–172. Springer, Cham (2022). https://doi.org/10.1007/978-3-031-05897-4_12
3. Alifieris, C., et al.: IOHIVE: architecture and infrastructure of an IOT system for beehive monitoring and an interactive journaling wearable device for beekeepers. In: Gervasi, O., et al. (eds.) ICCSA 2023, Part V, pp. 133–149. Springer, Heidelberg (2023). https://doi.org/10.1007/978-3-031-37117-2_11
4. Malisova, K., Stavrakis, M.: MyHive Service for Hive Adoption, GR. https://myhive.aegean.gr/. Accessed 14 Feb 2024
5. Patel, V., Pauli, N., Biggs, E., Barbour, L., Boruff, B.: Why bees are critical for achieving sustainable development. Ambio **50**, 49–59 (2021). https://doi.org/10.1007/s13280-020-01333-9
6. Bradbear, N.: Bees and their role in forest livelihoods: a guide to the services provided by bees and the sustainable harvesting, processing and marketing of their products. Non-Wood For. Prod. (2009)

7. Duarte Alonso, A., Kok, S.K., O'Shea, M., Koresis, A.: Pursuing competitiveness: A comparative study of commercial beekeepers. J. Foodserv. Bus. Res. **24**, 375–396 (2021). https://doi.org/10.1080/15378020.2020.1859962

8. Champetier, A., Sumner, D.A., Wilen, J.E.: The bioeconomics of honey bees and pollination. Environ. Resour. Econ. **60**, 143–164 (2015). https://doi.org/10.1007/s10640-014-9761-4

9. Hilmi, M.: Marketing research for micro and small-scale beekeepers (2021). https://www.researchgate.net/profile/Martin-Hilmi/publication/357380475_Marketing_research_for_micro_and_small-scale_beekeepers/links/61cb58b3b6b5667157b04c05/Marketing-research-for-micro-and-small-scale-beekeepers.pdf

10. Zacepins, A., Stalidzans, E., Meitalovs, J.: Application of information technologies in precision apiculture, 11

11. Gupta, S.G., Bhoomi: Securing Honey Supply Chain through Blockchain: An Implementation View. In: IoT Security Paradigms and Applications. CRC Press (2020)

12. Landaverde, R., Rodriguez, M.T., Parrella, J.A.: Honey production and climate change: beekeepers' perceptions, farm adaptation strategies, and information needs. Insects. **14**, 493 (2023). https://doi.org/10.3390/insects14060493

13. Guiné, R.P.F., et al.: Professional training in beekeeping: a cross-country survey to identify learning opportunities. Sustainability. **15**, 8953 (2023). https://doi.org/10.3390/su15118953

14. Burma, Z.A.: Digital transformation in beekeeping to carrying beehives into the future. Int. J. Nat. Life Sci. **7**, 89–99 (2023). https://doi.org/10.47947/ijnls.1372420

15. Huet, J.-C., Bougueroua, L., Kriouile, Y., Wegrzyn-Wolska, K., Ancourt, C.: Digital transformation of beekeeping through the use of a decision making architecture. Appl. Sci. **12**, 11179 (2022). https://doi.org/10.3390/app122111179

16. Costopoulou, C.I., Lambrou, M.A., Harizanis, P.C.: A framework for electronic trading of hive products. Bee World **81**, 172–181 (2000). https://doi.org/10.1080/0005772X.2000.11099491

17. Dar Indriani, M.H., Irmayanti, I.: Development of E-Commerce for Selling Honey Bees in the COVID-19 Era. Sink. J. Dan Penelit. Tek. Inform. 7, 165–175 (2022). https://doi.org/10.33395/sinkron.v7i1.11263

18. Wakjira, K., et al.: Smart apiculture management services for developing countries—the case of SAMS project in Ethiopia and Indonesia. PeerJ Comput. Sci. **7**, e484 (2021). https://doi.org/10.7717/peerj-cs.484

19. Dasig, D.D., Mendez, J.M.: An IoT and wireless sensor network-based technology for a low-cost precision apiculture. In: Pattnaik, P.K., Kumar, R., Pal, S. (eds.) Internet of Things and Analytics for Agriculture, Volume 2. SBD, vol. 67, pp. 67–92. Springer, Singapore (2020). https://doi.org/10.1007/978-981-15-0663-5_4

20. Kviesis, A., Zacepins, A., Stalidzans, E.: Future development perspectives of precision apiculture (precision beekeeping). 1

21. Catania, P., Vallone, M.: Application of a precision apiculture system to monitor honey daily production. Sensors. **20**, 2012 (2020). https://doi.org/10.3390/s20072012

22. British Beekeepers Association, Adopt a beehive, UK. https://www.bbka.org.uk/adopt-a-beehive-update-feb-2019. Accessed 14 Jun 2023

23. SW Honey Farms, UK. https://swhoneyfarms.com/adopt-a-beehive. Accessed 14 Feb 2024

24. The Bee Conservancy: Sponsor-a-Hive Eligibility. https://thebeeconservancy.org/sponsor-a-hive-eligibility/. Accessed 14 Feb 2024

25. 3Bee: Adopt a beehive, IT. https://www.3bee.com/en/adopt-a-beehive/. Accessed 14 Nov 2023

26. Adopt a Beehive, Bee the Change, AU. https://adoptabeehive.com.au/product/bee-the-change-and-adopt-a-beehive-of-honeybees-and-help-us-save-the-worlds-most-important-pollinators-be-the-change-you-want-to-see-in-this-world/. Accessed 14 Feb 2024

27. Grant Boys Honey, Adopt-A-Hive, US. https://grantboyshoney.com/products/sponsor-a-hive. Accessed 12024/02/14
28. BEE1, Sponsored Hive Option, UK. https://bee1.co.uk/sponsored-hive-option/. Accessed 14 Feb 2024
29. MOB Honey, Beehive Sponsorship US. https://mobhoney.com/products/beehive-sponsorsh ip-a. Accessed 14 Feb 2024
30. IntoTheBlue, Beehive Adoption, UK. https://www.intotheblue.co.uk/experiences/beehive-adoption/. Accessed 14 Feb 2024
31. Hunajalahde, Worker Bee beehive adoption, FI. https://www.hunajalahde.com/WORKER-BEE-beehive-adoption-permanent-orde. Accessed 14 Feb 2024
32. CrowdFarming. adopt a beehive. Organic Provence Honey de NectarPerty, FR. https://www.crowdfarming.com/en/farmer/nectarperty/up/adopt-a-beehive-provence-honey, https://www.crowdfarming.com/en/farmer/nectarperty/up/adopt-a-beehive-provence-honey. Accessed 14 Feb2024/02/14
33. Staunton Park, Bees & Hive Corporate Sponsorship, UK. https://staunton-park.co.uk/. Accessed 14 Feb 2024
34. Honey Farm L'Abeille de Ré, artisanal honey: Sponsor a Hive, FR. https://www.abeilledere.com/en/sponsor-a-hive. Accessed 14 Feb 2024
35. Bees, B.B.: Backed By Bees, Adopt Your Own Hive, US. https://backedbybees.com/products/adopt-a-hive. Accessed 14 Feb 2024
36. The Hive, Adopt a beehive, UK. https://the-hive.uk/adopt-a-beehive/. Accessed 14 Feb 2024
37. Burt's Bees, Bring Back the Bees Campaign. www.adoptabeehive.co.uk. Accessed 14 Feb 2024
38. Park, T., Mishra, A.K., Wozniak, S.J.: Do farm operators benefit from direct to consumer marketing strategies? Agric. Econ. **45**, 213–224 (2014). https://doi.org/10.1111/agec.12042
39. Shneor, R.: Crowdfunding models, strategies, and choices between them. In: Shneor, R., Zhao, L., Flåten, B.-T. (eds.) Advances in Crowdfunding, pp. 21–42. Springer, Cham (2020). https://doi.org/10.1007/978-3-030-46309-0_2
40. Cone, C., Myhre, A.: Community-supported agriculture: a sustainable alternative to industrial agriculture. Hum. Organ. **59**, 187–197 (2000). https://doi.org/10.17730/humo.59.2.715203 t206g2j153

Research on Individualized Design of Youth Clothing Based on QFD Method

Wenyu Chen and Sun Lei[✉]

Business School, Shanghai DianJi University, Shanghai 201306, China
`Rain.sun@126.com`

Abstract. The manufacturing industry is undergoing a transformation from a traditional manufacturing model to a service-oriented manufacturing industry due to the gradual deepening of Industry 4.0 and the rapid development of the economy. This transformation has brought about technological and process innovations and significant changes in consumer needs and behavior. Currently, individuals prioritize self-expression and personalized satisfaction, which is particularly evident in their shopping habits. Clothing, as a crucial component of self-expression and personal style, has evolved from a purely materialistic aspect to a more spiritual one. Young consumers in the modern era have distinct clothing preferences. They seek not only functional and visually appealing products, but also clothing that embodies their values, tastes, and attitudes towards life. However, the traditional clothing industry largely relies on standardized production and has yet to establish a personalized industrial production model. As a result, the homogeneity of clothing makes it difficult to meet the diverse aesthetic needs of consumers. The adoption of personalized product design has become a new aid for the development and transformation of apparel enterprises. This paper conducts an in-depth study on the personalized demand for apparel products of youth groups using the Quality Function Deployment (QFD) method. By analyzing the needs of young consumers, we gain a comprehensive understanding of their consumption habits and aesthetic preferences. This understanding is then used to transform consumer demand into specific design requirements. This paper uses the hierarchical analysis (AHP) method to determine the weights and priorities of user needs. It then constructs a quality house to transform user needs into product design requirements. The aim is to provide guidance for apparel companies to design products for this group.

Keywords: QFD · Clothing Industry · Product Personalization · AHP

1 Introduction

1.1 Background

The 21st century has seen the emergence of a new generation of young people who have grown up in an era of information explosion, cultural diversity, and advanced technology. This generation has distinct values, consumption concepts, and lifestyles, and they

J. Wei and G. Margetis (Eds.): HCII 2024, LNCS 14738, pp. 20–31, 2024.
https://doi.org/10.1007/978-3-031-60487-4_2

are more willing to improve their lifestyles by spending on unique things [1]. Being the main force in the clothing consumption market, the demand for clothing among young people presents new characteristics. Firstly, young people prefer fashion brands that show their personality and uniqueness [2]. They seek to differentiate themselves and express their attitudes, emotions, and values through clothing. Secondly, young people's awareness of the quality and price of clothing is also increasing. Quality consciousness refers to a consumer's perception of the quality of a product [3]. This means that consumers have higher expectations for the quality and comfort of clothing to meet their basic needs. Price consciousness, on the other hand, refers to an individual's sensitivity to price when purchasing a product [4]. Additionally, young people often have a strong desire for branded and fashionable clothing. Youth are not only concerned with the practicality of clothing, but also with the brand value and fashion sense of clothing [5]. They are often willing to pay for their favorite brands and fashion trends to become leaders and spreaders of fashion. In summary, the demand for clothing among youth reflects a trend towards personalization and diversification. The clothing industry faces new challenges and opportunities as consumers increasingly prioritize not only the practicality of clothing, but also the expression of personality, quality, and brand value.

1.2 Purpose

To gain useful insights insights in relation to consumers' preferences, the research should focus on a specific context [6]. Young consumer groups have unique characteristics and needs that present new opportunities and challenges in the apparel market. This study uses hierarchical analysis (AHP) to create a judgment matrix for determining user demand weights and priorities. It then constructs a quality house to translate user demand into product design requirements. The goal is to offer decision-making support for the design and production of apparel products. By conducting a thorough analysis of the needs and expectations of young people born between 2000 and 2005, specific fabric choices, process standards, and design requirements can be established to guide enterprises in product development. The main objective of this study is to investigate transformation methods that are appropriate for enterprise development, in order to meet the diverse and individualized demands of young people for clothing products.

2 Methods

2.1 Data Sources

During the stage of acquiring customer requirements, this paper uses online reviews as a data source. The Affinity Diagram (KJ) method is then employed to categorize the requirements. Subsequently, the Analytic Hierarchy Process (AHP) method is used to determine the relative importance of each requirement through expert questionnaires, in order to establish the comprehensive weights of user requirements.

2.2 Research Methodology

Quality Function Development (QFD) is a product development methodology that orig-inated in Japan. Its aim is to improve product quality and meet consumer expectations by accurately translating consumer demands into product characteristics. The concept of QFD was originally developed in Japan to enhance product quality and meet consumer expectations by accurately translating their needs into product characteristics. QFD can be summarized as a process of transformation, where the main purpose of QFD is to translate the voice of the customer into suitable engineering characteristics for product design [7]. This is accomplished through a series of 'Houses of Quality', each of which focuses on a specific aspect of the product. QFD house of quality matrix is widely used in the design fields of functional feature-oriented industrial design, interactive design, and engineering design [8]. The QFD method is used to study user requirements and explore user needs. By using the QFD method, design solutions that highly fit user needs can be output [9]. Because the importance score of QFD functional features is subjective evaluation with certain uncertainty [10]. This paper introduces the Analytical Hierarchy Process (AHP) method, which uses the data analysis method to convert the semi-quantitative and semi-qualitative problems [11].

3 Building the House of Quality

3.1 Customer Requirements Acquisition and Arrangement

The main concept behind Quality Function Deployment (QFD) is to focus on consumer needs and translate them into product design features. Therefore, it is essential to thor-oughly investigate consumer needs to improve user satisfaction and achieve customized design for specific groups. To gain a better understanding of the needs of apparel con-sumers, this paper utilizes two research methods: website review collection and literature review. The Internet's rapid development has led to an increase in online shopping. Enter-prises can extract valuable information from product reviews to improve and optimize their products or services [12]. This paper analyzes customer reviews of various clothing stores on online platforms to gain a deeper understanding of consumer needs. However, these reviews contain a wide variety of needs, some of which are vaguely expressed and difficult to classify uniformly. To parse these needs more precisely, this paper introduces the affinity diagram method (KJ method). The KJ method is not limited to numbers and is also suitable for text descriptions [13]. This paper describes a non-quantitative analysis method that utilizes inherent interrelationships to categorize information and simplify complex problems. The method involves hierarchical induction from chaotic and disordered information [14], resulting in a regular information architecture [15]. By organizing large amounts of complex data in an orderly manner, a clearer and more in-depth understanding of customer needs can be achieved. This paper collates several related literatures and online reviews of clothing stores from the past five years. Redun-dant and repetitive information is excluded. The direction of user needs is determined and the collected information is recorded on blank cards. The needs are categorized hierarchically according to their relevance and affinity, and a list of needs is made.

This study examines the fundamental requirements of young consumers for apparel items, classifying them into four primary categories: practicality, appearance, dependability, and affordability. As demonstrated in Table 1, with regards to practicality, customers are especially interested in the texture of the fabric and the accuracy of the design. They desire a comfortable and organic wearing experience. When it comes to clothing, consumers prioritize variety of styles and unique designs that showcase their personality and taste. Additionally, they value clothing that is easy to match and has reliable durability. To meet these demands, apparel products should be made with hard-wearing fabrics and reliable workmanship. Finally, when choosing apparel products, consumers cannot ignore affordability. Multi-occasion wearability is also a key factor to consider. They emphasize practicality and fashionability within a limited budget.

Table 1. Classification of customer requirements

Serial number	Primary Needs	Serial number	Secondary Needs
C1	Daily needs	C11	Soft material
		C12	Fits well
C2	Aesthetic needs	C21	Variety of styles
		C22	Unique design
		C23	Easy to match
C3	Reliability needs	C31	Wear-resistant fabrics
		C32	Reliable workmanship
C4	Economy needs	C41	Affordable price
		C42	Multi-occasion wearability

3.2 Importance of Customer Needs

To meet the diverse needs of youth in apparel product design, this paper presents a Analytic Hierarchy Process (AHP) model. The model focuses on youth's apparel product design and refines four key dimensions at the criterion layer: daily needs, aesthetic needs, reliability needs, and economic needs. To ensure the model's depth and practicality, corresponding user needs are further refined at the sub-criteria level.

Based on the user demand hierarchical model constructed above, a two-by-two judgment matrix was created using the AHP hierarchical analysis method to determine the weight relationship between the indicators. Additionally, a system of scaling and RI values was introduced during the arithmetic process [16] (Tables 2 and 3).

The arithmetic process for the first level indicator layer example is as follows (Table 4).

Construct a judgment matrix for the comparison of the importance degree of layers pairwise. Construct a judgment matrix for the comparison of the importance degree of layers pairwise C [17].

Table 2. Scale and its meaning

scale	Meaning
1	Two factors have the same importance compared to each other
3	When two factors are compared, the former is slightly more important than the latter
5	When comparing two factors, the former factor is significantly more important than the latter factor
7	The former factor is more important than the latter factor
9	The former factor is extremely more important than the latter factor when compared to both factors
2,4,6,8	The median value of the judgment of two neighboring factors
Reciprocal	Factor i compared to factor j scales as aij and factor j compared to factor i scales as 1/aij

Table 3. Criteria for RI

Order	1	2	3	4	5	6	7	8	9	10
RI	0.00	0.00	0.58	0.90	1.12	1.24	1.32	1.41	1.45	1.49

Table 4. Judgement matrix for the first level of the indicator hierarchy

	C1	C2	C3	C4
C1	1	1/2	2	4
C2	2	1	2	3
C3	1/2	1/2	1	4
C4	1/4	1/3	1/4	1

Weighting the matrix results.

The AHP calculation principle uses the square root method to calculate the eigenvector of the judgment matrix [18]. To calculate the maximum eigenvalue of the matrix, $\lambda_{max} = 4.1831$ is obtained. Next, the consistency test is performed, which involves calculating the consistency index CI and consistency ratio CR as shown in Eq. (1) (2)

$$CI = \frac{\lambda_{max} - n}{n - 1} = \frac{4.1831 - 4}{4 - 1} = 0.0610 \tag{1}$$

$$CR = \frac{CI}{RI} = \frac{0.061}{0.90} = 0.0678 \tag{2}$$

Based on the calculation results, the consistency ratio CR < 0.10 was obtained, indicating that the matrix has passed the consistency test and the results are valid.

The same method was applied to judge and calculate the weight of the second-level indicator layer, and after consistency tests, it was found that all results passed. Finally, the final weights of all user requirements can be calculated by multiplying the weights of the first-level indicators by the weights of the second-level indicator layers beneath them. The summary of the comprehensive calculation of requirements is shown in Table 5.

Table 5. Summary of consolidated calculations of needs

Objective	Level 1 Criterion	Weights(W)	CI	CR	Level 2 Criterion	Weights(W)	Combined weights	CI	CR
C	C1	0.3038	0.0610	0.0678	C11	0.2500	0.0760		
					C12	0.7500	0.2279		
	C2	0.3998			C21	0.2583	0.1033	0.0192	0.5800
					C22	0.6370	0.2547		
					C23	0.1047	0.0419		
	C3	0.2148			C31	0.3333	0.0716		
					C32	0.6667	0.1432		
	C4	0.0816			C41	0.2500	0.0204		
					C42	0.7500	0.0612		

In summary, the final weight of users' clothing needs is ranked in order of importance as follows: Unique design > Fits well > Reliable workmanship > Variety of styles > Soft material > Wear-resistant fabrics > Multi-occasion wearability.
> Easy to match > Affordable price.

3.3 Customer Needs and Design Requirements

Unique Design. Integrate trends and fashions: always keep a keen sense of the market and follow the current fashion trends. Pay close attention to global fashion trends and skillfully integrate the latest popular elements into our products.

Integrate youth culture elements: pay close attention to the dynamics and trends of youth culture, such as music, art, social media, etc., and incorporate them into clothing design.

Highlights individual style: Clothing should maintain consistency with the design language and brand tone, establishing a personalized brand image.

Fits Well. Consider the physical characteristics of youth groups: analyze the physical characteristics of youth groups, such as thinness and curvature, and design garments that fit their body types.

Provide a variety of sizes: Design a variety of sizes to meet the needs of youth with different body types and shapes. Provide detailed sizing charts to help consumers choose the right size for them. Consider elasticity and stretch in the design to accommodate different body shapes.

Reliable Workmanship. Details: Strive for excellence in garment detailing, including cuffs, collars, and hems, as well as thread and raw edge treatment.

Sewing: The sewing process is crucial to garment workmanship, encompassing line smoothness, splice accuracy, stitch uniformity, and thread treatment. High-quality clothing should have fine, neat sewing with no exposed threads.

Variety of Styles. Variety of Cuts: Different cuts can create various silhouettes and lines for garments, such as slim, loose, straight, or A-shaped. These adjustments can be customized to fit various body shapes and sizes, resulting in more comfortable and well-fitting garments.

Variety of color combinations: Color combinations can be selected based on various occasions and seasons to align the clothing with the overall appearance.

Soft Material. Use natural fibers: Priority is given to natural fibers such as cotton, linen, silk, wool, etc., which are breathable and comfortable.

Optimize fabric treatment process: When processing fabrics, use special treatment methods such as soft treatment, fabric finishing, etc. to improve the comfort of fabrics.

Fabric Abrasion Resistance. Enhanced Fabric durability and wrinkle resistance: high quality, abrasion-resistant fabrics are selected and their wrinkle resistance is enhanced by special treatment techniques.

Multi-occasion Wearability. Minimalist design: Design clothing that can be adapted to different occasions, such as leisure, business, sports, etc.

Easy to Match. Compatibility with other products: Focus on product versatility and compatibility in design to meet the diverse needs of different consumers.

Affordable price. Controls cost: use high quality materials and craftsmanship.

Offers a reasonable pricing strategy: in the design and production process, it always implements the principle of cost-effectiveness, and strives to ensure product quality while offering consumers reasonable and affordable prices.

Once the product design elements are determined, they are evaluated for autocorrelation. It is important to consider the interrelationships between elements before setting the target value of each product design element and formulating an improvement program, as the change of one element may affect other elements, and this effect may be positive or negative [19]. The correlation between each element is determined through research with relevant personnel in the apparel industry. A positive correlation between elements is indicated by a ' + ', a negative correlation is indicated by a '-', and no correlation is indicated by a blank space. This is also referred to as the 'roof' of the quality house.

The 'body' of the House of Quality (HOQ) is the matrix that correlates user requirements and technical features. It assigns a score based on the degree of correlation between the two, with a high degree of correlation receiving 5 points, a moderate degree receiving an intermediate score, and weak correlation being scored accordingly. Irrelevant correlations are not scored [20]. If a quality element does not have a corresponding demand, it is considered invalid and must be adjusted and canceled [21]. The degree of relevance is determined and marked by filling in the appropriate symbols, as shown in Table 6.

Table 6. Assignment of user requirements to technical characteristics

Degree of association	Strong correlation	Moderate correlation	Weak correlation	No correlation
Symbol	★	●	▲	
Score	5	3	1	0

Apparel product element importance $= \sum$ customer demand importance $\times$ apparel product element importance and customer demand relevance score, such as apparel product element "material soft" importance:

$$0.076 \times 5 + 0.2279 \times 3 + 0.0716 \times 3 + 0.1432 \times 1.5 = 0.8227$$

The relative importance of each apparel product element $=$ the importance of each apparel product element $\div \sum$ the importance of each apparel product element, and the relative importance of the apparel product element "beautiful color matching" is:

$$0.8227 \div (0.8227 + 1.5527 + 1.79 + 1.3768 + 0.621 + 0.9248 + 0.2856 + 1.9037) = 8.87\%$$

Similarly, calculate the importance of other measures of service quality and the relative importance of the specific results are shown in the table 10.

4 Results and Analysis

4.1 House of Quality (HoQ)

See Fig. 1.

4.2 Product Competitive Analysis

Technical Competitiveness Assessment: The quality characteristic indexes of our products and those of Company A and Company B are evaluated by technicians through tests and literature review. The technicians use a 5-stage judging method to score the products and obtain a technical competitiveness assessment.

To evaluate the competitiveness of the product, the QFD group analyzed and scored the characteristics of the subject product and the best-selling products in the current market of Company A and B from the user's perspective [22]. The information comparison analysis method was used to compare the competing products in the same dimension, with a full score of 5 points. The higher the score, the stronger the competitiveness. Upon comparison with other clothing brands, this study reveals that the subject product has a significant advantage in the competitiveness index.

The results indicate that the apparel products produced from the design practice of this study have several advantages over competing products. Firstly, this study emphasizes the reliability of the workmanship of the products to ensure their durability and stability.

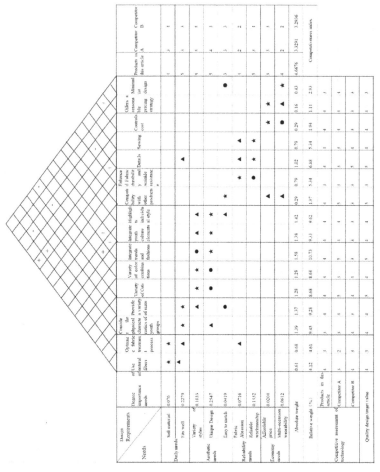

Fig. 1. HoQ

Secondly, this paper aims to enhance the comfort and fit of the product by combining the characteristics of suitable and soft materials to meet consumers' needs for a better wearing experience. Additionally, aesthetic product characteristics are introduced to improve the overall appearance and style of the product, meeting consumers' desire for personalization and beauty. In summary, this topic's product demonstrates stronger competitiveness by optimizing and enhancing workmanship reliability, fit, soft material, and aesthetic nature based on the existing product characteristics of competitors.

4.3 Product Design Analysis

The target value for specific quality characteristics is determined by considering the importance of quality characteristics, the results of technology competitiveness assessment, the difficulty and cost of technology implementation, the relationship matrix between quality requirements and quality characteristics, and the strengths and weaknesses of the current product. This target value represents the minimum standard of the specification value required to make the product competitive in the market [23], as shown in Table 10 under the column 'Quality design target values'.

Therefore, when designing products for youth, this paper focuses on quality control of clothing, based on the results shown in the quality house. Quality is a crucial factor for consumers, and it is the lifeline of a product. This involves not only the choice of materials but also the excellence of the sewing process. Quality sewing enhances the durability of the garment and highlights the craftsmanship of the product in the details, ensuring a comfortable and long-lasting wearing experience for young consumers. Apparel companies must identify and prioritize consumer needs, balancing satisfaction with maintenance costs [24]. Attention must also be paid to the youth's keen sense and pursuit of trends. The design team should monitor the latest fashion developments, interpret trends promptly, and seamlessly incorporate them into product design. Tailoring design should not only emphasize diversity but also consider the physical characteristics of the youth group to create a layout that meets their unique aesthetic and wearing needs.

5 Summary

5.1 Research Conclusions

The paper focuses on young people born between 2000 and 2005. The study utilized both qualitative and quantitative methods, namely the KJ method (affinity diagram method) and AHP (hierarchical analysis method), to systematically organize and calculate the importance of collected customer requirements. Based on this analysis, 16 key product design requirements were identified. Subsequently, the quality function development (QFD) method was used to translate these design requirements into specific product quality characteristics. An in-depth comparative analysis with competing products in the market was conducted. This paper draws several important conclusions from the research process. Based on the customer requirements and their importance, customers prioritized unique design, reliable workmanship, and fit. The research results indicate that several key elements among the 16 product design requirements are particularly important to the youth group and largely influence their purchasing decisions. Additionally, a comparative analysis with competing products identified potential advantages and shortcomings of this product in the market, providing a clear direction for subsequent product development and improvement.

5.2 Shortcomings and Prospects

To succeed in a competitive market, apparel brands must innovate, pay attention to changing consumer needs, provide personalized products and services, and establish a strong connection with consumers. This paper acknowledges that research on consumer psychology is still lacking in depth. As the field of consumer psychology and behavioral patterns of youth is complex and variable, more empirical research is needed to reveal its underlying mechanisms. Follow-up studies should consider integrating TRIZ, SWOT, and other methods to expand QFD. This paper aims to explore more personalized design methods to meet the growing needs of youth.

References

1. Su, J., Watchravesringkan, K., Zhou, J., Gil, M.: Sustainable clothing: perspectives from US and Chinese young millennials. Int. J. Retail. Distrib. **7**(11), 1141–1162 (2019)
2. What makes Asia–Pacific's Generation Z different? 2020/06/29. https://www.mckinsey.com/business-functions/growth-marketing-and-sales/ourinsights/what-makes-asia-pacifics-generation-z-different
3. Lang, C., Armstrong, M.C., Brannon, A.L.: Drivers of clothing disposal in the US: Drivers of clothing disposal in the US: An exploration of the role of personal attributes and behaviours in frequent disposa. Int. J. Consum. Stud. **37**(6), 706–714 (2013)
4. Lang, C., Armstrong, C.M.: Personal attributes: influences on clothing disposal reasons and frequency. J Family Ecol. Consum. Sci. **108**(3), 41–47 (2016)
5. Zhang, J.: Analyzing the creativity and practicality in clothing design. Art. Life **01**, 65–66 (2010)
6. Esteban, D.M., Sara, A., Calvin, W., et al.: Understanding young Chinese consumers' preferences for foreign clothing brands: a behavioural approach. Asia. Pac. J. Market Lo. **35**(12), 3032–3051 (2023)
7. Cho, J.I., Kim, J.Y., Kwak, C.: Application of SERVQUAL and fuzzy quality function deployment to service improvement in service centres of electronics companies. Total Qual. Manag. Bus. **27**(4), 368–381 (2016)
8. Li, Y.F., Xu, Y.W.: Research on user interface design of elderly mobile phone based on QFD. Packag. Eng. **14**(07), 95–99 (2016)
9. Zadry, R.H., Rahmayanti, D., Susanti, L., et al.: Identification of design requirements for ergonomic long spinal board using quality sunction deployment (QFD). Procedia Manuf. **3**, 4673–4680 (2015)
10. Govers, C.P.M.: What and how about quality function deployment (QFD). Int. J. Prod. Econ. **46**, 575–585 (1996)
11. Wong, J.K.W., Li, H.: Application of the analytichierarchy process (AHP) in multi- criteria analysis of the selection of intelligent building systems. Build. Environ. **1**(43), 108–125 (2008)
12. Tirunillai, S., Tellis, G.J.: Mining marketing meaning from online chatter: strategic brand analysis of big data using latent Dirichlet allocation. J. Mark, Res. **51**(04), 463–479 (2014)
13. Qiu, B.J., Li, X.K., Shuai, M.: Innovative design of office area lockers based on TRIZ theory and KJ method. Packag. Eng. **43**(24), 385–391 (2022)
14. Song, Y.B., Xuan, W., Jian, Y.S.: A study of all-age design of senior facilities in old communities based on the KJ-AHP method. Packag. Eng. **42**(22), 165–169 (2021)
15. Wang, W.R.: QC new seven tools of the fourth: KJ method. Chinese Health Qual. Manag. **25**(05), 137–139 (2018)
16. Song, X.L.: Research on the Design of AgingAdaptive Transformation of the Environment Outside the Old Urban Residential Area Based on Analytic Hierarchy Process. Qingdao Tehcnology University, Qingdao (2020)
17. Zhang, S.L., Zhang, Z.R.: Application of AHP and its application in enterprise decision-making. Sci. Technol. Manag. Res. (03), 204–207 (2006)
18. Li, L.H., Zhang, Y.: Application of AHP-fuzzy comprehensive evaluation method in psychology. J. Northeast Normal Univ. (Philos. Soc. Sci. Ed.) (03), 169–174 (2008)
19. Liu, H.E., Zhang, L.P.: Quality Function Expansion: Review and Perspectives. Industrial Eng. Manag. (05), 10–14 (2000)
20. Gong, P.H., You, J.X., Wang, Q.L.: Determination of the importance of quality characteristics based on the unfolding of improved quality functions. J. Tongji Univ. (Nat. Sci.) **47**(09), 1359–1368 (2019)

21. Wu, Z.X.: Research and application of QFD-based quality tool integration. Zhejiang University Press, Hangzhou (2015)
22. Shi, X.D., Chen, X., Wen, D.C.: Research on the optimization of e-commerce service quality oriented by customer demand. Stand. Sci. (07), 64–73+78 (2016)
23. Xiong, W.: Quality Function Development QFD from Theory to Practice. 64–65. Science Publishing Company, Beijing (2009)
24. Tang, Y.Z., Long, Y.L.: Research on personalized demand acquisition method based on kano model. Soft Sci. **26**(02), 127–131 (2012)

Augmented Reality Marketing: Factors that Affect the Intention to Use a Virtual Try-on Mobile Application

Elpida Efstathiou[ID] and Dimitris Drossos[(⊠)][ID]

Athens University of Economics and Business, 11362 Athens, Greece
drosos@aueb.gr

Abstract. This study aimed to examine the parameters that contribute to users' attitude and intention to use Virtual Try-on for beauty products. The study comprised of one-hundred eighty women who used the Virtual Try-on tool of a cosmetics website through their mobile devices and subsequently completed a questionnaire based on their experience assessing Virtual Try-on' ease of use, usefulness, enjoyment, attitude and behavioral intention. According to the results, ease of use, usefulness and enjoyment were positively associated with users' attitude towards Virtual Try-on, which in turn mediated the relationship between the aforementioned factors and behavioral intention.

Keywords: Augmented Reality marketing · Mobile Marketing · Virtual Try-on

1 Introduction

Augmented Reality (AR) is an effective technology which provides virtual information about products and services [1]. The main concept of this technology is to highlight information enriched with virtual and digital data displayed in the natural environment, in real time through the screen of a computer or a smart mobile device. [2]. AR is considered as a trend in digital marketing, while many retail companies offer AR services on their official website that give consumers the opportunity to try on various products virtually, such as eyeglasses [3], cosmetics [1], apparel [4] and furniture [5]. Previous research on Augmented Reality has highlighted its positive effects in fields, such as education, games and tourism. In addition, efforts have been made to research the AR technology impact on online shopping via mobile devices (mobile shopping) and to study the attitude of consumers towards this technology, as well as their intention to accept and use it.

Due to the fact that mobile devices and their use have changed completely the traditional retailing environment, AR has been integrated into mobile applications, something that makes easy the usage of Virtual Try-on tools as more people can use it on their mobile phones or tablets. Among all mobile devices, smartphones are considered to be the most common mobile AR device because of their high accessibility and proliferation.

Mobile Augmented Reality (MAR) experiences create new opportunities as they include embedded cameras and touch screens. Therefore, various industries have adopted

© The Author(s), under exclusive license to Springer Nature Switzerland AG 2024
J. Wei and G. Margetis (Eds.): HCII 2024, LNCS 14738, pp. 32–46, 2024.
https://doi.org/10.1007/978-3-031-60487-4_3

MAR technology in their marketing strategies in order to make their products and services more appealing to consumers. Several researchers have studied the attitude of consumers towards AR technology, along with their intention to accept and use it for online shopping [6].

The present study aimed to examine the parameters that contribute to the attitude of users towards Virtual Try-on for a beauty product (lipstick) and the mediating role of attitude to behavioral intention. This research employed Technology Acceptance Model (TAM) that is also utilized in several studies to examine the adoption of new technologies by users [7]. The research model consists of the following variables: ease of use, usefulness, enjoyment, attitude as regards the use of a new technology, along with behavioral intention to use AR in a shopping context. To our best knowledge there has been no previous research regarding the factors that may lead users to adopt Virtual Try-on for lipsticks, based on TAM.

The section that follows provides insights into the theoretical background of Augmented Reality and TAM with respect to an AR system (Virtual Try-on for lipsticks). The subsequent section presents the methods and the research design. Next, the study's results are presented. Finally, the paper concludes by discussing implications, limitations and proposing some directions for further research.

2 Theoretical Background

2.1 Augmented Reality

AR is defined as a technology that integrates digital elements and graphics into the users' physical world and allows real time interactions, while according to Azuma [8] mainly three are the features of AR technology: the first is that it combines the physical and the virtual world, the second is the users' interactivity in real time and finally, the virtual objects are three-dimensional, offering a clear representation of them in the physical world. AR has been utilized in several fields such as architecture [9], education [10], tourism industry [11], entertainment [12] and advertising [13]. Concerning systems based on Augmented Reality technology, Virtual Try-on is considered as a popular digital tool in the industry of beauty and cosmetics, apparel, fashion, etc., as it allows users to receive useful information about a product, which they can "try" on themselves virtually through smart devices or smart mirrors in the stores [13].

2.2 Technology Acceptance Model (TAM)

TAM was introduced and developed by Davis [7]. In research it has been utilized to understand and explore factors and motives that drive users to accept and adopt new technologies, as well as to investigate specific benefits for consumers that could help maintain a long-term relationship with an innovative technology [14]. Moreover, studies utilize TAM in various contexts, such as online banking systems [15], social networking sites [16] and e-learning systems in universities [17].

In particular, TAM examines the following main variables: ease of use, usefulness, attitude regarding usage and intention to use a technology system [7]. This model is also considered to be a suitable approach to examine adoption of AR in marketing and retailing [5]. Notably, TAM has been expanded with the addition of several variables, related to the functionality of AR applications, users' adaptability in processing and using technology, their beliefs and feelings about new technologies [14], as well as interactivity, response time, information and aesthetic quality provided by AR applications [3]. The research model of the latter, apart from the abovementioned variables that were investigated in the original TAM by Davis [7], also examined "perceived enjoyment" that was included in Perumal et al.' study [18].

Ease of Use. Ease of use, as perceived by users, refers to the absence of special effort during the use of a technology system [7]. In addition, according to previous research, when less effort is needed while using a system, users tend to develop positive attitude towards it, along with willingness to adopt it [4]. Previous studies have also showed that ease of use affects positively the attitude of users towards the Internet in order to send e-mails [4]. Moreover, in TAM research, attitude towards the use of technology has been considered to have a mediating role between ease of use and intention to use a system, such as the use of mobile banking systems [19]. Furthermore, studies have found that ease of use may affect intention through attitude towards the use of social media [20].

Therefore, we hypothesize that:

- H1a: Ease of use affects positively attitude towards Virtual Try-on use.
- H1b: Attitude mediates positively the association of ease of use with behavioral intention to use.

Usefulness. Usefulness refers to users' belief that a system will upgrade their performance [7]. Usefulness is often recognized as a fundamental factor regarding the use of a new system [21]. Virtual Try-on' usefulness for eyeglasses has been shown that it positively affects users' attitude towards the application [3]. In addition, relevant studies have found that attitude regarding a mobile banking system use mediates the association of perceived usefulness with intention to use it again [19]. Altawallbeh et al. [17] suggested that attitude towards e-learning systems had also a mediating effect on the association of usefulness with intention to use that type of systems.

Hence, we hypothesize that:

- H2a: Usefulness affects positively attitude towards Virtual Try-on use.
- H2b: Attitude mediates positively the association of usefulness with behavioral intention to use.

Enjoyment. Enjoyment refers to the degree that the usage of technology is considered as an enjoyable activity derived from the particular technology's performance [18]. As reported by Rese et al. [5] and Van der Heijden [22], enjoyment that stems from the usage of technology has been recognized as one of the most significant factors, together with ease of use and usefulness that might influence users' attitude towards a technology system and ultimately their intention to use it. Kim and Forsythe [4] in their study on Virtual Try-on systems' acceptance for online apparel shopping reported that perceived enjoyment significantly affects attitude towards this technology. Similarly, Praveena and Thomas [16] suggested that users' perceived enjoyment affects their attitude towards a particular social network. In addition, attitude towards use may mediate the association of enjoyment with intention to use, as according to Perumal et al. [18], attitude towards the use of smart retail technologies has a mediating effect on the association of enjoyment with users' intention.

Based on these findings, we hypothesize that:

- H3a: Enjoyment affects positively attitude towards Virtual Try-on use.
- H3b: Attitude mediates positively the association of enjoyment with behavioral intention to use.

Attitude. Users' attitude towards a new technology refers to the evaluation of a particular system's performance which may affect their intention to adopt it [4]. Of note, Roy et al. [14] found that attitude towards smart technology systems in retail stores, affects positively consumers' intention to accept and use them. Furthermore, according to Shanmugam et al. [19], attitude towards use is related with users' intention to use mobile banking systems and also mediates the association of ease of use, usefulness, enjoyment with intention.

Accordingly, we hypothesize that:

- H4: Attitude towards Virtual Try-on use affects positively behavioral intention to use.

3 Methodology

3.1 Design and Data

Data were collected through an online survey. Participants were informed regarding the aim of the study and the procedure by which data would be collected, while they were assured confidentiality and anonymity regarding their voluntary participation. Inclusion criteria comprised being adult and having used lipsticks in the past. Lipstick was selected as stimulus, as it is a cosmetic preferred by several women that can be worn at any time of the day [23].

After providing informed consent, participants were requested to use the Virtual Try-on tool of a cosmetics website on their mobile phone and then to answer a questionnaire that contained measures of ease of use, usefulness, enjoyment, attitude and intention, together with other measures of attitude towards the lipstick brand and product involvement to avoid any confounding effects. In addition, the questionnaire included items with respect to behavioral and demographic characteristics.

3.2 Measures

Three items were used to assess ease of use [24], four items to measure usefulness [25], four items for enjoyment [26], five items regarding attitude [5] and five items to evaluate behavioral intention [3]. In addition, nine items were used to measure product involvement [1] and four items to evaluate attitude towards brand [27]. All items were measured on a 7-point Likert scale (specifically from 1 = strongly disagree to 7 = strongly agree), while there were also questions regarding age, educational level, daily mobile usage and users' relationship with Virtual Try-on applications.

Regarding data analysis, SPSS Version 28.0 was used in order to describe the sample in terms of demographic and behavioral data, as well as to investigate the relationship between demographic and other study's variables. SmartPLS 3.2.7 was used for Confirmatory Factor Analysis, as well as Structural Equation Modeling (SEM) of Partial Least Squares (PLS) [28].

4   Results

4.1 Descriptive Characteristics

The sample consisted of 180 women aged 18 years or over, most of whom were between 25 and 34 years of age (47.8%, n = 86), followed by participants aged 18 to 24 years (19.4%, n = 35). Regarding education level, most participants had a university degree (43.3%, n = 78), while 36.7% had a Master's degree/PhD (n = 66). Regarding daily mobile usage, the median time spent was 4 h (IQR = 3–5). When asked if they knew what a Virtual Try-on system was prior to their participation in this research, 62.2% (n = 112) of the sample answered positively. Regarding previous experience of Virtual Try-on for cosmetic products, 40.6% (n = 73) reported that they had such experience in the past, while 30% (n = 54) reported that they had used Virtual Try-on tools or applications for products other than cosmetics.

4.2 Measurement Model

To evaluate the measurement model and the structural model, Confirmatory Factor Analysis (CFA) was carried out using the statistical analysis method PLS-SEM (Partial Least Squares – Structural Equation Modeling).

To assess the constructs' reliability, Indicator Reliability, Cronbach's alpha and Composite Reliability (CR) were investigated. Notably, all indicators' outer loadings were above 0.70, which shows sufficient levels of indicator reliability. All CRs were above 0.70, while each construct's Cronbach's alpha went beyond 0.70 [29]. Convergent Validity was also acceptable as the Average Variance Extracted (AVE) was above 0.50 [30] (Table 1).

Discriminant validity was confirmed using Cross Loadings, as the indicators' outer loadings on the related constructs were higher than their cross loadings with other constructs [29] (Table 2).

4.3 Structural Model

To assess a structural model, the R^2, Q^2 and the significance of the paths have to be examined. According to the data analysis, all R^2 values were above 0.70, thus the model's predictive capability was established. Furthermore, the results indicated that the Q^2 values were above 0.50 that shows that the model had predictive relevance as well. Moreover, there were no multicollinearity issues as the Variance Inflation Factor (VIF) values were lower than 5 (Table 1).

Table 1. Mean (Std), Loadings, Reliability, Convergent Validity, Collinearity, R^2, Q^2 for endogenous constructs.

Measures	Mean (Std.)	Outer Loadings	Cronbach's Alpha	Composite Reliability	AVE	VIF	R^2	Q^2
Ease of use	18.99 (2.35)		0.782	0.868	0.689			
I found the Virtual Try-on to be easy to use		0.929				1.955		
It was easy to understand how to use the Virtual Try-on		0.720				1.436		
Handling the Virtual Try-on was easy		0.828				1.774		
Usefulness	22.02 (4.38)		0.860	0.906	0.709			
For me the Virtual Try-on has great value		0.715				1.441		
The Virtual Try-on provides beautiful ideas for lipsticks		0.850				2.314		
The Virtual Try-on is very inspiring in terms of lipsticks		0.909				3.301		
The Virtual Try-on is a perfect aid to come to a decision in the selection of a lipstick		0.880				2.553		

(continued)

Table 1. (*continued*)

Measures	Mean (Std.)	Outer Loadings	Cronbach's Alpha	Composite Reliability	AVE	VIF	R^2	Q^2
Enjoyment	23.44 (3.89)		0.915	0.940	0.798			
Trying the different colors of lipsticks on the virtual try-on was.								
enjoyable		0.905				3.051		
fun		0.880				3.213		
pleasant		0.930				4.274		
interesting		0.856				2.342		
Attitude towards the use	28.29 (5.81)		0.929	0.946	0.780		0.808	0.618
I am positive about the Virtual Try-on		0.892				3.299		
The Virtual Try-on is so interesting that you just want to learn more about it		0.811				2.196		
It just makes sense to use the Virtual Try-on		0.914				3.928		
The use of the Virtual Try-on is a good idea		0.920				4.468		
Other people should also use the Virtual try-on		0.873				2.932		
Behavioral intention	25.18 (6.81)		0.916	0.937	0.749		0.784	0.576

(*continued*)

Table 1. (*continued*)

Measures	Mean (Std.)	Outer Loadings	Cronbach's Alpha	Composite Reliability	AVE	VIF	R^2	Q^2
If I were to buy lipstick in the future, I would use the Virtual Try-on		0.885				3.132		
If I were to buy lipstick in the future, I would give the Virtual Try-on priority over a cosmetics store		0.809				2.348		
If I were to buy lipstick in the future, I would give the Virtual Try-on priority over the images on the website		0.837				2.427		
I will recommend the Virtual Try-on for lipstick try-on to my friends		0.880				3.277		
I will use the Virtual Try-on for lipstick try-on regularly in the future		0.912				3.881		

4.4 Hypotheses Testing

PLS-SEM bootstrapping resample procedure was used to evaluate the significance level and path coefficients, including direct and indirect associations [29]. Table 3 summarizes

Table 2. Discriminant Validity - Cross Loadings

	Attitude towards use	Behavioral Intention	Ease of use	Enjoyment	Usefulness
ATT1	**0.892**	0.765	0.334	0.628	0.812
ATT2	**0.811**	0.683	0.421	0.717	0.685
ATT3	**0.914**	0.771	0.386	0.686	0.796
ATT4	**0.920**	0.806	0.322	0.592	0.811
ATT5	**0.873**	0.771	0.366	0.628	0.751
EU1	0.446	0.359	**0.929**	0.452	0.320
EU2	0.238	0.122	**0.720**	0.249	0.178
EU3	0.284	0.190	**0.828**	0.364	0.232
EN1	0.691	0.694	0.404	**0.905**	0.653
EN2	0.580	0.563	0.367	**0.880**	0.501
EN3	0.668	0.651	0.470	**0.930**	0.604
EN4	0.674	0.627	0.351	**0.856**	0.689
BI1	0.787	**0.885**	0.254	0.569	0.790
BI2	0.622	**0.809**	0.246	0.554	0.674
BI3	0.733	**0.837**	0.315	0.578	0.646
BI4	0.780	**0.880**	0.237	0.708	0.737
BI5	0.789	**0.912**	0.257	0.665	0.764
U1	0.620	0.603	0.311	0.542	**0.715**
U2	0.682	0.653	0.165	0.545	**0.850**
U3	0.793	0.716	0.307	0.627	**0.909**
U4	0.827	0.820	0.256	0.601	**0.880**

Note: EU: Ease of use, U: Usefulness, EN: Enjoyment, ATT: Attitude, BI: Behavioral Intention

the results for Hypotheses 1a, 2a, 3a, 4, Table 4 summarizes the results for Hypotheses 1b, 2b, 3b, while Fig. 1 presents the structural model with the path coefficients and respective p-values.

The results showed that the impact of ease of use on attitude towards technology is statistically significant with positive direction ($\beta = 0.106$, t = 2.847, p = 0.004). Consequently, H1a was confirmed. With respect to H1b (EU $\rightarrow$ ATT $\rightarrow$ BI), according to the Mediation Analysis results, it emerged that the Direct Effect of ease of use towards intention was not statistically significant ($\beta = -0.075$, t = 1.924, p = 0.054). However, the Indirect Effect of ease of use towards intention via attitude towards use was statistically significant ($\beta = 0.053$, t = 2.449, p = 0.014), while the Total Effect was statistically non-significant ($\beta = -0.021$, t = 0.482, p = 0.630). For this reason, H1b was confirmed as the association of Ease of Use with Behavioral Intention is mediated positively by Attitude towards use (Indirect-only Full mediation).

Concerning H2a, it was confirmed as the impact of usefulness on attitude towards technology use was statistically significant with positive direction ($\beta = 0.703$, t $= 9.001$, p < 0.001) (Table 3). Regarding H2b (U $\rightarrow$ ATT $\rightarrow$ BI), the mediation analysis indicated that the Total Effect was significant ($\beta = 0.658$, t $= 9.195$, p < 0.001), as well as the Direct ($\beta = 0.305$, t $= 2.969$, p $= 0.003$) and so was the Indirect Effect of Attitude on the association of Usefulness with Behavioral Intention ($\beta = 0.353$, t $= 3.976$, p < 0.001). Thus this hypothesis was confirmed (Complementary Partial Mediation).

H3a was also confirmed as the impact of enjoyment on attitude towards use was significant with positive direction ($\beta = 0.203$, t $= 2.485$, p $= 0.013$) (Table 3). Regarding H3b (E $\rightarrow$ ATT $\rightarrow$ BI), the Total Effect of enjoyment on behavioral intention was statistically significant ($\beta = 0.269$, t $= 3.699$, p < 0.001), as well as the Direct Effect ($\beta = 0.167$, t $= 2.873$, p $= 0.004$). Furthermore, the addition of the mediating variable led to the confirmation of the hypothesis, as the Indirect Effect of Attitude on the association of Enjoyment with Behavioral Intention was significant ($\beta = 0.102$, t $= 2.201$, p $= 0.028$) (Complementary Partial Mediation).

Finally, H4 was also confirmed as according to the results, attitude towards use was found to affect positively Behavioral Intention ($\beta = 0.503$, t $= 4.623$, p < 0.001).

Table 3. Path coefficients

	B	Std	t	p-value
Ease of use → Attitude towards use	0.106	0.037	2.847	0.004
Ease of use → Behavioral intention	-0.075	0.039	1.924	0.054
Usefulness → Attitude towards use	0.703	0.078	9.001	< 0.001
Usefulness → Behavioral intention	0.305	0.103	2.969	0.003
Enjoyment → Attitude towards use	0.203	0.082	2.485	0.013
Enjoyment → Behavioral intention	0.167	0.058	2.873	0.004
Attitude towards use → Behavioral intention	0.503	0.109	4.623	< 0.001

Table 4. Mediation analysis – Direct and Indirect effect of the mediating variable

	Total Effect	t	p-value	Direct Effect	t	p-value		Indirect Effect	t	p-value
EU → BI	−0.021	0.482	0.630	−0.075	1.924	0.054	**EU → ATT → BI**	0.053	2.449	0.014
U → BI	0.658	9.195	<0.001	0.305	2.969	0.003	**U → ATT → BI**	0.353	3.976	< 0.001
EN → BI	0.269	3.699	<0.001	0.167	2.873	0.004	**EN → ATT → BI**	0.102	2.201	0.028

Note: EU: Ease of use, U: Usefulness, EN: Enjoyment, ATT: Attitude, BI: Behavioral Intention

4.5 Additional Findings

With a view to investigating whether participants' demographic variables and in particular age (i.e., 18–24, 25–34) and education (i.e., high school, vocational training,

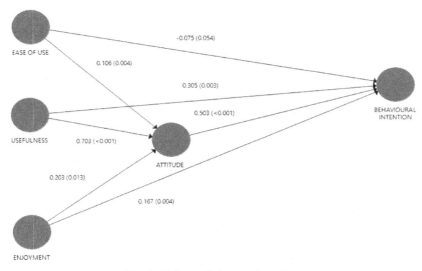

Fig. 1. Path coefficients and p-values

university) were related to ease of use, usefulness, enjoyment, attitude regarding Virtual Try-on, intention to use it in the future, as well as attitude towards the lipstick brand and product involvement, Analysis of Variance (ANOVA) was performed. According to the results, a significant relationship emerged among the age of the participants and their intention to use Virtual Try-on for lipstick try-on, with women aged 35–44 (M = 26.88, SD = 5.48) and 45 or over (M = 26.67, SD = 4.95) appearing more willing to use the Virtual Try-on than both women aged 18–24 (M = 22.23, SD = 7.93) and 25–34 (M = 25.28, SD = 6.99; F = 3.42. p = 0.019). No other statistically significant relationships emerged as regards age or education ($p > 0.05$).

Furthermore, women who were not aware of the Virtual Try-on applications prior to their participation in the current study compared to women with such knowledge, presented higher levels of perceived usefulness (M = 23.12, SD = 3.66 versus M = 21.36, SD = 4.65; $t = 2.82$, $p = 0.005$), as well as intention to use them again (M = 27.01, SD = 5.89 versus M = 24.06, SD = 7.11; t = 3.01, p = 0.003). There were not found any statistically significant differences regarding ease of use, enjoyment and attitude regarding the use of the application (p > 0.05). Moreover, participants with no previous experience (M = 23.99, SD = 3.59) of using Virtual try-on applications for cosmetics presented a higher mean in perceived enjoyment compared to the ones who had used it in the past (M = 22.64, SD = 4.18; t = 2.31, p = 0.022), while no other statistically significant differences were observed (p > 0.05).

5   Discussion

The aim of this study was to investigate the factors that contribute to users' attitude towards Virtual Try-on, as well as factors associated with their intention to use it again by utilizing the Technology Acceptance Model (TAM) through the mediation analysis.

According to the findings, ease of use, usefulness and enjoyment had an impact on attitude towards use (H1a, H2a, H3a). In addition, attitude towards the Virtual Try-on was found to affect the behavioral intention of users (H4). Notably, attitude displayed a significant mediating role among the factors ease of use, usefulness, enjoyment and intention (H1b, H2b, H3b).

In particular, it emerged that ease of use as perceived from the users, can lead to a positive attitude regarding the use of Virtual Try-on for lipsticks. Accordingly, Roy et al. [14] reported that ease of use of smart retail technologies influenced users' attitude towards these technologies.

Furthermore, this study found a relationship between usefulness and user's attitude. Similar results were reported by Pantano et al. [3], who reported a statistically significant impact of usefulness on attitude towards Virtual Try-on for eyeglasses. However, in Perumal et al.' [18] study regarding smart technologies, no statistically significant relationship was found between usefulness and attitude towards use.

Of note, perceived enjoyment was significantly associated with users' attitude towards Virtual Try-on, thus highlighting the importance of both hedonic (i.e., enjoyment) and utilitarian benefits (i.e., ease of use and usefulness) of this system. Kim and Forsythe [4] also found that the enjoyment which was attributed to the use of a Virtual Try-on application for apparel shopping may lead to positive attitude towards these applications. Notably, similar were the findings reported in Pantano et al. [3].

As regards attitude towards the use of Virtual Try-on, our findings suggesting that it affected users' intention to adopt and use it in the future were in accordance with findings of Roy et al. [14] who suggested that positive attitude affects customers' adoption of smart technologies.

Regarding the mediation analysis results, it emerged that attitude towards the Virtual Try-on for lipsticks fully mediates the association of ease of use with intention. Accordingly, Shanmugam et al. [19] reported that users' attitude towards a mobile banking system mediated the association of ease of use with intention to use the system. In fact, it is worth noting that full mediation was observed in the aforementioned study, which emerged in the present study as well. These findings suggest that the mediating role of attitude towards use is of crucial importance, as only through it an association of ease of use with behavioral intention can be established.

Regarding the association of usefulness with intention, it was found that it is mediated by attitude towards technology use (indirect effect), while usefulness can also influence behavioral intention directly (complementary partial mediation). Altawallbeh et al. [17] found a mediating effect of attitude towards the use of online education systems in the association of usefulness with intention. Conversely, Perumal et al. [18] reported that attitude towards use did not mediate the association of usefulness of smart technologies with users' intention to adopt them.

Furthermore, complementary partial mediation was also noted when assessing the mediating effect of attitude towards use on the association of enjoyment with behavioral intention. In accordance with our findings, Perumal et al. [18] found that attitude mediated the association of enjoyment with users' intention to accept and use smart technologies.

6 Conclusion

The purpose of the present study was to examine the parameters that potentially lead consumers who use a Virtual Try-on tool through mobile devices to a positive attitude towards this technological system, which could ultimately contribute to their intention to use it again. According to the results, factors such as ease of use, usefulness and enjoyment regarding Virtual Try-on were associated with attitude towards this system, while attitude also mediated their relationship to behavioral intention.

6.1 Implications

The results of this study could potentially contribute to a better understanding for cosmetics companies of users' perspective and needs. Specifically, it is crucial for companies in the beauty industry to recognize that customers wish to be able to try on a cosmetic product virtually, without having to be physically present at a store. Thus, adding Virtual Try-on tool on their website could benefit companies as it would potentially result in happier and more satisfied customers.

Furthermore, as this study showed, users who perceive the usage of Virtual Try-on as easy and enjoyable, may form a more positive attitude towards it. Consequently, firms should try to make their website mobile friendly and resolve any technical barriers in order to make navigation easier and improve mobile user experience in total. Moreover, increasing and promoting the availability of Virtual Try-on services in companies' websites is also of great importance as according to this study's findings 59.4% of the participants had never tried it before for cosmetics.

6.2 Limitations and Further Research

The findings of the present study have to be interpreted considering a number of limitations. First of all, the survey was conducted online and therefore it was not possible for people who did not have access to the Internet or use a mobile device to be informed and participate (sampling bias). Moreover, as self-report questionnaires were used, the possibility that some of the participants' responses may not have been accurate (possible response bias) needs to be acknowledged.

Concerning further research, it is recommended that the survey be conducted in person to reduce possible shortcomings related to the online sampling and data collection. Furthermore, additional characteristics of the Virtual Try-on applications could be investigated, such as interactivity, response time, information quality and aesthetic quality, as perceived by users. Additionally, technology readiness [30] related to a person's perceptions, beliefs and feelings about new technologies could be included and assessed in an expanded research model, as they are suggested to positively affect the adoption of Augmented Reality technology [25]. Moreover, users' privacy concerns could be investigated, as many brands take into consideration consumers' personal data and information and therefore, they take measures to protect them.

Acknowledgements. None.

Disclosure of Interests. None.

References

1. Whang, J.B., Song, J.H., Choi, B., Lee, J.H.: The effect of Augmented Reality on purchase intention of beauty products: the roles of consumers' control. J. Bus. Res. **133**, 275–284 (2021)
2. Javornik, A.: Augmented reality: research agenda for studying the impact of its media characteristics on consumer behaviour. J. Retail. Consum. Serv. **30**, 252–261 (2016)
3. Pantano, E., Rese, A., Baier, D.: Enhancing the online decision-making process by using augmented reality: a two country comparison of youth markets. J. Retail. Consum. Serv. **38**, 81–95 (2017)
4. Kim, J., Forsythe, S.: Adoption of virtual try-on technology for online apparel shopping. J. Interact. Mark. **22**(2), 45–59 (2008)
5. Rese, A., Baier, D., Geyer-Schulz, A., Schreiber, S.: How augmented reality apps are accepted by consumers: a comparative analysis using scales and opinions. Technol. Forecast. Soc. Chang. **124**, 306–319 (2017)
6. Qin, H., Osatuyi, B., Xu, L.: How mobile augmented reality applications affect continuous use and purchase intentions: a cognition-affect-conation perspective. J. Retail. Consum. Serv. **63**, 102680 (2021)
7. Davis, F.D.: Perceived usefulness, perceived ease of use, and user acceptance of information technology. MIS Q. 319–340 (1989)
8. Azuma, R.T.: A survey of augmented reality. Presence: Teleoper. Virtual Environ. **6**(4), 355–385 (1997)
9. Russo, M.: AR in the architecture domain: state of the art. Appl. Sci. **11**(15), 6800 (2021)
10. Hincapie, M., Diaz, C., Valencia, A., Contero, M., Güemes-Castorena, D.: Educational applications of augmented reality: bibliometric study. Comput. Electr. Eng. **93**, 107289 (2021)
11. Neuhofer, B., Buhalis, D., Ladkin, A.: Conceptualising technology enhanced destination experiences. J. Destin. Mark. Manag. **1**(1–2), 36–46 (2012)
12. Rauschnabel, P.A., Rossmann, A., tom Rossmanneck, M.C.: An adoption framework for mobile augmented reality games: the case of Pokémon Go. Comput. Hum. Behav. **76**, 276–286 (2017)
13. Raska, K., Richter, T.: Influence of augmented reality on purchase intention: The IKEA case. [Master's Thesis, Jönköping University] (2017). http://urn.kb.se/resolve?urn=urn:nbn:se:hj:diva-36421
14. Roy, S.K., Balaji, M.S., Quazi, A., Quaddus, M.: Predictors of customer acceptance of and resistance to smart technologies in the retail sector. J. Retail. Consum. Serv. **42**, 147–160 (2018)
15. Garaus, M., Wolfsteiner, E., Wagner, U.: Shoppers' acceptance and perceptions of electronic shelf labels. J. Bus. Res. **69**(9), 3687–3692 (2016)
16. Praveena, K., Thomas, S.: Continuance intention to use Facebook: a study of perceived enjoyment and TAM. Bonfring Int. J. Ind. Eng. Manag. Sci. **4**(1), 24–29 (2014)
17. Altawallbeh, M., Soon, F., Thiam, W., Alshourah, S.: Mediating role of attitude, subjective norm and perceived behavioural control in the relationships between their respective salient beliefs and behavioural intention to adopt e-learning among instructors in Jordanian universities. J. Educ. Pract. **6**(11), 152–159 (2015)
18. Perumal, S., Qing, Y., Jaganathan, M.: Factors influencing attitudes and intentions towards smart retail technology. Int. J. Data Network Sci. **6**(2), 595–602 (2022)
19. Shanmugam, A., Savarimuthu, M.T., Wen, T.C.: Factors affecting Malaysian behavioral intention to use mobile banking with mediating effects of attitude. Academic Res. Int. **5**(2), 236–253 (2014)

20. Verma, P., Sinha, N.: Role of attitude as mediator of the perceived ease of use and behavioural intention relationship. Int. J. Manag. Concepts Philos. **10**(3), 227–245 (2017)
21. Kim, H.Y., Lee, J.Y., Mun, J.M., Johnson, K.K.: Consumer adoption of smart in-store technology: assessing the predictive value of attitude versus beliefs in the technology acceptance model. Int. J. Fash. Des. Technol. Educ. **10**(1), 26–36 (2017)
22. Van der Heijden, H.: User acceptance of hedonic information systems. MIS Q. 695–704 (2004)
23. Matthaiou, E.: The effectiveness of an Instagram post when cooperating with an influencer: Mary Synatsaki and Sevastiana Kosta [Master's thesis, Athens University of Economics & Business] (2020)
24. Joerss, T., Hoffmann, S., Mai, R., Akbar, P.: Digitalization as solution to environmental problems? When users rely on augmented reality-recommendation agents. J. Bus. Res. **128**, 510–523 (2021)
25. Rese, A., Schreiber, S., Baier, D.: Technology acceptance modeling of augmented reality at the point of sale: can surveys be replaced by an analysis of online reviews? J. Retail. Consum. Serv. **21**(5), 869–876 (2014)
26. Smink, A.R., Frowijn, S., van Reijmersdal, E.A., van Noort, G., Neijens, P.C.: Try online before you buy: how does shopping with augmented reality affect brand responses and personal data disclosure. Electron. Commer. Res. Appl. **35**, 100854 (2019)
27. Handriana, T.: Consumer attitudes toward advertisement and brand, based on the number of endorsers and product involvement: an experimental study. Gadjah Mada Int. J. Bus. **19**(3), 289–306 (2017)
28. Ringle, C.M., Wende, S., Becker, J.M.: SmartPLS 3. Boenningstedt: SmartPLS GmbH (2015). https://www.smartpls.com
29. Hair Jr., J.F., Hult, G.T.M., Ringle, C.M., Sarstedt, M.: A Primer on Partial Least Squares Structural Equation Modeling (PLS-SEM). SAGE Publications (2017)
30. Parasuraman, A.: Technology Readiness Index (TRI) a multiple-item scale to measure readiness to embrace new technologies. J. Serv. Res. **2**(4), 307–320 (2000)

Branded App Usability Study Focuses on Beverage Apps

Xiaoning Fang[1]([⊠]) and Sunghyun R. Kang[2]

[1] Experience Design, VML, Atlanta, GA, USA
xiaoning.fang@vml.com
[2] Department of Graphic Design, Iowa State University, Ames, IA 50011, USA
shrkang@iastate.edu

Abstract. With the popularity of mobile devices and the increasing usage rate of mobile applications, more and more companies tend to develop branded apps for branding and marketing purposes [1]. Despite the growing interest in applications and their market influence, there is still a lack of research on why branded apps perform successfully as visual communication channels, branding tools, and loyalty-building platforms. Realizing the significant role of branded apps as a technology product, an online marketing tool, and a service product, the researchers developed a branded app in this study to investigate how it can be a marketing tool for a business, and conducted usability tests to learn how the interface and interaction design work in branded apps, with the goal to identify usability problems in the prototype, learn about users' preferences through observing interactions between the users and the interface, and improve the interface design based on the findings. Data was collected from 17 participants of usability tests.

Keywords: Branded app · usability test · beverage branded app design · user interface design · user experience design

1 Introduction

With the maturity of internet technology, the number of mobile phone users has been increasing, and the interface design of mobile applications (apps) has also been developing rapidly, forming a set of independent design languages. Smartphone usage rates is 85% in the United States, and research shows that 90% of smartphone users' screen time is spent on mobile apps [2]. The growing popularity of mobile devices and the increasing usage of mobile applications have enabled marketers to realize the possible business opportunities of branded applications [1]. By definition, a branded app is a mobile app that is produced by a company to help with promoting its brand. The brand identity is usually displayed through the app name, logo, icons, and other branding elements during the entire user experience [3].

The branded app is like a window, which is a sales platform of the products and even the culture of the brand. The experience of using the branded app directly affects the user's perception of the brand. Marketers have increased their interest in creating

J. Wei and G. Margetis (Eds.): HCII 2024, LNCS 14738, pp. 47–57, 2024.
https://doi.org/10.1007/978-3-031-60487-4_4

branded mobile applications as a consumer–brand relationship platform [3]. One of the explanations for why branded apps are highly effective as marketing tools is their extraordinary user engagement and positive impact on users' attitudes toward sponsored brands [4]. Branded apps allow consumers to get access to information easily, receive personalized messages and coupons from the brand, and interact with the brand on the move.

This study has three objectives: (1) to understand the relationship between branding, marketing, and interface design; (2) to design a branded app and investigate how it can be a marketing tool for a business; and (3) to conduct usability tests to learn how the interface and interaction design work in branded apps, with the goal to identify usability problems in the prototype, learn about users' preferences through observing interactions between the users and the interface, and improve the interface design based on the findings. Four research questions were generated to seek the answers: why does business use branded apps nowadays; how can branded apps be an effective marketing tool; what elements will affect the user interface design, common features, and functions in existing beverage-branded apps; and how can one provide a practical, aesthetic, and marketable user interface for branded apps?

2 Background

With the rapid development of mobile marketing, marketers have started to create a brand communication channel to get connected with their current and potential consumers through mobile devices, and this is known as branded mobile apps. Accordingly, a branded app of a company is a mobile application designed to promote its brand. It typically reflects the brand's identity, with features such as its visual identity, value, colors, logo, style, slogan, and other brand characteristics. Branded apps are linked to a business which differentiates them from other mobile apps. A branded app is considered as another communication approach for interactive advertising and marketing, and it is more engaging than the traditional website [3].

According to Distimo's research, among the top 100 brands, 91% of them have at least one app in major app stores [5]. One of the reasons why the branded apps become popular marketing tools is because their advertising messages are persuasive, thanks to their high user engagement [6] and how they influence users' attitudes toward brands positively [4]. The investment and development of a branded app will increase the younger consumers' loyalty to the brand. In summary, it has become more and more important for companies to provide branded apps that offer delightful customer experiences.

3 Development and Study Procedure

The main objective of this research was to study how branded apps were designed and to observe how users interact with the branded apps to improve the user experience design. The results help the researcher understand the relationship between branding, marketing, and user experience design. Also, the results can be used as a reference to assist the UX/UI designers with designing and producing the branded apps. This study includes three research methods: *1) A case study of four current branded apps on the market; 2) Designing a brand and a branded app prototype; and 3) Conducting a usability study to observe user experience with an exit survey to collect the feedback on the app design.*

3.1 Case Study

At the beginning of this study, four current branded drink apps, which are Starbucks, Dunkin', Scooter's Coffee, and Caribou Coffee, were examined to understand how the .branded apps were designed by these brands. The visual design branding elements were evaluated to discover how the brands deliver their brand message through the applications. The goal of this case study is to understand the interface design elements, common functions, and features of existing beverage-branded apps, and to establish guidelines for designing a branded app.

As beverage ordering branded apps, these branded apps have significant similarities, including functionality and mobile checkout experience. Although there are 14 common functions in these four branded apps, four main functions, including ordering, mobile pay, loyalty program and offers/coupons, are emphasized and prioritized in menu order by the brands. The scan and pay functions reduce the workload of the users and increase the efficiency of the checkout experience. These small considerate designs and user-centered UI elements make the mobile ordering experience with speed and ease, which definitely delights the users [7].

3.2 Design the Brand Identity

The brand's visual identity, which reflects the core brand identity and conveys the brand personality and characteristics, should strictly follow the brand identity's design guideline to avoid frequent redesign and rebranding [8]. The brand's visual identity was created using the existing bubble tea company named Liubai (留白)in China in the scenario of launching a new business in the USA. Through earlier marketing research, the researcher decided to position the market in the university campus town, with the target market being undergraduate students and graduate students. The enrollment statistics of a university were utilized to identify the demographic information of all adults. Most of the residents in the university campus town are students aged 18–35, who belong to the Millennial (Gen Y) and Gen Z generations. Based on the marketing strategy developed at the earlier stage, the researcher designed the new branding elements including logos, colors, typography, and the signature of brandmark for this research project.

The signature of the brandmark consists of a symbol, a logotype, and a tagline. The symbol was inspired by the Chinese character "白" from the Chinese brand name 留白 and the initial letters "W" and "S" from the English brand name "White Space", as well as Chinese calligraphy (see Fig. 1). The brush stroke not only represents the origin of the brand but also conveys a fluid feeling of the brand product. The negative space used in the logo represents the letters "W" and "S" which are capital letters of the brand name. To make sure the meaning of the brandmark is easy to understand, a tagline is added to clarify the attribute of the brandmark.

Fig. 1. Signature with tagline

3.3 Branded App Development

Information Architecture. By establishing the information architecture, navigation schemes were organized in a hierarchical way to allow users to move through the prototype effectively [9]. According to the results from the branded apps' case study, there are 14 features and functions commonly used in current beverage ordering branded apps such as order history, my favorite, gift card, reward, etc. The information architecture of the White Space tea café app was established by grouping these features/functions as shown in Fig. 2.

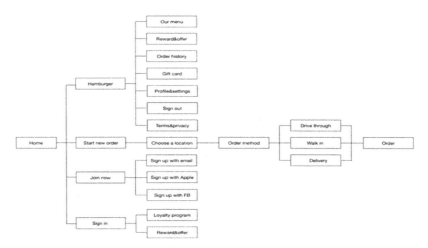

Fig. 2. The information architecture of branded app prototype

User Interface (UI) Design Development. The branded app design guideline was adopted into the development of White Space tea café app. Colors were carefully chosen from brand colors and adopted to the UI design to extend the brand visual identity. To ensure the legibility of fonts while the fonts share similarities with the brand's personality and characteristics, three fonts were carefully selected for the interface. "Brushstrokes" coming from the logo was chosen as the font for header in all the pages. Several types with different sizes and weights from Opificio font family were used in various locations, including subheaders and button texts. SF display pro, a flexible, neutral, and San-serif font, was chosen as a body text font to coordinate texts with the appearance of rounded UI elements in the design. Twenty icons (See Fig. 3) were developed for application by following seven icon design principles, including clarity, simplicity, readability, consistency, personality, transferability, and adaptability. They were designed in brush stroke style, which is a part of brand elements and evokes the brand personality.

Fig. 3. Iconography in branded app prototype

3.4 Prototype of Branded App

The prototype of White Space tea café app was developed in Adobe XD, which is one of the most popular design tools for website and mobile applications. The visual design in the app follows White Space tea café branded app design guideline that was explained in the UI design development section. The interaction design in the app was developed by following Nielsen Jakob's interaction principle [10]. Figure 4 shows the selected app screens.

3.5 Usability Study

The main objective of the usability study was to identify the usability problems in the prototype, learn about users' behavior and preferences through observing the interaction between users and the interface, and improve the interface design based on the findings.

With the Institutional Review Board approval, 17 undergraduate and graduate students from Iowa State University were recruited to participate in three phases of the usability study at different times (see Fig. 5). Five participants participated in the pilot study, four participants participated in the usability test 1, and eight students participated in the usability test 2. The usability tests were conducted virtually via Zoom/Webex. The app prototype link was provided for the test, along with a list of eight tasks in the Google slide during the usability test. The participants were asked to complete an exit survey after they finished the usability test.

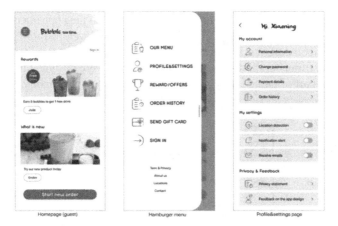

Fig. 4. Home page and hamburger menu of the prototype

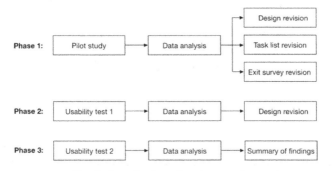

Fig. 5. Introduction of study procedure

After all the 17 usability test sessions were completed, each video recording was tabulated to calculate where and how many mouse clicks were used during the testing session. All the data was organized into a table using Excel. Feedback, comments, and suggestions from all the recordings were documented and analyzed using both qualitative and quantitative research data analysis methods. Besides the analysis data from usability test sessions, there are three groups of analysis data from exit surveys in three study phases: pilot study, usability test 1, and usability test 2. Each set of analysis data contains participants' demographic information, app usability evaluation scores, and opinions (qualitative interview answers). After data analysis for study phases 1 and 2, the app design was revised based on the results and findings. The design iterations improve not only the UI design of the app but also the user experience. The results also helped with the refinement of the branded app design guideline.

4   Results and Findings

4.1 Pilot Study

A pilot study was conducted with five participants, including three female and two male students from Iowa State University. Only one of the five participants has been constantly using an online beverage ordering app, the Starbucks app. The other four participants indicated that they rarely or never used such apps before.

When all four sessions were completed, the researcher reviewed the recorded videos, and summarized the results: All the participants had a hard time completing a task, "Customize your drink: Choose my own cup, 20% ice, and no sugar. Add it to your order." The main reason was related to the recognition and clarity of buttons. Participants needed assistance and explanation on how to operate the buttons even though there was an instruction before they entered the page. When the participants were asked to perform the next task, which was to choose another drink "milk tea" and customize the drink, they were able to operate the buttons better because of their previous experience. This pilot study found that the icons and irrelevant content caused confusions about the icons' meaning. The icons were then revised before the usability test 1.

4.2 Usability Test 1

Usability Test 1 was conducted with three female participants and one participant identifying as third gender, all aged from 18 to 35 years old. Regarding the beverage app experience, two participants used the Starbucks app regularly, and two of them did not use any beverage app.

After sessions were completed, this study found that two participants were confused with "Choose my own cup" in the task. They were not sure about where to find the option to click on in the app interface. Although interface clicks were all around 5–8 but one participant spent more than one minute to complete the task. As mentioned earlier, the reason for this performance was that the option was hidden under the drop-down menu. Two participants found the "my own cup" option in the drop-down menu because of their previous experience with a food ordering app. Three participants needed clarification with the icon on the top right of the home screen after signing in the app. Similar to the participants in the pilot study, the participants in usability test 1 also showed that unclear icons confused participants. The icons were again revised before usability test 2.

4.3 Usability Test 2

Eight participants with four female and four male participants from 18 to 35 years old participated in usability test 2. Regarding the beverage-ordering app experience, four participants indicated that they had been using online beverage-ordering apps, and three of them had never used such apps. Three participants had used the Starbucks coffee app frequently, and two participants had used the DoorDash and Uber Eats apps sometimes.

All eight sessions in usability test 2 followed the same procedure as in usability test 1. When the sessions were completed, the researcher reviewed the recorded videos, and summarized the findings as below: During usability test 2, three participants could not complete one of tasks that asks participants to read the customer review about black tea. They spotted the customer rating label on the top of the product page very quickly and tried to click the label, but it was not linked to the customer review page as expected. They did not try to scroll down the page and gave up after spending a relatively long time on the task with a few clicks. Two participants had previous food ordering experience. They thought the customer review rating label was clickable just like the other food ordering apps, and decided to scroll down to the end of the page to look for customer reviews when they found the label was non-interactive. At the end of the usability test, they mentioned that they expected the label to be clickable in the app.

4.4 Different Factors Affect Users' Behavior

Four factors derived from usability tests may affect users' interaction with the interface and should help the UX/UI designers develop a better application in the future.

Previous Experience. During usability test sessions, the researcher found that participants with previous experience on the beverage-ordering branded apps performed better in completing tasks than those without experience. They completed the task more efficiently. However, participants who had not yet gained experience with food-ordering branded apps could not employ existing mental models for how such apps work. This factor may affect their behavior when completing the task. The researcher found that some participants would try a different way to find the information when the first try failed. For example, one participant scrolled down the ordering page to find the customer review when he/she found the rating label was not clickable. He/she said it was because he/she usually found the customer review either at the top of the app page or at the bottom of the page.

Age Group. One of the most interesting factors that may affect participants' behavior was the different age groups. The researcher observed that Gen Z participants were more skillful in operating the system. They had the patience and curiosity to explore the interface of the branded app prototype by scrolling down the page and clicking on the buttons and links. However, Millennium participants focused more on the information in the app viewport. For example, in usability test 2, when participants experienced difficulties completing the task, "Read the customer review," three Millennium participants did not scroll down the page to look for the information since it was not presented in front of them. They stopped and moved on to the next task when they did not see the information in the app's viewport. In addition, Millennium participants paid more attention to the interface details and critiqued the app design at a higher level regarding their knowledge and educational background.

Language. During the Think-Aloud usability test session, non-native English speakers needed more assistance in understanding the tasks than native English speakers. For example, the most difficult-to-understand phrase for non-native English speakers was "pre-filled payment method." Also, the researcher tended to encourage non-native English speakers to think aloud more frequently. However, both native English speakers and non-native English speakers had similar verbalization patterns indicating the usability and interface design problems.

5   Discussion

Button. It is essential for designers to create a UI design style guide to make sure the UI elements with different purposes and functions have a consistent look in the interface. For example, users should easily identify which button is clickable and which is not. During usability test 2, the customer rating label with brown color was clicked by participants because of its rounded corner and color cue that confused the participants.

Color. As a critical part of UI interface design, colors help the brand communicate its value and shape users' positive emotions toward the branded app. Choosing the right color palette for the branded app is essential at the beginning stage of the design process. UI designers must ensure all the colors used in the branded app are from the brand colors to keep a consistent look for branded products online and offline. Light and dark shades of brand colors can increase the variety of color palettes and the contrast between UI visual elements. The UI style guide should include different usages of colors, such as the color of the title, subtitle, body text, link, text in the button, and label. To create a user-friendly branded app interface, UI designers must strictly follow UI design style guide other than the branded design guideline. According to Jakob Nielsen, relying on a UI design guide and standard improves user's ability to quickly learn interfaces and increase their productivity by reducing the operational errors [11].

Icon Design. To increase the recognizability and functionality of icons, icons should be accompanied with a text label. During this study, although the icons were rated easy to understand and participants' answers to the icon identification were positive, participants could not accurately identify all the icons' meanings without further assistance. During this study, when the drink icon without text label placed on the homepage, none of the participants understood its intended meaning given by the researcher. The icons in the app interface were easily recognized without any difficulty because of their text labels. Therefore, icons accompanied with text will provide an accurate cue, helping the users identify the icons efficiently. It also assists the UI designers in creating a positive user experience for the users.

Content. The word "content" in UX/UI design usually refers to information, images, videos, text, etc. The content of a branded app drives users' interest and builds the relationship between the brand and users. During this study, the researcher found that it is crucial for UI designers to ensure the information is accurate and the content in the branded app interface is well-written and strategic. Using strategic content for the branded app not only increases the users' awareness of the brand but also helps them visualize the stories that the brand wants to share with their consumers.

6   Conclusion

This study began with two research questions: Why do businesses use branded apps nowadays? And how can branded apps be effective marketing tools? Through the literature review, the researcher found that branded apps are popular because of their "anytime, anywhere" high engagement feature. The personalized, interactive, and convenient user experience that users gained from branded apps led to their positive attitudes about the brand, purchase intention, and purchase behavior. For example, the employment of digital loyalty programs in the branded apps instead of traditional physical loyalty cards increases the usage rate of branded apps and strengthens the relationship between loyal consumers and the brand, which also leads to a sale increase. Therefore, companies have been constantly improving the brand user experience by employing new technologies, embedding new features, and redesigning the UX and UI of the branded app [12, 13].

This study also tried to address the following question: what elements affect the user interface design, common features, and functions in existing beverage-branded apps? Four existing beverage-branded apps were selected for the case study: Starbucks, Dunkin', Scooter's Coffee, and Caribou Coffee. Through analyzing the branding elements and user interface design in the case study, the researcher found that branded colors, typography, icons, buttons, hierarchy, and layout collaborate to create a visually pleasing user interface in branded apps. These four beverage-branded apps share 14 common features and functions, including user-centered UI design elements in their branded apps. These 14 features/functions are vital in providing a convenient, efficient, and smooth user experience for beverage-branded apps.

Based on the findings from the case study, four new features, including guest orders, customer reviews, writing instructions to the order, and an order tracking system, were embedded into the branded app design based on the results of secondary user research. Through the UX/UI design process, the researcher learnt that knowing target users' lifestyles, behaviors, and preferences is crucial for developing a practical and marketable branded app. Building a solid understanding of the target users requires the marketing research team and the user researcher to collaborate on the market strategy before executing the UX and UI design.

Usability tests have been conducted to understand how the user interface and interaction design work in the branded app. The usability study helped address usability problems and interface-related issues, including button recognition, icon recognition, and information quality. The usability study findings also revealed the influence of demographic factors on the interaction between the users and the interface, and the users' understanding of the tasks. These factors include users' previous experience using beverage-branded apps, their age groups, and their native languages.

This study has some limitations. The first limitation is the limited diversity of the data sample. The age groups of 21–25 years old and 26–35 years old comprise the majority of the sample. Most of the participants are Gen Z members, i.e., 10 of the 17 participants are from the 21–25 age group, five are Millenniums, and none is from the 18–20 age group. Only university students were recruited for this study. The results cannot be used in a broader population. The second limitation is due to the adoption of the remote usability test. The researcher (test facilitator) and participants used laptop screens and a mouse for the usability tests, but not mobile screens or finger tabs. The third limitation is related to the second one. Different resolutions of laptop screens affected the appearance of colors, and this difference might have caused discrepancies in the evaluation results of colors in the usability exit survey.

There are several directions to be considered for future studies: (1) A/B testing can be conducted to examine the difference between the hamburger and tab navigation menu to help the researcher make a better design choice; (2) a usability study on the interaction between younger Gen Z members (18–20 years old) and the branded app prototype can be conducted by recruiting participants from this age group; (3) a group of diverse participants with different educational backgrounds and cultures can be recruited for the usability study to examine the influence factors on the interaction between the users and the interface; (4) the accessibility of icon design needs further investigation; and (5) Gen Z's preference for UI design elements including logos, icons, and button styles can be studied in the future.

References

1. Baek, T.H., Yoo, C.Y.: Branded app usability: conceptualization, measurement, and prediction of consumer loyalty. J. Advert. **47**(1), 70–82 (2018)
2. Wurmser, Y.: The majority of Americans' mobile time spent takes place in Apps. Insider intelligence (2020). https://www.emarketer.com/content/the-majority-of-americans-mobile-time-spent-takes-place-in-apps. Accessed 20 Sept 2021
3. Bellman, S., Potter, R.F., Treleaven-Hassard, S., Robinson, J.A., Varan, D.: The effectiveness of branded mobile phone apps. J. Interact. Mark. **25**(4), 191–200 (2011)
4. Hutton, G., Rodnick, S.: Smartphone opens up new opportunities for smart marketing. Admap **44**(11), 22–24 (2009)
5. Distimo: The 2011 Top 100 Global Brands and their App Store Status (2011). https://www.slideshare.net/zebs/the-2011-top-100-globalbrands-and-their-app-store-status. Accessed 16 Nov 2022
6. Calder, B.J., Malthouse, E.C., Schaedel, U.: An experimental study of the relationship between online engagement and advertising effectiveness. J. Interact. Mark. **23**(4), 321–331 (2009)
7. Kaley, A.: The Mobile Checkout Experience. Nielsen Norman Group (2018). https://www.nngroup.com/articles/mobile-checkout-ux/. Accessed 25 Dec 2022
8. Kotler, P., Pfoertsch, W., Michi, I.: B2B Brand Management, vol. 357. Springer, Berlin (2006)
9. Garrett, J.J.: The Elements of User Experience: User-Centered Design for the Web and Beyond. Pearson Education (2003)
10. Nielsen, J.: 10 Usability Heuristics for User Interface Design (2020). https://www.nngroup.com/articles/ten-usability-heuristics. Accessed 23 Oct 2022
11. Cooper, A., Reimann, R., Cronin, D., Noessel, C.: About Face: The Essential of Interaction Design. Wiley (2014)
12. Meisenzahl, M.: Dunkin' is revamping its rewards system and the new one looks a lot like Starbucks' (2022). https://www.businessinsider.com/dunkins-new-rewards-membership-looks-like-starbucks-rewards-2022-10. Accessed 23 Oct 2022
13. News, I.: Caribou Coffee to Refresh Loyalty Program with New Perks, App. QSR (2022). https://www.qsrmagazine.com/news/caribou-coffee-refresh-loyalty-program-new-perks-app. Accessed 23 Sept 2022

A Market-Ready Ecosystem for Publishing and Reading Augmented Books

David M. Frohlich[1(✉)], Haiyue Yuan[2], Emily Corrigan-Kavanagh[1], Elisa Mameli[1], Caroline Scarles[1], Radu Sporea[1], George Revill[3], Alan W. Brown[4], and Miroslaw Bober[1]

[1] University of Surrey, Guildford, UK
d.frohlich@surrey.ac.uk
[2] University of Kent, Canterbury, UK
[3] Open University, Milton Keynes, UK
[4] University of Exeter, Exeter, UK

Abstract. Many studies show the possibilities and benefits of combining physical and digital information through augmented paper. Furthermore, the rise of Augmented Reality hardware and software for annotating the physical world with information is becoming more commonplace as a new computing paradigm. But so far, this has not been commercially applied to paper in a way that publishers can control. In fact, there is currently no standard way for book publishers to augment their printed products with digital media, short of using QR codes or creating custom AR apps. In this paper we outline a new publishing ecosystem for the creation and consumption of augmented books, and report the lab and field evaluation of a first commercial travel guide to use this. This is based simply on the use of the standard EPUB3 format for interactive e-books that forms the basis of a new 'a-book' file format and app.

Keywords: Augmented paper · augmented reality · a-books

1   Introduction and Related Work

Paper and ink have evolved to be an integral part of our daily lives since their invention in ancient China. While this is still true, a range of screen-based reading alternatives have emerged with the development of the World Wide Web, mobile devices, and e-book standards and readers. These do not simply duplicate the reading of text on screen, but rather extend it to support new types of fragmented and networked reading through hyperlinks to multimedia content which is no longer linear and fixed [e.g. 1]. Debates about the future of paper in this context continue, but research suggests that it still has unique properties and will persist in parallel with screen reading for the foreseeable future. For example, research has revealed that paper still has advantages such as offering better reading comprehension [2, 3], better support for browsing and collaboration [4, 5], and providing better free-form annotation and bookmarking [6]. Some researchers suggest that the adoption of advanced technologies should not keep people away from

J. Wei and G. Margetis (Eds.): HCII 2024, LNCS 14738, pp. 58–75, 2024.
https://doi.org/10.1007/978-3-031-60487-4_5

paper, but rather integrate it with digital content [7, 8]. Media scholars now point to the emergence of cross-media and transmedia reading practices in which people move freely between paper and screen media for different purposes and experiences, for example in the consumption of entertainment or news [9, 10]. This effect has even led to a widening of the definition of textual literacy within pedagogy, to multiliteracies including the listening and watching of digital media [11]. In this context, it becomes a small step in everyday practice to accommodate augmented paper which begins to establish new connections between existing paper and screen content, and new affinities between the physical and the digital worlds for reading and writing [12].

Work on augmenting paper with digital resources dates back over 30 years to Wellner's Digital Desk [13]. Two core technologies have been used to establish links between pages and digital content, approximating broadly to what we would now call Augmented Reality (AR) and Internet of Things (IoT). AR approaches have used optical recognition of barcodes, QR codes, fiducial markers or pages themselves to trigger the display or playback of audiovisual or other content on adjunct devices [13–16]. IoT approaches have used electronic sensors embedded or printed in the paper itself, such as Radio Frequency Identification tags (RFID), or Bluetooth chips and capacitive touch regions to trigger content from manual reading actions [17–20]. Such IoT technologies add cost to paper and are still difficult to manufacture at scale, whereas AR technologies are relatively mature and have had most success commercially. This is described in a review of the application of AR in print media which lists numerous lab and commercial experiments in augmented print for storybooks, magazines and packaging [21]. However, these continue to remain one-off experiments rather than sustainable initiatives in publishing, because of the lack of guidelines and standards for augmented paper and a coherent approach to authoring augmented content alongside existing print media [20, 22, 23].

Some attempts have been made to develop authoring tools for augmented paper (AP). Lu and Lu [24] developed a publishing framework for pattern-embedding based AP. However, it relies on existing software BookMaker and the magic pen manufactured by Clevercode Corp. Similarly, a cluster of research [23, 25–27] has been contributing to developing frameworks and/or software tools for authoring pen and paper interactions such as such as Anoto pen and paper system, Livescribe smart pen, and LeapReader. These are tied to specific hardware and their own data formats and design protocols. This lack of standards impairs commercial uptake which requires a common but extensible approach with standard consumer technology. What is really needed is an augmented paper ecosystem with the following properties:

- A sustainable authoring and playback workflow for both professional and lay publishers.
- A legacy approach which allows the augmentation of any existing printed books retrospectively.
- Playback of augmented book content with standard consumer technology.
- A simple to use tool set with easy learning paths from current practice.

In the Next Generation Paper project, we have been tackling this issue for the authoring and playback of augmented books, or *a-books* for short [28]. Working with book publishers in the travel guide and photobook industries we have attended to their publishing work flows and requirements to create a new generic platform for both professional and amateur a-book publishing. This is compatible with both AR and IoT technologies which we refer to as second generation (2G) and third generation (3G) paper respectively. Printed hotlinks from paper are triggered by image/speech recognition or embedded electronics on a nearby smartphone, without the need for specialized pen or holder devices.

In this paper, we describe the ecosystem used to author and publish a complete augmented travel guide book, and its consumption by travellers using an a-book Player app. This was done in partnership with Bradt Travel Guides Ltd with whom we collaborated to make a commercial 'slow travel' guide to *Cornwall and the Scilly Isles*, 3rd Edition [29], augmented with additional digital content. This a-book was available free on a version of our a-book Player app for Android smartphones, using the AR (2G) image/speech recognition interface for triggering digital content from each page. This was 'market-ready' in the sense that it could be used reliably in this market test without adding extra cost to production of the printed book through printed or embedded electronics required in a 3G interface. In other publications, we have reported (a) experiments in the development of light-sensitive tags or bookmarks to support 3G paper interaction [30–32], (b) the design and use of an a-book Author app to create self-made augmented photobooks [33], and (c) the basic a-book approach and its implications for the future of reading and graphic design [34–36]. Here we publish more details of the ecosystem and the results of three new user studies with the commercial travel guide from lab, field and interview methods. We aim to show that it is feasible to create a professional and interactive a-book using standard book layout software such as Adobe InDesign, and to add user value of different kinds to a printed reference book with pre-designed image, audio, video and weblinks, together with personal media annotations. We begin by describing the ecosystem, the augmented travel guide book, and feedback from user and industry evaluations, before discussing the implications for augmented print publishing.

2   Platform and Media Design

2.1   The Ecosystem

Here we propose an ecosystem with the above properties for producing and consuming augmented paper/books that adopts the 'zero-delta' design philosophy. By this we mean that there should be minimal change to the existing practices of both publishing and reading augmented books, so that the approach is 'market-ready' with maximum chance of being adopted by the industry and consumer market. Elements of our ecosystem for Next Generation Paper are shown in Fig. 1.

Authors can use either a desktop or a mobile device (Fig. 1(1)) to create symbolic links between pages and regions of physical paper (Fig. 1(9)) and interactive digital content snippets such as video, audio, images, and web links (Fig. 1.(2)) available in the cloud or stored locally. It can also include real-time and updateable content such as airline/train/bus timetable, maps, opening time and etc. (Fig. 1.(3)).

These content and links with the physical paper/books will be processed and stored to an augmentation engine (Fig. 1.(4)). As most modern smartphones/tablets have enough computing powers and various built-in interaction features, we have chosen to have them in the ecosystem as the main playback devices for augmented content (Fig. 1.(8)). The

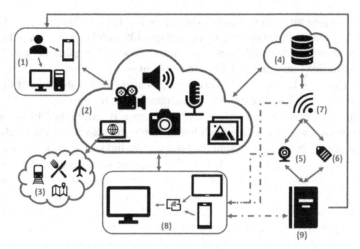

Fig. 1. The Next Generation Paper ecosystem

mobile device can also act as the camera for triggering content from the paper, or the Bluetooth receiver and processor of sensor data from the book itself (Fig. 1.(5), Fig. 1.(6), Fig. 1.(7)).

By using optical recognition (Fig. 1.(5)) or electronic tagging or sensing of some kind (Fig. 1.(6)) via wireless transmission (Fig. 1.(7)), the cross-linked content can be retrieved via the augmentation engine (Fig. 1.(4)) and delivered to the consumer playback device (Fig. 1.(8)) available to the users. The smart phone/tablet can also cast the content to a nearby big TV screen or monitor o offer a shared viewing experience. The entire process should ideally be effortless and seamless, so that users just point to the printed paper they wish to explore. This should be automatically recognised to trigger the delivery of the cross-linked digital content to the player device.

The proposed Next Generation Paper ecosystem explores two main types of linking interface between the digital content and the physical paper/book that are referred as 2G and 3G paper (Fig. 1.(5), Fig. 1.(6)). In the first 2G case, advanced optical recognition technology is applied to recognise the page content and retrieve the associated page number (Fig. 1.(5)). The second 3G linking interface involves special instrumentation of the pages and binding of the book with printed and embedded electronics that can automatically detect the active page and send signals to the smartphone/tablet via a Bluetooth connection (Fig. 1. (6)).

2.2 The a-book File Format

The current publishing practice of many book publishers is to publish a printed book with its corresponding stand-alone e-book. Consumers then have a choice of whether to buy the print or e-book version of the same book. Among all the e-book formats, the EPUB file format is one of the most widely supported open standards, published by the International Digital Publishing Forum (IDPF). This format supports the insertion of hotlinks in the text of a book, local or remote storage of links, and their presentation and playback in pop-up overlay windows on top of the displayed pages. Such links can be added in popular publishing design applications like Adobe *InDesign*, although the use of these varies between publishers and genres of books. For example, novels do not usually have hotlinks that might disrupt the flow of reading. They are simply screen-displayed versions of the print book, often repaginated ('reflowable') to fit the screen size of the reading device. In contrast, educational books for children may have audio or video links that pop up to illustrate or extend the text. By using the EPUB format for interactive e-books, we inherit the inbuilt hotlink authoring capabilities of modern book design applications, but choose to split the book and its links between paper and screen. The print book is printed as usual, but the links appear on a separate device nearby. We use a smart phone/tablet as the most popular and convenient consumer device for this, although the approach is extensible to other devices such as smart TVs. This leads to a paper-and-screen reading experience, consistent with emerging transmedia reading practices, that preserves the affordances of paper but combines them with the affordances of screen technology for playback of audiovisual materials in particular. This is already used in various niche products such as talking photo albums, recordable greeting cards, and books with audio. We are interested in whether this could be scaled up to support audio, video and other annotation of any book or document in the way we have described.

EPUB3 format file is implemented as an archive file consists of a number of HTML files along with supporting files such as video, audio, and images. The latest EPUB3 format is compatible with Hypertext Markup Language (HTML)5, Cascading Style Sheets (CSS)3 and JavaScript, supporting multimedia content integration and manipulation with interactive e-books. Creating a new format to support the proposed Next Generation Paper ecosystem from scratch is not cost effective and is more error-prone than adapting an established format. The adaptation of the EPUB3 format can have the following features to help realize the system properties outlined in Sect. 2.1 above:

- offers an easy learning curve to publishers to move from making a printed book and e-book to the proposed a-book, without modification to the original print design.
- allows us to develop a simple HTML and mobile based authoring tool, which can offer an easy learning curve to amateur users to design and author personal a-books using existing printed paper/books without change to the original print design.
- offers simplicity: the EPUB3' HTML5 features support simple integration of additional digital content with a printed paper/book, and easy review and validation of an a-book.
- supports backward compatibility: an EPUB3 based a-book is equivalent to a working version of an e-book and compatible with any EPUB3 supported eReader such as 'Apple Books' for iOS and 'Lithium eReader' for Android. Publishers could therefore release three versions of a book in the future: printed 'p-book', e-book & a-book.

2.3   The a-book Player App

While the (non-reflowable) EPUB3 file format specifies the mapping between printed pages and their digital hotlinks, and also holds any local link content such as audio, image or video files, a mechanism is still required to trigger the appropriate links from any printed page. This is done by an *a-book Player* app, originally developed for Android phones and later for Apple IOS phones. This app was designed to use 2G or 3G paper technology to identify which page the user is reading and what links are required. However, for the purposes of this paper we focus on the 2G technology which is closer to market and does not add cost to the printed book. As mentioned in Sect. 3.1, the main way of interacting with the physical book for 2G paper is using (our proprietary) optical page recognition from a smartphone camera [37]. The user takes a picture of the page and series of link options are presented on the smartphone for selection and playback (see Fig. 2). For fail-safe operation, we include two other approaches: 1) voice recognition provides hands free interaction. The user just needs to speak a page number to navigate to a specific page. As mobile operating systems such as Android and iOS normally have built-in light weight APIs for speech-to-text that can work offline, this linking interface could be considered as a fail-safe option if the optical recognition does not work due to internet connection issues; 2) manual page entry allows the user to manually enter a page number to access related digital content. This serves as another fail-safe option if both optical recognition and voice recognition do not work. The a-book Player app can be compared to an e-book Reader, in the sense that it is independent of the book files. Both require the importation of a library of books that can then be read or played upon selection. The big difference is that e-books are stand-alone and read on a tablet, phone or computer, while a-books comprise only links which are read in conjunction with their associated print book.

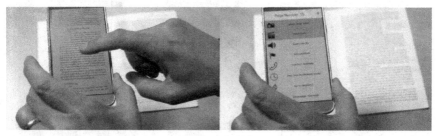

Fig. 2. The main method of triggering printed hotlinks from an a-book. The user activates the camera from the home page on the a-book Player app and takes a picture of the current page. Any available links are presented as highlighted options on the smartphone screen.

The main interface to the a-book Player is shown in Fig. 3. In addition to triggering augmented content published with the book from paper to screen, this supports the triggering of page references in the other direction from screen to paper, and the annotation of any page with personal content. This leads to the control of three forms of interaction as follows.

Print Book to Augmented Content. - this interaction allows the user to browse additional digital content given a page number. Users can select the camera, microphone or text-search icons on the home screen of Fig. 3a, to trigger printed hotlinks by taking a picture of the current page, speaking its page number or typing the page number. Seven different link types were used for the travel guide described below. These include generic links such as Image slideshow, Video, Audio and Weblinks, but also specific links such as Map, Phone numbers and Timetable information relating to the travel domain. The user can also bookmark pages of particular interest, using the 'BOOKMARK THIS PAGE' button at bottom of the Home screen. This creates a short cut to access specific pages of interest later, by tapping the Bookmarking button to see a list of selectable pages.

Augmented Content to Print Book. - this interaction links the digital content back to the book. A dynamic slide show of all extra images in the a-book appears at the bottom right of the Home Screen in Fig. 3a. This can be clicked to go to the other links for the page to which it is linked (e.g. Fig. 3b). This shows the printed page number at the top so the user can flick backwards or forwards to that page in the physical book. A similar facility 'Live map' facility appears at the top right of the Home screen. This shows the map of a location that is closest to the current location of the mobile device. Once the mobile device is near one of the locations included in the book, a notification appears on the phone to notify the user. The user can then turn to that physical page in the book and get the associated digital links on the phone by opening the location notification. Both features can lead the user back to the physical print book, which potentially give users the motivation to read and explore more of the print book.

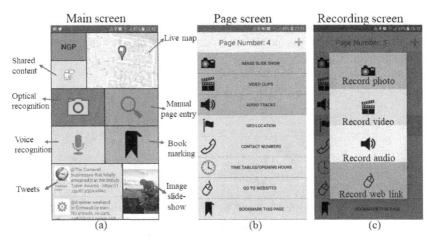

Fig. 3. a-*book Player* app interface, showing from left (a) home screen, (b) link types and (c) recording screen for adding further content to a page.

Print Book to Personal Content. - this interaction allows the user to personalise the current page of the a-book with their own personal media. The user can click on the ' +' button at the top right of the current page in Fig. 3b. This brings up the options of adding a Photo, Video, Audio or Weblink to the current page in Fig. 3c, either from a resident file on the smartphone or by recording a new media item. Multiple items of the same or different types can be added in this way. These appear alongside the professional published links which came with the a-book. In the travel context, tourists can link their own photographs, video clips or sound recordings to each page so that their guidebook becomes a personalised diary and memento of the trip for later reminiscing. An extension of this personalisation is also given in the Twitter feed shown in Fig. 3a. This shows public messages relating to the title of the book, and can also be queried and tuned by the user. Moreover, the app is configured to be available in the share list of other apps so that the user can share other apps' content including image, video, audio, and weblinks with the a-book Player app. For instance, the user might find an interesting video of the travel destination on YouTube, and share the video with the augmented travel guide. While we designed these interactions, we realised that the two-way interplay between the printed book and its digital augmentations could lead to new forms of paper-and-screen reading, and the blurring of boundaries between personal, published and publicly available information on the web [35].

2.4 Professional Authoring of a Guide Book

To test the feasibility and attractiveness of the augmented paper ecosystem and approach, we decided with our publishing partner Bradt Travel Guides to create a fully augmented travel guide book for sale in their collection. The book had 352 pages of which most were augmented. It could be read without augmented links as usual, but would also contain icons in the text representing hotlinks that could be accessed from our a-book Player app free to download by customers. The price point was set as identical to that of an ordinary guide book so that the extra digital content would be seen as an additional incentive to buy the book. The company chose to augment a new 3rd edition of an existing Slow travel guide to Cornwall and the Scilly Isles [29], since we could look at the 2nd edition print content as an indication of what we would be designing the augmentations for. We worked closely with the travel writer on the project and commissioned her to collect additional digital content in parallel to her additional printed content for the new edition. This comprised mainly audio interviews with local characters, additional photographs, voiceover, ambient sound and video recordings of landscapes and locations. We were also able to incorporate hotlinks for existing web URLs and phone numbers of organisations included in the print book, and to find publicly available timetables and map references for travel and locations mentioned in the text. The commercial guide was launched in early 2019 and was available for 3 years before being replaced with a 4th edition. This is itself a proof of concept that the approach works and can be used in a commercial context. In the rest of this section, we describe the technical steps and challenges involved. In the next section, we report feedback from both travellers and tourist associations/companies on the design and use of the guide.

Technically, the book was created in the following way and raised a number of issues for the approach. A number of EPUB3 compatible publishing tools could have been used to author the a-book with minimum alterations to the printed design, including Adobe InDesign, Sigil, Calibre, etc. The graphic designers in Bradt Travel Guides used InDesign as their primary book design tool, so this was used to lay out the print book as usual but also to add hotlinks to additional digital content from the travel writer and ourselves. The additional content was added by one member of our team who also has a graphic design background (Corrigan-Kavanagh). Essentially for every printed hotlink, an icon of the hotlink type was inserted into the text and made interactive using a button box over the top of it. This was linked to the content itself or a web reference to the content online. Seven different link types were defined for the travel guide as shown in Fig. 3b above, excluding the Bookmark icon which wasn't a link type but an operation to save a favourite page. The image, audio and video icons linked to actual files of those types stored locally within the e-book and eventual a-book. The geo location, timetable, map and website icons linked to URLs of corresponding web content, while the phone number icons linked to locally stored phone numbers which triggered a phone call in the a-book Player app. Any page could have none, 1 or more links of every type, making the design options very flexible. An example double page spread from the book is shown in Fig. 4. This is from a section in Chapter 2 describing the Camel estuary and its attractions, with a 1 min 15 s video interview with a local resident of Port Isaac, an extra picture of a Cornish singing group called Fisherman's Friend, a 56 s live recording of them singing a sea shanty, a web link to a walking tour company, and three maps of regions around Port Gaverne and Port Quin.

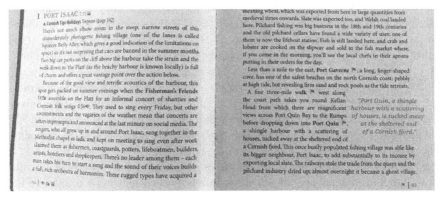

Fig. 4. Horizontal section of a double page spread from the augmented travel guide, showing one video, one photo and one audio link on page 56, plus three map links on page 57.

Once the full 352 print pages had been annotated with digital links in this way, an EPUB3 file was created for an interactive e-book that would normally be read/played on an e-book reader device or app. However, for our purposes this was made 'non-reflowable', meaning that it remained in a fixed print format with stable pagination, and could not be repaginated for different size screens. This is because we used the page images as reference images for our page recognition algorithm, and printed them as the print part of our a-book. Originally we intended to simply import the full EPUB3 file into our a-book Player app, to trigger the digital content from the pages as described in Sect. 3.3. However, the publisher raised a security issue with this because the file contains both the text of the print book and the digital links or references. Therefore, a user could in principle view the text of the print book alone from our free app, using other EPUB3 supported applications without purchasing the print book, thereby reducing sales. For this reason, we created a new '. Abook' file format for our app which was essentially the EPUB3 file with the print book stripped out of it. This also had the benefit of reducing file size.

Finally, the separation we had planned between the a-book Player app and the a-book files themselves came into question when considering how to make them available with the guide book. For convenience and ease of installation in this market test we decided to combine the a-book and the Player app into a single 'Cornwall a-book app' with restricted license terms and conditions. This prevented the app from being used for anything else and avoided the long-term practice of installing a generic Player app once, and importing multiple a-book files into it for playback. However, this remains our vision for the future of the approach, and we have since created a generic a-book Player app for Android and IOS that can be used with different a-books. Such commercial considerations are not normally considered in research projects but were an important lesson to us when designing the ecosystem to be as 'market-ready' as possible.

3 Evaluation

Three different forms of evaluation of the augmented Cornwall guide were conducted to understand user and industry reactions to the design. A lab study and field trial were carried out by prospective and actual travelers to Cornwall. In addition, a number of interviews were carried out with tourist organisations, involving a demonstration of the guide book for discussion. These will be briefly described in turn.

3.1 Lab Study

Fourteen participants were invited to attend a one-to-one 'technology elicitation style' semi-structured interview session in a home lab at the university campus. Essentially, we used the printed Cornwall a-book with companion Android smartphone and app to elicit usability and utility feedback following a hands-on period of free use. We also showed participants two interactive e-book versions of the Cornwall guide for comparison, complete with all the same digital annotations which popped up over the screen-displayed text on both an Android smartphone and tablet. This is because the interactive e-book is the main competitor to an a-book and perhaps a fairer comparison than a non-interactive e-book without digital links. Participants included 3 males and 11 females. Their age range was between 32 and 74. Four participants used print and digital media evenly in everyday life, 9 participants used mostly used digital media, and 1 participant only used digital media. First, an initial demonstration of using the Cornwall a-book Player app was carried out by a researcher with the participant. Then, each participant had unlimited time to interact with the app and printed book undisturbed within the context of UK travellers visiting Cornwall. Subsequently, each participant was allowed to play with the smartphone and tablet versions of the interactive e-book for comparison, and then interviewed about their impressions of reading and interacting with all the printed and digital materials.

All interview accounts were transcribed and analysed using the Corbin and Strauss's grounded theory [38] research methodology. Reflective memos, opening coding, axial coding and selective coding were applied to extract common themes and reactions from the group. Three main themes and findings on the a-book are shown below, before those on the comparison with the interactive e-books.

Semi-immersive imaginary reading. In general, participants appreciated the tangibility of the printed book combined with the additional digital content on a phone: "It's more gratifying to go through an actual physical book. Then the phone gives it the bonus of additional content. But I think because it's two separate things it's a bit more playful than the e-book and it's another layer" (Jenny). They liked the convenience of direct links to URLs and phones numbers already in the printed text, and additional up-to-date timetables and extra maps. However, their favourite content was the multimedia illustration of holiday destinations in image slideshows, audio recordings and video clips. These appeared to enhance their imagination of the look and feel of destinations before visiting: "I like the images, I like the slideshows, equally with the video clips it's nice to have a look around, and it's just, I suppose it just takes that one, it makes it easy when you get to a place because you recognize it" (Jim). Such links were also available locally on the smartphone without going online and fitted with a desire expressed by participants to relax and disconnect from too much technology when on holiday.

Social reading. A surprise finding for us was the mention by several participants that the a-book allowed more social reading in a group. The split content between book and smartphone could sometimes be awkward to manage by an individual, but became a perceived advantage for sharing and discussing content with others. Participants imagined that one person could hold the book, while one or more people could *each* hold their smartphones to access and discuss additional digital content: "I would use it at the same time as my husband, where I never would with my phone, so I could see myself sitting in bed looking through this with my husband. I could definitely picture me sitting down on the steps of a caravan where me and my mum will quite often sit with a cup of tea in the mornings and looking at this" (Sarah). Some participants also mentioned screen casting smartphone content to a shared TV.

Personal digital annotation. In addition to accessing the extra published digital content from the printed book, participants loved the idea of adding their own content to personalise it. Technically this could be done by adding photos, audio, video or weblinks on each page, or by tuning the Twitter feed to see local news and events of particular interest to the reader. Both methods were appreciated, either to extend the planning of a trip beforehand or to document it afterwards in a kind of travel journal: "You can save photos onto pages and stuff. It's a nice way you could have your holiday diary in the app" (Jenny). "I really like the fact that you've got, you know, up-to-date information about Cornwall… for example, if there was a new festival… you get updates or… any offers, that would be really good" (Annie). As an extension of the social reading practice above, some people imagined social writing of annotations shared within a group: "you know friends that live there, so they may give you extra information and *it would be nice asterisk here to add you know the extra bit of information here*" (Gareth). "*If you are able to look at the bookmarks page and see who's added what. Then you could have other people tick and say, I want to be able to go here. Then, you know what everyone wants to do*" (Mary).

Comparison with interactive e-books. Participants were able to see the augmented Cornwall guide in e-book form, on both a smartphone and tablet. Neither was considered to be entirely satisfactory, since the tablet was seen as too big and heavy to carry around on holiday and the phone screen was too small to allow the book text to be read properly. However, participants liked all the extra digital content on the phone, and felt that it might be useful to carry with them on a trip. This led to the unusual idea of using the a-book app and content alone for a bookmarked set of pages when travelling outdoors, after planning the trip with the book-and-phone together indoors: "A-book at home before I leave. Leave this [printed book] at home. Take this [smartphone] with me with all my bookmarks. Be able to access the relevant pages from here [a-book app]. That seems the most natural to me" [John].

3.2 Field Trial

Eleven one-to-one semi-structured interviews were conducted with adult travellers that visited Cornwall between June and mid-August 2021. All travellers were given a free augmented Cornwall guide book and app to use before and during their visit, and to keep thereafter. On return, they were asked for their feedback on the augmented guidebook with the aim of understanding of how the a-book can be adopted in practice during the planning and engagement stages of travel.

Collectively, the findings show that participants liked the concept and found it an interesting and innovative idea. Many participants said that were intrigued by the concept of integrating a paper guidebook and digital solutions. They especially appreciated how the book was nicely laid out and rich with detailed information. Regarding the augmented content, it was suggested that it was interesting, especially because it provides a better understanding of the culture and history of Cornwall. Similarly, some participants expressed positive comments on the local voices in the audio and video links: "Yeah, I like that stuff. Yeah, hearing the local voices describe things is great because you don't often get that chance when you're visiting as a tourist" (Brian). Most interviewees (7 of 11) indicated that they would recommend it to friends and family members. Some participants claimed that using the a-book improved the quality of their experience in Cornwall and offered an engaging reading experience. Overall, the findings show that the a-book could enrich travel experiences.

Whilst one participant did not show any interested in continuing using the a-book, all claimed that they would continue to use it for future travel in Cornwall. When asked about future purchase intention, they reported there are likely to buy an a-book if these become widely available in the market: "I maybe don't know the rest of Cornwall as well as I should do, given the amount of time spent there. So, the guide will be a good way of exploring the rest" (Adam).

However, participants were unanimous in the view that some features of the a-book needed improvement, particularly in regards to the augmented content and the app design. The majority of participants provided negative comments about the quality of the augmented content, since it did not meet their expectations: "I really liked the idea of the guidebook, but I just don't think the multimedia content is decent enough quality. It doesn't feel like the screen lives up to the book!" (Susan).

Concerns were also expressed about the quantity of the augmented content, since some pages were non-interactive. There were suggestions that every page should offer some type of augmented content. Some interviewees argued that since it is a heavy book, it was not practical for them to carry and use the a-book and smartphone together, especially for outdoor activities like walking and cycling. This led to the same suggestion as that made in the lab study, to carry a bookmarked set of pages and links on the phone alone "I wasn't going to take it out on my walking because it was too heavy to carry. So being able to perhaps to somehow access some of the content of the book on the app might be useful. If we could have saved like some key stuff from the book onto the app so when we were out we could look at it" (Emma).

Relatedly, some participants felt it was difficult even indoors to use the book with the phone: "it was just a bit strange getting used to using the two together because you almost tend to use them quite separately" (Martha). Five interviewees described the app as 'clunky', and a common view amongst them was that the app design needs to be enhanced and be more visually appealing in order to provide a more user-friendly navigation.

3.3 Interview Survey

Five online semi-structured interviews were conducted individually with representatives of four Destination Management Organisations (DMOs) and 1 attraction project manager working between the UK and Denmark. These were carried out between June and mid-August 2021 and involved hands on use of the Cornwall a-book and app by each participant to elicit reactions of how a-books might be adopted in a commercial context. Participants were recruited through emails and word or mouth and the interviews lasted 30 to 40 min. Data were analysed and interpreted through thematic analysis in accordance with Braun and Clarke's guidelines (2011) using the software NVivo 11.

Overall, all interviewees showed interest in the idea and agreed that the a-book is nicely laid out, detailed and easy to read. The majority of participants suggested that the a-book has the potential to increase visibility and raise awareness about aspects and locations that visitors usually do not realise about a tourist destination to diversify the audience. Notably, two participants appreciated the "Slow Travel" concept since it enables the promotion of a more profound travel experience: "But also, I think in my perspective, you know, the whole concept of slow travel when taking the time to pay attention to stuff is, you know, very much what we would be supporting as well" (Participant 1).

Regarding strategic partnerships, there was a general consensus amongst participants that the adoption of the a-book might foster possible collaboration with local attractions, accommodations and public transport to bring mutual benefits. As one interviewee put it: "Yes, yes, I think we could get this as a funded project from, say, VisitEngland, then it would be a great project for everyone to get behind together and something very physical to show at the end".

Relatedly, respondents reported that the a-book can create opportunities to offer more inclusive and accessible content, particularly for people with different disabilities. For example, Participant 4 commented: "It could be hugely advantageous if the virtual content or the digital content is coded or tagged to suit different disabilities. So, for instance, obviously there's a wheelchair one which is a common one. But that's you know that's only 15% of people with disabilities. So, 85% of people can be to do with difficulty to walk over rough terrain, deafness, autism, dementia".

Nonetheless, there were some negative comments about the quality of augmented content and suggestions for improvements were also advanced. Similar to the tourists' interviews, all participants agree that the mobile app was not intuitive and should provide more user-friendly navigation, in particular a short tutorial for first-time users: "you know like when normally in some apps, when it's the first time you download it, they give you a tutorial. You know when you can say, skip I know the tutorial, but sometimes it's like they offer you the chance to get to half a tutorial in the app. I think that would be a big help on the app because if it had a pop-up saying, "well, first time, we're so excited for you to be here and to explore the book in a more digital way" (Participant 3). In the same vein, the participants were unanimous in the view that significant improvement regarding the quality and quantity of the augmented content needs to be implemented.

Notably, Participant 5 questioned whether the a-book is more convenient to read in the pre-travel stage to learn about the destination from home while planning the vacation rather than during the stay in Cornwall: "Yeah, I think the thorough research to back that up that you know people do 80% of their planning before they go. And most of that is done digitally, these days. And I think also time is because your time is very precious and you have to put things in advance, particularly post COVID, I think you pretty much know what your, what you want to get what you want to go and see and do, before you leave. But I think this is a really impressive, fantastic tool for researching and inspiring you".

Moreover, there were some suggestions that the a-book can be adopted as a space for tourists to share their experiences and stories through visual contents: "To give it more value, it would be nice to if you did something like a user-generated thing so they could send in photos as well so it's not just the author's photos here in there, but you have, you know, a lot like a TripAdvisor thing where you have different sort of reviews or photos" (Participant 2). Overall, participants indicated that the tailor-made content, storytelling and possibly user-generated content (UGC) features could represent the USP to promote the augmented guidebook.

Furthermore, some participants stressed the importance of promoting the a-book to the right target market. Talking about this issue, Participant 4 said: "So, I think it's actually targeting it to the demographic that the buys that once information is information hungry. But there are probably 30–40% of the population that would use it, and probably 15% who would really love it. So, my view is, this is like a new tool, but it's got to be put in the right hands". In summary, these results indicate that the a-book has significant business potential for stimulating strategic partnerships with destinations, increasing the accessibility and attractiveness of travel guides, and improving the travel experience.

4 Discussion

Despite nearly 30 years of experimentation in the field of augmented paper, there is still a lack of consistency in the approach to authoring augmented documents and lack of a common format or standard. To make things worse, there are at least two core technologies derived from AR and IoT for triggering links from paper, and no consensus about what client devices to use to do this. Little wonder then that the approach has failed to influence the publishing industry as predicted, and is relegated to one-off initiatives that are custom made.

We have shown that one key to this puzzle may be the use of existing e-book standards which already allow for interactivity and augmentation designed to be read on e-book screens. By utilising a non-reflowable EPUB3 format we have been able to create an a-book comprising a printed book with hotlinks that play on a nearby smartphone. In effect we still use the screen to display such multimedia content, whilst printing the main part of the book as usual. This means that publishers can continue to use their existing book layout software such as InDesign to author a-books as well as e-books, creating a third book format for consumers. This leads to a 'third way' in the battle between print and e-books in which paper and screen are used together in a hybrid reading experience. We have also shown that this can be achieved on standard consumer products such as a smartphones or tablets, yet still accommodate AR and IOT linking mechanisms as triggers for content. While we referred to these as 2G and 3G paper, in practice we can see that combinations could be used in the future, depending on the maturity of the technology and the user experience that is desired. In general, the 2G AR approach is more awkward for the user who has to hold the phone in one hand and the book in the other to take a picture of the page. 3G paper approximates touch sensitive paper and is more seamless to handle with content being triggered more naturally from page turning or pointing actions over the paper. Future research should explore what might be called 2.5G mechanisms for combining the technologies as well as speech control as an alternative to image recognition.

This raises some questions about the stability of future book content, when that content is split between paper and screen. We have found that paper is generally good for stable visual content while screen is good for dynamic multimedia content that could change over time. This is accommodated weakly at the moment through weblinks to pages whose content could update. Stronger support could be provided by shifting the balance between local and remote content, and adding remote functionality to update content automatically, as with travel timetables for example. Longer term, there may be ways of generating augmented content automatically using AI by analysing the print content of documents and seeking ways to enhance it. At the moment, authoring of augmented books throws additional responsibility onto authors and publishers who now have to collect or create extra image, audio or video material for a publication. This gives them additional creative freedom of expression but is likely to extend the time and effort required to 'write' a book across paper and screen media. New writing and design guidelines are needed for such an enterprise, to make the most of this new paradigm for multimedia writing and responsive reading.

There is little doubt from our user evaluations of this first commercial a-book that the augmentation of a printed travel guide with additional smartphone content is seen by customers as an intriguing innovation with real value. Perhaps its strongest benefits were seen indoors in the planning of a trip or day out before travel and documenting or sharing of the experience of a trip afterwards. This is because the use of a book and smartphone together is easier when one of them is supported by a table or shared between people in a group. In this context, additional multimedia content from the publisher or traveller were especially seen to enhance both the imagination of a place and the memory of visiting it. Further design support might be provided for this kind of imaginary, immersive and social reading and writing in the travel domain, so that a printed travel guide might become an individual or group travel journal. This opens up new publishing possibilities for the co-authoring of travel guides by publishers and their readers through a kind of citizen travel journalism. Other user benefits were perceived for outdoor use of an augmented travel guide especially for practical and up to date information, but in a screen-only form combining print and digital content in a new way. This was not satisfied by the interactive e-book version of the Cornwall guide on a smartphone, and requires further innovation to allow bookmarked print content to be read on a small screen in series with its associated digital content.

Such user feedback was amplified by the positive comments of travel organisations about the approach. They saw its potential for improved storytelling about destinations, customised content for different audiences, increased accessibility, and partnership opportunities to market tourist attractions. They also began to suggest tailoring the additional digital content to different audiences and optimising the a-book paradigm to trip planning. This leads us to believe that the a-book approach we have outlined is truly market-ready, at least in the tourism domain, to add benefit and longevity to conventional travel guide books.

Acknowledgments. This work was funded by the UK Engineering and Physical Sciences Research Council (EPSRC) as part of the Digital Economy programme under grant number EP/P02579X/1. This was in response to a call entitled 'Content creation and consumption in the digital economy'. We also thank travel writer Kirsty Fergusson and CEO Adrian Phillips and his staff at Bradt Travel Guides Ltd for their collaboration to create the augmented Cornwall guide.

Disclosure of Interests. The authors have no competing interests to declare that are relevant to the content of this article.

References

1. Hillesund, T.: Digital reading spaces: how expert readers handle books, the web and electronic paper. First Monday (2010)
2. Jeong, H.: A comparison of the influence of electronic books and paper books on reading comprehension, eye fatigue, and perception. Electron. Libr. **30**(3), 390–408 (2012)
3. Mangen, A., Walgermo, B.R., Brønnick, K.: Reading linear texts on paper versus computer screen: effects on reading comprehension. Int. J. Educ. Res. **58**, 61–68 (2013)
4. Levy, M.D.: Scrolling Forward: Making Sense of Documents in the Digital Age. Arcade Publishing, New York (2001)
5. Sellen, A.J., Harper, R.H.: The Myth of the Paperless Office. MIT Press, Cambridge (2003)
6. Clark, D.T., Goodwin, S.P., Samuelson, T., Coker, C.: A qualitative assessment of the Kindle e, Äêbook reader: results from initial focus groups. Perform. Meas. Metrics **9**(2), 118–129 (2008)
7. Chen, S., Granitz, N.: Adoption, rejection, or convergence: consumer attitudes toward book digitization. J. Bus. Res. **65**(8), 1219–1225 (2012)
8. Zhang, Y., Kudva, S.: E-books versus print books: readers' choices and preferences across contexts. J. Am. Soc. Inf. Sci. **65**(8), 1695–1706 (2014)
9. Jenkins, H., Ford, S., Green, J.: Spreadable Media: Creating Value and Meaning in a Networked Culture. NYU Press (2013)
10. Schrøder, K.C., et al.: Audiences are inherently cross-media: audience studies and the cross-media challenge. CM Komunikacija i mediji. **6**(18), 5–27 (2011)
11. Cope, B., Kalantzis, M.: "Multiliteracies": New literacies, new learning. Pedagogies Int. J. **4**(3), 164–195 (2009)
12. Luff, P., Heath, C., Norrie, M., Signer, B., Herdman, P.: Only touching the surface: creating affinities between digital content and paper. In: Proceedings of the 2004 ACM Conference on Computer Supported Cooperative Work, CSCW '04. New York, NY, USA, pp. 523–532. Association for Computing Machinery (2004). https://doi.org/10.1145/1031607.1031695

13. Wellner, P.: Interacting with paper on the digital desk. Commun. ACM **36**(7), 87–96 (1993)
14. Billinghurst, M., Kato, H., Poupyrev, I.: The magicbook - moving seamlessly between reality and virtuality. IEEE Comput. Graphics Appl. **21**(3), 6–8 (2001)
15. Erol, B., Antúnez, E., Hull, J.J.: Hotpaper: multimedia interaction with paper using mobile phones. In: Proceedings of the 16th ACM International Conference on Multimedia, MM '08. New York, NY, USA, pp. 399–408. ACM (2008)
16. Liao, C., Liu, Q., Liew, B., Wilcox, L.: Pacer: fine-grained interactive paper via camera touch hybrid gestures on a cell phone. In: Proceedings of the SIGCHI Conference on Human Factors in Computing Systems, CHI 2010. New York, NY, USA, pp. 2441–2450. ACM (2010)
17. Back, M., Cohen, J., Gold, R., Harrison, S., Minneman, S.: Listen reader: an electronically augmented paper-based book. In: Proceedings of the SIGCHI Conference on Human Factors in Computing Systems, pp. 23–29 (2001)
18. Klemmer, S.R., Graham, J., Wolff, G.J., Landay, J.A.: Books with voices: paper transcripts as a physical interface to oral histories. In: Proceedings of the SIGCHI Conference on Human Factors in Computing Systems, CHI '03. New York, NY, USA, pp. 89–96. ACM (2003)
19. Chen, N.S., Teng, D.C.E., Lee, C.H., Kinshuk: Augmenting paper-based reading activity with direct access to digital materials and scaffolded questioning. Comput. Educ. **57**(2), 1705–1715 (2011)
20. Frohlich, D.M., et al.: Designing interactive newsprint. Int. J. Hum. Comput. Stud. **104**, 36–49 (2017)
21. Georgiadou, E., Margaritopoulos, M.: The application of augmented reality in print media. J. Print Media Technol. Res. **8**(1), 43–55 (2019)
22. Signer, B., Norrie, M.C.: Interactive paper: past, present and future. In: Proceedings of the 12th ACM International Conference on Ubiquitous Computing (UbiComp'10). Copenhagen, Denmark (2010)
23. Signer, B., Norrie, M.C., Weibel, N., Ispas, A.: Advanced authoring of paper-digital systems. Multimedia Tools Appl. **70**(2), 1309–1332 (2014)
24. Lu, X., Lu, Z.: A publishing framework for digitally augmented paper documents: towards cross-media information integration. In: Zhuang, Y., Yang, S.Q., Rui, Y., He, Q. (eds.) Advances in Multimedia Information Processing - PCM 2006, pp. 494–501. Heidelberg, Springer (2006)
25. Guimbretière, F.: Paper augmented digital documents. In: Proceedings of the 16th Annual ACM Symposium on User Interface Software and Technology, pp. 51–60 (2003)
26. Yeh, R.B., Paepcke, A., Klemmer, S.R.: Iterative design and evaluation of an event architecture for pen-and-paper interfaces. In: Proceedings of the 21st Annual ACM Symposium on User Interface Software and Technology, pp. 111–120 (2008)
27. Heinrichs, F., Steimle, J., Schreiber, D., Mühlhäuser, M.: Letras: an architecture and framework for ubiquitous pen-and-paper interaction. In: Proceedings of the 2nd ACM SIGCHI Symposium on Engineering Interactive Computing Systems, pp. 193–198 (2010)
28. Mackay, W.E., Pothier, G, Letondal, C., Bøegh, K., Sørensen, H.E.: The missing link: Augmenting biology laboratory notebooks. In: Proceedings of the 15th Annual ACM Symposium on User Interface Software and Technology, UIST '02, New York, NY, USA, pp. 41–50. ACM (2002)
29. Cornwall, F.K., the Isles of Scilly (3rd Edition). Bradt Travel Guides (2019)
30. Bairaktaris, G., Frohlich, D., Sporea, R.: Printed light tags and the magic bookmark: using light to augment paper objects. In: Extended Abstracts of the 2021 CHI Conference on Human Factors in Computing Systems, pp. 1–5 (2021)
31. Bairaktaris, G., Siderov, H., Celebiler, D., Kolii, C., Frohlich, D.M., Sporea, R.A.: Magic bookmark: a nonintrusive electronic system for functionalizing physical books. Adv. Intell. Syst. **4**(3), 2100138 (2022)

32. Bairaktaris, G., Le Borgne, B., Turkani, V., Corrigan-Kavanagh, E., Frohlich, D.M., Sporea, R.A.: Augmented books: hybrid electronics bring paper to life. IEEE Pervasive Comput. **21**(4), 88–95 (2022)
33. Corrigan-Kavanagh, E., Frohlich, D.M., Scarles, C.: Re-invigorating the photo album: augmenting printed photobooks with digital media. Pers. Ubiquit. Comput. **27**(2), 467–480 (2023)
34. Frohlich, D., et al.: The Cornwall a-book: an augmented travel guide using next generation paper. J. Electron. Publ. **22**(1) (2019)
35. Corrigan-Kavanagh, E., Scarles, C., Revill, G., Beynon, M., van Duppen, J.: Explorations on the future of the book from the Next Generation Paper Project. Publishing History **83**, 35–54 (2020)
36. Corrigan-Kavanagh, E., Frohlich, D., Yuan, H., Bober, M.: Designing for the next generation of augmented books. J. Des. Res. **18**(5–6), 356–374 (2020)
37. Husain, S.S., Bober, M.: Improving large-scale image retrieval through robust aggregation of local descriptors. IEEE Trans. Pattern Anal. Mach. Intell. **39**(9), 1783–1796 (2016)
38. Corbin, J., Strauss, A.: Strategies for qualitative data analysis. Basics Qualit. Res. Tech. Proc. Dev. Grounded Theory **3**(10), 4135 (2008)

Research on Tax Collection and Administration of Mobile Commerce Under Smart Taxation

Na Fu, Peiyan Zhou[✉], and Zhangxin Ma

Jilin University, 2699 Qianjin Street, Changchun, Jilin, China
zh-peiyan@163.com

Abstract. With the rapid development of the internet industry and the widespread use of mobile devices, mobile commerce has gradually become an important way of consumption in people's daily lives. Due to the characteristics of mobility, virtuality, real-time transactions, and borderless nature of mobile commerce, tax collection and management in this area have become a major challenge. In China, the tax system has undergone a transition from "experience-based tax management" to "invoice-based tax management" and further towards "data-driven tax management", which aims to improve the tax collection and management system by promoting the construction of intelligent taxation digital and intelligent management platforms for enterprises. Against this backdrop, this study combines intelligent taxation with mobile commerce, focusing on solving the tax collection and management issues of mobile commerce under intelligent taxation. It analyzes the implementation methods and characteristics of intelligent taxation, the current development status and taxation issues of mobile commerce, and deeply explores the connection and adaptability between the two. The study aims to provide policy recommendations for the digital upgrade of tax collection and management applied to the field of mobile commerce.

Keywords: Intelligent taxation · mobile commerce · tax collection and management · adaptability

1 Introduction

According to the policy data released by the Ministry of Commerce of the People's Republic of China on January 16, 2024, the total volume of e-commerce transactions in China increased from RMB 31.63 trillion in 2018 to RMB 43.83 trillion in 2022. The proportion of online retail sales of physical goods to total social retail sales exceeded 25%. As of early 2023, China has been the world's largest online retail market for 11 consecutive years. According to a report published by consulting firm Kawes Lab and reported by Chile's "Tres Puntos" on January 18, after explosive growth during the pandemic, e-commerce has declined for three consecutive years, with declines of 2.7%, 12.5%, and 1.5% respectively from 2021 to 2023. It is expected to rebound this year, and is expected to grow by 4.8% and 6.1% in 2024 and 2025, respectively. According to the report, 2024 will be a turning point for the development of the e-commerce industry. The report also discusses the technologies that will affect e-commerce this year. Firstly, mobile phones: more than half of online shopping is expected to be completed through mobile devices by 2023. Secondly, personalized services: consumers will value more personalized services such as product recommendations and customer service when shopping online. The use of mobile devices such as mobile phones in the e-commerce industry is actually entering the field of mobile commerce. Mobile commerce is an extension and expansion of e-commerce, which optimizes efficiency and other aspects based on e-commerce [1].

Mobile commerce has unique mobility characteristics and inherent virtuality and borderlessness, making it challenging for countries worldwide to manage its taxation effectively. Mobile commerce enterprises can choose to engage in cross-border online transactions and take advantage of different tax rates imposed by various countries. By establishing their presence in tax-free or preferential countries, these enterprises can evade high taxes in their home country, leading to significant erosion of tax bases and profit shifting issues [2]. In September 2013, the G20 leaders decided to implement the Base Erosion and Profit Shifting (BEPS) Action Plan for international tax reform, with the OECD leading the project. The signing of the BEPS Multilateral Convention by multiple countries indicated the international community's concern regarding this issue and the collective efforts to prevent tax base erosion and profit shifting. The Chinese government also signed the BEPS Multilateral Convention and delivered a speech on June 7, 2017, demonstrating China's commitment to addressing international issues and assuming its responsibilities as a major country.

This article explores the tax management issues in China's mobile commerce industry and combines them with the characteristics of China's advancement in the modernization process through the implementation of smart tax platforms. It aims to investigate the adaptability of smart tax systems in the taxation of mobile commerce and seek a Chinese solution that can serve as a reference for other countries in addressing tax issues in the mobile commerce sector. Additionally, it showcases China's substantial measures to prevent tax base erosion and profit shifting. The research significance of this article includes: (1) refining the tax issues of e-commerce into the field of mobile commerce, thereby increasing the depth of research in this area. Since mobile commerce is a development of e-commerce and largely follows its characteristics, this article analyzes the tax issues specific to mobile commerce based on existing research on e-commerce. (2) Broadening the channels for resolving tax issues in mobile commerce. This article innovatively combines China's construction of smart tax platforms in the digital economy era and examines whether smart tax systems are suitable for tax management in mobile commerce. This, in turn, helps address the issue of tax fairness between mobile commerce and traditional brick-and-mortar businesses. (3) Providing policy recommendations for China's early realization of the modernization process to some extent. The construction of smart tax platforms is an essential step for China to achieve tax modernization. By combining mobile commerce with smart tax systems and improving the existing digital and intelligent tax management systems, this article further provides solutions to promote China's tax modernization process.

2 Mobile Commerce

2.1 The Implications of Mobile Commerce

Extensive research findings suggest that most definitions based on a transaction perspective consider mobile commerce as an extension of electronic commerce. On the other hand, definitions from a systemic perspective view mobile commerce as a system built upon a certain economic and technological foundation [3]. However, this article argues that mobile commerce refers to a new form of electronic commerce transaction that relies on mobile communication technology and mobile devices to achieve real-time and mobility characteristics, based on a certain technological and value chain circulation.

2.2 The Necessity of Mobile Commerce Taxation

In the early stages of the development of the mobile commerce industry, many countries implemented tax exemption policies to promote its growth. In 1998, the United States Congress passed the Internet Tax Freedom Act, which established a three-year tax exemption period and principles such as origin-based taxation to avoid double taxation and tax discrimination. In 2000, the US Electronic Commerce Advisory Commission extended the tax exemption period through the Internet Tax Freedom Act. In 2004, the US Congress passed the Internet Tax Nondiscrimination Act, expanding the scope of tax exemption for internet access services [4]. The European Union also proposed that EU residents enjoy e-commerce services tax-free when obtained from non-EU residents, while non-EU residents are exempt from value-added tax.

However, with the widespread use of mobile devices, the tax-exempt online business model in mobile commerce has created significant market displacement issues for the physical economy. The physical economy bears a more comprehensive tax management system, and the tax burden is partially transferred to the sales prices of goods purchased by consumers. In addition to providing consumers with more convenient and diverse shopping options, the tax advantages of mobile commerce also result in lower market prices. This severe price competition of mobile commerce poses a threat to the development of the physical economy. In 2013, the US Senate passed the Marketplace Fairness Act, which stipulates the collection of local sales tax and use tax on e-commerce companies under the premise of simplifying state tax regulations. The European Union also levies taxes on non-residents providing e-commerce services to ensure tax fairness for EU residents. The shift in tax collection systems in e-commerce by the United States and the European Union also provides guidance for China. From a developmental perspective, both the physical economy and mobile commerce inherently satisfy the principles of profitability and non-public interest taxation. They only differ in the way they provide transactions to consumers. Therefore, mobile commerce should also assume its own tax obligations after implementing promotion measures [5]. In China, the mobile commerce industry, including e-commerce, has experienced rapid development. The increasing reliance of residents on mobile commerce reflects that the industry has passed the survival stage and consumers have widely accepted the convenience brought by mobile commerce in their lives. Mobile commerce should improve relevant tax systems and establish tax fairness between mobile commerce and the physical economy to avoid tax evasion issues during the transformation from the physical economy to mobile commerce, which can harm the national and regional tax bases. The Electronic Commerce Law of the People's Republic of China, promulgated by the Standing Committee of the National People's Congress on August 31, 2018, demonstrates China's efforts to regulate and lead the e-commerce sector. Mobile commerce will gradually improve while complying with the law, and taxation in this area will eventually be addressed in China.

2.3 Tax Collection and Administration of Mobile Commerce

This article will analyze the existing difficulties in taxing mobile commerce based on its own characteristics and the current relevant laws and regulations in China's business field.

Tax Location Determination. Due to the virtual and concealed nature of mobile commerce, it is difficult to determine the tax objects and tax locations of mobile commerce transactions [4]. The real-time and mobile nature of mobile commerce transactions may span multiple regions, making it difficult to determine tax attribution. Existing international literature primarily focuses on analyzing whether the United States and the European Union should adopt origin-based or destination-based taxation for electronic commerce. The determination of the tax jurisdiction for electronic commerce can provide some insights for mobile commerce. Most scholars support the principle of destination-based taxation, and their analysis is often based on production efficiency [6]. The reasons for destination taxation are still considered valid. Policy makers in the European Union for digital products taxation also mostly agree with the principle of destination-based taxation. Generally speaking, the destination principle is considered superior to the origin principle [7]. Some studies also suggest that if destination-based taxation is implemented for e-commerce while maintaining the origin-based principle for in-store purchases, local governments may have more incentive to encourage residents to choose online shopping over cross-border in-store shopping. As a result, tax competition among different regions becomes more intense, and there is a greater possibility of overall tax revenue decline due to tax reductions [8]. China has a more centralized tax system where local governments have limited authority to set tax rates. They can only make adjustments to taxes through tax exemption policies and appropriate taxation measures for local industries. In contrast, the central government has stronger control over taxation, and local governments have limited freedom in tax matters. This relatively limited tax competition ability in China's mobile commerce sector is due to these factors. The destination-based taxation principle is more suitable for China's mobile commerce. However, the implementation of destination-based taxation and how to collect taxes at the destination is still a problem that needs to be addressed.

Definition of the Nature of Income. According to international tax rules, different types of transactional income are subject to different tax policies. The classification of mobile commerce transactional income into categories such as products, services, royalties, rent, and licensing fees remains a challenge [9]. The ambiguity in classification can lead to tax planning opportunities for mobile commerce businesses, allowing them to shift income that should be taxed at higher rates into categories with lower tax provisions. This practice seriously undermines the tax base of the country.

The Existence of International Tax Avoidance. The borderless nature of mobile commerce also allows businesses to choose different countries for transactions, and the traded goods or services may be transported from one country to another. In terms of taxation, this cross-border mobile commerce poses challenges as the flow of goods may not align with the flow of funds, making it difficult for tax authorities to determine the sales revenue. For example, in mobile commerce transactions, the goods or services are directly delivered from the provider to the consumer, but the funds involved in the transaction are collected from the consumer by an intermediary platform, which deducts its fees before transferring the remaining amount to the provider [10]. The source of goods for providers in mobile commerce may also be cross-border, as mobile commerce businesses may set up companies in countries with lower tax rates and remotely control them to transfer goods to consumers in other countries. This increases the difficulty of monitoring the tax compliance of mobile commerce businesses.

Tax Avoidance Punishment Mechanism. Due to the incomplete punitive mechanism for tax evasion in the field of mobile commerce taxation in China and other countries [11], mobile commerce businesses have a significant imbalance between the benefits and costs of tax evasion. Mobile commerce breaks the time and space limitations of physical transactions, creating a gap between the real-time nature of transactions and the lag in tax collection, providing opportunities for businesses to evade taxes. From a cost perspective, the traditional tax control and physical verification management model, coupled with lenient tax policies, make it difficult for tax authorities to obtain information on mobile commerce businesses [12]. Furthermore, the trade information of businesses is internal and exclusive, and the tax authorities mainly rely on information uploaded by businesses, exacerbating the tax operation space in mobile commerce. The punitive mechanism for tax evasion has yet to be established and implemented, resulting in lower costs for tax evasion in the mobile commerce industry. However, in terms of revenue, tax evasion is a direct benefit, which also encourages mobile commerce businesses to conceal tax information as much as possible.

Relevant Laws and Regulations. On August 31, 2018, China issued its first law on the field of e-commerce, the "E-commerce Law," which plays a guiding role in regulating the e-commerce sector. However, as it is the first law specifically related to e-commerce, it has been in effect for five years, and its exposed issues have become increasingly significant. The law's provisions are overly general, only providing principle-oriented guidelines [13]. The ambiguity of the legal provisions will lead to challenges in implementation and operation for relevant departments [19]. There are no specific regulations regarding how e-commerce operators who are not required to register as market entities, as stated in Article 10 of the E-commerce Law, should handle tax registration, where to handle tax registration, how to declare taxes, and how to regulate such operators [11]. The formulation of laws in the e-commerce sector faces serious operational difficulties, let alone in the more specific field of mobile commerce, where there are no targeted laws and regulations. Only the general guidelines of the E-commerce Law, which lack specificity, can be used for regulation. The imperfect development of taxation laws in the mobile commerce sector will further limit the industry's healthy development.

3 Smart Taxation

3.1 The Historical Development of Smart Taxation

Since China began tax reform in 1978, the tax system has been refined from a broad and crude system to a classification of various types of taxes. The taxation system has become more meticulous, targeted, and management-focused. However, "experience-based management" was the main form of tax management at that time. The low efficiency of national tax management did not match the rapidly developing market trade, and tax evasion was rampant. In order to solve the problem of tax evasion caused by false invoices, the Chinese tax authorities launched the Golden Tax Project Phase I in 1994, which has undergone tax system reforms from Golden Tax Phase I, Golden Tax Phase II, Golden Tax Phase III to today's intelligent taxation. The first phase focused on verifying the authenticity of value-added tax invoices. The second phase was "from point to line," focusing on building a management chain of functions such as value-added tax invoice issuance, declaration, and review. The third phase was "from line to face," aiming to build an information management system for all taxes, all links, and all institutions. The goal of "intelligent taxation" is to establish a multi-dimensional and comprehensive tax-sharing system for government departments, financial institutions, taxpayers, and tax authorities through diversified information sharing. It realizes the full-process tax governance through "digital twins" and further expands new scenarios of intelligent taxation.

3.2 The Connotation of Smart Taxation

The Implementation of Smart Taxation. Intelligent taxation integrates digitalization and intelligence, utilizing modern information technologies such as big data, cloud computing, and artificial intelligence. It aims to promote the convergence of internal and external tax-related data, bridging online and offline channels. This drives innovation and development in tax services, tax supervision, and tax enforcement. Simultaneously, it improves data management mechanisms, optimizes the allocation of tax administration resources, and enhances the efficiency and effectiveness of tax governance. This process involves continuous learning and improvement to achieve iterative upgrades in tax governance.

Specifically, intelligent taxation involves the following aspects:

1. Tax authorities utilize tax big data for intelligent collection and efficient management, enabling controllable tax enforcement processes, assessable outcomes, traceable violations, and accountable responsibilities. This transforms the tax management approach from "invoice-based" to "information-based" and further to "data-driven".

2. Taxpayers and payment obligors benefit from intelligent gathering and monitoring of tax-related data through "one-stop" and "individual" digital tax accounts. This promotes self-monitoring, self-identification, self-response, and self-prevention of tax risks, transforming their compliance behaviors from "passive obedience" to "active obedience" and eventually to "automated compliance".

3. Other stakeholders involved in taxation, such as financial institutions, customs, market regulators, public security agencies, and payment platforms, contribute to tax governance through intelligent collection and presentation of tax-related data. This promotes data collaboration, sharing, coordination, and governance, facilitating the modernization of the digital government and tax governance system.

The Characteristics of Smart Taxation

High Efficiency of Data Technology. The construction of intelligent taxation is based on "tax big data as the driving force" and promotes the integration of data from multiple stages, departments, and perspectives. At the technological level, modern information technologies such as cloud computing, Internet of Things, blockchain, artificial intelligence, and 5G are integrated to innovate and promote the construction of intelligent taxation platforms. This achieves breakthroughs in "computing volume, algorithms, and computing power," enhances data protection and traceability capabilities, and ensures the management of taxpayer identities under the real-name system, data sharing, and information application [14]. The application of data technology will greatly shorten the time for tax administration and verification, enable online monitoring of actual transaction content, rapidly analyze market transaction trends, promptly curb fraudulent transactions, and cooperate with legal measures to crack down on tax evasion and avoidance activities.

Linkage of Information Sharing. Intelligent taxation utilizes cloud computing and efficient algorithms based on big data to accurately process the vast amount of market transaction data. It can quickly identify fraudulent transactions. However, to achieve the desired effect of "tax governance through numbers," it is essential to have a reliable and extensive database as the foundation for this fast and accurate algorithm technology. The coordination and collaboration among various tax administration departments are crucial in realizing this goal. In order to facilitate interdepartmental data supervision, the tax administration system has established an information sharing platform. The tax administration system continuously shares real-time information from various regions with other departments through cloud space, enabling dynamic data monitoring [15, 18]. This allows timely verification and capture of fraudulent data based on upstream and downstream transaction information. Intelligent taxation greatly promotes the coordinated cooperation among tax administration departments to create a favorable tax environment.

Transparency of Oversight Throughout the Process. Compared to the traditional system, intelligent taxation focuses on verifying not only value-added tax invoices but also the essence of transactions. It matches the tax conditions of multiple tax types and enables detailed examination of the actual transactional business for tax purposes. In addition to value-added tax, intelligent taxation plays an equally important role in other tax types such as personal income tax and corporate income tax. The application of big data can create data profiles for taxpayers and payment obligors. While businesses or individuals independently report transaction information, tax authorities can compare this information with a large collection of data on the timing, location, and other details of transaction activities. This allows for precise reporting of income tax [15]. Through its powerful data allocation and processing capabilities, intelligent taxation simplifies tax administration workflows and meets the higher service demands of taxpayers and payment obligors.

Current Issues of Smart Tax Implementation. The existing implementation issues in intelligent business mainly stem from an excessive reliance on the development of existing algorithm technologies. Faced with a large pool of data, only more sophisticated algorithms can accurately reconstruct transaction facts. However, there is still room for improvement in current algorithms, which reflects the limitations of excessive reliance on manual tax assessment. The purpose of intelligent taxation operation is to transform the tool-oriented thinking of traditional tax systems into a concept centered around serving taxpayers and payment obligors. However, in the current practical operation, the overly automated tax system quickly processes tax payments after uploading transaction data, without openly displaying the process to taxpayers. As a result, taxpayers lose certain rights such as the right to information, knowledge, and participation [16].

4 The Application of Smart Taxation in Mobile Commerce Taxation

4.1 The Application of Data Technology in Mobile Commerce

With the development of data technologies such as cloud computing and big data, their characteristics of large capacity, diversity, and high speed have led mobile commerce enterprises in competitive fast-paced markets to quickly adopt these data technologies to achieve digitalization and intelligence transformation in order to gain more market share.

1. Data technologies can reduce the investment cost for mobile commerce enterprises. In the mobile commerce industry, operations are primarily conducted through a mobile commerce platform system, which serves as the core for connecting service providers and consumers. Maintaining this platform system requires talented individuals with high knowledge and technical capabilities, and the significant number of personnel involved in platform maintenance and data analysis can increase costs for mobile commerce enterprises. The use of data technologies can significantly reduce the expenditure on talent recruitment while achieving precise transaction data analysis. This drives mobile commerce enterprises towards intelligent transformation.
2. Cloud storage established by data technologies helps safeguard enterprise data security. By purchasing data technology algorithms from data technology providers, enterprises can upload their transaction data to data centers, where data technology providers offer meticulous data protection. This reduces the risks associated with internal data leakage prevention and harassment by hacker groups for mobile commerce enterprises [20].

3. Data technologies enable precise data analysis, providing the basis for enterprise decision-making. Through comprehensive analysis of mobile commerce enterprise operational processes, data technologies integrate and analyze seemingly dispersed and unrelated process data to identify the root causes of existing operational issues. By achieving fine-grained decomposition and business integration throughout the entire process, and leveraging the powerful data mining and data analysis functions of big data, data technologies provide data-based support for precise marketing by enterprises.

4.2   The Suitability of Smart Taxation and Mobile Commerce

By analyzing the benefits brought by the use of data technologies for mobile commerce enterprises, we can see that as a data tool, data technologies can facilitate the matching application of intelligent taxation and mobile commerce. Mobile commerce enterprises need to upload transaction data to the cloud, and after data classification by data technologies, it becomes easier for them to quickly submit the tax reporting materials required by tax authorities. Through the intelligent tax platform, tax authorities can again use data technologies to achieve information sharing among departments and horizontal and vertical comparison of enterprise data, analyze the authenticity of the data, restore the various business processes of the enterprise, categorize them into relevant tax categories, and carry out tax collection. The tax management issues in the mobile commerce industry are fundamentally related to its virtual, mobile, borderless, and real-time transaction characteristics. These characteristics can be weakened in intelligent taxation, achieving fair and legitimate tax collection.

1. The intelligent taxation system dynamically tracks and analyzes business processes in real-time to clarify the location of transactions and the nature of income. For commodity or service transactions, the intelligent taxation system can match the business data provided by mobile commerce enterprises with the itinerary information provided by logistics providers and other relevant business information uploaded by enterprises, to restore the entire actual transaction process. This helps to determine the tax attribution of the corresponding transaction and alleviate the ambiguity caused by the virtual nature of mobile commerce through the clarification of business processes.
2. Intelligent taxation facilitates cross-time data information comparison and prevents international tax evasion by enterprises. With the implementation of the BEPS action plan led by the OECD, several countries have united to solve the problem of erosion of national tax bases and profit shifting caused by international tax evasion. While internationally cooperating to prevent tax evasion, the intelligent taxation system also helps the Chinese government to supervise mobile commerce businesses within China. Considering that international tax evasion may involve cross-time operations, the intelligent taxation system can vertically compare and analyze enterprise business process data to more accurately identify tax evasion behavior. This to some extent increases the risk of being caught for mobile commerce enterprises attempting to evade taxes, thereby reducing their motivation to evade taxes.
3. Intelligent taxation identifies key areas of tax evasion, and the transparency of tax evasion behavior facilitates the development of reward and punishment mechanisms as well as the implementation of laws and regulations. Through data technology,

intelligent taxation detects abnormal points in the declaration information of mobile commerce business processes. By conducting comprehensive analysis across multiple enterprises, it identifies the frequent occurrence of tax evasion behavior in the mobile commerce industry [21]. Enhanced business transparency provides reliable data support for the punishment mechanisms against tax evasion. The comprehensive restoration of the entire process by intelligent taxation also enables the rapid identification of areas where relevant laws and regulations need improvement, thus improving the operability of corresponding laws and regulations.

5 Conclusion and Suggestion

This article analyzes the tax administration issues in mobile commerce based on its characteristics and the current status of Chinese laws and regulations. It also examines the implementation methods and features of intelligent taxation, linking the two together to analyze their compatibility. It concludes that intelligent taxation can greatly mitigate the tax administration issues in mobile commerce, providing technological and tax system support for taxation in the mobile commerce sector. However, it is evident that the primary role of intelligent taxation in the field of mobile commerce taxation is to enhance business transparency, ensure data integrity, and improve the ability to identify transaction anomalies for tax authorities. In other words, it serves as a convenient taxation tool.

Based on the above analysis, this article proposes the following suggestions:

Firstly, in order to truly implement the concept of intelligent taxation centered on serving taxpayers and fee payers, it is necessary to safeguard taxpayers' rights and improve service satisfaction in the actual implementation of intelligent taxation. Secondly, while intelligent taxation provides operational possibilities for taxing mobile commerce, overcoming tax administration issues in the mobile commerce sector requires the improvement of laws and regulations specific to mobile commerce. Based on the comprehensive understanding of mobile commerce operations by intelligent taxation, it is important to define clearly the tax objects, tax bases, and other related issues for each tax category in the laws and regulations, further refining the legal provisions. This will enable the combination of sound laws and regulations, efficient tax systems, and professional tax personnel to achieve fairness and transparency in mobile commerce taxation, creating a fair tax administration environment. Lastly, to promote the development of intelligent taxation, it is necessary to enhance the accuracy and adaptability of the data technology algorithms based on intelligent taxation. It is important to utilize existing advanced technological tools effectively, leveraging their advantages while improving any shortcomings to ensure seamless integration with reality.

References

1. Wu, X., Chen, X.: Comparative study of mobile commerce and electronic commerce: based on the perspective of value creation. J. Intell. **29**(08), 19–21+44 (2010). (in Chinese)
2. Chen, C.: Application of tax planning in E-commerce enterprises in China. Enterp. Sci. Technol. Dev. (08), 128–129 (2019). (in Chinese)

3. Wu, X., Qi, C., Sheng, L.: Research on the value chain of mobile commerce industry. J. Chongqing Univ. (Soc. Sci. edn.) (06), 22–26 (2017). (in Chinese)
4. Yang, X.: Discussion on tax issues and countermeasures in E-commerce. Foreign Trade Econ. (02), 149–151 (2016). (in Chinese)
5. Mao, X., Deng, Y., Wang, Q., et al.: Analysis of controversy over "E-commerce Tax." China Market **36**, 163–165 (2022). (in Chinese)
6. Keen, M., Hellerstein, W.: Interjurisdictional issues in the design of a VAT. Tax Law Rev. **63**(2), 359–408 (2010)
7. Agrawal, D.R., Fox, W.F.: Taxes in an e-commerce generation. Int. Tax Public Financ. **24**, 903–926 (2017)
8. Aiura, H., Ogawa, H.: Does E-commerce ease or intensify tax competition? Destination principle versus origin principle. Int. Tax Public Financ. **19**, 781–803 (2023)
9. Argilés-Bosch, J.M., Somoza, A., Ravenda, D., García-Blandón, J.: An empirical examination of the influence of E-commerce on tax avoidance in Europe. J. Int. Account. Audit. Taxation **41**, 100339 (2020)
10. Jiang, Y.: Tax management measures for cross-border E-commerce under the digital economy. Investment Cooperation (08), 63–65 (2021). (in Chinese)
11. Li, Y.: Difficulties and countermeasures of tax collection and administration in E-commerce. Market Modernization (02), 36–38 (2020). (in Chinese)
12. Yuan, C.: Tax compliance in the digital economy: evidence, models, and response suggestions. Econ. Financ. Rev. (05), 24–33(2022). (in Chinese)
13. Yang, Y., Shi, J.: Impact and strategies of the implementation of E-commerce law on China's cross-border E-commerce platforms. J. Hangzhou Dianzi Univ. (Soc. Sci. Edn.) **17**(05), 28–33 (2021). (in Chinese)
14. Zhou, K.: Value implication, logical mechanism, and practical path of smart tax construction. Tax Res. (08), 52–56 (2022). (in Chinese)
15. Wang, Y., Liu, Z.: Research on several issues of modernization of tax collection and administration in the context of "Tax Governance with Numbers". Financ. Supervision (07), 75–81 (2022). (in Chinese)
16. Li, J., Li, S.: Reshaping taxpayer rights: the underlying logic of the "Tax Governance with Numbers" era. J. Huazhong Univ. Sci. Technol. (Soc. Sci. Edn.) **36**(06), 79–89 (2022). (in Chinese)
17. Liu, J., Luo, L.: Basic conditions, restricting factors, and realistic paths of smart tax construction. Tax Res. (09), 139–143 (2022). (in Chinese)
18. Zhao, L.: Smart taxation promotes the transformation of tax governance from "Tax Control with Invoices" to "Tax Governance with Numbers". Int. Bus. Account. (13), 71–75 (2023). (in Chinese)
19. Wang, X.: Analysis of relevant regulatory models of mobile E-commerce economic law. Legal Expo (06), 46–48 (2022). (in Chinese)
20. Zhang, C.: Application of cloud computing and big data technology in mobile E-commerce. Inf. Comput. (Theor. Edn.) **33**(09), 22–24 (2021). (in Chinese)
21. Xue, W., Huo, Z., Tang, J.: Practice analysis of modernization construction of corporate income tax. Tax Res. (04), 42–48 (2023). (in Chinese)

Interactive Elements in E-commerce Live Streaming: Key Influencing Factors in Consumer Purchase Decisions

Tao Huang[✉]

Ningbo University of Finance and Economics, Ningbo, People's Republic of China
huangtao@nbufe.edu.cn

Abstract. With the rapid development of internet technology, the live streaming industry is booming, and e-commerce companies are adopting live streaming marketing methods. Through live streaming, consumers can more intuitively understand the products. This interactive format not only stimulates consumers' purchase intentions, but also brings more traffic to businesses. Based on the SOR theory, this study explores the characteristics of e-commerce live streaming, focusing on variables such as visibility, authenticity, interactivity, entertainment, and preferential treatment. The research results show that the visibility, interactivity, and authenticity of live streaming have significant positive effects on consumer satisfaction, and the entertainment and preferential treatment also play positive roles. At the same time, consumer satisfaction positively promotes purchase intentions. Among the characteristics of e-commerce live streaming, the preferential treatment of live streaming has a significant mediating effect on purchase intentions, while the mediating effects of authenticity is relatively limited. These findings provide important references for e-commerce companies to formulate strategies in live streaming sales.

Keywords: E-commerce live streaming · Consumer satisfaction · Purchase intentions · SOR theory

1 Introduction

Since the emergence of e-commerce live streaming in 2016, it has experienced explosive growth, relying on live streaming technology to continuously expand the market size with rich content, intuitive displays, and frequent interactions. Businesses are rapidly adopting the new profit model of live streaming sales on e-commerce platforms, making live streaming shopping a popular new way for contemporary consumers to purchase. The new "e-commerce + live streaming" model can not only take into account the advantages of both "online" and "offline", but also showcase the details of the items being sold in a more intuitive and visual way, allowing consumers to have a deeper understanding of the product's characteristics. Under this new marketing method of "e-commerce + live streaming", companies need to fully utilize the traffic generated by various live streaming platforms to enhance their competitiveness.

J. Wei and G. Margetis (Eds.): HCII 2024, LNCS 14738, pp. 87–93, 2024.
https://doi.org/10.1007/978-3-031-60487-4_7

2   Research Framework and Hypotheses

2.1   The Impact of Live Streaming Characteristics on Purchase Intentions

The interactivity of live streaming is one of the important factors that influence consumers' purchase intentions. Live streaming marketing has a significantly positive impact on customer purchase intentions. Among the four dimensions of perceived value, economic value has a significant mediating effect on customer purchase intentions, while cognitive value, functional value, and entertainment value have weaker mediating effects (Lee & Wan, 2023). This study further explores the impact of social media advertising on purchase intentions from three perspectives: perceived usefulness, entertainment, and excitement (Balroo, 2023). Therefore, this study hypothesizes:

- H1: Live streaming characteristics have a positive correlation with purchase intentions.

2.2   The Impact of Consumer Satisfaction on Purchase Intentions

Exploring the mechanism of consumer satisfaction on purchase intentions is crucial. Factors such as live streaming platforms, e-commerce hosts, and consumers have an impact on continuous purchase intentions (Jie Meng & Xin Chen, 2021). Factors such as information security perception positively affect consumer satisfaction and positively impact consumers' continuous purchase intentions (Flanagin & Metzger, 2001). Perceived trust and consumer satisfaction play a partial mediating role between independent variables and consumers' continuous purchase intentions (Liu & Zhang, 2024). Therefore, we propose the hypothesis:

- H2: Consumer satisfaction has a positive impact on purchase intentions.

2.3   The Mediating Role of Consumer Satisfaction

Consumer satisfaction may play an important mediating role in the impact of e-commerce live streaming on consumers' purchase intentions. By introducing consumer satisfaction as a mediating variable from the perspective of interaction, a model between interaction and trust is constructed, and the internal mechanism of online interaction on consumers' satisfaction in online shopping is studied (Li et al., 2023). In online clothing product experiences, sensory experience, perceived experience, practical experience, and associative experience all have a positive and significant impact on consumers' re-purchase intentions (Xian, 2022); customer satisfaction plays a partial mediating role between online clothing product experience and consumers' re-purchase intentions (Pang & Pang, 2022). Therefore, we propose the hypothesis:

- H3: Consumer satisfaction plays a mediating role between live streaming characteristics and purchase intentions.

2.4   Theoretical Model Building

Based on the analysis of e-commerce live streaming, consumer satisfaction, and purchase intentions, this article combines the S-O-R theory to propose the following model construction ideas (Fig. 1):

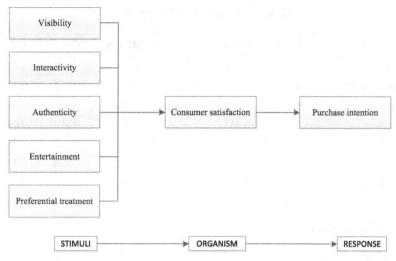

Fig. 1. Proposed Research Model

3   Research Methodology

In this study, the questionnaire was developed based on mature scales from other researchers. By combing the relevant literature on e-commerce live streaming and consumer purchase intentions, and combining with the research object and content of this study, the questionnaire was designed to collect data for subsequent analysis. The measurement methods of the questionnaire in this study selected a five-level scale. The questionnaire was developed based on reference to other scales, including the measurement items for live streaming visibility, which referenced Liu & Zhang (2024) and other scales on live streaming visual attractiveness. The measurement items for live streaming authenticity was adopted from Beverland et al. (2008). Live streaming interactivity was measured with the items created by Flanagin & Metzger (2001) and Jiang (2019). The measurement items for entertainment was adopted from Chen (2022). And preferential treatment was measured with the items developed by Dittmar & Beattie (1995). The measurement items for consumer satisfaction were adopted from Oliva (1995) and Szymanski (2001). The measurement items for purchase intentions were adopted from Fang Rui (2022).

4   Reliability and Validity

4.1   Reliability and Validity

See Table 1.

Table 1. Measurement of constructs

Constructs	Items	Cronbach's Alpha	Rho_A	CR	AVE
Interactivity	4	0.881	0.908	0.918	0.736
preferential treatment	4	0.870	0.877	0.911	0.720
Visibility	4	0.859	0.934	0.901	0.696
Entertainment	4	0.852	0.873	0.899	0.690
Satisfaction	4	0.877	0.880	0.915	0.730
Authenticity	4	0.890	0.896	0.924	0.753
Purchase Intention	4	0.854	0.857	0.901	0.695

4.2 Hypothesis Testing

Path Analysis. See Fig. 2.

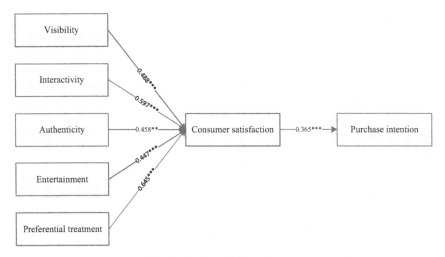

Fig. 2. Path coefficient diagram

The results of the regression analysis show that the impact of live streaming characteristics on consumer satisfaction is significant, with a coefficient of 0.577 (P = 0.000***).
This indicates that live streaming characteristics have a significant positive impact on
consumer satisfaction. Similarly, the impact of consumer satisfaction on purchase intentions is also significant, with a coefficient of 0.365 (P = 0.000***). This suggests that
consumer satisfaction has a significant positive impact on purchase intentions. Therefore, we can draw the conclusion that the impact of live streaming characteristics on
purchase intentions is partially mediated by consumer satisfaction (Table 2).

Mediating Effect of Consumer Satisfaction. In the established model of this study,
consumer satisfaction is used as the mediator variable. It is hypothesized that there is a

Table 2. Regression Coefficients of the Model

Factor	Item		Non-standardized Coefficient	Standardized Coefficient	Standard Error	Z-value	P-value
Live broadcast	→	Satisfaction	0.867	0.577	0.139	6.234	0.000***
Satisfaction	→	Purchase intention	0.312	0.365	0.061	5.123	0.000***

Note: ***, **, * represent significance levels of 1%, 5%, and 10%, respectively

mediating effect of consumer satisfaction on the impact of live streaming characteristics on consumer purchase intentions. To investigate the existence of mediating effects of consumer satisfaction, this study uses the Bootstrap method to conduct a mediating effect test (Table 3).

Table 3. Summary of Mediating Effect Test Results

Item	c Total effect	a	b	$a*b$ Mediating effect value	$a*b$ (Boot SE)	$a*b$ (z value)	$a*b$ (p value)	$a*b$ (95% BootCI)	c' Direct effect	Conclusion
Preferential treatment → Satisfaction → Purchase intention	0.136*	0.263**	0.115*	0.03	0.019	1.578	0.114	−0.003 ~ 0.073	0.106	Full mediation
Entertainment → Satisfaction → Paction → Purcurchase intention	0.195**	0.078	0.115*	0.009	0.009	0.965	0.334	−0.005 ~ 0.032	0.186**	Not significant
Interactivity → Satisfhase intention	0.091	0.099	0.115*	0.011	0.01	1.101	0.271	−0.002 ~ 0.036	0.08	Not significant
Authenticity → Satisfaction → Purchase intention	0.197**	0.173**	0.115*	0.02	0.014	1.372	0.17	−0.002 ~ 0.055	0.178**	Partial mediation
Visibility → Satisfaction → Purchase intention	0.04	−0.007	0.115*	−0.001	0.008	−0.108	0.914	−0.017 ~ 0.015	0.041	Not significant

* $p < 0.05$ ** $p < 0.01$; Bootstrap type: percentile bootstrap method

5   Discussion

According to the above analysis, the hypothesis test results of this study are summarized, and the results are as follows.

- H1a: The visuality of online live streaming characteristics has a significant positive impact on consumer purchase intentions. Supported
- H1b: The authenticity of online live streaming characteristics has a significant positive impact on consumer purchase intentions. Supported
- H1c: The interactivity of online live streaming characteristics has a significant positive impact on consumer purchase intentions. Supported
- H1d: The entertainment of online live streaming characteristics has a significant positive impact on consumer purchase intentions. Supported
- H1e: The preferential nature of online live streaming characteristics has a significant positive impact on consumer purchase intentions. Supported

- H2: Consumer satisfaction has a significant positive impact on purchase intentions. Supported
- H3a: Consumer satisfaction plays a mediating role between the visuality of online live streaming characteristics and purchase intentions. Not supported.
- H3b: Consumer satisfaction plays a mediating role between the authenticity of online live streaming characteristics and purchase intentions. Supported.
- H3c: Consumer satisfaction plays a mediating role between the interactivity of online live streaming characteristics and purchase intentions. Not supported.
- H3d: Consumer satisfaction plays a mediating role between the entertainment of online live streaming characteristics and purchase intentions. Not supported.
- H3e: Consumer satisfaction plays a mediating role between the preferential nature of online live streaming characteristics and purchase intentions. Supported.

The present study has conducted empirical analysis and arrived at the following conclusions: In the context of e-commerce live streaming, the five dimensions of e-commerce live streaming, namely live streaming visibility, interactivity, authenticity, entertainment, and preferential treatment, have a positive impact on consumer satisfaction. Consumer satisfaction, in turn, has a positive impact on purchase intentions. Among the five dimensions of e-commerce live streaming, preferential treatment has a significant mediating effect on customer purchase intentions, while authenticity plays a partial mediating role. The mediating roles of visibility, interactivity, and entertainment are not significant.

6　Limitations

This study has only explored five key factors in e-commerce live streaming. However, the complexity of the e-commerce live streaming environment means that there are many more factors that affect consumer purchase intentions. Although this study has reached academic findings, more research efforts are needed to further explore potential antecedents influencing consumer purchase intention, particularly in the field of live streaming.

The current research may have overlooked some important variables, such as the technical quality of live streaming, consumers' trust in live streaming, and the relationship between hosts and consumers. These factors may have a significant impact on consumer purchase intentions, but they have not been fully considered in the current research.

In addition, the study mainly focuses on the impact of the characteristics of live streaming itself on consumer purchase intentions, while ignoring the differences between different consumer groups. Consumers of different ages, genders, and educational backgrounds may have different perceptions and reactions to live streaming, and these factors also need to be further explored.

Acknowledgement. This article is funded by Zhejiang Provincial Philosophy and Social Science Planning Project (21NDJC173YB).

References

Balroo, S.A.: Social media advertisements and purchase intention: attitude as a mediator. J. Econ. Manag. Trade **29**(10), Article 10 (2023). https://doi.org/10.9734/jemt/2023/v29i101152

Beverland, M.B., Lindgreen, A., Vink, M.W.: Projecting authenticity through advertising: consumer judgments of advertisers' claims. J. Advert. **37**(1), 5–15 (2008). https://doi.org/10.2753/JOA009-3367370101

Chen, B., Wang, L., Rasool, H., Wang, J.: Research on the impact of marketing strategy on consumers' impulsive purchase behavior in livestreaming e-commerce. Front. Psychol. **13** (2022). https://www.Frontiersin.org/articles/https://doi.org/10.3389/fpsyg.2022.905531

Dittmar, H., Beattie, J., Friese, S.: Gender identity and material symbols: objects and decision considerations in impulse purchases. J. Econ. Psychol. **16**(3), 491–511 (1995). https://doi.org/10.1016/0167-4870(95)00023-H

Flanagin, A., Metzger, M.: Internet use in the contemporary media environment. Hum. Commun. Res. **27**(1), 153–181 (2001). https://doi.org/10.1111/j.1468-2958.2001.tb00779.x

Lee, D., Wan, C.: The impact of mukbang live streaming commerce on consumers' overconsumption behavior. J. Interact. Mark. **58**(2–3), 198–221 (2023). https://doi.org/10.1177/10949968231156104

Li, L., Yuan, L., Tian, J.: Influence of online E-commerce interaction on consumer satisfaction based on big data algorithm. Heliyon **9**(8), e18322 (2023). https://doi.org/10.1016/j.heliyon.2023.e18322

Liu, J., Zhang, M.: Formation mechanism of consumers' purchase intention in multimedia live platform: a case study of taobao live. Multimedia Tools Appl. **83**(2), 3657–3680 (2024). https://doi.org/10.1007/s11042-023-15666-6

Oliva, T.A., Oliver, R.L., Bearden, W.O.: The relationships among consumer satisfaction, involvement, and product performance: a catastrophe theory application. Behav. Sci. **40**(2), 104–132 (1995). https://doi.org/10.1002/bs.3830400203

Pang, X., Pang, Y.: Evaluation model and influencing factors of consumer satisfaction with e-commerce platform. Ingénierie Des Systèmes d Information **27**(6), 983–990 (2022). https://doi.org/10.18280/isi.270615

Xian, Q.: A study of consumers impulsive buying behavior under the interactive situation of live webcast—taking individual impulsive characteristics as a moderating factor. Acad. J. Bus. Manag. **4**(10) (2022). https://doi.org/10.25236/AJBM.2022.041014

Rui, F.: Research on the influence of interaction with the streamer on customers' purchase intention in the context of live-streaming e-commerce. Soc. Sci. (6) (2022). https://doi.org/10.11648/j.ss.20221106.14

Jie, M., Xin, C.: Consumers' satisfaction with live delivery in the post-epidemic era research. In: 2021 International Conference on Enterprise Management and Economic Development (ICEMED 2021), Nanjing, China (2021). https://doi.org/10.2991/aebmr.k.210601.065

Prediction and Analysis of Mobile Phone Export Volume Based on SVR Model

Ruizhi Li and Haibo Tang[✉]

School of Business, Shanghai Dianji University, Shanghai 201306, China
18561208951@163.com

Abstract. Electronic products occupy an important position in the export structure of China's trade, and mobile phone products occupy a place in the export of electronic products. With the change of China's export trade structure, it is of great significance to accurately predict the future trend of mobile phone export market. In order to effectively predict China's mobile phone export volume, this paper selects China's mobile phone export volume and other macro data that affect mobile phone export volume since 2008, normalizes the data to better reflect the essential relationship between the data, and finally uses the Gauss radial basis kernel function. In order to reflect the prediction accuracy of SVR model, this paper introduces ARIMA model for comparison. By comparing the two models, it is found that the support vector regression model can predict the export volume of mobile phones more accurately and verify the accuracy of its prediction of China's mobile phone export volume.

Keywords: SVR · Prediction · Mobile Phone · Export Volume

1 Introduction

In the past decade, amidst the evolution of scientific knowledge and technological advancement, China's mobile phone production capacity has been rapid growth, which makes China an important base for global mobile phone manufacturing. However, with the rapid development of the market, the speed of mobile phone update iteration far exceeds the replacement cycle of per capita mobile phones, and the Chinese mobile phone market is close to saturation [1]. As the growth rate of China's mobile phone sales has diminished in recent years, there has been an accumulation of inventory within the China's market, leading to increasingly intense competition among mobile phone manufacturers, resulting in a significant reduction in the profits of related enterprises in the Chinese market [2]. According to relevant reports, the overall shipment volume in 2022 is less than 300 million units; sales data is also not optimistic, China's smart phone sales fell by 14%, down for five consecutive years. In addition, China's mobile phone export market has also been sluggish in recent years. According to customs statistics, China's mobile phone exports in 2023 were USD 138.89 billion, a year-on-year decrease of 2.7%. On the one hand, the Sino-US trade war has directly affected the pattern of the overseas market for mobile phones from China. The cost of China's mobile phone

J. Wei and G. Margetis (Eds.): HCII 2024, LNCS 14738, pp. 94–105, 2024.
https://doi.org/10.1007/978-3-031-60487-4_8

exports has soared due to US tariffs and non-tariff barriers [3]; on the other hand, the outbreak of the novel coronavirus epidemic has increased the customs clearance cost of mobile phones and the risks in transit, exposing enterprises to various destabilizing factors. Although the overall scale of China's mobile phone export is huge, there are also frequent negative growth in export scale, continuous trade frictions, and intensified competition in the international market. These problems have restricted the development of China's mobile phone export trade.

Therefore, it is very important to be able to predict a country's mobile phone exports more accurately. The aim of this research is to utilize the support vector machine model in machine learning to carry out support vector regression, establish a prediction model of China's mobile phone export volume, and predict the mobile phone export volume in recent years. The outcomes of the study demonstrate that the support vector regression model can proficiently predict the export volume of China's mobile phones. After training and testing the model, it is discovered that the support vector regression exhibits minimal error in predicting the quantity of mobile phones exported from China, which can accurately predict the export volume of China's mobile phones, and here is no substantial disparity between the data of the forecasting model and the data of the actual situation.

2 Literature Review

2.1 Support Vector Regression and Prediction

The research on support vector regression originated from a machine learning algorithm Support Vector Machines (SVM) put forth by Vapnik (1997) in the decade of 1990s. Support Vector Machines are usually employed for categorization and estimation, among which Support Vector Regression (SVR) model is utilized for estimation. Support vector regression possesses a broad spectrum of applications across various domains. SHANG-GUAN L X and Yin Y [4] put forward a hybrid enhanced SVR algorithm for the purpose of predicting the freezing duration of the road surface by the enhanced operation of the response surface method (RSM) and particle swarm optimization (PSO). Patel J, Shah S and Thakkar P [5] use the two-stage fusion method of SVR to form SVR-ANN, SVR-RF and SVR-SVR integrated forecasting models. The experimental assessment of index data of two stock exchanges in the Indian stock market. Syriopoulous and Tsatsarons, [6] incorporated cutting-edge advancements in the dynamic realm of artificial intelligence and machine learning algorithms. Furthermore, introduced a groundbreaking and inventive prediction framework to generate fresh ship-building price forecasts for diverse ship categories and shipping markets. Leveraging the strengths of the support vector machine framework, a support vector regression (SVR) model suitable for ship price forecasting is proposed, tested and verified. Due to the dynamic and nonlinear structural nature of exchange rate time series, FU S, Li Y and SUN S, [7] Developed two evolutionary support vector regression models for predicting the four prominent RMB exchange rates against the dollar, euro, yen and pound with the aim of enhancing the precision of exchange rate forecasting. To assess the efficacy of the sample foreign exchange rate prediction, four evaluation criteria were employed. Levis and Papageorgiou [8] proposed a support vector regression (SVR) customer demand forecasting approach centered on system optimization. The algorithm is built upon past sales data and has a regression function that is both flexible and adaptive. By leveraging available training data, it has the capability to discern potential patterns in customer demand, effectively capturing customer behavior and generating precise predictions. By comparing the prediction accuracy of the traditional ARIMA model, it is found that SVR is more accurate than the traditional prediction method and can more accurately predict the needs of customers.

Based on this, support vector regression is a prediction tool that can be used in many industries and aspects. Compared with traditional prediction methods, it has higher accuracy and can provide reference value for practitioners in all walks of life more effectively.

2.2 Export Forecast

In recent years, the technology of export forecasting has been greatly developed. DAI C [9] used back propagation neural network to estimate export volume in international trade, predicted export volume of a single city in China, and contrasted it against the factual export volume. It is found that the accuracy of back propagation neural network exhibits an approximately 30% increase compared to conventional forecasting techniques. Gerasimov, Gromov [10] created dynamic econometric models to predict regional-level production, sales, and export of primary livestock products. The constructed dynamic econometric model is employed to assess the export potential of principal commodities in the regional agricultural market. Eckert and Hyndman [11] proposed a new predictive adjustment framework using Bayesian spatial methods to predict and analyze Swiss exports. Karabay and Kilic [12] used ANN (artificial neural network) to predict Turkish clothing for seven of its major export countries. And compared the accuracy of the predictions through three precision tests. SHEN M L [13] also uses a multivariate LSTM-based method utilize advanced techniques to analyze temporal variations in trade data, enabling the generation of robust and effective trade forecasts. Comparisons are made to comprehensively assess the performance of the proposed method by leveraging time series analysis and economic structure models, thereby gaining a deep understanding of its effectiveness. Empirical findings indicate that this method can accurately simulate temporal variations and uncertainty trends in foreign trade data, effectively capturing time-related information. This method achieves almost perfect prediction performance for previously unpredictable data.

2.3 Support Vector Regression and Export Forecast

Due to the instability, volatility and uncertainty of export volume, it is difficult to predict and there is a large error in prediction. In the use of support vector regression technology to predict the export volume, Chinese and foreign scholars have certain research. In China, the literature on the use of support vector regression technology for export forecasting can be traced back to 2005.Due to the fact that the data analysis related to China's import and export activities in international trade business and status still stays on the basis of traditional time series analysis and regression analysis, Some China's scholars proposed a foreign trade export forecast based on support vector machine, and used support vector machine to predict the export volume of motorcycles in Chongqing.

The purpose is to improve the prediction effect and alleviate the problem of large volatility and strong nonlinearity in product export. It is found that the prediction of motorcycle export volume by support vector machine has higher fitting degree and accuracy than MA model, and the overall error is maintained at about 10%. In recent years, the research on the prediction of export volume has also developed to a certain extent. FAN L W, PAN S J and LI Z M [14] use independent component analysis (ICA) performing an analysis of crude oil prices. The decomposition of crude oil prices is performed to isolate independent components, each representing a unique set of factors that affect oil prices. Through the development of a new SVR model, the predicted independent components are integrated together, and the autonomous elements are used as inputs to predict crude oil prices. Empirical evidence suggests that ICA-SVR2 represents a reliable and effective approach to predicting crude oil prices. KUO, RJ and LI, P [15] proposed A three-stage prediction model is proposed, which integrates wavelet transform as a key component. And support vector regression (SVR) based on K-means calculation of firefly algorithm. Through testing, it has been discovered that the predictive efficacy of the firefly algorithm has demonstrated superior performance compared to other two algorithms, and it can predict Taiwan's exports more accurately.

Based on the above research, It can be observed that support vector regression model has achieved certain results in the field of export forecasting, but the export forecasting of mobile phones is a blank in this field. The support vector regression model can make the best use of sample information and make full use of historical data. Continuous self-learning, especially in the case of small samples, has a good performance in inferring future mutation points. Using the support vector regression model to predict the export volume of mobile phones can broaden the data sources for the government and the enterprise sector, which has certain practical significance.

3 Methodology

3.1 Support Vector Machine

Support Vector Machine (SVM) was formally proposed by Cortes and Vapnik [16]. Due to its excellent performance in classification tasks, it soon became the mainstream technology of machine learning, and set off a wave of 'statistical learning' around 2000.

Support vector machine can be understood as, in order to distinguish the two types of dimension data, N is the number of samples of data, M is the number of dimensions, how to design an M-1 dimension hyperplane, namely:

$$W_1 X_1 + W_2 X_2 + \ldots \cdots + W_m X_m + B = 0 \tag{1}$$

This plane is used to distinguish the two types of data, W is the weight of the corresponding x. However, there are many problems in the determination of the decision hyperplane, which may lead to the wrong classification of samples near the decision hyperplane. Therefore, the concept of support vector is introduced, and it is assumed that the decision hyperplane moves up and down C to form the upper and lower boundaries. Since the upper and lower boundaries must pass through some sample data points, and these sample points are closest to the decision boundary, the position and interval distance of the upper and lower boundaries are determined. These sample data are also called support vectors. When new data needs to be added, it can be judged according to the relative position of the decision hyperplane, so as to classify the new data and solve the problem of abnormal values and low fault tolerance in the sample data when classifying the sample data. The formula is:

$$\begin{cases} min\frac{1}{2}\|w\|^2 \\ st. \ y_i(wx_i + b) \geq 1, \forall i \end{cases} \tag{2}$$

3.2 Support Vector Regression

Support vector regression (SVR) is a kind of support vector machine. And it is commonly used in regression forecasting The study of support vector regression was given a more comprehensive introduction by Smola in 2004 [17]. It is a nonlinear regression model for establishing training data. The support vector regression model can be interpreted as constructing an 'interval band' surrounding the linear function. This interval band, with a width of 2ε, effectively captures the majority of sample points beyond its upper and lower boundaries (Fig. 1).

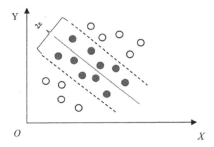

Fig. 1. Support vector regression diagram

3.3 Kernel Function

Kernel function is the core of support vector regression. By introducing kernel function, it can effectively solve the problem that high-dimensional mathematical calculation is too complicated, so that support vector machine can process samples more effectively and predict.

The commonly used kernel functions are Linear Kernel, Polynomial Kernel, Gaussian Kernel and Sigmoid Kernel [18]. Because the number of samples and the dimension of sample characteristics are limited, As the kernel function for support vector regression, the Gaussian kernel function is selected. The formula is as follows:

$$K(x, x') = exp\left(-\frac{\|x - x'\|^2}{2\sigma^2}\right) \tag{3}$$

3.4 Linear Control Model (ARIMA Model) and Prediction Ideas

The application of time series model has greatly promoted the prediction research of macroeconomic indicators, and it has also evolved into a classic control model that serves as the foundation for various emerging prediction methods. Therefore, this paper selects ARIMA model as a control model to evaluate SVR support vector regression [19]. Aiming at China's mobile phone exports, the prediction idea of ARIMA model is as follows: firstly, the logarithm of China's mobile phone exports is taken, and the optimal difference order is selected by ADF test to obtain a stationary sequence. Secondly, according to the AIC rule, the model parameters are selected and the sequence modeling is carried out. Finally, the ARIMA model is utilized for sequence forecasting, and the model flow chart is shown in the diagram.

3.5 Accuracy Test Method

In order to verify the feasibility of the SVR model, this paper uses four verification methods to evaluate the effect of model prediction, which are absolute error, relative error, regression coefficient R ^ 2 and root mean square error RMSE [20].

The absolute error represents the absolute value of the difference between the measured value and the real value, and the relative error accounts for the percentage of the real value. The calculation formula of the two is:

$$absolute\ error = x - \mu \tag{4}$$

$$relative\ error = (x - \mu)/\mu \times 100\% \tag{5}$$

The coefficient of determination (R ^ 2) is a statistical index to measure the goodness of fit of the prediction model. The fitting degree of the model improves as R^2 approaches 1. The calculation formula is:

$$R^2 = \frac{\Sigma(\hat{y}_i - \overline{y})^2}{\Sigma(y_i - \overline{y})^2} \tag{6}$$

where $\hat{y}_i$ is the estimated value of the regression, and $\overline{y}$ i s the mean value of the actual value.

The root mean square error (RMSE) represents the expected value of the squared difference between the estimated and true values of a parameter. It serves as a measure to assess the data's variability. A lower RMSE indicates a higher level of model accuracy in fitting the experimental data. The calculation formula for RMSE is as follows:

$$RMSE = \sqrt{\frac{1}{m}\sum_{i=1}^{m}(y_i - \hat{y}_i)^2} \tag{7}$$

where m is the number of samples. y_i is the Predicted value. And $\hat{y}_i$ is the real value.

4 Experimental Process

4.1 Data Acquisition

China's mobile phone exports were obtained from UN Comtrade, and the National Bureau of Statistics obtained China's 2008–2023 gross domestic product (GDP), foreign direct investment (FDI), technology investment and other characteristic variables.

4.2 Data Pre-processing

The export volume of mobile phone is affected by many factors. The influence factors are different in dimension and the problem of huge difference in numerical range leads to non-convergence of training or other problems, which affects the accuracy of prediction. Therefore, the data is normalized.

The dataset is divided into a training set and a test set. And set input variables and output variables.

By normalizing the data, each variable in the training set and the test set is mapped between [0,1], and the formula is:

$$x^{'} = \frac{x - x_{min}}{x_{max} - x_{min}} \tag{8}$$

where x' represents the normalized data, x represents the original data, x_{max}, x_{min} The upper and lower bounds of the original data are indicated.

The training set, which has been normalized, and the variables in the test set are utilized to estimate the original target values.

The data is adjusted to the input format of the adaptive model through the transposition operation, that is, the input feature matrix of the training set and the test set is transposed from the row vector to the column vector.

4.3 Selection of Kernel Function

In this paper, the ε-SVR function is selected and the Gauss kernel function [21] is used. There are three parameters to be determined in the ε-SVR model.

The linear equation of the support vector regression model is:

$$f(x) = w \cdot x + b \tag{9}$$

where, w represents the weight, and b represents the bias value. In order to ensure the flatness of the linear equation, the minimum w needs to be selected. The values of w and b can be transformed into the regression model by introducing relaxation factors $\xi_i > 0$, $\xi_i^* > 0$:

$$min\frac{1}{2}\|w\|^2 + C\sum_{i=1}^{n}\left(\xi_i + \xi_i^*\right) \tag{10}$$

Constraint conditions:

$$\begin{cases} y_i - w \cdot x_i - b \le \varepsilon + \xi_i \\ y_i - w \cdot x_i - b \ge \varepsilon + \xi_i^* \\ \xi_i \ge 0 \\ \xi_i^* \ge 0 \end{cases} i = 1, \ldots, n \tag{11}$$

The penalty coefficient, represented by C, will affect the generalization ability of the model, which is the tolerance of the error. If C is too high or too low, the over-fitting or under-fitting will be more serious.

After selecting the Gauss function as the kernel function, its own coefficient σ, σ determines the count of support vectors, and its size is positively correlated with support vector.

The coefficient in the penalty coefficient is represented by ε. In this paper, the optimal ε value is selected through experience.

4.4 Parameter Optimization and Prediction

In this paper, the optimal parameters are obtained by grid search method and cross validation method. After obtaining the optimal parameters, the support vector regression output is used, and the obtained parameters are used for simulation test. After the simulation test, the output data is denormalized to obtain the predicted export volume.

4.5 Precision Measurement

To facilitate a more thorough assessment of the prediction performance of both models, the absolute error, relative error determination coefficient R^2 and mean square error root RMSE are used to compar two models, and the prediction effect of the two models is compared more intuitively. Where R^2 is the closer to 1, the better the regression effect; the smaller the RMSE, the smaller error.

5 Results and Analysis

This paper obtains China's mobile phone export volume, export volume, export volume in the previous year and export volume to major countries from 2008 to 2023 through UN Comtrade. Through the National Bureau of Statistics, China's GDP, FDI, scientific research investment and China's mobile phone production from 2008 to 2023 were obtained, of which China's mobile phone volume was the output variable and the remaining seven were the input variables. The proportion of the training set to the data set was 0.8. In this paper, we will use the support vector module in MATLAB to carry out experiments. Finally, the penalty coefficient C is 64, the coefficient σ of the Gauss function is 0.0039, and the coefficient ε in the penalty coefficient is 0.04. The results are as follows:

5.1 Outcome Evaluation

According to Fig. 2, the prediction effect of the two models is better, but the prediction curve of the ARIMA model fluctuates greatly, and the prediction curve of the SVR model is closer to the real value.

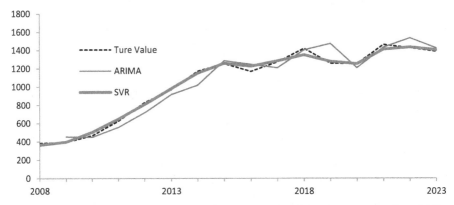

Fig. 2. The fitting and forecasting results of China's total mobile phone exports from 2008 to 2023.

5.2 Accuracy Evaluation

According to Table 1, From the observations, it is evident that the SVR model exhibits a significant disparity between the predicted value and the true value of the commercial mobile phone export in 2010, and the predicted value in other years is in proximity to the true value. According to the relevant information, there are two reasons for the large deviation of the predicted value in 2010.First, the shipment of mobile phones in 2010 increased by 20.8%, reaching 1.425 billion. The second is the transformation of mobile phone motherboard suppliers into OEMs. The MediaTek platform makes it extremely easy to make a mobile phone solution, and even a person can complete a complete mobile phone solution. In addition, comparing the absolute percentage error of the predicted value of the two models, Evidently, the absolute percentage error of the predicted value of the ARIMA model is larger and more volatile, while the absolute percentage error of the predicted value of the SVR model is smaller and more uniform, so the SVR model demonstrates superior prediction performance.

For further compare prediction effect of SVR model and ARIMA model, The R^2 and RMSE are computed for both the SVR model and ARIMA model (Table 2).

The R^2 and RMSE of the SVR model are comparatively lower than those of the ARIMA model, indicating that the predicted value of the SVR model is in proximity to the true value. Therefore, it is concluded that the fitting accuracy based on SVR model is very high, which can better fit the trend of China's mobile phone export volume. The model shows great advantages and reference value in dealing with the prediction and analysis of similar small samples and multiple influencing factors. And can provide

Table 1. The comparison between the actual value and the predicted value of China's total mobile phone exports from 2008 to 2023.

Year	Ture Value	ARIMA	SVR	Absolute Error		Relative Error	
				ARIMA	SVR	ARIMA	SVR
2008	385.39	NA	364.817	None	−20.57	NA	−5.34
2009	395.57	453.6425	397.782	58.0725	2.21	14.68	0.56
2010	467.4	450.8693	504.922	−13.76	37.52	−2.94	8.03
2011	627.6	557.8795	648.482	−176.73	20.88	−28.16	3.33
2012	829.87	717.8257	809.536	−271.99	−20.33	−32.78	−2.45
2013	971.53	918.9252	982.997	−253.7	11.47	−26.11	1.18
2014	1172.6	1020.349	1151.65	−253.67	−20.95	−21.63	−1.79
2015	1255.09	1287.505	1259.38	−234.74	4.29	−18.7	0.34
2016	1170.82	1247.948	1227.36	116.69	56.54	9.97	4.83
2017	1274.44	1210.257	1285.36	−26.49	10.92	−2.079	0.86
2018	1421.72	1405.547	1352.22	−211.46	−69.5	−14.87	−4.89
2019	1259.51	1474.561	1280.15	146.04	20.64	11.59	1.64
2020	1254.53	1210.089	1254.18	220.03	−0.35	17.54	−0.03
2021	1463.21	1432.537	1411.09	−30.67	−52.12	−2.1	−3.56
2022	1426.7	1535.265	1435.17	108.57	8.47	7.61	0.59
2023	1387.99	1424.54	1404.61	36.55	16.62	2.63	1.2

Note. NA represents a null value, because of the differential operation, the beginning will be less than one bit

Table 2. The prediction effect evaluation of SVR and ARIMA model.

Mode	R^2	RMSE
SVR	0.9967	30.4893
ARIMA	0.9710	89.6934

reference for China's government departments, macroeconomic workers and customs related departments. Thus, using the SVR model to predict 2024 China's mobile phone exports of $ 142.059 billion.

6   Conclusion and Suggestion

In this paper, SVR model and ARIMA model are used to test export value of China's mobile phones in the past 16 years. The experimental results indicate that the SVR model demonstrates superior predictability. And can predict the export value of Chinese mobile phones more accurately. The forecast results show that China's mobile phone exports in 2024. Based on this, this paper proposes the following recommendations to promote China's mobile phone export market.

For the government, China's mobile phone exports will show an increasing trend in 2024, so the government should do a good job in the supervision of mobile phone exports, enhance the quality of exported mobile phones, reduce the occurrence of detention and return events due to quality, further stimulate China's mobile phone export market, stimulate China's mobile phone market potential, and promote the domestic and foreign dual cycle [22].

For mobile phone enterprises, combined with the predicted value of 2024, they should further adjust the industrial structure, accelerate industrial transformation and upgrading, change from labor production factor monopoly to technology monopoly, and improve the competitiveness of Chinese mobile phones in the international market.

References

1. Liu, Z.J., et al.: Gradient boosting estimation of the leaf area index of apple orchards in UAV remote sensing. Remote Sens. **13**(16), 3263 (2021)
2. Zhu, X.D., Liu, X.: Research on the evolution of global electronics trade network structure since the 21st century from the Chinese perspective. Sustainability **15**(6), 19 (2023)
3. Li, P.F., Xu, J.G., Ai-Hamami, M.: Application of machine learning in stock selection. Appl. Math. Nonlinear Sci. **12**, 2413–2424 (2022)
4. Shangguan, L.X., Yin, Y.F., Zhang, Q.T., Liu, Q., Xie, W., Dong, Z.J.: Icing time prediction model of pavement based on an improved SVR model with response surface approach. Appl. Sci. **12**(16), 8109 (2022)
5. Patel, J., Shah, S., Thakkar, P., Kotecha, K.: Predicting stock market index using fusion of machine learning techniques. Expert Syst. Appl. **42**(4), 2162–2172 (2015)
6. Syriopoulos, T., Tsatsaronis, M., Karamanos, I.: Support vector machine algorithms: an application to ship price forecasting. Comput. Econ. **57**(1), 55–87 (2021)
7. Fu, S., Li, Y., Sun, S., Li, H.: Evolutionary support vector machine for RMB exchange rate forecasting. Physica A-Stat. Mech. Appl. **521**, 692–704 (2019)
8. Levis, A.A., Papageorgiou, L.G.: Customer demand forecasting via support vector regression analysis. Chem. Eng. Res. Des. **83**(A8), 1009–1018 (2005)
9. Dai, C.: A method of forecasting trade export volume based on back-propagation neural network. Neural Comput. Appl. **35**(12), 8775–8784 (2023)
10. Gerasimov, A.N., Gromov, E.L., Skripnichenko, Y.S., Grigoryeva, O.P., Skripnichenko, V.Y.: Models and forecasts of the export potential of the regional economic system. Regionologiya-Regionology Russian J. Reg. Stud. **30**(4), 762–782 (2022)
11. Eckert, F., Hyndman, R.J., Panagiotelis, A.: Forecasting Swiss exports using Bayesian forecast reconciliation. Eur. J. Oper. Res. **291**(2), 693–710 (2021)
12. Karabay, G., Kilic, M.B., Saricoban, K., Günaydin, G.K.: Forecasting of Turkey's apparel exports using artificial neural network autoregressive models. Industria Textila **74**(2), 143–153 (2023)
13. Shen, M.L., Lee, C.F., Liu, H.H., Chang, P.Y., Yang, C.H.: Effective multinational trade forecasting using LSTM recurrent neural network. Expert Syst. Appl. **182**, 115199 (2021)
14. Fan, L.W., Pan, S.J., Li, Z.M., Li, H.P.: An ICA-based support vector regression scheme for forecasting crude oil prices. Technol. Forecast. Soc. Change **112**, 245–253 (2016)

15. Kuo, R.J., Li, P.S.: Taiwanese export trade forecasting using firefly algorithm based K-means algorithm and SVR with wavelet transform. Comput. Ind. Eng. **99**, 153–161 (2016)
16. Drucker, H., Burges, C.J.C., Kaufman, L., Smola, A., Vapnik, V.: Presented at the 10th Annual Conference on Neural Information Processing Systems (NIPS), Denver, Co (1996)
17. Brereton, R.G., Lloyd, G.R.: Support Vector Machines for classification and regression. Analyst **135**(2), 230–267 (2010)
18. Thomas, S., Pillai, G.N., Pal, K.: Prediction of peak ground acceleration using ε-SVR, ν-SVR and Ls-SVR algorithm. Geomat. Nat. Hazards Risk **8**(2), 177–193 (2017)
19. Latif, N., Selvam, J.D., Kapse, M., Sharma, V., Mahajan, V.: Comparative performance of LSTM and ARIMA for the short-term prediction of bitcoin prices. Australas. Account. Bus. Financ. J. **17**(1), 256–276 (2023)
20. Roozbeh, M., Rouhi, A., Mohamed, N.A., Jahadi, F.: Generalized support vector regression and symmetry functional regression approaches to model the high-dimensional data. Symmetry **15**(6), 21 (2023)
21. Shi, T., Chen, S.G.: Robust twin support vector regression with smooth truncated Hε loss function. Neural Process. Lett. **45** (2023)
22. Hao, D., Kihyung, B., Meng-Ze, Z.: A study on the trade potential of electronic products based on trade gravity expansion model between China and Korea. J. Korea Contents Assoc. **22**(7), 216–226 (2022)

Research on the Taxation of Mobile Commerce Digital Assets

Zhangxin Ma, Peiyan Zhou[✉], and Na Fu

Jilin University, 2699 Qianjin Street, Changchun, Jilin, China
15943595913@163.com

Abstract. In recent years, with the development of Internet and other technologies and the popularization of smart phone mobile terminals, people's ideas and shopping methods have changed, and the mobile commerce market has developed rapidly. In this context, the use of massive data elements to empower business development will also become an important starting point for the improvement of business performance in the future, and at the same time, enterprises can also enrich the connotation of products and services through digital productization to create new business growth points. As a result, data elements will become an indispensable asset for future mobile commerce enterprises. Since digital assets are a new type of production factor, whether the traditional tax system is suitable for its characteristics, how to determine the occurrence of tax liability of digital assets, how to tax collect and manage digital assets, especially how to measure the value of digital assets and empower entities, and then clarify taxpayers, tax bases and other tax factors are all issues that need to be solved urgently. Therefore, this paper studies the tax management of China's mobile commerce digital assets based on regional interests, China's actual situation and the characteristics of mobile commerce.

This paper first defines the related concepts of digital assets, and analyzes the composition and characteristics of enterprise digital assets in the mobile commerce environment. Secondly, this paper analyzes the pre-taxation and taxation obstacles of mobile commerce digital assets, and finally puts forward corresponding countermeasures and suggestions, hoping to provide some reference for the tax department to carry out its work in the future.

Keywords: Mobile commerce · Digital Assets · Taxation First Section

1 Introduction

With the popularization of the Internet, the scale of mobile commerce is gradually expanding, and the use cases of data in mobile e-commerce enterprises are also increasing: after collecting, processing, and analyzing data on daily business activities, mobile e-commerce enterprises can gain valuable insights, such as consumer preferences and market demand. This information not only helps businesses optimize their products and make the right decisions in a competitive market, but it can also increase the overall profitability of the company by improving internal business processes and increasing

J. Wei and G. Margetis (Eds.): HCII 2024, LNCS 14738, pp. 106–118, 2024.
https://doi.org/10.1007/978-3-031-60487-4_9

operational efficiency. At present, it is already a big trend for e-commerce companies to commercialize dagital assets, and various data products, such as Alibaba Database and Sesame Credit, have appeared in the Chinese market. With the rapid development of new technologies such as big data, cloud computing, and artificial intelligence, dagital assets have become an indispensable part of the development of mobile e-commerce enterprises, and more and more enterprises have paid attention to them.

On the other hand, in 2019, the Fourth Plenary Session of the 19th Central Committee of the Communist Party of China proposed to "improve the mechanism for the contribution of factors of production such as labor, capital, land, knowledge, technology, management, and data to be evaluated by the market and the remuneration determined according to the contribution", which for the first time regarded data as a factor of production and emphasized the need to gradually form an income distribution mechanism on data. As one of the important means for the state to participate in the distribution of income, taxation should participate in the distribution of data production factors. In December 2022, the "Opinions of the Central Committee of the Communist Party of China and the State Council on Building a Data Basic System to Better Play the Role of Data Elements" pointed out that "data, as a new factor of production, is the foundation of digitalization, networking, and intelligence, and has been rapidly integrated into all links such as production, distribution, circulation, consumption, and social service management". The operation mechanism of property rights such as the separation of the right to operate data products promotes a new model of "joint use and shared benefits" of non-public data in a market-oriented manner, and provides a basic institutional guarantee for activating the value creation and realization of data elements." This not only fully affirms the status and role of data in the economy and society, but also puts forward the principles, methods and objectives of data rights confirmation, and also lays the foundation for the taxation of digital assets. For a long time, China's tax collection and management objects are mainly the real economy, tax collection and management methods are mainly managed by enterprises, the distribution of tax sources is relatively stable, and the innovation requirements for tax management level are not high, and the rapid development of the digital economy in the world has brought many challenges to the current tax law, and how to build a data tax system has become an important issue of great concern at home and abroad.

This paper makes a detailed analysis of the composition of digital assets in the context of mobile commerce and the path selection of taxation of mobile commerce digital assets, so as to make up for the lack of theoretical content related to the taxation of digital assets in the context of mobile commerce, and promote the reform and improvement of the legal system in related fields.

2 Overview of Digital Assets in the Context of Mobile Commerce

2.1 The Concept of Digital Assets

There are many concepts related to digital assets that are widely used in existing academic literature and practice: the concept of digital assets is derived from data. At present, there are many definitions of digital assets in theory and practice, among which the more authoritative definitions come from the China Asset Appraisal Association and the

China Academy of Information and Communications Technology. The Asset Valuation Expert Guidelines No. 9 - Mobile Commerce Data Asset Valuation issued by the China Asset Appraisal Association defines digital assets as "data resources that are legally owned or controlled by a specific entity, can continue to play a role, and can bring direct or indirect economic benefits". The White Paper on Data Asset Management Practice Version 5.0 released by the China Academy of Information and Communications Technology (CAICT) defines digital assets as "data resources legally owned or controlled by an organization, recorded electronically or otherwise, and can be measured or traded, which can directly or indirectly bring economic and social benefits". It is not difficult to see that these data asset concepts are derived from the current accounting asset concept, and have the following characteristics: one is to emphasize the ownership or control of data resources, and the other is to emphasize that they can bring economic or social benefits.

2.2 Composition of Mobile Commerce Digital Assets

According to the 50th China Internet Development Statistics Report, as of June 2022, China has about 1.051 billion Internet users, 80% of whom have participated in online shopping. The resulting huge purchase volume has brought a large amount of data, which is widely used in electronic payment, express logistics and other industries, providing strong support for the development of e-commerce. In the context of mobile commerce, the main components of digital assets can be divided into the following types:

User Data. As one of the most important resources of mobile e-commerce enterprises, user data is also the core resource for maximizing the value of data in their operation. In the marketing process of e-commerce enterprises, user data provides necessary auxiliary data for the daily operation of e-commerce enterprises, including the age structure of users, the gender structure of users, the source of users, and the browsing patterns of users. User data is real-time data, which can be updated independently according to the user's preferences and needs at different times, and the information and products that meet the user's needs can be selected. This helps manufacturers and distributors build user profiles and improve and update products based on users' preferences, allowing them to carry out targeted marketing and make their products more competitive. E-commerce companies can use data analysis to collect and monitor consumer behavior data in real time to accurately judge user needs and user consumption preferences, so as to provide them with targeted personalized services and improve their shopping experience and transaction efficiency.

Product-Related Information. When consumers buy products, they will interact with sellers through the platform in all aspects of sales, and express complaints and feedback through comments, customer service chats or directly on the platform to meet the needs of consumers and express their interest and satisfaction with the purchased products; Sellers can also use this to advertise and promote products and events, which will make consumers buy more products. E-commerce businesses use a variety of technological tools to capture and extract this unstructured data to produce structured data that can be used for analysis. A large and complete database and relevant information is a key way to drive consumer traffic. By monitoring products across the network, timely product information, real-time price updates, and intelligent consumer and product matching can be achieved.

Consumption Data. Consumption data includes consumers' payment information, credit information, etc. Based on consumer data, e-commerce companies can filter out financially healthy consumers and focus on integrity. When trading on the platform, it is inevitable that some data related to other industries will be generated, so that businesses can use this data to collaborate with other businesses. For example, the logistics data generated by consumer shopping can be used to cooperate with logistics companies to improve the deployment of logistics routes, improve the resource utilization rate of frequent shopping areas, and implement logistics routes in other regions accordingly.

Social Data. Social data encompasses a range of data that consumers share before, during, and after purchasing a product. This data helps e-commerce businesses understand what consumers really want, optimize products, and provide actionable recommendations to other shoppers.

Operational Data. Operational data refers to the financial data generated by e-commerce enterprises through various activities in the operation process, which can help e-commerce enterprises clearly understand their operating conditions, so as to have a comprehensive grasp of their own development. This data can help e-commerce companies plan their business effectively and make business decisions to ensure they stand out from the competition.

2.3 Features of Mobile Commerce Digital Assets

With the development of information technology and the improvement of mobile terminal functions, compared with traditional e-commerce, payment functions and information access are more convenient and efficient, prompting more and more users to use mobile commerce to complete shopping. In addition, compared with traditional e-commerce, mobile commerce needs to collect more user information, so as to provide users with more accurate services, make customized services and personalized services possible, and then improve the user's experience. This paper analyzes the digital assets of enterprises in the context of mobile e-commerce and finds that they have the following characteristics:

Non-substantial. A mobile commerce data asset is an asset that has no physical form and must rely on the physical medium, but its value depends on the data itself. Mobile commerce digital assets, like traditional intangible assets, are non-consuming resources that do not degrade or deplete over time. Therefore, mobile commerce digital assets can be stored for a long time, so that the enterprise business continues to grow and develop.

Dependence. The data must be stored on a specific medium. There are different types of media such as paper, disk, tape, CD-ROM, hard disk, etc. The same data may exist in different forms on several mediums at the same time. Like other intangible assets, mobile commerce digital assets cannot exist in isolation and often rely on tangible assets to function.

Diversity. Each type of data processing is different for different use cases, such as databases, networked storage, and more. The same m-commerce data asset can be used for different purposes, such as intellectual property and business value, but due to the uncertainty of data use, it has high variability. In addition, due to technological advancements and changes in the market environment, the same type of data may be reclassified or redistributed. Mobile commerce data asset value generation is a process that integrates data and technology, which is also known as mobile commerce data asset generation and transformation.

Machinability. Data is retained, updated, and supplemented to increase data capacity, but it also brings more potential value. Deleting, summarizing, and grouping are meant to eliminate redundancies in order to make the data valid so that it can be better analyzed, refined, mined, and processed. Processability enables enterprises to obtain deeper data resources through continuous processing, thereby increasing the value of their mobile commerce digital assets to better meet the needs of business operations and growth.

Value Variability. The volatility of the value of mobile commerce digital assets is mainly manifested in three aspects. First, data can not only reflect different forms of representation, but also classify different data processing methods, such as text data and image data, which will be processed differently. In addition, the same mobile commerce data asset may be used for different purposes, which leads to uncertainty in the use of the data, which can lead to significant changes in the value of the mobile commerce data asset. Second, the data is time-sensitive, and its asset value may decrease over time, but it is likely to continue to grow. Third, data is fluid, and the flow between different subjects, especially within the enterprise, may bring about changes in value. In the context of mobile commerce, the digital assets of the e-commerce industry themselves have high value, and by collecting more user information, it can provide users with more accurate services, make customized services and personalized services possible, and then improve the user's experience.

3   Prerequisites for Taxation of Mobile Commerce Digital Assets

The current research on the taxation of mobile commerce digital assets takes data transactions as the object of taxation, which not only promotes it to play an important role in the study of tax governance in the digital economy, but also supports the development of data elements and promotes the continuous vigorous development of the digital economy to a large extent. In order to better construct the system and system of taxation of mobile commerce digital assets, the theoretical roots of the taxation of mobile commerce digital assets should be clarified and defined.

3.1   Definition of Mobile Commerce Digital Assets

As a special asset, the legal status of mobile commerce digital assets has not been clarified in the current tax law, resulting in a lack of unified tax management. From this, it is necessary to determine what kind of property type mobile commerce digital assets belong to, which needs further attention. This is due to the fact that different types of property have unique attributes of value, and the tax rules are also different from different types of property, which will also cause various detailed differences and differences in tax treatment. Mobile commerce digital assets exist as virtual symbols, and are generally not classified as tangible objects.

The definition of intangible assets is not entirely consistent in the Implementation Measures for the Pilot Program of Replacing Business Tax with Value-Added Tax and Accounting Standard for Business Enterprises No. 6 – Intangible Assets. In addition to the possibility of no physical form, economic gain, Guideline 6 also stipulates that the criteria of identifiability and ownership or control must be met. In practice, since accounting standards stipulate that the accounting treatment of intangible assets is based on fair value, the ownership attribute of the data must be considered when determining whether there is a digital asset. In China's current tax system, data is not clearly defined as an intangible asset. Like general dagital assets, mobile commerce digital assets also have the characteristics of no physical form, possibility of income, controllability, and independent trading, which are the basic properties of intangible assets in the sense of tax law, so they can be regarded as one of the special types of intangible assets.

3.2 Value-Based Data Elements of Mobile Commerce Based on Value Chain Theory

The economic theory of value chain can specifically analyze how the actors involved in it create value, their competitive position in the market and the links they participate in. With the help of the theory of value chain, we can see how the source of tax revenue is formed, and can concretely and directly show how the data elements are gradually circulated and circulated in the market business behavior. This also ensures the reliability of the tax source.

In the past economic behavior, traditional enterprises intervened in the process of production through data elements, and the process of data value creation was not only manifested in internal data exchange and cooperation, but also through data interaction and cooperation with official organizations, digital platform enterprises and other external departments. Data can be used to cooperate with other factors of production in a simple and convenient way to realize its own innovation potential, and realize the utilization and innovation of means of production. The process by which data obtains other factors of production through the exchange process reflects its exchange value and the effect of circulation. At the same time, data elements can play a synergistic role through coordination and cooperation with other elements to jointly create value-maximizing products, and when data products or services can achieve economic returns through transfer, data creates maximum value through transactions.

4   The Dilemma of Taxation of Mobile Commerce Digital Assets

At present, China's tax collection and management regulations related to digital assets are still not clear enough. Digital assets are the product of data intensification, and the tax base, tax source, taxpayer and other elements are different from those of general VAT levy objects, which hinder the tax collection and management of digital assets. Therefore, there are different dilemmas on how to impose a new tax on mobile commerce digital assets.

4.1 Confirmation of Ownership of Mobile Commerce Digital Assets

The Opinions of the Central Committee of the Communist Party of China and the State Council on Constructing a Basic Data System to Better Play the Role of Data Elements requires that "the legitimate rights enjoyed by each participant in the process of data production, circulation and use shall be defined separately according to the data source and data generation characteristics", and due to the reproducibility, non-competition, non-exclusivity and other characteristics of mobile business data, the rights and interests of data sources, data processors, and data users are intertwined and overlapped, and it is difficult to determine.

The Source of Mobile Commerce Data is Difficult to Determine. For example, if the personal location information and personal browsing records generated by consumers with the help of the platform involve relevant individuals, but the information is naturally generated from the platform, is the source of such information an individual or the platform? 4.1.2 Mobile commerce data processors are difficult to identify.

For example, if an enterprise or individual authorizes a third-party technology company to invest in algorithms to process data to obtain processed data-mobile commerce digital assets, is the data processor an enterprise, an individual, or an authorized third-party technology company?

The Ownership, Use, and Income Rights of Mobile Commerce Digital Assets are Often Intertwined and Difficult to Determine. Due to the uncertainty of the source of mobile commerce data and the uncertainty of the data processor, it is difficult to determine the right to hold, use, and benefit from the digital assets involved in the rights and interests of the digital assets. For example, a shopping platform records customer review data, and the result of processing this data – mobile commerce digital assets – becomes the basis for formulating business strategies and thus obtaining operating revenue. As a mobile commerce data asset, the property rights of the processed shopping platform review data seem to be attributable to the data processor, the platform enterprise, but the buyer's personal account information, consumption records, geographical location and other information recorded in the platform are also important components of the digital assets. If so, how should it be determined? The right to hold, use, and benefit from mobile commerce digital assets usually does not belong to a specific entity such as the data source, data processor, or data user, but may belong to different entities.

4.2 Valuation of Mobile Commerce Digital Assets

Because mobile commerce digital assets have the characteristics of physical virtuality, their value is directly proportional to the effective information content. However, the assessment of the value of information is subjective in nature, and it is difficult to adopt a single or standard evaluation model. Therefore, on the road to improving the tax governance system, it is necessary to solve the problem of how to reasonably evaluate the value of mobile commerce digital assets and the value created by mobile commerce digital assets for enterprises.

Reprocessing of Mobile Commerce Digital Assets Will Change Their Value. Mobile commerce digital assets are reproducible, and the process of reworking them may create an entirely new data asset. And in general, the value of the reprocessed mobile commerce digital assets will be much greater than the value of the individual mobile commerce digital assets before the processing is combined. In addition, different valuation models and estimation methods will also change the value of mobile commerce digital assets, making the accurate evaluation of the value of mobile commerce digital assets more complex.

The Increase in the Number of Uses Will Also Move the Value of Business Digital Assets. Unlike traditional assets, the infinite nature of mobile commerce digital assets allows them to be used multiple times by different people, but also by many people at the same time, and even in different ways depending on their purpose. In addition to this, mobile commerce digital assets are non-consumable. This infinite and non-consumable nature makes it difficult to accurately quantify the value of digital assets.

The Value of Mobile Commerce Digital Assets of the Same Quality May Be Completely Different. This is because different consumers have different needs, so different people may evaluate the value of the same mobile commerce data asset in diametrically opposed ways. For example, an advertisement for a health supplement for the elderly may be very valuable for some older people who have a demand for the benefits that the product brings. However, most young people or children will feel that the ad is not valuable and may even be seen as a waste of time. From this, it can be concluded that sometimes mobile commerce digital assets may have the same quality, but their value is different, and this issue must be taken into account when valuing the value of mobile commerce digital assets.

5 Policy Recommendations

5.1 Suggestions for Confirming the Ownership of Mobile Commerce Digital Assets

According to the requirements of the "Opinions of the Central Committee of the Communist Party of China and the State Council on Building a Basic Data System to Better Play the Role of Data Elements", the confirmation of the right to digital assets includes the establishment of a separate property rights operation mechanism such as the right to hold data resources, the right to process and use data, and the right to operate data products. Therefore, unlike the traditional sense of the organic unity of ownership, the right to use, the right to benefit, etc., the confirmation of the right to mobile commerce digital assets needs to determine the holding, use and income rights of the digital assets on the basis of determining the data source, data processor, and data user, and establish a multiple rights and interests structure of the property rights of mobile commerce digital assets.

First, identify the data source, data processor, and data consumer. The sources of mobile commerce data mainly include information provided by individuals (such as information registered and browsed by individuals on shopping platforms) and information owned or collected by enterprises, so the data sources are individuals, enterprises, etc.

Mobile commerce data processors are entities that process raw data from individuals, enterprises, etc., through algorithms, which may be enterprises, individuals, or third-party technology enterprises authorized by enterprises or individuals. The data processor invests the original data into the algorithm to form a data asset.

Enterprises or individuals use these digital assets, put them into production and operation and obtain benefits, and enterprises or individuals are the users of digital assets. For example, a shopping platform mentioned above is the data source, the user who evaluates after consumption on the platform is the data source, the platform is the data processor when it invests in the algorithm to process the data to form the data asset, and the user who uses the data asset after the algorithm processing and generates income is the data user.

Second, determine the rights and interests of mobile commerce data sources, data processors, and data users.

The source of mobile commerce data has the ownership of the data provided, and this right is embodied in the right to access, correct, delete and other rights to the information provided. Of course, data processors who process these raw data are obliged to keep these raw data confidential.

Mobile commerce data processors (except for entrusted third-party technology enterprises or individuals) and those entrusted to third-party technology enterprises or individuals to carry out data processors enjoy the right to hold digital assets. For enterprises, if the source of data is an enterprise, then the enterprise is not only the owner of the original data, but also has the right to hold the digital assets because it is a data processor; If there is data collected or purchased in the data source, then because it has paid a certain cost in the collection or purchase, the data processor has the right to use the data collected or purchased, and has the right to hold the digital assets formed after processing and processing using these original data. For third-party technology enterprises entrusted by enterprises or individuals to process and process raw data, the ownership of the processed digital assets shall belong to the entrusting party, the enterprise or individual, not the third-party technology enterprise.

Mobile business data users enjoy the right to use and operate digital assets. Mobile commerce data users have the right to use and operate the digital assets obtained from the data processor.

Finally, determine the property rights of the mobile commerce digital assets. For the mobile commerce data source, if its data is not processed, its value will not be reflected, so the data source does not have the right to hold the digital assets, nor does it enjoy the right to benefit from the digital assets. Both the processor and the user of the mobile commerce digital assets have the right to receive the benefits of the digital assets. Processors and principals of digital assets who have the right to hold mobile commerce digital assets have the right to receive income from the sale or use of these digital assets. For users of mobile commerce digital assets, they have the right to receive benefits after using the purchased digital assets. That is, the holder of mobile business digital assets has the right to use, operate and benefit from mobile business digital assets; Those who have the right to use mobile commerce digital assets have the right to operate and benefit from the mobile commerce digital assets. The above definition of mobile commerce digital assets can solve the problem of data ownership and the division of rights and interests of digital assets from data sources, and clarify the relationship between the right to hold, use, operate and benefit of digital assets. Of course, the state should participate in the distribution of income by taxing the income obtained by data processors and data users who receive the benefits of mobile commerce digital assets.

5.2 Recommendations on Taxation of Mobile Commerce Digital Assets

Determine the Type of Tax. First, according to the principle of "capital per se shall not be taxable", no property tax should be levied on mobile commerce digital assets. Secondly, based on the principle of scientific and reasonable taxation, VAT should not be levied on mobile commerce digital assets. Finally, based on the fact that the income should be regulated, and the adjustment should be moderate, scientific and reasonable, it is recommended to levy data use tax and income tax on the income of mobile commerce digital assets. The levy of data use tax on mobile commerce digital assets is levied on the premise that digital assets generate income, which can not only play the role of tax regulation in the development and use of digital assets, but also will not form a tax burden on digital assets that do not generate income, will not inhibit the development of the digital economy, and will also balance the tax burden between the production factors of digital assets and non-data asset production factors such as capital. The income tax on the income of mobile business digital assets is mainly based on the fair principle of taxation when there is income, so that the income tax burden of the digital economy is consistent with the income tax burden of the non-digital economy.

Determination of Taxpayers of Mobile Commerce Digital Assets. Taxpayers of mobile commerce data asset use tax are data asset holders and data asset users. The taxpayer of mobile commerce data asset income tax is the holder of the data asset, the user of the data asset or the third-party enterprise entrusted with the processing of the data asset.

The mobile commerce data asset holder receives income from the sale of its digital assets, and therefore the mobile commerce data asset holder is a taxpayer of data asset use tax and income tax. The user of mobile commerce digital assets purchases digital assets from the data asset holder for production and operation and benefits, and thus is a taxpayer of data asset use tax and data asset income tax. Although the third-party enterprise entrusted with the processing of digital assets does not have the right to hold the mobile business digital assets, it is a taxpayer of income tax on mobile business digital assets because it has income related to the processing of digital assets.

Determine the Tax Base of Mobile Commerce Digital Assets
(1) The tax base of the mobile commerce data asset use tax is the income of the data asset. The value assessment of mobile commerce digital assets should take into account risk factors, transaction scenarios and related party transactions, and the legal attributes,

information attributes, transaction attributes, value volatile attributes and specific performance of the assessed digital assets should be clarified. Influencing factors such as market and quality are taken into account. Specifically, the data potential energy model can be used to measure the value of digital assets in different dimensions. The data potential energy model incorporates the legal attributes, information attributes, transaction attributes, value volatile attributes and specific performance of digital assets into the correction factors, and different factors can be adjusted according to different adaptation scenarios, so that the model can be widely used in the value evaluation of digital assets in different application scenarios. The specific operation method is as follows: firstly, on the premise that the mobile commerce digital assets are used in a specific application scenario, based on the quality evaluation of the digital assets, the legal attributes, information attributes, transaction attributes, value volatile attributes and specific performance of the digital assets are included in the correction factors to determine the costs that may occur in the formation of the digital assets; Secondly, according to the characteristics of mobile commerce digital assets, such as non-entity, dependence, value volatility and timeliness, the costs that may occur in the formation of digital assets are adjusted. Thirdly, according to the characteristics of the industry where the application scenarios of mobile commerce digital assets are located, combined with the scarcity or monopoly degree of digital assets applied to specific scenarios, the cost of digital assets is corrected. Finally, based on the replicability characteristics of mobile commerce digital assets, there are potential market development contributions in different scenarios, and this part of the value contribution is included in the value correction factors of digital assets to determine the value of digital assets. Since the data trading market is not active at this stage, it is more feasible and reliable to conduct systematic economic analysis of the value and cost of digital assets from multiple dimensions.

(2) The tax base of income tax on mobile commerce digital assets is the taxable income of digital assets.

Taxable income is taxable income minus costs (expenses). According to Article 13 of the Regulations for the Implementation of the Enterprise Income Tax Law, the amount of income from intangible assets shall be determined at fair value. Under the premise that market transactions are limited and market prices are difficult to obtain effectively, it is a feasible choice to use the above data potential energy model to measure the value of digital assets in different dimensions. At the same time, this method is used to evaluate the cost of mobile commerce digital assets in different scenarios, so as to determine the taxable income of data asset income tax by subtracting the valuation cost from the appraised value of the data asset. Under the premise that market transactions are limited and market prices are difficult to obtain effectively, the use of the above-mentioned data potential energy model to measure the value and cost of digital assets between different dimensions is also in line with the principle of determining the taxable income of digital assets in Article 8 of the Regulations for the Implementation of the Individual Income Tax Law.

6   Epilogue

In the process of developing the digital economy, it is inevitable to establish and improve the taxation system for mobile commerce digital assets. The ever-expanding volume of mobile commerce data asset transactions has challenged the establishment of tax relations between countries and the design of global tax regimes. This paper mainly takes the taxation mechanism of value-added tax on mobile commerce digital assets under the digital economy as the starting point of research, and analyzes the dilemma of regulating the taxation of mobile commerce digital assets from three aspects: the confirmation of ownership, value composition and tax collection and management of mobile commerce digital assets. At the same time, in combination with the international legislative practice of mobile business data asset transactions, the legislative concept of levying value-added tax on mobile business digital assets under China's national conditions is proposed.

As the "visible hand" in the factor market, the tax collection and management of mobile commerce data asset transactions is a distribution tool for countries to divide economic benefits in the era of digital economy. Due to differences in national systems, economic environments, and the level of science and technology, the positions of different countries are often very different. In the long run, China, as a major Internet country, should actively explore and study the establishment of a tax collection and management system for mobile business digital assets, and build a tax collection and management system that complements modern society. Standing at the forefront of the development of the times, on the basis of giving full play to data as the basic production factor of market development, a theoretical framework for the self-consistency of the development of mobile commerce data asset market is formulated. At the same time, on the basis of a thorough understanding of the nature of the development law and the actual situation of mobile business digital assets, with policies as incentives, blockchain technology as guarantees, taking into account innovation and fairness, properly solving the problems in the process of establishing a tax system for mobile business digital assets, and designing a tax system for mobile business digital asset transactions that is not only in line with national conditions but also in line with international standards.

References

1. Digital Asset Monetary Network Inc. (OTC: DATI) Drives Innovation with Social Impact and Value Investing. M2 Presswire (2024)
2. Mohammad, Q.A., Hanan, A.: Digital assets should be included in advance care planning discussions for patients receiving palliative care. Evidence-Based Nurs. (2023)
3. Hanqing, J.: Research on the impact of digital asset management on broadcast media consumption patterns. Acad. J. Bus. Manag. **5**(21) (2023)
4. Arjun, H.R., Wei, W., Ming, L., et al.: Blockchain-enabled digital asset tokenization for crowdsensing in environmental, social, and governance disclosure. Comput. Ind. Eng. **185** (2023)
5. Vien, G.T., Vo, H.M.T.: Digital assets in the context of the fourth industrial revolution, international integration, and Vietnamese law. Cogent Soc. Sci. **9**(1) (2023)
6. Alma, A., Tracy, A., Gene, B., et al.: The case for self-regulation for the digital assets industry. J. Finan. Compliance **7**(1), 15–34 (2023)

7. Zhou, P., Wei, Q., Zhang, X., et al.: China's legislative challenges regarding income taxes on mobile commerce. Int. J. Mobile Commun. **19**(6), 683–707 (2021)

8. Huang, X., Zhang, J.: Investigation on tax planning and risk prevention based on financial big data. Finan. Eng. Risk Manag. **6**(7) (2023)

9. Gong, L.: Study on tax governance of data assets in the context of digital economy. Int. J. Manag. Sci. Res. **6**(6) (2023)

10. Chen, Y., Zhao, Y., Xie, W., et al.: An empirical study on core data asset identification in data governance. Big Data Cogn. Comput. **7**(4) (2023)

11. Zhang, Q.: An introduction to accounting recognition and measurement of data assets. Acad. J. Bus. Manag. **5**(15) (2023)

12. Wen, C., Wang, N., Fang, J., et al.: An integrated model of continued m-commerce applications usage. J. Comput. Inf. Syst. **63**(3), 632–647 (2023)

13. Yu, S., Kong, X., Wang, W.: Tax system choices for the development of digital economy: data use tax. Tax Res. (12), 39–43 (2023). (in Chinese)

14. Faizah, F.S., Solan, R.S., Ridzwan, M.Y., et al.: Impact of Google searches and social media on digital assets' volatility. Humanit. Soc. Sci. Commun. **10**(1) (2023)

15. Chu, R.: Data resource tax: a systematic investigation of a legislative model of data tax. Tax Res. (09), 66–72 (2023). (in Chinese)

Analysis of Food Safety Issues in Cross-Border Mobile E-commerce Platforms Based on BTM–Taking Amazon US User Reviews as an Example

Yue Wang[1], Zhongwei Gu[1], and June Wei[2(✉)]

[1] Shanghai Dianji University, Pudong, Shanghai, China
zwgu@qq.com
[2] University of West Florida, Pensacola, FL, USA
jwei@uwf.edu

Abstract. As the cross-border mobile e-commerce food market is rapidly booming, food safety issues are becoming more and more prominent. To effectively respond to this challenge, this study applies the BTM (Biterm Topic Model) thematic model to deeply analyze the food safety user reviews on cross-border mobile e-commerce platforms. We first selected and collected platform data that met the research requirements and performed the necessary preprocessing. Subsequently, the review texts were analyzed using the BTM model, including topic intensity distribution, word cloud mapping, word frequency weight visualization, and quantitative output of word item relevance. Through these analyses, we delved into the manifestation of food safety issues in three aspects: topic intensity, topic domain, and subject structure, identified five specific types of food safety issues, and revealed the reasons behind them. The findings suggest that AMAZON US cross-border mobile e-commerce platform has some problems with food safety regulations. In response to these findings, we propose a series of targeted recommendations for improvement, which are relevant to other cross-border e-commerce platforms. These discoveries will offer valuable insights for the operation and oversight of cross-border mobile e-commerce platforms, fostering the sustainable growth of the cross-border food trade, safeguarding consumer rights and interests, mitigating platform risks, and ultimately promoting the long-term expansion of the industry.

Keywords: cross-border mobile e-commerce · BTM model · food safety · user reviews big data

1 Introduction

As globalization and the rapid advancement of the Internet intersect, cross-border mobile e-commerce has emerged as a fresh option for consumer shopping, delivering unprecedented convenience and diversity to the shopping experience. In recent years, China's cross-border e-commerce has exhibited a positive development trend, with its market

© The Author(s), under exclusive license to Springer Nature Switzerland AG 2024
J. Wei and G. Margetis (Eds.): HCII 2024, LNCS 14738, pp. 119–132, 2024.
https://doi.org/10.1007/978-3-031-60487-4_10

scale expanding rapidly. The total volume of China's cross-border e-commerce imports and exports has consistently grown between 2019 and 2021, breaking through the trillion level, of which China's cross-border e-commerce import and export scale is up to 1,923.7 billion yuan in 2021, a year-on-year increase of 18.6% compared with 2020 [1].

Today's emerging business models bring brand-new business opportunities; however, they are also accompanied by a series of challenges. Particularly on cross-border e-commerce platforms, food safety issues frequently arise, which not only threaten the health and rights of consumers but also directly jeopardize the credibility and sustainable development of e-commerce platforms. The characteristics of cross-border e-commerce, such as inter-temporal transactions and inaccessibility, increase the difficulty of regulating food safety. Against this backdrop, a large number of food safety issues have emerged, the obvious ones of which include unclean food, spoilage, odor, decay, inconspicuous production dates, false advertising, and counterfeit product information. In addition, the timeliness of cross-border logistics is in dire need of improvement, as untimely logistics can also lead to food safety problems. The complexity, diversity, and dynamics of food safety issues are becoming more and more prominent, thus forcing us to adopt a more systematic and scientific approach to addressing these challenges.

BTM topic modeling, as an unsupervised learning method, can uncover structures and features in datasets without labeling information. In the past decades, BTM topic models have been widely used in the fields of text mining, and topic modeling, and applied to education, policy governance, and product reviews. By collecting user review information on cross-border e-commerce platforms and screening and processing the data, analyzing food reviews on cross-border mobile e-commerce platforms by using BTM topic modeling may be effective in finding out the reasons for the emergence of food safety problems and providing new ideas and methods for regulatory issues.

2 Literature Review

2.1 Research on Thematic Modeling

Topic mining in text analysis has seen the prevalent utilization of the LDA (Latent Dirichlet Allocation) topic model, initially introduced by Blei et al. [2] This model relies on patterns of word co-occurrence within documents, where the subject matter of the document is represented as a probability distribution through various stages including preprocessing, modeling, and similarity calculations, which can realize multi-domain topic discovery [3], text clustering [4], semantic annotation [5], topic recognition, etc., and thus is widely used for text topic extraction. However, the majority of text content on web mobile platforms exists in the form of short texts. Due to the limitations posed by the brevity of this content, traditional topic models often struggle to establish connections between different topics when processing short texts. This results in a relatively sparse pattern of word co-occurrence within each document [6]. The rhetorical expression of consumer review content often possesses a certain degree of arbitrariness, so it is also easy to use some unfounded, worthless, and insubstantial rhetoric, or even some unfounded and worthless advertisement slogans [1]. The validity of the model is greatly affected by the above two reasons. To solve this problem, Xiaohui Yan [7] and others proposed the Bi-term Topic Model (BTM), which counts co-occurring word pairs consisting of any two words occurring in the target corpus, and models the corpus with co-occurring word pairs, thus solving the problem of data sparsity in the short text corpus. Compared with traditional research methods, the BTM model can effectively explore the potential semantic information in the text, especially in the topic mining of short texts.

2.2   Research on Cross-Border E-commerce Food Safety Issues

In Theory and Practice of Cross-Border E-Commerce, Ke Limin and Hong Fangren (2016) provide a comprehensive explanation of the current state of cross-border e-commerce and retail imports, highlighting key characteristics of their development. They also delve into the evolving regulatory framework, discussing both the opportunities and challenges that lie ahead for cross-border e-commerce. Furthermore, they offer targeted suggestions for constructing an effective regulatory model to address these challenges [8]. Li Yufang holds that there are problems in the risk information mechanism of the cross-border e-commerce food market in China, the collection of risk information is not standardized, the disclosure is not sufficient, and the related regulatory model is problematic [9]. Wu Peng and Huang Sijun found that there are problems in cross-border e-commerce imported food safety supervision, including defective regulatory systems, insufficient risk management, and information traceability dilemmas [10]. Huang Lu, Peng Zhongqin, and Tan Yue argued there are problems in the regulation of food safety with the development of China's cross-border e-commerce platforms and food safety hazards [11]. Based on actual data, the study of Zhang Bei, Ye Danmin, and Ma Ruqiu analyzed the subject, object, channel, and situation of cross-border e-commerce food safety risk, and proposed to realize the collaborative governance of cross-border e-commerce food safety risk by improving the risk warning mechanism, perfecting the risk regulation standard, and constructing an information sharing platform [12]. Guo Xin believes that at present, China's cross-border e-commerce food supply chain management is relatively chaotic, with shortcomings in suppliers, transportation channels, and receiving channels, and an imperfect regulatory system [13]. In terms of quality supervision, Zhou Feng, Yan Yingpeng, Su Rina, and Qiu Hui proposed a method for risk assessment of cross-border e-commerce imported food quality and safety to provide feasible countermeasures for food quality and safety [14]. Chen Yi et al. used big data visualization techniques to analyze food safety issues and provide new tools for food safety monitoring and control [15].

Although the existing studies have achieved results to a certain extent, there are still some shortcomings and limitations. There are relatively few studies on food safety issues in the field of cross-border mobile e-commerce, and there is a lack of systematic theoretical framework and empirical analysis. Currently, research predominantly centers on the viewpoints of policymakers and enterprises, often neglecting the underlying reasons for food safety concerns and the regulatory challenges that underlie these issues. In addition, traditional qualitative analysis methods prevail, lacking quantitative analysis and big data support.

Against this background, in-depth analysis of food reviews on cross-border mobile e-commerce platforms is carried out through big data information collection and mining techniques to strengthen the application of empirical analysis in cross-border e-commerce food safety issues, and to explore in-depth the causes, impacts, and regulatory recommendations of cross-border mobile e-commerce food safety issues. This will not only help to reveal the nature of food safety problems but also provide effective coping strategies for regulators and enterprises, to better protect consumers' rights and health.

3   Research Design

3.1   Research Framework

The purpose of this study is to analyze user reviews on cross-border e-commerce platforms using data processing techniques and BTM topic models to explore the causes of food safety problems and to make regulatory attributions of the results presented by the topics, to provide relevant recommendations for regulatory bodies. First, we collected consumer reviews of various food products on the AMAZON US platform. Second, after the data collection was completed, we used the NLTK (Natural Language Toolkit) tool to pre-process the review text, as well as to implement the BTM topic model and visualization, among other steps. Through these steps, we obtained the topic intensity distribution of food safety issues and performed topic intensity analysis; then we used word cloud mapping to perform topic domain analysis; and finally, we performed topic structure analysis using word frequency gravity viewable and word item relevance quantitative output. Through achieving steps, we can understand which themes have greater intensity, which food safety problems account for a larger proportion, and the main categories that cause the occurrence of food safety problems, ultimately, we will attribute these frequent food safety problems to regulation and make suggestions to the regulator. The research framework is shown in Fig. 1.

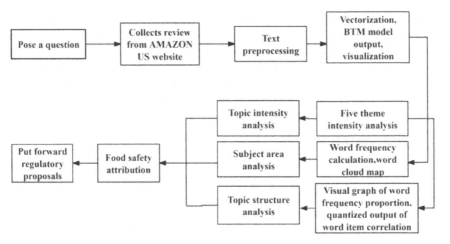

Fig. 1. Research framework

3.2 Research Process

Data Sources and Pre-processing. Data source: the research data comes from the AMAZON US cross-border mobile e-commerce platform, and this study mainly collects the comment data about food types on this platform through the Octopus platform.

Data pre-processing: the collected data were first filtered to retain only the comment texts containing keywords about food safety issues. Then, the filtered text was preprocessed using the NLTK tool, which included removing HTML tags, converting the text to lowercase, processing formatting symbols, removing stop words, and performing word form reduction. By pre-processing the data, the consistency and accuracy of the data were ensured, laying the foundation for the subsequent thematic analysis.

BTM Theme Model Construction. BTM (Biterm Topic Model) is a probabilistic graphical model for discovering potential topic structures in text data. It achieves topic modeling and analysis of textual content by capturing the association relationships between words in a document and transforming textual data into a representation of topic distribution. In constructing the BTM model, the text data is first preprocessed and then converted into a vocabulary-document matrix representation. Then, using biterms as input data, the BTM model is initialized and run to set the hyperparameters of the model, such as the number of topics and the number of clusters, as well as the values of the hyperparameters alpha and beta. Through iterative training, the BTM model learns the topic distribution and topic-vocabulary distribution of the document, revealing the underlying topic structure and topic distribution in the text data.

The core idea of BTM is to use the collection of word pairs in the whole corpus to model the topics contained in short texts. Compared with traditional topic modeling, BTM is efficient and flexible. It generates topics directly from the probability distributions of all co-occurring word pairs extracted from a short text, instead of taking the entire document content as the modeling object, which improves the efficiency of topic modeling. In addition, BTM models topics through the aggregation patterns in the whole corpus, which solves the data sparsity problem faced by traditional models when modeling topics in short texts. The modeling process of the BTM model consists of four steps: constructing a corpus with the word pairs extracted from the text to be modeled; training BTM with the constructed corpus; calculating appropriate parameters for the model; and obtaining word distributions and topic distributions in the built corpus based on the parameters. Word distribution and topic distribution in the built corpus based on the parameters.

3.3 BTM Thematic Model Parameter Settings

Model Parameter Setting. For BTM, inferring the global parameters θ and φ is a very important step because these parameters are not directly accessible in BTM, but need to be derived by inference. θ represents the distribution of topics within a document, while φ represents the distribution of words within a specific topic. To effectively model the topics present in short texts, it is imperative to determine the topic distributions across the entire corpus and the word distributions within each individual topic. The BTM employs an approximation inference method, specifically Gibbs sampling, for estimating these parameters. Specifically, Gibbs sampling is a Markov Chain Monte Carlo method, which progressively approximates the true a posteriori probability distribution by sampling samples from conditional probability distributions.

In Gibbs sampling, each vocabulary word in each iteration is sampled and the topic assignment of the current vocabulary word is updated by known other vocabulary words and topics. This process is repeated over many iterations to obtain a set of samples, which are eventually used to estimate the values of θ and φ. Gibbs sampling has two advantages: first, it improves sampling accuracy by incrementally approximating the correct distributions; second, Gibbs sampling requires only the maintenance of the counter results and the prescribed variables, which improves the efficient use of memory and makes it more suitable for dealing with large-scale data sets. This sampling method is widely used in BTM models and provides an effective numerical inference tool for topic modeling of short texts.

Number of Topics and Related Parameter Settings. To determine the optimal number of topics (K) in the topic modeling process, we utilize the BTM topic perplexity metric. Typically, a smaller perplexity value indicates better predictive performance of the topic model on the text, thereby guiding us towards selecting the most appropriate number of topics. Perplexity is calculated as follows:

$$Perplexity = \exp(-\frac{1}{N} \sum_{d=1}^{N} \log p(wd|\theta d)) \tag{1}$$

where N is the number of documents. p(wd|θd) denotes the product of the probabilities of each lexical item of document d, where wd is the lexical item in document d and θd is the topic distribution of document d. The log-likelihood function log p(wd|θd) denotes the logarithm of the probability of the model predicting the lexical item wd given document d. The lower the perplexity, the better the model fits the data. In addition, empirically, α is generally set to $\alpha = 0.1$, and β is set to $\beta = 0.01$. By calculating the perplexity degree, we obtained the optimal number of topics as 4. However, given that the textual data is larger and covers a wider range of food safety issues, we decided to increase the number of topics to 5. Doing so enhances the discriminatory and diverse nature of the model, and better captures the underlying structure and themes in the data.

In addition, we used perplexity and consistency as metrics to evaluate model performance. Perplexity reflects how well the model fits the data, with lower values indicating a better fit, while consistency assesses the interpretability and coherence of the themes learned by the model, with higher values representing stronger thematic relevance. By adjusting the parameters and selecting the evaluation indicators, we ensure that the BTM model can effectively analyze food review data and provide accurate support for food safety.

4   Empirical Analysis and Discussion

4.1   Thematic Intensity Analysis

When using BTM (Biterm Topic Model) for topic analysis of food review texts, we focus on the relative importance of each topic in the whole corpus, i.e., topic intensity. Usually, topic strength can express the intensity of the occurrence of different categories of food safety issues, and a high topic strength represents the more frequent occurrence of that category of food safety issues.

Typically, the theme intensity calculation is publicized as:

$$Pk = \frac{\sum_{i=1}^{N} \theta ki}{N} \tag{2}$$

where in Eq. Pk denotes the strength of the kth topic, i.e., the relative component of the topic in the corpus; P(z) is the topic, N is the total number of documents in the corpus, and θki denotes the probability that the kth topic is in the i-th document. This formula calculates the average probability of occurrence of each theme in all documents, thus indicating the strength of each theme.

Figure 2 illustrates the marginal topic distributions analyzed by the BTM model, where the circle size represents the topic strength or salience, i.e., frequency of occurrence and importance in the corpus. The distance between the centers of each circle then reflects the similarity or difference between the themes. As can be seen from the figure, the similarity among the five themes is low, with intensities of 20.1%, 16.8%, 11.9%, 7%, and 0.9%, respectively, from highest to lowest. Theme 0 and Theme 3 have higher intensity while Theme 1 has the lowest. This suggests that Theme 0 and Theme 3 are more prominent in the corpus, reflecting the high frequency of related issues in the area of food safety and therefore more likely to be under-regulated.

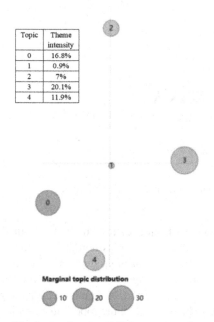

Topic	Theme intensity
0	16.8%
1	0.9%
2	7%
3	20.1%
4	11.9%

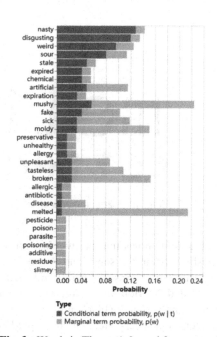

Fig. 2. Review text BTM output results

Fig. 3. Words in Theme 1 &word frequency weights

4.2 Thematic Area Analysis

After analyzing the topic strength, we proceeded to analyze the text in terms of topic domain, firstly by using Python's NLTK library for word segmentation. By splitting words, removing deactivated words, and calculating word frequency, we obtained word frequency statistics. Subsequently, we generated word cloud maps for the preprocessed text to visualize the frequency of food safety issues and their major manifestations. Compared with the word cloud map generated after BTM topic analysis, the word cloud map generated directly on the preprocessed text will be more comprehensive, because the word cloud map generated based on BTM topic analysis is constructed based on the word item weights of the topics, which only shows the keywords in each topic, and some information points will be missing. On the other hand, the word cloud map generated directly on the preprocessed text contains all the lexical information in the retained text, which is more comprehensive. Therefore, we chose to generate a word cloud map for the preprocessed text.

The generated word cloud map is shown in Fig. 4, where word items closer to the center and with a larger font size indicate a higher word frequency, while word items with the same color have the same word frequency. This analysis helps us to understand which food safety issues are more prominent and helps us to find out what causes food safety issues so that we can provide relevant recommendations for regulatory topics.

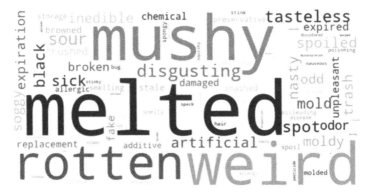

Fig. 4. User comments on cross-border e-commerce platforms (food)

Figure 4 shows that the words with the highest frequency are "melted", "rotten", "mushy", "weird", "sour" and so on. It can be found that cross-border e-commerce food safety problems are mainly reflected in the field of frozen products melting, food rotting and deteriorating, acidic meat in mushy form, strange taste, etc. There are also some embodied in the blackening of food, expiration of period, broken food packaging, counterfeit products, etc., which are predicted to be possible in the food transportation, food hygiene, product quality and other aspects of food. Transportation, food hygiene, product quality and other aspects of inadequate supervision.

4.3   Thematic Structure Analysis

After analyzing the comment text for topic strength and topic domain, we analyzed the user comment text for topics using the BTM topic model, which resulted in a quantitative output of the word frequency weight viewable for each topic as well as the word item relevance. Utilizing the BTM topic model, we derived a topic-word distribution that encapsulates the structure of each potential topic. This structure is explicitly represented by the probability values assigned to each word, where a higher probability value signifies a stronger relevance of the word to the corresponding topic. Figure 3, using theme 3 as an example, presents the top 30-word items in the text with the highest degree of association with theme 3, which are, in descending order, "nasty," "disgusting," "weird," "sour," "expired," "stale," "chemical", and so on. We brought these words into the review text, they mainly refer to nasty taste, sour and unpleasant flavor, excessive chemical additives, and expired or near expiration date of the product. The distribution of the top ten lexical items and their probability values in each category of themes are shown in Table 1.

Table 1. Lexical items and relevance of user review texts

Topic	Food damage or spoilage		Unclean food and abnormal food production		Product quality issues		
	Lexical item	frequency	Lexical item	frequency	Lexical item		frequency
User comment text	melted	0.095283018	damaged	0.110000000	illness		0.121428571
	rotten	0.095283018	bug	0.010000000	trash		0.026190476
	replacement	0.010377358	spider	0.010000000	sick		0.073809523
	smashed	0.029245283	misleading	0.010000000	fake		0.050000000
	black	0.057547169	inspection	0.010000000	artificial		0.026190476
	crushed	0.066981132	broken	0.110000000	odd		0.097619047
	molded	0.076415094	stink	0.010000000	smelling		0.026190476
	squishy	0.029245283	browned	0.010000000	storage		0.026190476
	insect	0.019811320	smashed	0.010000000	unpleasant		0.050000000
	crashed	0.019811320	discolored	0.010000000	speck		0.050000000
Topic	Food preservation and approaching shelf		Food appearance and taste issues				
	Lexical item	frequency	Lexical item	frequency			
User comment text	nasty	0.127777777	soggy	0.084722222			
	disgusting	0.119841269	spoil	0.070833333			
	stale	0.048412698	spot	0.154166666			
	expired	0.040476190	inedible	0.098611111			
	weird	0.096031746	dis-coloration	0.029166666			
	sour	0.080158730	mushy	0.126388888			
	chemical	0.040476190	tasteless	0.070833333			
	allergy	0.016666666	damaged	0.029166666			
	fake	0.040476190	weird	0.152777777			
	unhealthy	0.166666666	mold	0.056944444			

By examining the theme structure of each topic through the visualization of word frequency weights and the quantitative assessment of word item relevance, we were able to determine the content distribution across the five themes. Then, we classify the themes according to the words that occupy a higher frequency under each theme, for example, the words that occupy a higher frequency in theme 0 are "melted", "rotten"," black", "crushed", "molded", "squishy", according to the meanings of these words, we categorized Theme 0 is categorized as damaged or spoiled food. Similarly, Themes 1 to 4 were categorized as unclean food and abnormal food production, product quality problems, food preservation and approaching shelf life, and food appearance and texture, respectively. Overall, these categories directly reflect the main types of food safety issues that lead to the occurrence of food safety problems on cross-border e-commerce platforms. This analysis helps us further explore the regulatory issues that exist behind food safety problems. For example, under Theme 0, based on the keyword information "crushed", "crashed", "smashed", food damage or spoilage may be caused by improper handling during storage and transportation. In other topics, product quality problems may be caused by uncleanliness or cutting corners in the production process. The results of these detailed analyses provide regulators with specific regulatory directions and recommendations for improvement.

4.4 Types and Regulatory Attribution of Food Safety Problems

We conducted an in-depth analysis using the BTM topic model and combined it with tools such as word cloud mapping and word frequency weight viewable to provide an exhaustive analysis of the types of food safety issues. First, through the BTM topic model analysis, we identified five major topics and their intensity distributions and visualized food safety issues, such as frozen products melting, rotten and spoiled food, mushy and sour meat, and strange taste. Finally, we categorized food safety problems into five major groups: damaged or spoiled food, food hygiene and abnormal food production, product quality problems, food preservation and approaching shelf life, and food appearance and texture problems.

By scrutinizing the results of the BTM thematic model analysis (Table 1), we can understand the reasons for the different types of food safety problems and the possible regulatory issues. Under the theme of food damage or spoilage, high-frequency words such as "melted," "rotten," and "crushed" suggest that improper transportation and storage may be the root cause of the problem. These include broken packaging, improper temperature control, and so on. Under the theme of food hygiene and mis-handling, high-frequency words such as "broken", "damaged" and "spider" were used, which could be attributed to inadequate hygiene supervision and quality control of raw materials in the production process. This may be due to the lack of hygiene supervision and quality control of raw materials in the production process, resulting in unclean food and poor packaging. Under the theme of product quality, high-frequency words such as "illness", "fake" and "odd" may be related to factors such as substandard food quality, low factory standards, and enterprises selling counterfeit products. This may be related to factors such as substandard food quality, low factory standards, and enterprises selling counterfeit products. Under the theme of food preservation and shelf-life approaching, high frequency words such as "nasty", "sour" and "expired" may be due to consumers' low awareness of storage. This may be due to consumers' low awareness of storage, improper storage temperature, long storage time, and other factors. Under the theme of food appearance and taste problems, the high-frequency words are "inedible", "tasteless" and "spot", which may be related to the appearance of the food and improper techniques in processing. For example, improper handling of the color, shape, texture, etc.

4.5 Recommendations for Relevant Regulators

Based on the conclusions of the study, we offer the following recommendations and countermeasures aimed at regulating cross-border mobile e-commerce platforms:

1. Enhance transportation and storage supervision: Tighten the supervision of cross-border mobile e-commerce platforms in terms of food transportation and storage. This involves ensuring compliance with temperature control, packaging integrity, and humidity standards. Irregularities in the storage and transportation process must be regulated and managed to minimize food damage, corruption, and acidification.
2. Strengthen the supervision of food production: on the one hand, strengthen the supervision and management of production enterprises to ensure that the sanitary conditions in the production process are up to standard and the operation of employees is standardized, so as to reduce the presence of food uncleanliness and other food hygiene problems. On the other hand, strengthen the monitoring and inspection of food quality, timely detection and treatment of product quality problems, especially food preservation and shelf-life approaching and other aspects of the problem, to protect the legitimate rights and interests of consumers.
3. Strengthening supplier qualification auditing: formulate stricter supplier auditing standards and management regulations, establish a mechanism for recording and evaluating supplier violations, and take appropriate punitive measures against enterprises that sell counterfeit goods or chemical additives that do not meet standards, so as to enhance food safety protection at the source.
4. Strengthen consumer education: strengthen publicity education on food safety knowledge of consumers. On the one hand, they will pay attention to the ingredients of products when purchasing them in order to avoid purchasing unqualified food products. On the other hand, they may pay attention to the preservation date of the products and the storage conditions to avoid the occurrence of food allergies and food poisoning.

Based on the conclusions of the study, we propose the following suggestions and countermeasures for the regulators themselves:

1. Strengthen the construction of laws and regulations: improve the food safety laws and regulations of cross-border mobile e-commerce platforms, and clarify the main body of supervisory responsibility and the boundaries of authority and responsibility. For example, when dealing with food damage or spoilage, regulations can stipulate that protective packaging must be used during food transportation to prevent food contamination due to broken packaging.
2. Establish an efficient regulatory mechanism: set up a specialized food safety regulatory agency responsible for the overall supervision and management of food safety issues on cross-border mobile e-commerce platforms. A regulatory system combining regular inspections and random sampling can effectively monitor food quality.

In addition, regular return visits to users who have given poor reviews can timely identify and solve problems in supervision.

3. Enhancement of regulatory capacity: strengthen the training and education of regulatory personnel and improve the standards for food exports. For example, for products with unclear food labels and unclear sources, regulators can take measures to refuse export. Advanced testing technology and equipment can also be introduced to improve the accuracy and efficiency of food safety testing.

4. Strengthen international cooperation and exchange: Strengthen cooperation and exchange with international food safety regulators to jointly develop food safety standards and regulatory measures for cross-border mobile e-commerce platforms. For example, cooperate with food regulatory agencies in other countries to jointly conduct food safety training programs and share best practices and advanced technologies in order to improve the food safety level of cross-border mobile e-commerce platforms globally.

Through the above regulatory recommendations and countermeasures, the food safety level of cross-border mobile e-commerce platforms can be further enhanced to protect the health rights of consumers and promote the sustainable development of cross-border e-commerce. At the same time, there is a need to continuously summarize lessons learned and to continuously refine and improve regulatory measures to better meet food safety challenges.

5 Conclusions and Outlook

5.1 Research Summary and Findings

In this study, we applied the BTM thematic model to deeply analyze users' evaluations about food of cross-border e-commerce platforms, and explored the reasons for the emergence of food safety problems as well as the regulatory issues behind them. Through the BTM thematic analysis, we found the main types of food safety issues on cross-border e-commerce platforms, including food damage or spoilage, improper food hygiene and handling, product quality issues, food preservation and approaching shelf life, and food appearance and taste. At the same time, problems in food safety supervision were also identified, such as inadequate qualification audits of suppliers, lagging logistics services, and inadequate laws and regulations.

Through the results of the study, we provide targeted regulatory recommendations for AMAZON US cross-border e-commerce platforms in the supervision of food safety issues, and also provide a reference for other cross-border e-commerce platforms. With the help of big data technology and modeling analysis, we actively promote the solution of food safety-related problems, promote the sustainable development of the platform and the continuous improvement of food quality management, to actively protect the health and safety of consumers.

5.2 Research Limitations and Directions for Improvement

Despite the innovation of this study in the methodology of analyzing food safety issues in cross-border mobile e-commerce platforms, there are still some limitations that need to be considered and improved:

First, the scope of data collection in this study is limited to specific cross-border mobile e-commerce platforms, which may not be fully representative of the entire industry. In the future, consideration can be given to expanding the data sources to cover more cross-border e-commerce platforms to improve the representativeness and universality of the study.

Second, this study adopted the BTM model for theme analysis, and although it can discover the hidden theme structure in user reviews, the model itself has certain limitations, such as being sensitive to parameter settings and requiring certain specialized domain knowledge for theme interpretation. In the future, we can try to combine other topic models or deep learning methods to improve the accuracy and comprehensiveness of the analysis.

Finally, this study did not perform a time series analysis on user review data, which makes it difficult to capture the trend of food safety issues over time. In the future, time series analysis methods can be introduced to dig deeper into the development dynamics of food safety issues and provide more timely and effective decision support for regulatory authorities.

In summary, in the future, we can further enhance the comprehensiveness and scope of this study by continuously refining our research methods and broadening our perspectives. This will enable us to provide more insightful analyses and effective solutions to food safety challenges on cross-border mobile e-commerce platforms.

References

1. Liu, Q.: Influence of cross-border e-commerce platform product reviews on consumer behavior. Zhejiang University (2023). https://doi.org/10.27461/d.cnki.gzjdx.2023.001086
2. Blei, D.M., Ng, A.Y., Jordan, M.I.: Latent dirichlet allocation. J. Mach. Learn. Res. **3**, 993–1022 (2003)
3. Lili, L., Xufeng, M.: Discovery and evolutionary analysis of domestic library intelligence research themes based on LDA model. Intell. Sci. **37**(12), 87–92 (2019)
4. Zhang, T., Ma, H.Q.: Research on a policy text clustering method based on LDA topic model. Data Anal. Knowl. Disc. **2**(9), 59–65 (2018)
5. Blei, D.M., Lafferty, J.D.: Correlated topic model. In: Advances in Neural Information Processing System 17. MIT Press, Cambridge, MA (2005)
6. Cui Jindong, D., Wenqiang, G.Y., et al.: Research on LDA evolution analysis of personalized recommendation topic model for microblog user information. Intell. Sci. **35**(8), 3–10 (2017)
7. Yan, X., Guo, J., Lan, Y., et al.: A biterm topic model for short texts. In: Proceedings of the 22nd International Conference on World Wide Web, pp. 1445–1456 (2013)
8. Ke, L.-M., Hong, F.F.: Theory and Practice of Cross-Border E-commerce. China Customs Press (2016)
9. Yufang, L.: Research on risk information mechanism of cross-border e-commerce food market development. China Bus. J. **9**, 43–46 (2023)
10. Peng, W., Sijun, H.: Dilemma and way out of cross-border e-commerce imported food safety supervision. Food Sci. **015**, 043 (2022)
11. Huang, L., Zhongqin, P., Yue, T.: Exploring the regulatory issues of import and export food safety on cross-border e-commerce platforms in China. Food Saf. J. **36**, 14–16 (2021)
12. Zhang, B., Ye, D. M., Ma, R.: Cross-border e-commerce food safety risk characterization and collaborative governance. J. Hum. **000**(010), 115–121 (2021)

13. Xin, G.: Exploring food safety governance strategies in cross-border e-commerce based on supply chain perspective–a review of research on sustainable supply chain management and food safety governance. J. Food Saf. Qual. Testing **14**(09), 325 (2023). https://doi.org/10.19812/j.cnki.jfsq11-5956/ts.2023.09.036

14. Zhou, F., Yan, Y., Su, R., et al.: Construction and application of risk assessment model for cross-border e-commerce imported food quality and safety. Economist (5), 3 (2021)

15. Chen, Y., Sun, M., Wu, C., et al.: Visual correlation analysis of food safety big data. Big Data **7**(02), 61–77 (2021)

Mobile Security, Privacy and Safety

Voyager: Crowdsource Application for Safe Travelling Experience

Richie Ang and Owen Noel Newton Fernando[✉]

Nanyang Technological University, Singapore 639798, Singapore
richie002@e.ntu.edu.sg, ofernando@ntu.edu.sg

Abstract. Tourism has always been an important economic sector around the world with millions of tourists travelling every year. As the world emerges from the COVID-19 pandemic, the tourism industry is rapidly recovering, and it is projected that global traveler numbers will reach 90% of pre-pandemic levels by the end of 2023. While it is a significant contributor to global economy, it is also a great source of danger for tourists. Research studies have found that tourists are vulnerable to a variety of dangers and risk, including injury and death, while visiting attractions around the world. Compared to domestic populations, tourists face up to 16 times higher risks of fatalities from road accidents, drowning, falls, and crimes. It has been found that in a study done in New Zealand, an estimated 20% of overseas visitor injuries and 22% of fatalities are by tourism related activities. As such, we have developed a mobile application called Voyager is focused to help users be more informed about the dangers and safety culture of their travel destinations. The Voyager aims to help tourists identify safe locations, understand local law and safety culture. By providing this information, the Voyager aims to minimize the risks associated with tourism and enhance the overall travel experience for users.

Keywords: Safety mobile app · Human computer interaction · Social computing

1 Introduction

Tourism has always been an important economic sector around the world with millions of tourists travelling every year. With the easing of covid restrictions around the world, the tourism industry has been recovering fast and resuming its upward climb. In the final quarter of 2022 alone, tourism saw an impressive 55% recovery with 965 million international travelers [7]. Projections indicate that by the close of 2023, the industry will rise to approximately 90% of its pre-pandemic levels [21].

While international tourism is a significant contributor to the global economy, it is also a source of danger for tourists. Foreign travels expose travelers to unfamiliar infectious diseases, as well as dangers brought on by a greater exposure to unfamiliar transportation and leisure activities. The health and safety risks encountered by foreign travelers are substantially different from their original country and can be increased with the lack of traveler familiarity with the new environment. As such, tourists travelling to unfamiliar locations are vulnerable to a variety of dangers and risks, including injury and

J. Wei and G. Margetis (Eds.): HCII 2024, LNCS 14738, pp. 135–156, 2024.
https://doi.org/10.1007/978-3-031-60487-4_11

death. Out of millions of tourists travelling globally every year, it is estimated that 30% to 50% are either injured or become ill while overseas. [9] Some of the most common causes of tourist injuries and fatalities include road traffic accidents, drowning, falls, and crimes [1]. Tourists experiences a higher risk of injury mortality rate, with relative rate of injury death being up to 16 times more likely than domestic populations [22]. According to a study done in New Zealand, an estimated 20% of overseas visitor injuries and 22% of fatalities are caused by tourism-related activities [1]. As the tourism industry recovers, the number of incidents resulting in tourist injuries and fatalities will likely increase.

Tourist safety has been tackled by many existing applications, such as the Emergency App by the US Red Cross and Smart Traveller by the US State Department. The scope of these existing apps covers a limited geographical scope and are limited in their set of functionalities. In contrast, this study aims to improve upon existing useful features and adding new features into a single application.

This study advances beyond previous solutions by implementing a new platform for travelers to obtain safe travel information. A mobile application called Voyager is developed to help users be more informed about the dangers and safety culture of their travel destinations. The objective of the app is to help tourists identify locations that are reviewed as safe by other tourists, understand local laws, and culture, and allow for user to choose recommended travel locations so that travelers can minimize the risks associated with tourism and have a better travel experience.

2   Background and Related Works

Given the significance of the problem when it comes to tourist safety, there exist several existing solutions in the market. In this section, existing solutions that aim to tackle or enhance travelers' safety experience in an unfamiliar environment will be reviewed. Specifically, the review will be divided into two areas, namely (a) research into the use of technology and awareness of tourist safety and (b) the features and functionalities of relevant and popular traveler's safety mobile application. The section ends with a reiteration of the objectives behind the investigation.

2.1   Related Research

The concept of implementing a technology solution for an existing problem is not new, many studies such as technology acceptance modal (TAM) [10] and the information system success modal (ISSM) [11] have been done to identify the key factors that would enable new technology to benefit the users. It has been found that information quality factor is the most important dimension of technology and that it affects user satisfaction the most, with the second most important dimension being system quality [12–14]. Crucial information that is to be presented to the user for their safety should be verifiable or managed by government bodies to ensure that they are unmodified. In recent years, multiple government initiatives around the world have provided east access to open government data that could allow for innovation using credible data [15].

The use of data and technology has brought many opportunities to the tourism industry. Much research has also been done to examine the impacts of smart tourism technology, with multiple sources identifying that accessibility of information, ease of use, and perceived benefits to be positively correlated to travel experience satisfaction [16, 17, 19]. Smart tourism apps that are implemented effectively have been known to significantly reduce safety risks and augment the perceived safety of the users [18]. Smart tourism technology has shown its effectiveness when implemented with proven modals [18, 20]. The implementation of Voyager aims to reduce safety risks of the general traveler in a new environment through accessible and quality data.

2.2 Related Applications

Within the United States of America, there are two mobile applications that are released by the government or state bodies that aim to provide travel safety information to US travelers. They are the Smart Traveler by the US Department of State and the Emergency App by the American Red Cross. Other popular apps used by users around the world include GeoSure, the travel location ratings app, and Trip Lingo which help travelers overcome language and cultural barriers overseas. The Table 1 provides information on existing applications with features aimed to provide more awareness of tourist safety have been compiled to identify features that incorporated in the Voyager mobile application.

Smart Traveler is a mobile application developed to help US citizens traveling abroad stay safe by providing up-to-date travel advisories and warnings for countries around the world, as well as information on the local laws, customs, and visa requirements of the destinations [3]. Emergency App is a mobile application designed to provide users with a range of tools and resources for emergency responses. The app includes features such as real-time weather alerts, information on American Red Cross shelters, and instructions for first aid and CPR procedures. The application is mainly made to be a comprehensive resource for travelers to prepare for and respond to emergency situations within the United States of America [4]. GeoSure is developed to provide user-reviewed safety and security ratings for over 200 countries and territories around the world, which are based on a range of factors such as crime rates, political stability, and environmental hazards [5]. Trip Lingo is mainly used by travelers to overcome language hurdles when it comes to communicating with the locals. The application provides a voice translator, a phrasebook with phrases for a variety of situations, and a cultural guide on local etiquette [6].

Despite the number of existing popular applications that aim to tackle the problem of tourist safety, each of them provides a feature that focuses on one component that a general traveler needs while travelling. The Smart Traveler and Emergency App are useful applications when it comes to travelling to new environments, however their services are mainly catered to use within the United States with most of the solutions being limited to the general American citizens. As for the GeoSure, it provides an innovative social solution that allows users to have an informed travel plan, the application lacks information on safety risks and guides upon reaching the location. Lastly, Trip lingo is mainly a communication application and does not provide much safety information.So far, there has been a considerable amount of research and solution provided worldwide to combat the issue of tourist safety, however, more could have been done to allow for

Table 1. Comparison on different mobile applications

	Smart Traveler [3]	Emergency App [4]	Geo Sure [5]	Trip Lingo [6]	Voyager
Weather Information		✓			✓
Location Review			✓		✓
Map		✓	✓		✓
Local Emergency Contact		✓		✓	✓
Location Safety Rating			✓		✓
Travel Warning & Alerts	✓	✓			✓
Map of shelters		✓			
Medical phrases in different language				✓	✓
Local Do's and Don'ts, Culture Notes				✓	✓
Local Law	✓				✓
Entry, Exit & Visa Requirements	✓				✓
Emergency Responses		✓			✓

a more convenient way to access all the useful safety information for travelers who are on foreign lands. Therefore, the Voyager application in this paper aimed to provide an all-in-one platform with relevant features from existing applications for the user to effectively plan for their travels and be informed of the local laws and safety responses to minimize the risk associated with tourism.

3 Design

3.1 System Perspective

The Voyager mobile application is a one-stop platform for travel safety information, available on both Android and IOS devices. It serves as a social utility tool that allows users to see and share travel safety information worldwide. Voyager's crowdsourced reviews enable people to pinpoint specific locations' cultures and major safety risks. Users can stay informed about potential threats by the application, which provides instant real-time weather and warning alerts based on location data. Ultimately, Voyager seeks to empower average users with the knowledge that locals and seasoned travelers have on each location.

3.2   Use Case Diagram

The figure below shows the use cases for a typical user (Fig. 1).

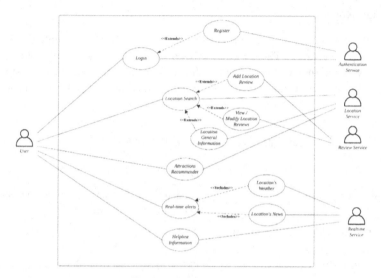

Fig. 1. Use Case Diagram

3.3   Colour Theme

The color palette shown in Fig. 2 is chosen for the Voyager theme. The colours were chosen with consideration of colors and their effects on human psychology and emotions. Blue is often associated with calming effect and feelings of trust and reliable [23]. It is commonly used to portray professionalism and trustworthiness. Whereas green is often linked to nature and growth, representing health, environment, and wellness [23]. As such, the mix of blue and green color is used to represent both intended effects, giving the Voyager its turquoise-like colour theme. Figure 2 also shows the distribution and hierarchy of importance of the colours, with the lighter tones appearing more with less importance and the darker tones appearing less with more importance.

Fig. 2. Color Palette

3.4 Design Rules

During the design phase of Voyager, design rules and principles are employed for the design of user interfaces. This is done to meet usability requirements and ensure a user-friendly experience while navigating the application. There are many design rules to follow but Voyager design references the Schneiderman's Eight Golden Rules [24], shown in Table 2.

Table 2. Schneiderman's Eight Golden Rules

	Rule	Description
1	Strive for Consistency	All actions such as layout, terminology should maintain consistent sequences
2	Enable Frequent Users to use Shortcuts	Shortcuts should be available to use regular actions very quickly
3	Offer Informative Feedback	Proper system feedback should be provided for all user action
4	Design Dialog to Yield Closure	Indication to let user know that the task has been completed
5	Offer Simple Error Handling	Prevent the user from making big mistakes and errors and provide instructions to recover from small errors
6	Permit Easy Reversal of Actions	Allow for user to return to previous state, good for exploration
7	Support Internal Locus of Control	Provide the feeling of control for experienced user over the system interfaces
8	Reduce Short-Term Memory Load	Keeping load time quick and simple to allow user time to learn action sequences

3.5 Hi-Fi Prototype

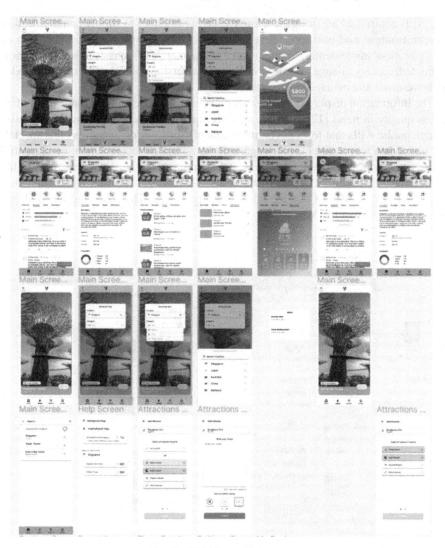

Fig. 3. Hi-Fi Latest Prototype

4 Implementation

4.1 System Overview

During the design of the system architecture, various principles and approaches are considered to ensure optimal functional and non-functional requirements. Firstly, every component in the frontend and backend is made with modularity and separation of concerns in mind. Every page and major component in the frontend implementation are modular and managed independently. In the backend, different parts of the Voyager application are broken down into smaller independently hosted and managed micro-services

[25]. APIs controllers are designed using RESTful principles to simply communication between frontend and backend. There is also a focus on performance optimization of the application, implementing caching and minimal network requests to reduce latency. Additionally, every change to code goes through a version control, Git, to ensure codes can be restored and managed efficiently (Fig. 3).

The information displayed on Voyager must be up-to-date and accurate. With information quality in mind [12], the data and information utilized for Voyager are mostly through public APIs that from government data platforms or organizations that specialized in the data we require [15]. Voyager utilizes attraction recommendation algorithm that are based on user's preference data and location to recommend attractions in the user interface. In addition, Voyager acts as a social platform for users to provide additional feedback or insights into the information presented. The following Fig. 4 shows a general overview of the Voyager application.

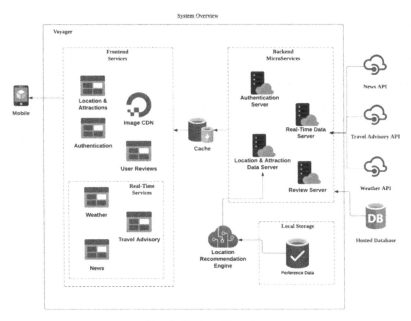

Fig. 4. System Overview

4.2 System Architecture

Going deeper into the system architecture, it defines the structure and organization of the Voyager application. It shows the specific components and modules and how they interact to meet its functional and non-functional requirements. The architecture addresses key aspects like scalability, performance, security, and modularity. Other factors such as cost, ease of administration is taken into consideration for the design as well. Figure 5 below shows the architecture diagram of Voyager.

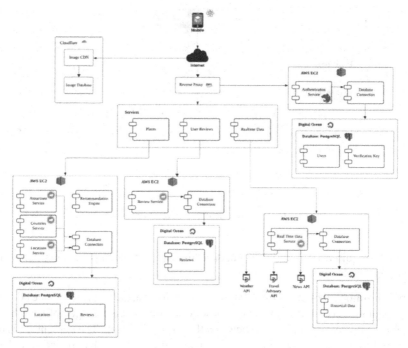

Fig. 5. Architecture Diagram

The development of each microservice follows the Controller-Service-Repository (CSR) design pattern [26], which adheres to the separation of concern and single responsibility principle. Each component is modular and maintainable independently.

4.3 Search Implementation

The search feature is implemented through reactive streams within the location WebFlux service [39]. Whenever the search endpoint is called with a search parameter, the main controller within the location WebFlux service will be subscribed for data emitted from individual country, location and attraction service with data filtered based on the search parameter. The data emission is performed asynchronously and runs simultaneously, but the merge process on the main controller will merge the stream of data based on the order of country, followed by location and finally the attraction emitted data. These data are then returned as the data response for the client that called the search endpoint (Fig. 6).

4.4 Review

The creation process for reviews starts at the attraction level, with the city/state and country level compiling the reviews for all the attractions within its geographical region the area covers. The reviews can be created with the no hazard option or with the selection of all the appropriate hazards for the location. Reviews cannot be created with

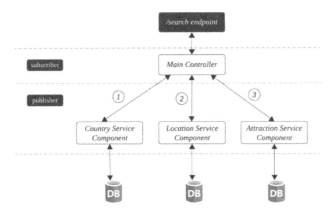

Fig. 6. Location Search Backend Process

any missing required information is checked for any malicious comments before it is stored in the database.

Hazard Summary. For the hazard summary on each page, the location service performs an aggregation query on the review database to obtain the percentages of each hazard option for the reviews over all the reviews on the chosen location. The percentage is then returned to the frontend where it is used to generate the bar graph length and sorted with the no-hazard option followed by the other hazards. That way users obtain a quick view on the summarized hazards of the location selected.

Risk Rating. For the general risk rating shown for the chosen location, the location service performs an aggregation query on the review database to obtain the percentages of the general risk rating provided for each review filtered on the location. The good, mid, and poor risk rating percentages associated with each symbol of tick, dash and cross respectively is then returned to the front end for further processing. Depending on the good, mid and poor percentages, a non-linear model is used to determine the general risk rating context of either "Highly Rated Safe", "Relatively Safe", Moderately Safe", "Relatively Unsafe", "Highly Rated Unsafe" and "Unrated". User can then identify the overall general rating for the location.

4.5 Recommendation Engine

The recommendation engine is responsible for delivering real-time suggestions for safe attractions on the explore page of the application. It incorporates two trained models, leveraging user and attraction data alongside historical swipe data on attractions. The first model utilizes collaborative filtering to identify users with similar swipe patterns to the current user and recommends attractions that the user has not yet viewed. These recommendations then undergo processing by a trained ranking model, which assesses the likelihood of the user swiping right on each suggestion, determining the final ranking. The selected attractions are then presented to the user for exploration. This entire process relies on a real-time streaming data service to continually provide new and relevant safe attractions for the current user to explore. Figure 7 shows the architecture for the recommendation engine.

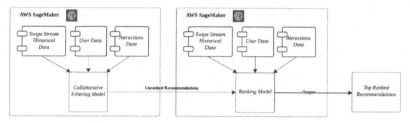

Fig. 7. Recommendation Engine System Architecture

5 Application Walkthrough

5.1 Main

The main page of Voyager is where most of the safety information are for the user. The user has the ability to search locations through the search bar, view the weather, alerts, helplines and other helpful information. Figure 8 shows a breakdown of the main page of Voyager.

Fig. 8. Main Page Breakdown

Overview. The overview tab is the default tab opened after the app starts up or after a location search. The overview contains the general description of the place and some extra information regarding them. To view the extra information requires user to scroll down to view more with the key focus on the safety ratings, weather, and icons when user first look up a place. Figure 9 shows an example of the scroll down in the overview section.

Fig. 9. Overview Scroll Down

Search. Upon clicking on the search bar with the current location, the user will be brought to the search page. Search results will automatically update with user's input. The search results returned will have the countries result be on top of cities or regions followed by attractions results. When the user selects a result from the list, the user will be brought back to the main screen with the information updated to match the selection. Figure 10 shows an example of this search in action.

Fig. 10. Search example

Weather. The weather panel on the main page shows the current temperate and cloud condition of the selected location. When the user clicks on the panel, a bottom sheet will appear. The weather sheet allows the user to have a clear idea of the current weather condition, with details on UV, humidity and wind speeds collected from public weather API as well as a forecast of the weather for the next few days (Fig. 11).

Fig. 11. Weather Panel

Helplines. On the main page, there will be an icon that is called helplines with the clear phone icon. Clicking on the icon will bring the user to the helpline page where emergency contacts are listed. International emergency contacts will always be available with options for location-based contacts shown if data exists. Figure 12 shows an example of the helpline.

Fig. 12. Helpline example

Alerts. Figure 31 shows what is shown when the user clicks on the Alerts icon. If there are any travel advisory alerts or weather alerts, it will be displayed on the panel. Additionally, there will be push notifications to inform user of any real-time weather or travel advisory alerts based on user's last known location. Figure 13 shows the alert panel.

Reviews. The main feature of voyager is that it allows user to create user safety reviews of any location and the review will determine the safety rating of the location along with the most common highlighted hazards. The user will provide also provide an overall

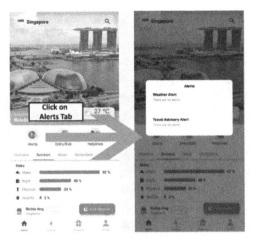

Fig. 13. Alert Panel

rating with a tick, dash or cross to indicate general safety level felt by the user. If the user who reviewed the place is from the same country as the location reviewed, a tag beside the name will indicate it. The same will happen if the user who reviewed the place is from the same country as the user browsing it. Figure 14 and 15 shows the review tab and the process of creating a new review.

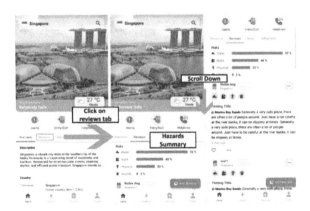

Fig. 14. Reviews tab

Click on add review brings the user to the add review page, the location for the add review will be based on the location in the main page. The user will be brough to a page to choose the hazards of the location followed by a write up on the location there, before giving an overall general safety rating.

News. The news tab shows the headline news of the selected country, the news comes from the real-time service which calls public news API. A general description, date published, and news source is provided to the user. Figure 16 shows the news tab.

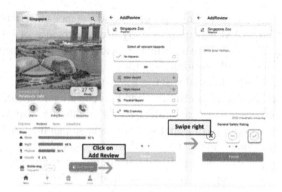

Fig. 15. Add Reviews

Fig. 16. News tab

6   Study on Intention to Use

A study is conducted to understand the user's behavior and intention to use the Voyager mobile application. Data collected from the study is done through a questionnaire and analyzed to understand how to enhance the experience for users. The questionnaire makes use of psychology models TAM and ISSM to understand user expected intention towards the usage of an application. The number of target samples was determined with the Slovin formula [41] to get a sufficient sample size for the approximation of the total population.

6.1   TAM Model

Technology Acceptance Model (TAM) was first proposed by Davis et al. [26] and was developed based on a social psychology theory called theory of reasoned action (TRA)

[27]. TAM is commonly used to examine the use and acceptance of technological solution for a practical problem. TAM was used to study user acceptance of information technology in many existing technology tools that are widely used today such as blackboard [28], websites [29], and e-collaboration tools [30].

TAM proposes that an individual will use a new technological tool if they are influenced by two factors, perceived usefulness, and perceived ease of use. Perceived usefulness and perceived ease of use will affect user's intention to use Voyager. For the perceived usefulness, travelers will want to use Voyager so that they may read up on the hazards that a place may have and prepare for them. Voyager also have various methods to explore difference places on the application itself, either through the search function or the explore page. While they are on the actual destination itself, they can use Voyager to get real time information such as weather, news, or any warning alerts for the area. These are potential benefits developed for the users and could increase the level of us of the technology. For the perceived ease of use, users will use Voyager if the application is easy to use, simple and hassle-free. Based on these theories, the research hypotheses that can be developed are as follows:

- **H1**: perceived usefulness has a positive and significant impact on the travelers' intention to use Voyager
- **H2**: perceived ease of use has a positive and significant impact on the employee's intention to use Voyager

6.2   ISSM Model

Information System Success Model (ISSM) was first developed by DeLone and McLean [31]. Originally 6 dimensions were theorized to be factors for intention of use, they were system quality, system use, impact on individuals and impact on organization. However, a revised model published by the original authors cut down to only 3 dimensions [32], namely system quality, service quality and information quality to have a positive influence on intention to use and user satisfaction.

System quality factor implies that the better the quality of the system, the higher the intention to use the system. It is usually measured by the ease of use, ease of understanding and system performance. Service quality factor is based on the system performance including the response time and information availability with attention to user's needs. Information quality factor implies that the data is easy to read or interpret, useful to user, and the presentation of data is clear and easy to understand.

- **H3**: system quality has a positive and significant influence on perceived usefulness
- **H4**: information quality has a positive and significant influence on perceived usefulness
- **H5**: service quality has a positive and significant influence on perceived usefulness
- **H6**: system quality has a positive and significant influence on perceived ease of use
- **H7**: information quality has a positive and significant influence on perceived ease of use
- **H8**: service quality has a positive and significant influence on perceived ease of use

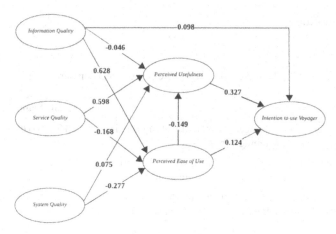

Fig. 17. Conceptual Diagram and Path Coefficients

6.3 Questionnaire

The questionnaire is adopted from a previous studies done to examine similar acceptance rate of application [33, 37] and theories were chosen based on suitability for Voyager application. The questionnaire is created through Google Forms and distributed to friends and family who have seen and interact with Voyager. The questionnaire consists of 6 sections and each of questions are answered using the Likert scale [35] with 5 points across a linear scale for respondents to choose from. The 6 sections in the questionnaire are (Fig. 17):

1. Demographic and Background
2. Perceived Usefulness
3. Perceived Ease of Use
4. System Quality
5. Information Quality
6. Service Quality

6.4 Results and Analysis

Demographic and Background. There was a total of 20 respondents with majority (65%) being males and (35%) being females. Majority of the respondents lie within the age range of 21–30 (70%), with other rage range of < 20 (5%), 31–40 (10%), 51–60 (15%). It is also found that majority of respondents do not use any safe travel applications when travelling abroad (70%) while the remaining (30%) do. Lastly, majority of respondents (80%) faces some sort of potential danger while travelling abroad whereas the rest (20%) do not (Tables 3, 4, 5, 6, 7).

Perceived Usefulness

Table 3. Perceived Usefulness from Questionnaire

Question	Mean	Standard Deviation
How likely are you to use Voyager to obtain travel information and safety tips for your upcoming trips?	4.15	0.670
Do you believe that using Voyager will help you make informed decisions about the safety of your travel destinations?	4.2	0.696
How much do you agree that Voyager can improve your overall travel experience by providing safety information shared by locals and other travelers?	4.5	0.688

Perceived Ease of Use

Table 4. Perceived Ease of Use from Questionnaire

Question	Mean	Standard Deviation
How easy is it for you to navigate and use the Voyager mobile application?	4.35	0.745
Do you find it easy to access and understand the safety information provided by Voyager?	4.55	0.604
To what extent do you agree that using Voyager is a hassle-free way to obtain travel safety information?	4.6	0.502

System Quality

Table 5. System Quality from Questionnaire

Question	Mean	Standard Deviation
How would you rate the overall quality of Voyager's mobile application in terms of performance, responsiveness, and reliability?	4.25	0.550
Did you encounter any technical issues or glitches while using Voyager?	4.3	0.732

Information Quality

Table 6. Information Quality from Questionnaire

Question	Mean	Standard Deviation
How accurate and reliable do you find the safety information provided by Voyager?	4.45	0.510
Do you feel confident in the credibility of the safety information shared by locals and other travelers on Voyager?	4.3	0.571

Service Quality

Table 7. Service Quality from Questionnaire

Question	Mean	Standard Deviation
How satisfied are you with Voyager updates?	4.15	0.489
Did you find the services offered by Voyager, such as notifications and alerts, helpful in ensuring your safety during travel?	4.2	0.523

6.5 Measures

The reliability analysis was carried out to ensure the internal validity and consistency of the results for defining each variable. Heale & Twycross [38] stated that the Cronbach's test is the most common internal consistency test of an instrument. The survey is considered reliable when results are consistent across the questions. Cronbach alpha values proposed by Lee Cronbach [36] suggested that values between 0.6 and 0.7 represent the lower threshold of acceptability. An alpha value exceeding 0.7 indicates that the items are consistent and of minimum acceptability. The reliability of the measurement scales is presented in Table 1. The Cronbach's alpha reliability scores exceeding 0.8 is considered highly favorable according to Nunnally [37]. Therefore, the results affirm that the questionnaire is a dependable measurement instrument (Table 8).

Table 8. Cronbach Values

Factors	Cronbach Value
Perceived Usefulness	0.706
Perceived Ease of Use	0.722
System Quality	0.816
Information Quality	0.736
Service Quality	0.875

7 Conclusion and Future Work

In this paper, the mobile application called Voyager is presented, it is a novel system that uses preference data to provide safe and popular tourist attractions recommendations. The app also allows users to access relevant safety information and emergency responses for their current location. Unlike other solution that provides a focused safety solution, Voyager provides all the effective component of existing applications into one consolidated platform and is adaptive to the user's location and preferences. There are a few information whereby public APIs does not provide and will be researched upon to enhance the experience for user.

In future work, we plan to improve the user experience of the Voyager client, which is an important factor during emergencies. Since majority of the safety information derives from multiple public APIs, we intend to enhance the system by eliminating such dependencies as much as possible. On top of that, the safety rating on tourist attractions and locations can be further analyzed to identify consistently hazardous locations for user to avoid.

References

1. Reid, C.: The global epidemiology of tourist fatalities. Journal 3–4 (2017)
2. Bentley, T., Page, S., Meyer, D.: How safe is adventure tourism in New Zealand? An exploratory analysis. Journal 329–331 (2001)
3. Smart traveler app. https://2009-2017.state.gov/r/pa/ei/rls/dos/165020.htm. Accessed 2 Feb 2023
4. Emergency app. https://www.redcross.org/about-us/news-and-events/news/2022/check-out-the-new-and-improved-red-cross-emergency-app.html. Accessed 2 Feb 2023
5. GeoSure app global homepage. https://geosureglobal.com/. Accessed 2 Feb 2023
6. Trip lingo app homepage. http://triplingo.com/. Accessed 2 Feb 2023
7. UNWTO.: tourism recovery gains momentum as restrictions ease and confidence returns. UNWTO.org. Accessed 22 Feb 2023
8. Leff, A., Rayfield, J.T..: Web-application development using the model/view/controller design pattern. In: Proceedings Fifth IEEE International Enterprise Distributed Object Computing Conference, pp. 118–127 (2001)
9. McIntosh, I.B.: The pre-travel health consultation. J. Travel Med. **22**, 143–144 (2015)
10. Marangunić, N., Granić, A.: Technology acceptance model: a literature review from 1986 to 2013. Univ. Access Inf. Soc. **14**, 81–95 (2015)

11. Jeyaraj, A.: DeLone & McLean models of information system success: critical meta-review and research directions. Int. J. Inf. Manage. **54**, 102139 (2020)
12. Alzahrani, A.I., Mahmud, I., Ramayah, T., Alfarraj, O., Alalwan, N.: Modelling digital library success using the DeLone and McLean information system success model. J. Librariansh. Inf. Sci. **51**(2), 291–306 (2019)
13. Zaied, A.N.H.: An integrated success model for evaluating information system in public sectors. J. Emerg. Trends Comput. Inf. Sci. **3**(6), 814-825 (2012)
14. Chiu, P.-S., Chao, I.-C., Kao, C.-C., Pu, Y.-H., Huang, Y.-M.: Implementation and evaluation of mobile e-books in a cloud bookcase using the information system success model. Library Hi Tech **34**(2), 207–223 (2016)
15. Calvin, M.L.C.: From open data to open innovation strategies: creating e-services using open government data. In: 46th Hawaii International Conference on System Sciences (2013)
16. Pai, C.K., Liu, Y., Kang, S., Dai, A.: The role of perceived smart tourism technology experience for tourist satisfaction, happiness and revisit intention. Sustainability **12**(16), 6592 (2020)
17. Choi, K., Wang, Y., Sparks, B.: Travel app users' continueduse intentions: it's a matter of value and trust. J. Travel Tour. Mark. **36**(1), 131–143 (2019)
18. Garvey, M., Das, N., Su, J., Natraj, M., Verma, B.: PASSAGE: a travel safety assistant with safe path recommendations for pedestrians. In: IUI (2016)
19. Chen, C.C. and Tsai, J.L.:. Determinants of behavioral intention to use the personalized location-based mobile tourism application: an empirical study by integrating TAM with ISSM. Future Gener. Comput. Syst. **96**, 628–638 (2017)
20. Hossain, E., Karim, M.R., Hasan, M., Zaoad, S.A., Tanjim, T., Khan, M.M.: SPaFE: a crowd-sourcing and multimodal recommender system to ensure travel safety in a city. IEEE Access **10**, 71221–71232 (2022)
21. UNWTO.: tourism recovery gains momentum as restrictions ease and confidence returns. UNWTO.org. Accessed 2 Dec 2023
22. Wyler, B.A., Young, H.M., Hargarten, S.W., Cahill, J.D.: Risk of deaths due to injuries in travellers: a systematic review. J. Travel Med. **29**(5), taac074 (2022)
23. LondonImageInstitute: color psychology: how do colors affect mood & emotions. London-imageinstitute.com. Accessed 8 Oct 2023
24. Mazumder, F.K., Das, U.K.: Usability guidelines for usable user interface. Int. J. Res. Eng. Technol. **3**(9), 79–82 (2014)
25. What are microservices?. microservices.io. https://microservices.io/
26. Bandara, C., Perera, I.: Transforming monolithic systems to microservices-an analysis toolkit for legacy code evaluation. In 2020 20th International Conference on Advances in ICT for Emerging Regions (ICTer), pp. 95–100. IEEE, November 2020
27. Davis, F.D.: Perceived usefulness, perceived ease of use, and user acceptance of information technology. MIS Q. **13**(3), 319–340 (1989)
28. Fishbein, M.: A theory of reasoned action: some applications and implications (1979)
29. Landry, B.J., Griffeth, R., Hartman, S.: Measuring student perceptions of blackboard using the technology acceptance model. Decis. Sci. J. Innov. Educ. **4**(1), 87–99 (2006)
30. Koufaris, M.: Applying the technology acceptance model and flow theory to online consumer behavior. Inf. Syst. Res. **13**(2), 205–223 (2002)
31. Dasgupta, S., Granger, M., McGarry, N.: User acceptance of e-collaboration technology: an extension of the technology acceptance model. Group Decis. Negot. **11**(2), 87–100 (2002)
32. DeLone, W.H., McLean, E.R.: Information systems success revisited. In: Proceedings of the 35th Annual Hawaii International Conference on System Sciences, pp. 2966–2976. IEEE, January 2002
33. DeLone, W.H., McLean, E.R.: The DeLone and McLean model of information systems success: a ten-year update. J. Manag. Inf. Syst. **19**(4), 9–30 (2003)

34. Gupta, A., Dogra, N.: Tourist adoption of mapping apps: a utaut2 perspective of smart travellers. Tourism Hospitality Manage. **23**(2), 145–161 (2017). https://doi.org/10.20867/thm.23.2.6

35. Lee, Y.H., Hsieh, Y.C., Hsu, C.N.: Adding innovation diffusion theory to the technology acceptance model: Supporting employees' intentions to use e-learning systems. J. Educ. Technol. Soc. **14**(4), 124–137 (2011)

36. Nemoto, T., Beglar, D.: Likert-scale questionnaires. In: JALT 2013 Conference Proceedings, pp. 1–8 (2014)

37. Cronbach, L.J.: Coefficient alpha and the internal structure of tests. psychometrika **16**(3), 297–334 (1951)

38. Nunnally, J.C.: Psychometric Theory, 1st edn. McGraw-Hill, New York (1967)

39. Deinum, M., Rubio, D., Long, J.: Spring WebFlux. In: Spring 6 Recipes: A Problem-Solution Approach to Spring Framework, pp. 205–240. Apress, Berkeley (2023)

40. Schafer, J.B., Frankowski, D., Herlocker, J., Sen, S.: Collaborative filtering recommender systems. In: Brusilovsky, P., Kobsa, A., Nejdl, W. (eds.) The Adaptive Web, LNCS, vol. 4321, pp. 291–324. Springer, Berlin (2007). https://doi.org/10.1007/978-3-540-72079-9_9

Cyber Risk Assessment Approach in Connected Autonomous Vehicles

Marcielo Bell[1（✉）], June Wei[2], and Guillermo Francia III[3]

[1] Department of Cybersecurity, University of West Florida, Pensacola, FL, USA
mjb120@students.uwf.edu
[2] Department of Business Administration, University of West Florida, Pensacola, FL, USA
jwei@uwf.edu
[3] Center for Cybersecurity, University of West Florida, Pensacola, FL, USA
gfranciaiii@uwf.edu

Abstract. The rise of automated technologies due to recent advances in Intelligent Transportation systems (ITS) from autonomous delivery services to physical transportation is rapidly developing and public availability is imminent with the active deployment and testing of teleoperation models launching this reality. With the inaugural release of the National Roadway Safety Strategy in 2022, the U.S. National transportation industry initiative aims for a goal of zero roadway fatalities and part of the solution is in designing safer autonomous or self-driving vehicle systems as viable forms of transport [14]. This initiative is prompted by the fact that worldwide vehicle related accidents result in 1.3 million deaths annually [13]. Further, this ambitious commitment to deliver safety and reliability in automotive teleoperations is commendable and will require further intentional efforts to focus on mitigating existing cybersecurity vulnerability and threat concerns. Additionally, the automotive industry supports integration of cybersecurity risk assessment and management through enforcing the joint *International Organization for Standardization and Society of Automobile Engineers* (ISO/SAE) 21434 standard and governance on road vehicle systems design and development. This ongoing research aims to develop a comprehensive framework to aid in threat mitigation by providing a conceptual information exchange flow model on Connected Autonomous Vehicle (CAV) and utilizing existing knowledge of threats to general information system security. By identifying the information flow, threat analysis and risk assessment risk based on threat vectors may be combined hybrid model approach annotating a ranked list to display classify risk factors into three severity levels: high, medium, low. This is an integral part of an overarching research on the design and development of a set of methodologies supporting the automotive industry toward the prevention of connected automotive cybersecurity vulnerability exploitation and promoting risk mitigation.

Keywords: connected autonomous vehicles · risk · threat assessment · risk management · cybersecurity

1 Introduction

Due to increasing adoption, development, and approaching societal and economic integration of ITS, complex autonomous or teleoperation automotive technologies have risen in popularity. The fundamental realization is that traffic safety could be improved through adopting automation with cyber physical systems (CPS) while promoting ancillary benefits such as reduced traffic congestion and enhanced safety. While the application of autonomous technology with a goal of safe mobility may benefit society, the implementation simultaneously creates safety issues and security threats that complicates the overall notion of protection. Indeed, several autonomous vehicle systems are currently in testing and data gathering stages with the intent of eventually releasing them as primary methods of common public transit.

A promise of impending public release indicates a dire need to address underlying security concerns in information exchanges related to vulnerabilities in its CPS including hardware, electronic and software related components. Cyber Physical systems are a combination of the digital and physical expressed by embedding software in devices utilizing "sensors and actuators" [3] which connect with one another and are also linked to "human operators by communicating via interfaces" [3]. A key aspect of vehicular network functionality is connectivity so that they may operate in rapidly disseminating and exchanging critical information through wireless communication networks which act as the basis for vehicular ad-hoc networks (VANETs).

2 Literature Review

A current review of studies indicates the need for a more comprehensive approach to defining the information flow to better understand the underlying threats for more effective cybersecurity risk management as alluded to in the ISO/SAE 21434 standard. The purpose of the standard is to establish trusted ITS as automated systems that is warranted by concerns over "safety-critical driving control" especially as there is no "direct driver input" [12]. From security surveys in VANET systems by Azees et al. [1], there had generated an extensive list of existing cyberattacks, proposed countermeasures and identified which five core security services including confidentiality, integrity, and availability (CIA), authentication and non-repudiation were targeted based on topology and vulnerabilities inherent in design of vehicular wireless and ad-hoc communication functionality.

An article by Parekh et al. [13] sparks discussion on the evolution of traditional mechanical design to modern intelligent automated safe transport solutions to decrease risks from human error and provides insight to AV architecture, functionality, and the promotion for security testing and Threat Assessment and Remediation Analysis (TARA). Autonomy related tasks and common taxonomy are defined such as sensors, cameras, RADAR, Light Detection and Ranging (LIDAR), and Ultrasonic technology to aid in object and event detection and response (OEDR), Dynamic Driving Task (DDT), and the six levels of automation as detailed by the Society of Automotive Engineers (SAE).

With the current six levels of automated ability starting from zero as per the SAE, this work will focus on developing a risk assessment model on information flows toward envisioning the advent of level five automation, which has not yet been implemented [9]. For a summary of SAE automated levels, a level zero vehicle is considered to have no automation, level one will have minor assistive features, level two systems incorporate partial automation, level three is conditionally based automation, level four has substantial automation ability and lastly, level five indicates a fully autonomous system [9]. It is important to note that levels below four will require some active level of human intervention [16] whether that is an individual in the vehicle or at a distance through teleoperation. As of current, there are products in testing that are mostly operating at level four automation or lower and most notably, companies such as Waymo and Cruise that are currently in a trial and data collection phase. There is only speculation around a research and development timeline for the more advanced and completed driving automation with level five ready systems.

Although vehicular data storage is not the main emphasis in this paper, the risk associated with stored data is inherent and authors Kang et al. [8] shared relevant insight over cloud computing operations which are critical to cybersecurity concerns within the information flow. In a comparison of cloud models, it was highlighted that vehicular cloud setups may have risks with the high level of interaction between automotive connections and coined as vehicular cloudlets [2]. For example, v-cloud architecture could be presented in three modes: stationary as in "parked vehicles similar to conventional clouds" [8], infrastructure-based where the automotive relies on road side units (RSUs), and dynamic in which V2V is utilized mostly for traffic management services [2] and/or emergency management [8]. Due to vehicular cloudlet formation being composed of multiple vehicular networks for "communication strategies" [2], attack vectors that are network focused such as eavesdropping, replay, message delay, and on path attacks will also pose risks through V2X communication, storage functions and other cloud connected aspects such as camera, LIDAR or other sensor technologies in AV systems [8].

In an article by Yurtsever et al., sensor technologies largely involve monitoring tasks of internal vehicle state and operations of movement through actuators; sensing features are all reliant on hardware systems and therefore warrant "high sensor redundancy" [16] which should be an urgent consideration and requirement in risk management. Sensors make up a large portion of functionality for enabling intelligent monitoring of driving environments in advanced automation [4] so reliability of these sensors remain a source for vulnerability. Another primary function are localization and mapping for navigation of AV systems and currently rely on techniques such as simultaneous localization and mapping (SLAM), a priori map-based and a specific form of Global Positioning system to name a few, which may rely on pre-built maps matching destinations, position readings or a blend of using available mapping with current vehicle environment to varying degrees of efficiency [16]. Decision making with mapping take either a global or local route approach and while in global, precomputed shortcuts may offer solutions to entire navigation sequences, they also may become cumbersome with vehicular data storage limitations [16].

By and large, connected autonomous vehicle systems rely heavily on interconnected parts with "decision making units, and data fused from multiple sources to conduct driving tasks with different levels of automation" as expressed by He et al. [7]. In autonomous robotic systems, the intelligent system of decision making (ISD) in development has been modeling a human-like "hybrid cognitive architecture" when processing multi-sensory data and blended memory storage types which is paving a pathway for a system "to orientate itself in its environment" for localization and object detection and also "to imitate of human ways of solving problems" that may parallel to how future level six automation techniques may also eventually develop [10].

3 Research Model

In this study, the focus is on examining an overview of the data flow processes in an advanced CAV system. By identifying each primary and critical information flow, three major sources of threats designated as human error, computer crime and natural disasters [11] can be linked; every specific instance of threat sources may be further collocated and analyzed with a quantitative system to evaluate the levels of associated risk and subsequently determine classification severity. There are generally six basic concise flow steps (F1:F6) described in the following flow breakdown and displayed in Table 1, which encompass a high-level overview of the information flow for a future level six connected autonomous vehicle system with an established advanced automated driving system.

Flow F1: The user enters the current location to destination choice through modalities such as voice or keyboard entry, then the GPS calculates and plans the optimal route from current location to destination which relays the functionality of vehicle actions for motion.

Flow F2: Current status of the CAV relayed to the Monitoring System as relayed though technologies such as Basic Safety Message (BSMs) [5].

Flow F3: Monitored information relayed to the Intelligent System for Machine Learning processing and communication to the CAV.

Flow F4: Crisis management from either internal or external data sources during emergencies will be relayed to the Intelligent System for analysis and real-time response.

Flow F5: External sources of data: traffic, road, and weather information intake for continuous monitoring and evaluation by the Monitoring System.

Flow F6: Intelligent System relays the necessary adjustments required for the CAV to remain safe, secure, and efficient on the road.

As depicted in Fig. 1 below, a visual representation of the information flow model as previously defined.

Subsequently, Table 2 illustrates a non-exhaustive list of potential cybersecurity threats in modern connected autonomous vehicle's automated driving systems in three categories involving: human factors, malicious threat actors, and natural disasters. A large part of attack surface is in the inherent infrastructure with "Vehicle-to-Everything (V2X) communication technologies" and constant influx of vehicle data streamed for an intelligent decision-making process while convenient for users, they pose risks of insecurity of these connected channels [4].

Some of the sources listed such as human negligence towards implementation security controls may lead to V2X exploits by creating a channel for eavesdropping

Table 1. Intelligent Self-Driving Information Flow Model

Information Flows	Description
F1 Navigation System	Creating route based on user input and with GPS cloud data and/or data from in-vehicle storage and localization process
F2 Monitoring System	Current CAV status continually relayed to the Monitoring system
F3 Intelligent System	Relay of Monitored information to the Intelligent System for Machine Learning processing and communication to the CAV
F4 Emergency System	Crisis management data of external or internal (vehicle) sources. Emergency data analyzed by Intelligent Decision system for analysis with real-time response to crisis
F5 External Sources	External data reliance on streams of traffic, road and weather conditions and information as constantly monitored and evaluated
F6 Iterative Decision Cycle	Intelligent system facilitates decision-making in an iterative cycle for continuous adjustments for safety and security in transit

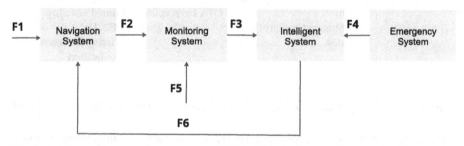

Fig. 1. Intelligent Connected Autonomous Vehicle Risk Assessment Information Flow Model.

among other modalities for adversaries thus impacting confidentiality of data. Furthermore, operating systems integrated into autonomous vehicle architecture was originally intended for robotics, which did not account for security measures in the slightest thus making in naturally vulnerable to cyber-attack [6]. While not all encompassing, Table 2 seeks to deliver an overview of security threat types impacting core data confidentiality, integrity, and availability within highly advanced connected automotive systems.

With data accumulated of three possible threat sources and twenty-two specific security threats in the information flow of CAVs in Table 2, the following Table 3 builds upon the previous collocated data and provides quantitative results, which key automotive industry entities such as manufacturers and associated supply chain software and hardware from original equipment manufacturer (OEM) can further examine for security risk management. From Table 3, each security threat vector is tallied with a number from zero to six correlating with each of the information flows that could be potentially impacted by any of the three main section of threats. For instance, AC1 signifying a lack

Table 2. CAV System Threat Model

Security Threats	Sources of Security Threats		
	A. Human Factors	B. Malicious Threat Actors	C. Natural Disasters
A. Data confidentiality	AA1. Unencrypted devices AA2. User Negligence AA3. Sabotage (Insider)	BA1. Intercepted data BA2. Unauthorized access to wired components (i.e. OBD-II)	CA1. Accidental data release CA2. Abnormalities
B. Data integrity	AB1. Inconsistencies of traffic data AB2. Navigation Errors AB3. Software & Architecture Misconfiguration	BB1. Spoofed traffic alerts BB2. Keyless entry signal manipulation	CB1. Degradation of sensor data streams CB2. Abnormal data transmission
C. Data Availability	AC1. Lack of automotive security controls AC2. Storage Capacity Exceeded	BC1. USB Ransomware attacks BC2. OTA Interception	CC1. Automated Driving System limited visibility CC2. Delay or Missing Emergency Notification

of automotive security controls impacts all six information flows resulting in a total of six.

However, other areas pose a lower level of risk with security and an example of which is abnormality development threats in CA2 that were only impacted in three data flows primarily from Natural Disaster area at a medium risk. Overall, the majority security root causes existed in Human Factors followed by both even quantities of Malicious Threat Actors and Natural Disasters in the High-risk level classification block. This order will change dependent on other factors as demonstrated in the Medium-risk class where most risk resides in natural disasters with a level of human factors presenting as vulnerabilities for consideration. On the lower end were human factors related to navigation input errors from users, teleoperators and/or devices such as "reliability of sensors" [15].

Table 3. CAV System Risk Level Classification

AV Security threats	Security Risk Level per AV threat	Average Security Risk Level	Sources of AV Threats	Risk Level Classification
AC1	6	100.00%	Section A: Human Factors	High
BC1	6	100.00%		
CB1	6	100.00%		
AB1	5	83.33%		
AC2	5	83.33%		
BC2	5	83.33%	Section B: Malicious Threat Actors	
CB2	5	83.33%	Section C. Natural Disasters	
AA1	4	66.67%	Section A: Human Factors	Medium
AA2	4	66.67%		
AB3	4	66.67%		
BB1	4	66.67%	Section C. Natural Disaster	
CA1	4	66.67%		
CC1	4	66.67%		
CC2	4	66.67%		
CA2	3	50.00%		
AA3	2	33.33%	Section B: Malicious Threat Actors	Low
BA1	2	33.33%		
BA2	2	33.33%		
BB2	2	33.33%		
AB2	1	16.67%	Section A: Human Factors	

4 Conclusion

This ongoing study seeks to develop a comprehensive risk management framework for a level five automation of a CAV system based on critical functions where vulnerability may exist in the six generalized information flow stages such as during automated driving system navigation and monitoring of external sources for road condition. Due to the complexity of a fully autonomous system, there is a potential for overgeneralization with fewer stages. Therefore, a more detailed information flow may account for nuances of key data flows that are targets to malicious actors. Three fundamental security threat sources: human factors, malicious threat actors, and natural disasters are utilized from established information systems security management strategies while twenty-two CAV threat factors are identified for use in quantitative calculation [11]. However, the CAV threat factors listed are not all inclusive. Additional vulnerabilities may lead to different results and greater risks to CAVs in light of a more comprehensive quantitative analysis.

5 Future Research Considerations

As aforementioned, a future research direction will expand upon the information flow stages and will provide detailed tasks of dataflow in CAV systems. By considering additional CAV threat factors a larger dataset may provide additional insights on the quantitative analysis and confirm which of the three categories require greater concern of risk management. Connected automated driving systems with intelligent "decision-making mechanisms are more vulnerable" [3] to attackers targeting this information flow; therefore, it is imperative for automotive designers and manufacturers to recognize and adopt a CAV risk framework to ensure the efficiency and safety of all levels of automation for CAVs.

Acknowledgments. This work is partially supported by the University of West Florida (UWF) Argo Cyber Emerging Scholars (ACES) Program funded by the National Science Foundation (NSF) CyberCorps® Scholarship for Service (SFS) Program under grant number 1946442. Any opinions, findings, and conclusions or recommendations expressed in this document are those of the authors and do not necessarily reflect the views of the NSF.

References

1. Azees, M., Vijayakumar, P., Deborah, L.J.: Comprehensive survey on security services in vehicular ad-hoc networks. IET Intel. Transport Syst. **10**(6), 379–388 (2016). https://doi.org/10.1049/iet-its.2015.0072
2. Boukerche, A., De Grande, R.E.: Vehicular cloud computing: architectures, applications, and mobility. Comput. Netw. **135**, 171–189 (2018). https://doi.org/10.1016/j.comnet.2018.01.004
3. Cardin, O., Derigent, W., Trentesaux, D.: Digitalization and Control of Industrial Cyber-Physical Systems: Concepts, Technologies and Applications. Wiley, New York (2022)
4. El-Rewini, Z., Sadatsharan, K., Selvaraj, D.F., Plathottam, S.J., Ranganathan, P.: Cybersecurity challenges in vehicular communications. Veh. Commun. **23**, 100214 (2020). https://doi.org/10.1016/j.vehcom.2019.100214

5. Francia III, G.A., Snider, D., Cyphers, B.: Basic Safety Message (BSM) test data generation for vehicle security machine learning systems. In: Proceedings of the 2023 International Conference on Security and Management (SAM 2023), Las Vegas, NV (2023)
6. Gao, C., Wang, G., Shi, W., Wang, Z., Chen, Y.: Autonomous driving security: state of the art and challenges. IEEE Internet Things J. **9**(10), 7572–7595 (2022). https://doi.org/10.1109/jiot.2021.3130054
7. He, Q., Meng, X., Qu, R.: Towards a severity assessment method for potential cyber-attacks to connected and autonomous vehicles. J. Adv. Transp. **2020**, 1–15 (2020)
8. Kang, J., Lin, D., Bertino, E., Tonguz, O.: From autonomous vehicles to vehicular clouds: challenges of management, security and dependability. In: 2019 IEEE 39th International Conference on Distributed Computing Systems (ICDCS), pp. 1730–1741 (2019). https://doi.org/10.1109/icdcs.2019.00172
9. Kershaw, J.: SAE International's Dictionary for Automotive Engineers (2023). https://doi.org/10.4271/9781468604078
10. Kowalczuk, Z., Czubenko, M.: An intelligent decision-making system for autonomous units based on the mind model. In: 2018 23rd International Conference on Methods & Models in Automation & Robotics (MMAR), pp. 1–6 (2018). https://doi.org/10.1109/MMAR.2018.8486009
11. Kroenke, D.M., Boyle, R.J.: Experiencing MIS, 8th edn. Pearson Education, Washington (2018)
12. Krontiris, I., et al.: Autonomous vehicles: data protection and ethical considerations. In: Computer Science in Cars Symposium (CSCS 2020), pp. 1–10 (2020). https://doi.org/10.1145/3385958.3430481
13. Parekh, D., et al.: A review on autonomous vehicles: progress, methods and challenges. Electronics **11**(14), 2162 (2022)
14. United States Department of Transportation, "National Roadway Safety Strategy," USDOT National Roadway Safety Strategy, version 1.1, pp. 1–38, January 2022
15. Xu, W., Chen, Y., Jia, W., Ji, X., Liu, J.: Analyzing and enhancing the security of ultrasonic sensors for autonomous vehicles. IEEE Internet Things J. **5**(6), 5015–5029 (2018). https://doi.org/10.1109/jiot.2018.2867917
16. Yurtsever, E., Lambert, J., Carballo, A., Takeda, K.: A survey of autonomous driving: common practices and emerging technologies. IEEE Access **8**, 58443–58469 (2020). https://doi.org/10.1109/ACCESS.2020.2983149

ChatAlone: An Anonymous Messaging Application for Enhanced Privacy and Open Communication

Jordan Yuen Jia Jun[(⊠)] [iD] and Owen Noel Newton Fernando

Nanyang Technological University, 50 Nanyang Avenue, Singapore, Singapore
JYUEN006@e.ntu.edu.sg, ofernnado@ntu.edu.sg

Abstract. Instant messaging application is widely used around the world containing a huge pool of active users help solidify their roots and it is here to stay for a long time, having an application to communicate and meet new people is something everyone loves, but there are a handful of people who are introverted and will be shy to approach or speak freely, through the use of anonymous messaging application helps free break free from the fear which may help people to interact comfortably. ChatAlone goal is to break such barrier and help create a safe and productive environment for people to make friends and conduct discussions with the power of being anonymous.

Keywords: Anonymous messaging · Privacy enhancing technologies · Offline communication · Mobile applications · User anonymity

1 Introduction

Messaging applications are very common, they contain a wide range and variety of users, it allows to connect with one another without the need to be there, a large amount of people around the world uses messaging application as it is effective and simple to use, [1] and get the message across no matter where you which is why it is so popular today [2], as it slowly evolves as many more features are yet to be discovered and explored messaging application is here to stay for many years to come, they require users to sign up and tag their personal information before being able to use such service. Based on research done by multiple research websites WhatsApp, WeChat, Facebook Messenger, and Telegrams are the top few applications that are popular in today life [3, 4]. However, these applications require a constant network connection to function. Using these applications for general discussion and giving feedback most comments are usually more controlled and not directed towards the main issue which might not provide enough feedback for improvements and sometimes even missed, as compared to being anonymous [5]. During general discussion being able to stay anonymous helps in providing ideas that might not be commonly used but could be sufficient to be investigated this helps ensure an open discussion [6]. The market also contains applications that allow users to be anonymous [7] but also requires network connections these applications are

ChatOus and Whisper. Having the protection of anonymous seems to be a drawing factor for people to be able to be more open be it asking of questions to answering of questions [8]. Being able to communicate anonymously helps improve the number of questions as it helps people who are more reserved and judgement of their peers to express their thoughts freely which helps in participating rates [9]. As Offline messaging does not rely on a stable internet connection which allows users to constantly be able to communicate without worrying [10], application that requires no network connection do exist but do also have their own flaws some of these applications are Bridgefy, Briar and FireChat. Each has their own benefits but also contains benefits but also has their own flaws, FireChat, Briar which still require some form of internet connection. And Bridgefy recommends tagging your mobile number to help improve discovery [11]. The use of Bluetooth where devices can discover devices and set up a connection to be able to send packets that consist of data [12].

1.1 Project Purpose

The purpose of this project is to create a mobile application which serves as a platform for users to be able to communicate with other users anonymously and provide a place for people who might be a little reserved or afraid to ask questions or raise feedback. And allow users to create groups for discussions. This application can be used and applied for many different scenarios such as classroom to raise feedback or questions, conferences, or events where users will be able search for groups of their interest the use case application are limitless. However, with so many benefits there are flaws of having anonymous communication such as abusive messages or username that may offend or contain profanity, as these are all ill-intention behaviors of human, there are precautions to be taken where this paper will cover.

1.2 Project Scope

This project aims to develop an offline where users can remain anonymous, ChatAlone will allow users to have a platform to communicate without the need of an active internet connection, communications will be done through Bluetooth. Users can communicate with the following functions peer to peer, group and through broadcasting of messages. Data will be stored locally as this application will not require internet access and at no time will the application ask the user for their private information this helps ensure that users are able to completely be anonymous while using this application.

2 Related Works

2.1 Bridgefy

Bridgefy SDK 3.0 provides user with the ability to communicate via Bluetooth Low-Energy through Peer-to-peer or through broadcasting of messages through a mesh chat also without the need of an active internet connection it allows users to be able to send image files and messages. They advertise themselves being useful for schools, large events, and natural disaster [13].

2.2 Briar

Briar provides the ability to communicate with Bluetooth through Peer-to-peer or through private group chats without the need for an active internet connection but however it only allows users to be able to send messages, Briar also allows user to be able to use internet for communication.

2.3 FireChat

FireChat provides the ability to communicate with Bluetooth through Peer-to-peer, through broadcasting of message through a mesh chat and private group chat without the need for an active internet connection it allows users to send message and images, however FireChat has been discontinued.

2.4 Comparison

Comparing the three solutions that have already existed before ChatAlone, the difference between these application to ChatAlone is that they do not allow for anonymous communication and some of the applications do not contain three features of Peer-to-peer, broadcasting, and group chat, where ChatAlone contains. Therefore, ChatAlone will be able to bring a new flavour into the market which allows user to be able to communicate anonymously and at the same time enjoy the features that most of the existing solutions has.

3 Methodology

With my different framework being available there is always an endless amount to choose from. However, in order to be optimized to its fullest, ChatAlone is developed using Flutter as the frontend for its application because of the vast amount of libraries and ability to function on multiple platforms on a singular codebase, and for the backend it uses Hive as data are stored locally Hive uses a Box function to store its data which can store simple and light weight data as ChatAlone does not require a server to store its data thus all data are stored locally on the respective devices.

3.1 Bluetooth

As Bluetooth is a wireless technology that is designed for short range communications. ChatAlone uses Bluetooth for its communication as it allows for short range proximity communication where users can communicate within classroom, event, or campus settings, in these scenarios an active internet connection is not required. Using a package dependency flutter_nearby_connection enables devices to be able to transfer bytes and data to other connected devices through User Datagram protocol. After a user has successfully connected to another device the status will be changed and the user can begin with communication through the chat feature.

3.2 Flutter

Flutter designed by Google helps enable cross platform singular codebase for the most independent and developed platforms Android and Apple. This helps in the development of the program as there is no need for two different program files. The framework creates widgets for its view rather than producing a web view as each component are rendered. Compared to other frameworks Flutter does not require bridging which results in better performance.

3.3 Hive

Hive is local database for Flutter, it is designed to be efficient and lightweight, it requires minimal setup making it very easy to integrate into an application, initializing Hive boxes allows for quick storing and retrieving of data. ChatAlone does not require an active internet connection therefore Hive is able to function best as data can be stored locally on the device.

3.4 Message Packet

Users message that will be sent out will be packed in a format similar to a network packet the format of the message packet will contain the type of message, content of the packet, name of receiver and sender. This is to help to ensure when the message is unpacked the correct functions will be called to decode the contents of each packet.

3.5 Image Byte Converter

Using the convert library from Flutter, it allows images that often takes a large amount of time to transfer over Bluetooth to be sent quickly, ChatAlone uses a function which converts the image to bytes, after the bytes are turned into string before sending it, this helps improve the time taken to transfer text file as the receiver will be able to convert the text back into an image file through a decoder function.

4 ChatAlone: Anonymous Communication

ChatAlone allows users to be able to pair with other devices within the vicinity through the function of the library allowing users device to be a listener or broadcaster to detect or allow users to detect their devices, after pairing has been established users will be able to send messages to connected devices. This service will ensure that the user remains anonymous, user will not be required to enter their personal information throughout the usage of the application, all data will be stored locally as there is no need for an internet connection.

4.1 Anonymous Communication

By being anonymous it allows users to be able to freely communicate and express their opinions, this will help user who may be afraid of judgement by their fellow peers to speak, this will result in the increase in class participation and feedback which will be able to benefit both students and professors, based on a research conducted where there are many different cases where students who are not confident or afraid to speak up or ask questions in classroom due to having bad grades or are not performing well, these are some of the factors that affect the ability to speak up or answer questions during lessons [14]. When meeting new people some people are much more reserved as they might how they act or behave might change others perspective on them or they are shy because they are introverted, but if one does not have their identity revealed they are able to act naturally and express their inner thoughts through texts.

4.2 Platform of Possibilities

The use cases for this application can cater to many needs such as in classroom discussions, conference networking, campus communications and many more, only through communication is how relationships begins and some may find it difficult to walk up and strike a conversation however with the power of ChatAlone one is able to search for users and be able to connect and communicate. Looking for an interest group in an event? ChatAlone caters to having group creation where users can create groups and other user who find the title of the group interest can join and communicate with users in it.

5 Design

ChatAlone has a simple but sturdy design, devices can pair with one another as long as they are within the vicinity of each other through the broadcasting and listening feature of Bluetooth, after the pairing is done, users are allowed to communicate by transferring data, each data are packed like a network packet this allows for easier unpacking when data is transmitted. Users can create groups and join them, broadcast their message to nearby users or create a private chat. All this data will be stored locally as there is no internet connection required by the user therefore storing the data on the local device is the most optimal solution (Figs. 1 and 2).

ChatAlone's UI allows for users to easily navigate and utilise all the functions available as the design is simple and straightforward. Users can send message by text or image if they are connected to another user. The username of the recipients is shown at the top of the chat. Messages are color coded to show which message belong to which user the green shaded color represents the message being sent by the user while the grey shaded color represents the message being received by the user (Fig. 3).

In an event where user feels that their identity might have been figured out, they are able to change their username this allows for the randomness and masks their identity which helps them remain anonymous. This does not affect the messages that they have previously sent.

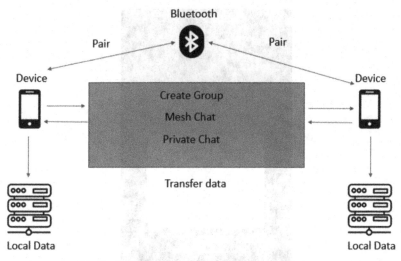

Fig. 1. ChatAlone's application design architecture

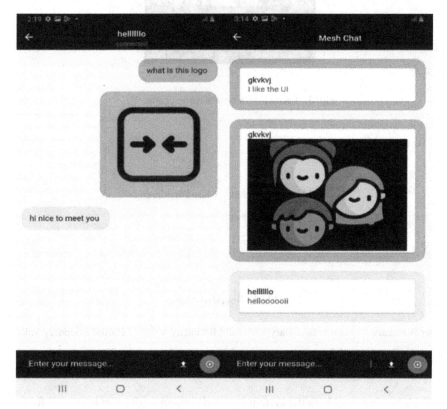

Fig. 2. ChatAlone Chat UI's Design

Fig. 3. ChatAlone's profile name change UI.

5.1 Testing of Scenarios

Table 1. Equivalence Class Partitioning

Valid	Invalid	
1 < X < 20	X > 20	X < 1

Table 2. Boundary Value

Lower Boundary: 1	Upper Boundary 15	Valid Boundary Values	Invalid Boundary Values
0,1	20,21	1,20	0,21

Black box testing where the system is tested without prior knowledge and for each input and test cases is recorded by the tester this is to help simulate an actual person using the application [15]. A black box testing was conducted to ensure that username values shall checks shall be in place to ensure that it does not prevent users from entering a high

Table 3. Test Results

Test Case	Expected Output	Actual Output
"" (x = 0)	"Invalid, do no leave blanks for username"	"Invalid, do no leave blanks for username"
Mike (x = 4)	"Valid"	"Valid"
Testing (x = 7)	"Valid"	"Valid"
IamTesting12345678910 (x = 21)	"Invalid, username over character limit"	"Invalid, username over character limit"
"(Profanity)"	"Valid"	"Invalid, contains profanity"

number of characters which may cause overflows or the display to cross boundaries. There will also a detection of profanity, so users are not allowed to use names that are offensive (Tables 1, 2 and 3).

6   Risk and Management

6.1   Power of Being Anonymous

With the power of being anonymous comes with drawbacks as anonymity allows for users to be toxic to others as there are not accountability through the application, this may result in messages that will harm peoples feeling, however for ChatAlone there will be some measures taken place and further improvements could be made in the future a profanity detector will be set in place to ensure that user's message that contain profanity will not be sent out, this can be countered if the users mask the profanity with as there are many different ways and shortcuts to enter them. However, this can be further improved in the future when AI creates a large dataset for all other different types and ways to enter a certain profanity [6].

6.2   Losing Credibility

By being anonymous acknowledgements might not be given to those who deserve due credit as ChatAlone is an anonymous communication platform this might not help in class participation if a student would like to give their feedback openly. But however, as ChatAlone may be an anonymous chat application users are able to freely declare their identity if they are comfortable on the application [6].

6.3   Bluetooth Range

The limitation of Bluetooth is where the range might not suffice if in scenarios where a campus is too big this might not allow for optimal communication, there ChatAlone at its current position only allows for optimal communication within a Classroom, conferences and events held at a certain venue.

7 Conclusion

ChatAlone application provides a platform for users to freely express their thoughts and feelings without the being judge, as users can communicate through Bluetooth, but with some of the limitations due to the length of Bluetooth and some disadvantages of being anonymous, as there are many more ways to improve ChatAlone this application will be able to reach its optimal state in the near future.

7.1 Future Works

Some of the possible ideas for future works to be able to investigate is beaconing services which allows for the range to be increased but however this requires for another device to be acting as a beacon which requires a network of users for this to work [16]. Another suggestion would be to allow the user to constantly still be able to receive messages without having the application to be opened this will require to keep the Bluetooth connection on constantly. With many ways to type profanity people can play around with the constraints set such as using symbols or numbers to represent letters with the help of AI it may be possible to deal with such situations in the future.

Disclosure of Interests. The authors have no competing interests to declare that are relevant to the content of this article.

References

1. Sultan, A.J.: Addiction to mobile text messaging applications is nothing to "lol" about. Soc. Sci. J. **51**, 57–69 (2014)
2. Huang, H.-H., Lin, C.-N.: Influencing factors of mobile instant messaging applications between single- and multi- platform use cases. Comput. Stand. Interfaces **83**, 103658 (2023)
3. March, L.: Most popular messaging apps in 2023. https://www.similarweb.com/blog/research/market-research/worldwide-messaging-apps/
4. Dixon, S.J.: Most popular messaging apps 2023. https://www.statista.com/statistics/258749/most-popular-global-mobile-messenger-apps/
5. Corelli, A.: Direct vs. anonymous feedback: teacher behavior in Higher Education, with focus on technology advances. Procedia – Soc. Behav. Sci. **195**, 52–61 (2015)
6. Scott, C.R.: Benefits and drawbacks of anonymous online communication: legal challenges and communicative recommendations. Free Speech Yearbook **41**, 127–141 (2004)
7. Hoang, N.P., Pishva, D.: Anonymous communication and its importance in social networking. In: 16th International Conference on Advanced Communication Technology (2014)
8. Ong, A.D., Weiss, D.J.: The impact of anonymity on responses to sensitive questions. J. Appl. Soc. Psychol. **30**, 1691–1708 (2000)
9. Yang, J.-Y., Choi, C.: Enhancing interactiveness of problem-based programming course using anonymous chatting service. In: 2017 16th International Conference on Information Technology Based Higher Education and Training (ITHET) (2017)
10. Junio, O.M., Chavez, E.P.: Development of offline chat application: framework for resilient disaster management. In: 2018 IEEE International Conference of Safety Produce Informatization (IICSPI) (2018)
11. Offline messaging, Bridgefy. https://bridgefy.me/

12. Verma, M., Singh, S., Kaur, B.: An overview of bluetooth technology and its communication. https://www.researchgate.net/publication/276251559_An_Overview_of_Bluetooth_Technology_and_its_Communication_Application
13. Albrecht, M.R., Blasco, J., Jensen, R.B., Mareková, L.: Mesh messaging in large-scale protests: breaking bridgefy. In: Paterson, K.G. (ed.) CT-RSA 2021. LNCS, vol. 12704, pp. 375–398. Springer, Cham (2021). https://doi.org/10.1007/978-3-030-75539-3_16
14. Dreher, H., Maurer, H.: The worth of anonymous feedback. https://www.researchgate.net/profile/Heinz-Dreher/publication/249905933_The_Worth_of_Anonymous_Feedback/links/542a30e20cf27e39fa8e7a87/The-Worth-of-Anonymous-Feedback.pdf?origin=publication_detail
15. What is Black Box Testing: Techniques & Examples: Imperva. https://www.imperva.com/learn/application-security/black-box-testing/
16. Bluetooth beacons technology- how does it work in 2023, Mapsted Blog. https://mapsted.com/blog/what-you-must-know-about-bluetooth-beacons-before-purchasing

Mobile User Experience and Design

Automating Mobile App Review User Feedback with Aspect-Based Sentiment Analysis

Vasileios Ballas$^{(\boxtimes)}$ (ID), Konstantinos Michalakis(ID), Georgios Alexandridis(ID), and George Caridakis(ID)

University of the Aegean, University Hill, 81100 Mytilene, Greece
cti22007@ct.aegean.gr, {kmichalak,gealexandri,gcari}@aegean.gr

Abstract. Effective user feedback is crucial for enhancing the user experience (UX) of mobile applications. However, manually analyzing user reviews can be time-consuming and labour-intensive. This paper investigates the application of state-of-the-art aspect-based sentiment analysis (ABSA) algorithms to automate user review analysis and feedback. We scrape the most relevant Google Play Store user reviews for 6 distinct applications of unrelated categories and we separate them into single sentences. We employ and fine-tune a BERT-based ABSA model – Aspect Sentiment Triplet Extraction by PyABSA – to extract sentiment triplets (aspect, opinion, polarity) from the review sentences. The results demonstrate that ABSA models can effectively capture user feedback by identifying specific aspects and sentiments related to app features and functionalities. Our framework, which utilizes the ABSA model along with filtering methods via Topic Modeling, can automatically extract sentiment triplets and provide additional suggestions and statistics for the app developers. This framework facilitates efficient and comprehensive user feedback collection, enabling developers to make informed decisions for UX improvement.

Keywords: Aspect-based Sentiment Analysis · User Feedback · Mobile Application · User Experience Evaluation

1 Introduction

When developing an application for mobile users, the most important thing to take into account is the users and their needs [15]. An application cannot be successful if it doesn't cover the requirements of the people who are supposed to use it [3]. To quote usability consultant, Don Norman, "Two of the most important characteristics of good design are discoverability and understanding.", as he references in his book "The Design of Everyday Things" [20]. Developers need to be aware of their users' opinions and feelings to offer the most optimal version of their product. In other words, they need to be able to receive User Feedback and listen to what the users expect from the applications [35]. Nowadays there are

J. Wei and G. Margetis (Eds.): HCII 2024, LNCS 14738, pp. 179–193, 2024.
https://doi.org/10.1007/978-3-031-60487-4_14

multiple ways to get feedback from people, especially in the mobile application field as users have many options to place their opinions such as in-app surveys, newsletter forms, app store ratings, etc. With the rapidly increasing amount of applications in the mobile app stores, people spend more time browsing through their options than they used to [5]. One of the most common criteria people have to check to install an application is its rating and the reviews other users write about it [12]. Applications with low ratings or bad reviews may leave negative impressions on possible users and it is the responsibility of the developers to fix the issues that users complain about to minimize the amount of bad reviews the application receives [31]. On the other hand, positive reviews not only motivate people to try out the application but also the feedback they provide can help the developers understand what aspects of their product are successful and which new features are welcomed by their audience [19]. It is safe to say that collecting User Feedback from app store reviews is essential for the well-being of an application [21]. In this paper, we propose a framework that automates the collection and analysis of user feedback from these reviews by the use of advanced Aspect-based Opinion Extraction and Sentiment Analysis models.

2   Previous Work

Before the mainstream use of Artificially Intelligent tools, researchers were analyzing user reviews using manual or semi-automated methods such as "handpicking" a small sample of reviews to summarize and using tools like Microsoft Excel for frequency and sentiment analysis. This method was time-consuming, prone to bias and error and limited by the scalability of the tools. It also couldn't handle unstructured text data and the complexity of user feedback [1]. AI-powered tools have revolutionized the analysis of user reviews by automating and streamlining the process, enabling businesses to extract valuable insights from vast amounts of customer feedback. Natural language processing (NLP), a field dedicated to enabling computers to understand human language, plays a central role in these tools. Two widely used NLP tools for user feedback analysis are Sentiment Analysis and Topic Modeling. Sentiment analysis delves into the emotional polarity of user reviews, classifying them as positive, negative, or neutral and assigning scores like 1 to 5 stars. This allows businesses to quickly gauge overall customer satisfaction. Topic Modeling, on the other hand, uncovers hidden themes or topics within user reviews, revealing common concerns, areas of interest, and recurring patterns. By employing sentiment analysis and topic modeling, businesses can identify specific product or service shortcomings that need improvement and areas that are consistently praised by customers. These insights can guide product development and marketing strategies. Sentiment analysis and topic modeling utilize machine learning techniques such as naive Bayes, maximum entropy, and support vector machines for sentiment classification, and Latent Dirichlet Allocation (LDA) for topic modeling. These methods can extract relevant information and patterns from large amounts of text data. They can also compare features like words, phrases, and part-of-speech tags to assess analysis performance. Influential research papers like "Thumbs up? Sentiment Classification using Machine Learning Techniques" [22] and "Latent Dirichlet Allocation (LDA)" [8] have introduced and evaluated these tools, inspiring further advancements in user feedback analysis. These tools have become indispensable for businesses seeking to understand customer sentiment and improve their offerings.

2.1   Sentiment Analysis

At the current time of writing this paper, the state of the art in Sentiment Analysis is dominated by deep learning models, such as recurrent neural networks (RNNs) [11] and convolutional neural networks (CNNs) [9]. These models have been shown to outperform traditional machine learning methods, such as support vector machines (SVMs) [23], on a variety of sentiment analysis benchmarks. One of the most significant recent advancements in text sentiment analysis is the development of pre-trained language models (PLMs), such as BERT (Bidirectional Encoder Representations from Transformers) [4], RoBERTa (Robustly Optimized BERT Pretraining Approach) [14] and DistilBERT (a distilled version of BERT) [32]. PLMs are trained on massive amounts of text data, can be fine-tuned for domain-specific tasks and have been shown to achieve state-of-the-art performance on a variety of NLP tasks, including sentiment analysis [4]. BERT is a deep neural network that uses the Transformer architecture to encode text from both left and right contexts, capturing the full meaning and nuance of words and sentences. It was introduced by Google researchers in 2018 and has since revolutionized the field of natural language processing, achieving state-of-the-art results on many tasks, including sentiment analysis. One of the advantages of BERT for sentiment analysis is that it can leverage large amounts of unlabeled text data to learn general language representations, which can then be transferred to sentiment analysis and other tasks, reducing the need for task-specific data and improving performance across domains and languages. For example, Sun et al. (2019) [34] showed that BERT can achieve better results than previous models on several cross-domain and cross-lingual sentiment analysis tasks, such as Amazon reviews and Twitter data. Another advantage of BERT for sentiment analysis is that it can capture the context and the sentiment of the whole input, not just individual words or phrases, which can be crucial for understanding the polarity and the intensity of the expressed opinion. For example, Yang et al. (2020) [38] demonstrated that BERT can handle negation, sarcasm, irony, and other linguistic phenomena that can affect the sentiment of the text, and proposed a method to enhance the sentiment representation of BERT using a sentiment lexicon.

2.2   Aspect-Based Sentiment Analysis

ABSA is a subtask of sentiment analysis that aims to identify the aspects or targets of an object and their opinion polarities. For example, given a review of a restaurant, ABSA can extract the aspects or targets, such as food, service, or price, and assign a sentiment polarity (positive, negative, or neutral) to each of them [13]. ABSA can be divided into multiple subtasks depending on the goal of the model: Aspect Extraction (AE), Aspect-based Opinion Extraction (AO), Aspect Term Sentiment Extraction (ATE), Aspect-Category Sentiment Extraction (ACES), Aspect-Sentiment(-Opinion) Triplet Extraction (ASOTE or ASTE), Aspect-Category-Opinion-Sentiment Quadruplet Extraction (ACOSE), Aspect-Oriented Sentiment Analysis (AOSA), Aspect-Level Sentiment Analysis (ALSA), Multi-Aspect Sentiment Analysis (MASA) [23]. Aspect extraction is the process of detecting and extracting the aspects or targets from a given text, while sentiment classification is the process of assigning a sentiment polarity to each extracted aspect or target [27]. From the techniques above we will focus our interest in ASTE and the generation of "triplets" (aspect, opinion, polarity) which we elaborate more in the next section.

BERT Models for ABSA. BERT and its variants have been used for both subtasks of ABSA, either as feature extractors or as end-to-end models. Sun, Huang, Qiu, and Dai (2019) [34] showed that BERT can improve the performance and the interpretability of ABSA, and outperform other models on four datasets from different domains, by using BERT as a feature extractor and constructing an auxiliary sentence for each aspect. Xu, Liu, Zhang, and Sun (2019) [37] showed that BERT can handle multiple aspects and targets of sentiment within the same input, and achieve state-of-the-art results on several ABSA datasets, by using BERT as an end-to-end model and adding a pointer network and a gate mechanism to the BERT encoder. However, using BERT models for ABSA has some risks for researchers as fine-tuning BERT requires a large amount of labelled data, which may not be available or sufficient for some ABSA domains or languages. Moreover, fine-tuning BERT may cause "catastrophic forgetting", which means that the model may lose its general knowledge and ability to perform other tasks after being adapted to a specific task [16].

Instruction-Based Models for ABSA. Because of the challenges that can be faced using the BERT models, some researchers have proposed to use of instruction-based models for ABSA, which can leverage the power of BERT and the flexibility of natural language instructions to perform various subtasks with minimal supervision and data. Instruction-based models are a type of few-shot learning methods that use natural language instructions to guide the model to perform a specific task. The instructions can be either predefined or learned from data. Instruction-based models have been applied to various ABSA subtasks [25,39]. In 2020, Wang et al. [36] proposed E2E-ABSA, a framework that uses manually designed instructions for ATE and ATSC while Scaria et al. (2023) [33] recently introduced InstructABSA, a paradigm that uses data-driven instructions for ABSA and its subtasks. Instruction-based models have shown competitive or superior performance to state-of-the-art supervised models on several ABSA benchmarks. However, they also face some challenges and limitations, such as the quality, diversity, and robustness of the instructions, the trade-off between instruction length and performance, and the generalization ability of the models across different domains and languages.

3   Research Method

Based on the literature review above, we understand that both types of ABSA models have their benefits and drawbacks in specific situations and we decided to explore the possibility of combining the outcomes of both approaches to confirm if our hypothesis of redounding with data of higher accuracy will be correct. The goal of this research is to propose a novel framework that combines both BERT and instruction-based models for analyzing user reviews and generating opinionated word conjunctions (triplets). The framework aims to address the challenges and limitations of the current methods and to improve the performance and the interpretability of user feedback analysis. The framework also aims to fine-tune the models for a domain-specific result.

3.1   Triplet Definition

Before we get into further detail on the data and our method, we first need to explain what we consider a triplet, as this term will be used significantly throughout this research. The clearest way to express our definition is with a simple example of manual Sentiment Analysis. Considering the sentence *The user interface is very nice*, we understand that the aspect of the sentence, meaning the attribute of a given more general concept [2], is the phrase *user interface*. Regarding this aspect, there is a sentimental term that describes it, we call it an opinion and in this example, it is the word *nice*. The aspect and the opinion are usually connected syntactically or semantically in a sentence [2]. The opinion, since it is an emotionally charged word or phrase has a sentiment polarity. The three options are positive, negative or neutral (if the phrase contains a balanced amount of emotionally charged words such as the opinion *not great*). In our example's case the opinion, *nice*, has *positive* sentiment polarity, thus we end up with the three-term combination for the sentence as demonstrated in Table 1.

Table 1. Example of a manual Aspect Sentiment Triplet Extraction (ASTE).

Sentence	Aspect	Opinion	Polarity
The user interface is very nice	user interface	nice	Positive

3.2   ABSA Model Selection

To approach our hypothesis of getting an enhanced ABSA tool by combining a BERT-based and an Instruction-based model, we have to sort and filter the available options. As we mentioned earlier, we aim to generate triplets and explore the State-of-the-art models in this topic. The Aspect Sentiment Triplet Extraction subtask of ABSA can offer the format that we want and multiple models on this subtask reportedly reach optimal scores for generic datasets [24]. We want to employ models that are trained with non-domain specific data to attempt to also fine-tune them with Android application reviews and compare which version provides higher accuracy results and better scores overall on our test data. Analyzing the public rankings for ABSA models [23], we focus on the ones that provide a pre-trained version from a Machine Learning Hub [7] or open-source models that we can have access to the code and the training checkpoints. For the BERT-based model, we decide to work on the ASTE feature of the PyABSA framework [40] that uses an enhanced version of pretrained bert and includes checkpoints for multiple non-domain specific trainings such as the SemEval 14 dataset [10]. On the other hand, for the instruction-based models, according to the same rankings as above, we conclude that the InstructABSA framework has the greater results in the ABSA scores and we can apply it for sentiment analysis since its ABSA model is available via huggingface. Unfortunately, after contacting the team behind this project, we can confirm that the ASTE version of this model is still under development and the training stage of the models was not available open-source. Nevertheless, we still believe that this framework can still offer a lot to our research. But since the ABSA model can only return doublets of aspect-polarity, as it cannot single out the opinionated term and draws the polarity from the context of the whole sentence related to the aspect [26], the use of InstructABSA will be only supplementary and advisory to the PyABSA framework.

3.3 Data Sampling

Since we want to analyze the reviews that users leave in the stores of applications, we attempt to use real data from actual application stores. Unfortunately, we were not able to use annotated data from related previous research works as most proclaimed datasets for ABSA-ASTE contained reviews from different topics [26, 27] which were not worth analyzing for our domain-specific goal. Given, also, the fact that the few datasets with mobile app reviews annotations [29] didn't offer the information (aspects, opinions, polarity) or a format that benefited the research we decided to generate our own data.

Google Play Scraper. Our initial goal was to use the sentiment analysis models to increase the User Feedback generated for a mobile application so it is important to deal with high-profile applications that have a great amount of users and, as a result, a variety of reviews we can sample from. With the use of a python library called google-play-scraper [17], we managed to scrape 3900 user reviews in total from 6 apps of 6 different Google categories of the Google Play Store. The reviews picked are the first 650 for each app, sorted by "most relevant" based on Google's algorithm about helpful reviews [30]. The selected applications along with the categories and amount of reviews are listed in Table 2.

The decision to retrieve data from apps that don't have a common goal was taken because we also wanted to investigate if the topic of the application is crucial for the model's results. We tried to get access to as many user reviews as possible to eliminate any doubt about not having enough data.

3.4 Data Processing

The collected data contain information about multiple aspects of each review in addition to its content, such as the review ID, the reviewer's username, the rating score (1 to 5), the date of the review, the version of the application when the review was made, and more. For the magnitude and the aim of this research, we only maintained for each review the name of the related application, the review ID and the content for analysis. We group the reviews by the name of the apps to separate them easily and we use the review ID to have a unique identification for each review since the content can be identical among user reviews. With these details, we generate the first version of our dataset containing 3900 rows (6 apps with 650 reviews each). Next, we are also going to process the text of the rows. A user review may contain more than one sentence and might evaluate multiple aspects in each sentence. To lower the complexity of each text sample for the ABSA models we split the reviews into full-stops, exclamation points and question marks. With this separation, we also increase the amount of different sentences we have and as a result the total of rows in the collective dataset. Finally, to have clear data to be read by the models, we pass the sentences through segmentation. That way the words are spaced from symbols and numbers that could be misinterpreted by the models.

Dataset Annotation. Having all the review sentences collected, we proceed to annotate the data with correct triplets, to be able to evaluate the results that the models will return. Given the fact that our research lab consists of people with expertise in extracting user feedback, the most optimal direction would be to manually analyze the reviews and annotate the dataset. But considering that we have access to pre-trained generic ABSA models we decided to do an AI-assisted annotation. We feed the review sentences to the PyABSA ASTE model and it returns the triplets that it found. We, then, collect the answers in a dataset and evaluate them manually, keeping the correct ones, removing the wrong ones, and adding some more correct answers that the model missed. That way, we get a first sight of what the chosen model is capable of, and in addition, the evaluation was less time and energy-consuming for our annotators as some of the answers are already filled by the model. During the manual annotation we also remove the sentences that contain no triplets at all, either because of no actual aspect, or no opinion regarding the aspect syntactically or semantically. The result of all the processing and filtering of the data is a new amount of annotated sentences for each of the selected applications. We now have almost double the amount of rows of the starting dataset and the exact values can be compared in Table 2.

Table 2. Selected Android Applications with Google Play Store ID, categories, scraped reviews, and final annotated sentences.

Application	Google AppID	Google Category	Reviews	Sentences
Uber Eats	com.ubercab.eats	Food Delivery	650	1471
Amazon Shopping	com.amazon.mShop .android.shopping	Product Shopping	650	1196
Netflix	com.netflix.mediaclient	Streaming Service	650	1249
Duolingo	com.duolingo	Education	650	1536
Any.do	com.anydo	Productivity	650	1433
Booking.com	com.booking	Travel	650	995

3.5 Training and Testing

Before we present the methodology we follow, we explain how we distributed the data respectively. The dataset of Booking.com will be destined for testing as it is the smallest one and the review sentences of the remaining five applications are registered for training.

Training Stage. Setting up and training the PyABSA ASTE model is quite demanding as the framework requires a specific and detailed way to organize the data for the training of the models with dataset folders following specific rules [40]. We pick the ASTE model from an already trained checkpoint called "English" [40]. The data had to be split into three simple Text files one for training, one for validating, and one for testing. In our case, the train and validation files will contain data from the testing app, as they need to be related [6], while the test file will contain data from the Booking.com reviews. Also, these text files must contain the annotations in a strict indexing format. Using the earlier triplet example from Table 1 we show how the format of each sentence must be:

The user interface is very nice .####[([1, 2], [5], 'POS')]

After fulfilling all the requirements, we train the ASTE model with our converted data. We let the model run through each application's dataset for 10 epochs thrice, we compare the F1 scores and keep the generated checkpoint of the highest one. After running each app separately we also run all five training app datasets together as a greater "Play Store bundle" in an attempt to fine-tune the pre-trained model with a massive amount of sentences compared to the previous approaches to investigate what results such an increase in the dataset rows will have.

Testing Stage. The trained models are tested on the Booking.com dataset and their F1 scores are compared to the score of the pre-trained model (English checkpoint). The testing dataset will be split into 2 parts to be proportional to the training sets. The first part with 480 sentences is added during the training as the file on which the model is tested after training and validation. Judging how the models will behave in the first testing part will affect the strictness regarding the semantic connections in the annotation of the second part with the remaining 515 sentences. Meanwhile, to support the greater goal of the research which is the increment of User Feedback, we collect the triplets that the models generate for the testing data and we evaluate their utility towards the maintenance and improvement of the testing app.

4 Results and Discussion

4.1 PyABSA Results

We collect and analyze the F1 scores after training and testing the ASTE model in multiple apps to see the effect of the domain-specific context in obtaining the correct triplets and also train it. The model is trained on each of the 5 training apps separately and also on all of them together. As we can see in Table 3 the models tested on the two Booking datasets are the pre-trained ASTE model from PyABSA, the five separately trained models for each app, and the model trained on all the apps together.

Testing Dataset Part 1. The results of the first attempt to test the performance of our fine-tuning didn't go as expected with the original pre-trained model outperforming the rest by a great margin. Analyzing further the F1 scores we notice that the score of the Play Store bundle, which contained all the smaller training datasets ranked second by a significant range outperforming the separately trained models which have closer scores to each other. An interesting point on these scores is the fact that their ranking in this test is almost equivalent to their ranking in the amount of sentences each training dataset has. We believe that this analogy is relevant as it seems like the more training sentences a model has the better it performs to the testing. Unfortunately, even the bundled model with the sentences of all the apps couldn't compete with the original ASTE model which has been trained on all Laptop and Restaurant SemEval datasets [27]. Even if the most evident reason behind these results might be the unsatisfying amount of training data, we also want to investigate further the nature of the results given by the models. We notice that the precision of the pre-trained ASTE model is lower on our testing data than on the reported benchmarks of the model's documentation [40]. After analyzing the results, we detected a lot of "False-positive" triplets, meaning triplets that the model found but were not in the annotations. Our opinion is that the pre-trained model relies a lot on the semantic connection between aspects and opinions and attempts to suggest triplets that match all the aspects with all the opinions of a sentence, which is not a fact.

Testing Dataset Part 2. To explore further the above case, we decided to re-annotate the second part of the Booking dataset more strictly, based mainly on the syntactic connections between aspects and opinions and less on the semantic ones. After that, we apply all the models to the dataset and collect the new F1 scores. As expected the original ASTE model scores notably lower in this set than the previous one and since the rest of the models are fine-tuned versions of it, they also score lower than their first test. Although not better, the "Play Store bundle" model seems to have a lower rate of decrease in its F1 score between the two tests than the pre-trained model, which might be a positive point for the fine-tuning process.

Table 3. Testing results for each model version sorted by the F1-scores of the Booking dataset part 1.

Model version	Sentences	Booking part 1	Booking part 2
pretrained (English checkpoint)	unknown	0.7985	0.6440
Play Store bundle	6885	0.6713	0.5711
Duolingo	1536	0.6137	0.5203
Any.do	1433	0.6119	0.5156
Uber Eats	1471	0.6006	0.5354
Netflix	1249	0.5798	0.5366
Amazon Shopping	1196	0.5797	0.5417

4.2   Discussion

Based on the results presented, we believe that if the whole annotation process of our data sentences was similar to the Booking dataset part 2 then both the training and the testing stage outcomes would improve. Furthermore, even if the manual annotation proved to be a massively time-consuming task for our team, an even bigger dataset for fine-tuning with more review sentences could provide better results and a clearer view of the potential that a domain-specific ABSA model has.

Overall Review. Regardless of the results that the fine-tuning produced, our statement about automating and accelerating User Experience Feedback through the ABSA method still stands. The triplets that come out of the ASTE model are stored in dataset files with the original review ID, app name, and review content. Every term in the dataset rows is utilizable for further analysis and at this part, we have enough data to experiment with the multiple options of harnessing the triplets, either as a whole or each term independently. The first action we take is to use the instruction-based ABSA model, InstructABSA, that we introduced earlier and reportedly scores higher on aspect-polarity doublets, to filter out the triplets that seem debatable between the two models. We do this by running the review sentences through the InstructABSA model and collecting its doublets. After that, we match the aspects from the two models referring to the same review sentence and see if their polarities match too. We suggest this method as both models are arguably well-performing but when handling Big Data mistakes may come up. With this filtering action, the final data will be more error-proofed. The next action we do is not related to the collection of the data but to their presentation. Most of the triplets might not be useful for the developers aiming to rectify the application that is set for analysis, so we have to keep the range of the aspects presented to the developers focused on topics about the application. This is possible through Topic Modeling which, as we mentioned before, locates themes and areas of interest on text samples. Apart from applying the LDA topic modeling method to the review sentences, we experiment with extracting topics from the official description of the Google Application too. For each topic, LDA lists some aspects detected in the text samples. Both the number of topics and aspects per topic are customizable and our suggestions are getting 1 or 2 topics from the application's description and 2 to 3 topics from the reviews with 5 aspects per topic. A simplified alternative to this is by using the "Term Frequency - Inverse Document Frequency" (TF-IDF) measure method [28] but while this guarantees that we receive the most important terms in the set, it does not provide the concept of grouping and relation to a specific topic as LDA does.

Framework Configuration. Following these processing methods preferably in the said order, we compose the framework that we aim to promote as the optimal way of acquiring feedback data from user reviews. The premise is a tool that receives a Google application ID, proceeds to scrape the 5000 most relevant reviews if available, refines the reviews and runs them through the ABSA models, then filters the results and presents the most applicable to the user of the tool. The framework can also provide statistics about the final aspects and opinions, such as ranking of aspect occurrences in the whole dataset, most

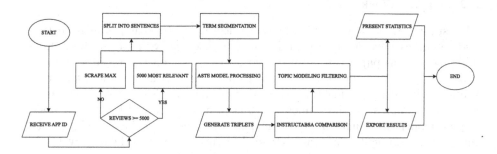

Fig. 1. Flowchart of the framework with the steps of the process

common negative opinions, etc. All steps are optional depending on the user's intentions and a detailed flowchart of the framework is depicted in Fig. 1.

5 Conclusion

Summing up, we believe that our research as an input in this field has a valid stand and provides qualities that can be utilized both in academic and industrial territories. Our attempt for a domain-specific ABSA model on Mobile user Reviews has the potential to offer higher scores than its generic counterpart but in our time and situation, we were not able to prove it. On the other hand, the guidelines we suggest for a user feedback analysis framework that can be adapted to a digital tool are supported by the literature review presented. The environment of this research is dedicated to accelerating the communication between mobile app developers and their user base but this framework is highly encouraged to be used also by everyone interested in domain-specific sentiment data about an application. It is structured in a flexible system to be embraced effortlessly by the User Experience community.

5.1 Limitations

Arguably there were a few constraints in our research because of the nature of this field [18]. A primary setback has been the fact that our selection of the focused models for the research was more limited than expected because we never aimed our study to include building an ASTE model but rather fine-tuning the State-of-the-Art models available. In addition to this, we didn't expect finding a proper open-source pre-trained model for this use to be the challenge that it turned to, costing the team time and resources. Finally, while we tried to optimize the manual annotation process as much as possible, this part of the research proved to be time-consuming, as evaluating 3900 reviews was a massive process motivated by our need for a secure amount of data, which judging from our results was a justified decision.

5.2 Future Work

This study was structured as a Master's degree level research and both time and resources were of equivalent magnitude. We believe that the limitations addressed in this paper can be surpassed if the research is continued at a higher academic level. We aim to insist on developing the domain-specific attribute of the system and improving the fine-tuning of the models. Moreover, our main target is to implement the framework concept as a functional UX tool to assist app developers in visualizing and analyzing User Feedback. Meanwhile, we also intend to experiment with some extended features related to the current result. One approach we want to handle is accessing also Apple App Store user reviews, to increase the variety of the sample and of course, cover more potential corrections and improvements. Another direction that also interests us is investigating models that provide more complex sentiment information about a sentence than our current triplet format, such as detecting sarcasm, categorizing the aspect and more. We are confident that our research and the proposed directions for future work can significantly contribute to the advancement of ABSA and the enhancement of the Mobile App User Experience.

Acknowledgments. This research has been co-financed by the European Union and Greek national funds through the Regional Operational Program "ATTICA 2014–2020" of the National Strategic Reference Framework (NSRF) - Research Funding Program: Smart Tourism Recommendations based on Efficient Knowledge Mining on Online Platforms-ATTP4-0349847.

References

1. Anastasiei, I.D., Georgescu, M.R., Cuza, A.I.: Automated vs manual content analysis—a retrospective look. Sci. Ann. Econ. Bus. **67**(SI), 57–67 (2020). https://doi.org/10.47743/saeb-2020-0025
2. Augustyniak, Ł, Kajdanowicz, T., Kazienko, P.: Comprehensive analysis of aspect term extraction methods using various text embeddings. Comput. Speech Lang. **69**, 101217 (2021). https://doi.org/10.1016/j.csl.2021.101217
3. Dalpiaz, F., Sturm, A.: Conceptualizing requirements using user stories and use cases: a controlled experiment. In: Madhavji, N., Pasquale, L., Ferrari, A., Gnesi, S. (eds.) REFSQ 2020. LNCS, vol. 12045, pp. 221–238. Springer, Cham (2020). https://doi.org/10.1007/978-3-030-44429-7_16
4. Devlin, J., Chang, M.W., Lee, K., Toutanova, K.: BERT: pre-training of deep bidirectional transformers for language understanding, May 2019. https://doi.org/10.48550/arXiv.1810.04805
5. Fernandez, C.: The paradox of choice: why more is less. Vikalpa **42**(4), 265–267 (2017). https://doi.org/10.1177/0256090917732442
6. Hastie, T., Tibshirani, R., Friedman, J.: Model assessment and selection. In: Hastie, T., Tibshirani, R., Friedman, J. (eds.) The Elements of Statistical Learning: Data Mining, Inference, and Prediction, pp. 219–259. Springer Series in Statistics. Springer, Cham (2009). https://doi.org/10.1007/978-0-387-84858-7_7
7. Hugging Face: Models, December 2023. https://huggingface.co/models
8. Jelodar, H., et al.: Latent Dirichlet Allocation (LDA) and topic modeling: models, applications, a survey, December 2018
9. Kim, Y.: Convolutional neural networks for sentence classification, September 2014. https://doi.org/10.48550/arXiv.1408.5882
10. Kirange, D.K., Deshmukh, R.R.: Emotion classification of restaurant and laptop review dataset: SemEval 2014 Task 4. Int. J. Comput. Appl. **113**(6), 17–20 (2015). https://doi.org/10.5120/19829-1680
11. Li, C., Xu, B., Wu, G., He, S., Tian, G., Hao, H.: Recursive deep learning for sentiment analysis over social data. In: 2014 IEEE/WIC/ACM International Joint Conferences on Web Intelligence (WI) and Intelligent Agent Technologies (IAT), vol. 2, pp. 180–185, August 2014. https://doi.org/10.1109/WI-IAT.2014.96
12. Liang, T.P., Li, X., Yang, C.T., Wang, M.: What in consumer reviews affects the sales of mobile apps: a multifacet sentiment analysis approach. Int. J. Electron. Commer. **20**(2), 236–260 (2015). https://doi.org/10.1080/10864415.2016.1087823

13. Liu, B.: Sentiment Analysis and Opinion Mining. Synthesis Lectures on Human Language Technologies. Springer, Cham (2012). https://doi.org/10.1007/978-3-031-02145-9

14. Liu, Y., et al.: RoBERTa: a robustly optimized BERT pretraining approach, July 2019. https://doi.org/10.48550/arXiv.1907.11692

15. López, M.I.C., Cervantes, A.L.E., Martínez, G.d.l.C., Arjona, J.L.O.: Agile, user-centered design and quality in software processes for mobile application development teaching. Int. J. Softw. Eng. Appl. **14**(5), 01–17 (2023). https://doi.org/10.5121/ijsea.2023.14501

16. McCloskey, M., Cohen, N.J.: Catastrophic interference in connectionist networks: the sequential learning problem. In: Bower, G.H. (ed.) Psychology of Learning and Motivation, vol. 24, pp. 109–165. Academic Press, January 1989. https://doi.org/10.1016/S0079-7421(08)60536-8

17. Mingyu, J.: Google Play Scraper for Python, January 2024

18. Nazir, A., Rao, Y., Wu, L., Sun, L.: Issues and challenges of aspect-based sentiment analysis: a comprehensive survey. IEEE Trans. Affect. Comput. **13**(2), 845–863 (2022). https://doi.org/10.1109/TAFFC.2020.2970399

19. Noei, E., Zhang, F., Zou, Y.: Too many user-reviews! What should app developers look at first? IEEE Trans. Software Eng. **47**(2), 367–378 (2021). https://doi.org/10.1109/TSE.2019.2893171

20. Norman, D.A.: The Design of Everyday Things. MIT Press, Cambridge (2013)

21. Palomba, F., et al.: User reviews matter! Tracking crowdsourced reviews to support evolution of successful apps. In: 2015 IEEE International Conference on Software Maintenance and Evolution (ICSME), pp. 291–300, September 2015. https://doi.org/10.1109/ICSM.2015.7332475

22. Pang, B., Lee, L., Vaithyanathan, S.: Thumbs up? Sentiment Classification using Machine Learning Techniques, May 2002

23. Papers with Code: Aspect-Based Sentiment Analysis (ABSA). https://paperswithcode.com/task/aspect-based-sentiment-analysis

24. Papers with Code: ASTE Benchmark (Aspect-Based Sentiment Analysis (ABSA)). https://paperswithcode.com/sota/aspect-based-sentiment-analysis-absa-on-aste

25. Peng, B., et al.: Few-shot natural language generation for task-oriented dialog, February 2020. https://doi.org/10.48550/arXiv.2002.12328

26. Peng, H., Xu, L., Bing, L., Huang, F., Lu, W., Si, L.: Knowing what, how and why: a near complete solution for aspect-based sentiment analysis. Proc. AAAI Conf. Artif. Intell. **34**(05), 8600–8607 (2020). https://doi.org/10.1609/aaai.v34i05.6383

27. Pontiki, M., Galanis, D., Pavlopoulos, J., Papageorgiou, H., Androutsopoulos, I., Manandhar, S.: SemEval-2014 Task 4: aspect based sentiment analysis. In: Nakov, P., Zesch, T. (eds.) Proceedings of the 8th International Workshop on Semantic Evaluation (SemEval 2014), pp. 27–35. Association for Computational Linguistics, Dublin, Ireland, August 2014. https://doi.org/10.3115/v1/S14-2004

28. Rajaraman, A., Ullman, J.D.: Data mining. In: Mining of Massive Datasets, pp. 1–17. Cambridge University Press, October 2011. https://doi.org/10.1017/CBO9781139058452.002

29. Rathi, P.: Google Play Store Reviews (2021). https://www.kaggle.com/datasets/prakharrathi25/google-play-store-reviews

30. razorclicks: The Top 5 Factors for a Review to be marked Most Relevant|Local Reviews, June 2019. https://localsearchforum.com/threads/the-top-5-factors-for-a-review-to-be-marked-most-relevant.54376/

31. Sällberg, H., Wang, S., Numminen, E.: The combinatory role of online ratings and reviews in mobile app downloads: an empirical investigation of gaming and productivity apps from their initial app store launch. J. Mark. Analytics **11**(3), 426–442 (2023). https://doi.org/10.1057/s41270-022-00171-w

32. Sanh, V., Debut, L., Chaumond, J., Wolf, T.: DistilBERT, a distilled version of BERT: smaller, faster, cheaper and lighter, February 2020. https://doi.org/10.48550/arXiv.1910.01108

33. Scaria, K., Gupta, H., Goyal, S., Sawant, S.A., Mishra, S., Baral, C.: InstructABSA: instruction learning for aspect based sentiment analysis, November 2023. https://doi.org/10.48550/arXiv.2302.08624

34. Sun, C., Huang, L., Qiu, X.: Utilizing BERT for aspect-based sentiment analysis via constructing auxiliary sentence, March 2019. https://doi.org/10.48550/arXiv.1903.09588

35. van Oordt, S., Guzman, E.: On the role of user feedback in software evolution: a practitioners' perspective. In: 2021 IEEE 29th International Requirements Engineering Conference (RE), pp. 221–232, September 2021. https://doi.org/10.1109/RE51729.2021.00027

36. Wang, X., Xu, G., Zhang, Z., Jin, L., Sun, X.: End-to-end aspect-based sentiment analysis with hierarchical multi-task learning. Neurocomputing **455**, 178–188 (2021). https://doi.org/10.1016/j.neucom.2021.03.100

37. Xu, H., Liu, B., Shu, L., Yu, P.S.: BERT post-training for review reading comprehension and aspect-based sentiment analysis, May 2019. https://doi.org/10.48550/arXiv.1904.02232

38. Yang, A., et al.: Enhancing pre-trained language representations with rich knowledge for machine reading comprehension. In: Korhonen, A., Traum, D., Màrquez, L. (eds.) Proceedings of the 57th Annual Meeting of the Association for Computational Linguistics, pp. 2346–2357. Association for Computational Linguistics, Florence, Italy, July 2019. https://doi.org/10.18653/v1/P19-1226

39. Yang, C., Zhang, H., Jiang, B., Li, K.: Aspect-based sentiment analysis with alternating coattention networks. Inf. Process. Manage. **56**(3), 463–478 (2019). https://doi.org/10.1016/j.ipm.2018.12.004

40. Yang, H., Zhang, C., Li, K.: PyABSA: a modularized framework for reproducible aspect-based sentiment analysis, August 2023

The Differences of Choice Preference on WeChat Mini Program and Native Apps Between Utilitarian and Hedonic Programs

Fei Chen[✉]

College of Business Administration, Ningbo University of Finance and Economics (NBUFE),
Ningbo, China
chenfei@nbufe.edu.cn

Abstract. In the realm of mobile internet, as products and services become increasingly homogenized, user experience has emerged as a pivotal factor in product success. User experience is an activity involving user participation, stimulating emotional responses, forming perceptions, and ultimately influencing consumer behavior. The current research conducts a quantitative analysis of consumer behavior to specifically examine the role of user experience in the selection of native Apps and WeChat Mini Program. We verified the selection differences between hedonic and utilitarian mobile internet products. The findings reveal significant differences in interaction and functional experience-based choices between these two categories of programs depends on the product types (hedonic vs. utilitarian), while differences in visual experience are not pronounced. This discovery offers valuable strategic guidance for mobile internet enterprises, especially in enhancing user experience. Furthermore, it provides a novel perspective and empirical support for academic research in related fields.

Keywords: Mobile · internet · User experience · Hedonic products · Utilitarian products · Consumer behavior

1 Introduction

With the increased usage of smartphones and wearable devices, a variety of mobile applications (commonly referred to as apps) have arisen (Gera et al., 2020; Kim et al., 2016). Which have brought human high-profile convenience in their daily lives. Over the past decades, the growing usage in mobile applicants has spurred extensive research interests among scholars (Ali et al., 2023; Hew et al., 2015; Khan et al., 2023; Linnhoff and Smith, 2017; Meena and Sarabhai, 2023). WeChat Mini Programs were officially launched on January 9, 2017, and at that time, they were still in their infancy compared to native apps. However, in the short time since their launch, these Mini Programs have made a significant impact (Cheng et al., 2019; Staykova and Damsgaard, 2016). Unlike native apps, WeChat Mini Programs do not require installation or uninstallation, are instantly accessible, and meet the immediate needs of users perfectly, which led to their rapid spread in people's daily lives (Bresnahan et al., 2014; Tilson et al., 2012; Tiwana,

2015; Yang et al., 2016). On the first anniversary of its public testing, the "2017–2018 WeChat Mini Program Market Development Research Report" indicated that, after just one year of development, the monetization potential of WeChat Mini Programs became evident, with the monthly revenue growth of Mini Programs in both retail e-commerce and the catering industry exceeding 60% in August 2017 (Cheng et al., 2019; Hao et al., 2018). Such rapid development pace raises questions: Will users gradually shift towards WeChat Mini Programs? Will native apps continue to be favored by users?

The current research aims to answer those important yet unclear questions. More specifically, based on the user experience theory, we try to reveal consumers' choice intention between native apps and WeChat Mini programs when they faced with different program types (hedonic vs. utilitarian). Furthermore, we analyze the extent to which different factors in user experience influence the choice of program types.

The rest part of this research is structured as follows: in the second part, we discuss the key theories that related to this research in theorical backgrounds. Then, we expound our research methodology and illustrate the results of our research, followed by a discussion of the findings and their implications.

2 Theorical Backgrounds

2.1 User Experience Theory

User experience has induced considerable debate among scholar trying to define it (Jay, 2005). Comparing to the knowledge consumers gained through consumption, user experience is described as meaningful and unforgettable event consumers encountered during their consumption (Forlizzi and Battarbee, 2004; Kahneman et al., 1999). User experience encompasses various aspects, including beauty, emotion, affective or feeling. It has been imbued with many meanings (Forlizzi and Battarbee, 2004). An interesting phenomenon: the user experience is widely adopted into human-computer interaction (HCI) by many scholars and practitioners. It might be the fact that HCI related researchers have found the limitation of traditional usability framework, which basically focused on the performance and efficiency in human-machine interactions (Law et al., 2009). However, user experience emphasizes none of such aspect, and targeting on users' feeling, emotion, meaning, opinion etc. feedback of such interactions. Consequently, this line of researches arisen during past decades (Bate and Robert, 2023; Fahrudin and Wahyudi, 2023; Hassenzahl, 2018; Wright et al., 2003).

Subsequently, user experience was widely applied in fields such as medicine, marketing, and consumer behavior, becoming a commonly used term in everyday vocabulary. In this context, (Japutra and Song, 2020) aimed to explain the mechanism by which user experience through retailer applications lead to loyalty towards the retailer. Perceived value mediated the impact of customer experience on satisfaction and loyalty to the retailer applications. (Qin et al., 2021) and colleagues investigated the impact of mobile augmented reality applications on user attitudes and shopping behaviors. In their empirical research, they delved into user experience and examined its effect on consumers' perceptions of both hedonic and utilitarian satisfaction, the amount of information, and perceived ease of use. In a related study, Jin Ming (2022) focused on vocational education apps, arguing that their goal-oriented, real-time online nature, and resource integration significantly shape user experience. This led to the identification of three distinct dimensions of user experience in these apps: visual experience, functional experience, and interaction experience.

2.2 Hedonic vs. Utilitarian Product

To explain the reference effects from product types, we first introduce two distinctive consumption types: hedonic consumption and utilitarian consumption (Batra and Ahtola, 1991). The preference in hedonic product consumption is often marked by a multi-sensory, emotive experience that encompasses elements such as flavor, auditory sensations, aromas, tactile feedback, and visual stimuli, predominantly leaning towards subjective rather than objective description (Hirschman and Holbrook, 1982). While utilitarian consumption refers to consumptions that are more cognitively driven. Consumers pay more attention to products' actual functionality and value to fulfill some particular goal or task (Dhar and Wertenbroch, 2000). More specifically, Utilitarian products primarily satisfy consumers' basic needs or functional benefits, whereas hedonic products offer emotional or other sensory experiences, providing value through the experience or emotional resonance derived from the product itself. Consequently, consumer preferences for hedonic products can vary significantly due to various subjective criteria. In contrast, preferences for utilitarian products tend to be more homogeneous, as they are often based on objective standards.

According to (Varshney and Vetter, 2000) research, the users of mobile devices believe that technology satisfies their purpose in different dimensions. Mobile devices provide consumers with utilitarian functions such as distance education, medical and shopping. As well deliver new services to individuals such as entertainment, communication and music on demand (Wakefield and Whitten, 2006). Thus, mobile devices provide consumers with utilitarian and hedonic value depending on their app types (Chang et al., 2023; Hu et al., 2023; Rodríguez-Ardura et al., 2023).

In current research, WeChat Mini Programs and mobile applications are categorized by product type into utilitarian and hedonic applications; utilitarian apps are akin to DiDi (ride-hailing), JD.com (shopping), and Ctrip (travel services), while hedonic apps resemble games like Happy Landlord, Candy Crush Saga, and Sheep Game. In this context, we explore user preferences for different app types of WeChat Mini Programs and native mobile applications across three dimensions of user experience, to ascertain whether users lean more towards WeChat Mini Programs or native mobile applications.

2.3 Consumer Preference Theory

Preference is a fundamental concept in modern microeconomic value theory and consumer behavior theory (Drakopoulos, 1992). It is manifested as the ordinal relation of consumption choices with a tendency. Evidently, preference is subjective and relative (Brown-Iannuzzi et al., 2015; Crettaz and Suter, 2013; Frey and Stutzer, 1999). It is defined and interpreted differently across various disciplines. Hoeffler and Ariely (1999) assessed the consumer learning process, or the preference stabilization process, from two perspectives: revealed preferences and stated preferences. When consumers first enter a new domain, they construct their preferences, which then stabilize with the accumulation of experience in that field. In consumer behavior research, preference is used to reveal the consumer's choice of a certain product or service (Font-i-Furnols and Guerrero, 2014; Govers and Schoormans, 2005). Based on the study of attitudes, Cai Pei (2009) defined preference according to the "tri-component" theory of attitude as cognitive preference, affective preference, and behavioral intention preference. Cognitive preference refers to preferences based on the thoughts and beliefs about the attributes of the attitude object; affective preference, which is formed based on feelings and values rather than the pros and cons of an object, is known as affective preference; behavioral intention preference, based on behavior, generally refers to the potential actions and tendencies an individual takes toward the attitude object.

Based on the connotation and definition of preference. Preference in current research refers to the consumers' attitudinal and actual usage tendencies between choosing WeChat Mini Programs or native mobile applications based on user experience.

3   Research Methodology

3.1 Overview of Current Research

Current research believes that consumers' mobile apps preference (WeChat Mini Programs vs. native mobile applications) depends on the app types (Hedonic vs. Utilitarian). In hits context, based on the user experience theory, the dimensions of consumer experience determine their overall perception and satisfaction with the apps, and thereby influence their final choice.

Study Design. In order to verify our hypotheses, current research takes a post-hoc evaluation (Miltenberger et al., 2003). More specifically, the study is a 2 (app types: Hedonic vs. Utilitarian) between-subjects design. In hedonic/utilitarian questionnaire, when participants are going to play Happy Landlord, or Candy Crush Saga/book a flight ticket with Ctrip or shopping clothes with JD.com, they were asked to indicate their app types of preference with a 4-item scale developed by Hein et al. (2008). Then, participants were asked to indicate their experiences about the previous choice making. In this part, the user experience was measured by a 12-items scale developed by Jin Ming (2022). Among the 12 items, four of them were used to measure visual experience, four of them were used to measure functional experience, and four of them were used to measure interaction experience.

Participants. The study was conducted online with the samples of netizen who show reliance on mobile device. 300 questionnaires were delivered to them, and 279 of them were finally collected with an effective response rate of 93%. All of them are used to process the current research analysis.

4 Results

4.1 Demographic Analysis Results

Among the total 279 questionnaires, 53.8% (N = 150) of them are female and 46.2% (N = 129) of them are male. Besides, 48.2% of them were aged between 21–30 years old, 34.4% of them were 31–40 years old and 17.6% of them were over 40 years old. More details are shown as bellow in Table 1.

Table 1. Demographic Analysis Results

variable		Frequency	Percentage%
Gender	Male	129	46.2
	Female	150	53.8
Age(years)	21–30	135	48.4
	31–40	96	34.4
	Over 40	48	17.2
Educational background	Junior high and below	91	32.6
	High school	90	32.3
	College and above	98	35.1
Household incomes	Below 4000RMB	20	7.2
	4000–7000RMB	53	18.9
	7000–10000RMB	124	44.5
	Above 10000RMB	82	29.4

4.2 Reliability and Validity

We use we statistical product service solutions 22.0 and Amos to verify the reliability and validity of constructs of current research, the results was shown in detail as seen in Table 2. All Cronbach's α are above 0.7 refer a good internal consistency among those constructs. The average variance extracted (AVE) are above 0.5, which means that the metrics in the construct are consistent in measuring the same concept. Composite Reliability (CR) are above 0.8, which means indicators within a construct have a high degree of consistency in measuring the same concept. Besides, as shown in Table 3. by comparing the squared values of the correlations between the constructs with the AVE values, it was identified that all AVE values were higher, thereby demonstrating discriminant validity among the constructs.

4.3 Main Verification

Additionally, a fundamental analysis was conducted using the ANOVA program in SPSS 22.0 to examine the differences between the WeChat Mini Program group and

Table 2. Measurement of constructs

Constructs	Items	Component				Cronbach'sα	CR	AVE
		1	2	3	4			
Functional Experience	FE1	.027	.992	.005	.051	.850	.858	.607
	FE2	.115	.772	.065	.059			
	FE3	.094	.778	.139	.115			
	FE4	.109	.801	.071	.030			
Interaction Experience	IE1	.078	.045	.912	.097	.833	.846	.585
	IE2	.168	.128	.767	.071			
	IE3	.115	.067	.741	.086			
	IE4	.036	.032	.786	.136			
Visual Experience	VE1	.912	.044	.048	.048	.826	.833	.557
	VE2	.822	.052	.052	.114			
	VE3	.790	.158	.097	.049			
	VE4	.763	.111	.222	.014			
Choice Preference	CP1	−.022	−.020	.038	.904	.857	.863	.614
	CP2	.085	.154	.195	.746			
	CP3	−.001	.083	.055	.788			
	CP4	.171	.041	.117	.755			

Table 3. Correlation between constitute concepts

	Functional Experience	Interaction Experience	Choice Preference	Visual Experience
Functional Experience	.607			
Interaction Experience	.173**	.585		
Choice Preference	.215**	.249**	.614	
Visual Experience	.161**	.246**	.151*	.557

the native app group in terms of visual experience, functional experience, and inter-action experience. The results, as presented in Table 4, indicate that, except for visual experience, significant differences were observed at the 5% significance level for the other dimensions.

Table 4. Table of Between-Group Differences Analysis

Group	Average (Standard Deviation)		
	visual experience	functional experience	interaction experience
Native App Group (148)	4.1689 (1.16249)	3.7044 (1.34847)	3.7669 (1.27063)
WeChat Mini Program Group (131)	4.4504 (1.29586)	4.2156 (1.27504)	4.3168 (1.31040)
Mean Difference Analysis	F (1,277) = 1.077, P > 0.1	F (1,277) = 0.883, P < 0.05	F (1,277) = 0.195, P < 0.00

Lastly, regression analysis was conducted to examine the different effects of visual experience, functional experience, and interaction experience on choice preferences between the WeChat Mini Program group and the native app group. As shown in Table 5. The regression equation of Native App Group is $Y = 0.181X1 + 0.228X2 + 0.096X3 + 2.482$ indicated visual experience, functional experience, and interaction experience had a positive effect on choice preference, $R2 = 0.636$ indicated a good explanation of choice preference. At the same time, the regression equation of WeChat Mini Program group is $Y = 0.206X1 + 0.271X2 + 0.096X3 + 4.463$ indicated visual experience, functional experience, and interaction experience had a positive effect on choice preference, $R2 = 0.701$ indicated a good explanation of choice preference.

Table 5. Comprehensive Table of Regression Model Results

Group						Statistical Indicators of the Model		
		B	SE	t	P	F	P	R^2
Native App Group	constant	2.482	0.353	7.037	.000	5.827	0.015	0.636
	functional experience(X1)	0.181	0.060	3.034	.003			
	interaction experience(X2)	0.228	0.061	3.757	.000			
	visual experience(X3)	0.096	0.041	2.330	.020			
WeChat Mini Program Group	constant	4.463	0.237	18.802	.000	3.642	0.003	0.701
	functional experience(X1)	0.206	0.076	2.754	.000			
	interaction experience(X2)	0.271	.041	6.609	.015			
	visual experience(X3)	0.096	0.039	2.462	0.00			

5   Discussion

With the development of technology, the emergence of mobile devices has brought great convenience to people's lives (Kane et al., 2009). This includes a range of utilitarian functions such as education (Dashtestani, 2016), security (Souppaya and Scarfone, 2013), academic (Qi, 2019), healthcare (Vrhovec, 2016), as well as entertainment functions like game (Ramírez-Correa et al., 2019), music (Krause et al., 2015). Many applications of mobile and wearable devices are developed to adapt those functions. Under this circumstance, the current research was designed to conduct the difference of user experience between the WeChat Mini Program group and the native app group when consumer use either utilitarian or hedonic applications. The contributions of current research are as follows.

First, the current research focuses on mobile devices related to applications by discovering usage preferences. Which makes significant contribution to mobile devices literature. With more and more attention are paid to mobile devices (Amatya and Kurti, 2014; Dunaway et al., 2018; Gavalas and Economou, 2010), research is still needed to discover the mechanisms between mobile device usage and consumers. The current research reveals the choice preferences between the WeChat Mini Program group and the native app group by dividing applications into utilitarian and hedonic type. To data, most scholars pay much attention to WeChat Mini Program itself by exploring its development (Hao et al., 2018), and usage in different areas (Cheng et al., 2019; Wan et al., 2019; Zhang et al., 2021). Only Ryu et al. (2022) has studied the value perception between WeChat Mini Program and the native app by exploring user perceived value. Seldom study has combined WeChat Mini Program and the native app together to process a horizontal comparison study. The current research addresses this gap by using a post-hoc evaluation (Miltenberger et al., 2003).

Furthermore, the results of current research also have great implications for technical developer, enterprises and businessman. Firstly, technical developer and enterprises should acknowledge the shortcoming in their applications. And aware influence of WeChat Mini Program on native apps. According to our research, consumers' choice preference on WeChat Mini Program is significantly due to their performance in functional and interaction experience. While visual experience has similarly impact when choosing both type of applications. Besides, businessman can carry out reasonable advertising strategy and commercial layout by familiar with consumers' choice preference and habits.

6   Limitations and Future Research Directions

The current research is subject to some limitations. First, the research adopted only a post-hoc evaluation method to verify users experience about WeChat Mini Program and native apps. Which might lead to a result bias. A pre-hoc evaluation method should be also adopted simultaneously to eliminate this potential bias. Besides, all variables related to current research was measured by a self-reported questionnaire, which might contain participants subjective bias although it has been not founded. Lastly, the sample of current research only includes 279. Expanding the sample size may lead to differences in the results and can increase the credibility of the outcomes.

References

Ali, A., Hameed, A., Moin, M.F., Khan, N.A.: Exploring factors affecting mobile-banking app adoption: a perspective from adaptive structuration theory. Aslib J. Inf. Manag. **75**(4), 773–795 (2023)

Amatya, S., Kurti, A.: Cross-platform mobile development: challenges and opportunities. In: ICT Innovations 2013: ICT Innovations and Education, pp. 219–229 (2014)

Bate, P., Robert, G.: Bringing User Experience to Healthcare Improvement: the Concepts, Methods and Practices of Experience-Based Design. CRC Press, Boca Raton (2023)

Batra, R., Ahtola, O.T.: Measuring the hedonic and utilitarian sources of consumer attitudes. Mark. Lett. **2**, 159–170 (1991)

Bresnahan, T.F., Davis, J.P., Yin, P.-L.: Economic value creation in mobile applications. In: The Changing Frontier: Rethinking Science and Innovation Policy, pp. 233–286. University of Chicago Press, Chicago (2014)

Brown-Iannuzzi, J.L., Lundberg, K.B., Kay, A.C., Payne, B.K.: Subjective status shapes political preferences. Psychol. Sci. **26**(1), 15–26 (2015)

Chang, Y.-W., Hsu, P.-Y., Chen, J., Shiau, W.-L., Xu, N.: Utilitarian and/or hedonic shopping–consumer motivation to purchase in smart stores. Ind. Manag. Data Syst. **123**(3), 821–842 (2023)

Cheng, A., Ren, G., Hong, T., Nam, K., Koo, C.: An exploratory analysis of travel-related WeChat mini program usage: affordance theory perspective. In: Information and Communication Technologies in Tourism 2019: Proceedings of the International Conference in Nicosia, Cyprus, 30 January–1 February 2019, pp. 333–343 (2019)

Chen, F., Yan, C.C., Wang, L., Lou, X.J.: The effect of alternative vs. focal identity accessibility on the intent to purchase products: an exploratory study based on Chinese culture. Front. Psychol. **13**, 852505 (2022)

Crettaz, E., Suter, C.: The impact of adaptive preferences on subjective indicators: an analysis of poverty indicators. Soc. Indic. Res. **114**, 139–152 (2013)

Dashtestani, R.: Moving bravely towards mobile learning: Iranian students' use of mobile devices for learning English as a foreign language. Comput. Assist. Lang. Learn. **29**(4), 815–832 (2016)

Dhar, R., Wertenbroch, K.: Consumer choice between hedonic and utilitarian goods. J. Mark. Res. **37**(1), 60–71 (2000)

Drakopoulos, S.A.: Keynes 'economic thought and the theory of consumer behaviour. Scottish J. Polit. Econ. **39**(3), 318–336 (1992)

Dunaway, J., Searles, K., Sui, M., Paul, N.: News attention in a mobile era. J. Comput.-Mediat. Commun. **23**(2), 107–124 (2018)

Fahrudin, N.F., Wahyudi, A.D.: Modeling inventory systems using the user experience design model method. J. Data Sci. Inf. Syst **1**(1), 9–16 (2023)

Fonti-i-Furnols, M., Guerrero, L.: Consumer preference, behavior and perception about meat and meat products: an overview. Meat Sci. **98**(3), 361–371 (2014)

Forlizzi, J., Battarbee, K.: Understanding experience in interactive systems. In: Proceedings of the 5th Conference on Designing Interactive Systems: Processes, Practices, Methods, and Techniques, pp. 261–268 (2004)

Frey, B.S., Stutzer, A.: Measuring preferences by subjective well-being. J. Inst. Theor. Econ. (JITE)/ZeitschriftFür Die Gesamte Staatswissenschaft, 755–778 (1999)

Gavalas, D., Economou, D.: Development platforms for mobile applications: status and trends. IEEE Softw. **28**(1), 77–86 (2010)

Gera, R., Chadha, P., Ahuja, V.: Mobile app usage and adoption: a literature review. Int. J. Electron. Bus. **15**(2), 160–195 (2020)

Govers, P.C., Schoormans, J.P.: Product personality and its influence on consumer preference. J. Consum. Mark. **22**(4), 189–197 (2005)

Hao, L., Wan, F., Ma, N., Wang, Y.: Analysis of the development of WeChat mini program. J. Phys.: Conf. Ser. **1087**(6), 062040 (2018)

Hassenzahl, M.: The thing and I: understanding the relationship between user and product. In: Funology 2: From Usability to Enjoyment, pp. 301–313 (2018)

Hein, K.A., Jaeger, S.R., Carr, B.T., Delahunty, C.M.: Comparison of five common acceptance and preference methods. Food Qual. Prefer. **19**(7), 651–661 (2008)

Hew, J.-J., Lee, V.-H., Ooi, K.-B., Wei, J.: What catalysis mobile apps usage intention: an empirical analysis. Ind. Manag. Data Syst. **115**(7), 1269–1291 (2015)

Hirschman, E.C., Holbrook, M.B.: Hedonic consumption: emerging concepts, methods and propositions. J. Mark. **46**(3), 92–101 (1982)

Hoeffler, S., Ariely, D.: Constructing stable preferences: a look into dimensions of experience and their impact on preference stability. J. Consum. Psychol. **8**(2), 113–139 (1999)

Hu, L., Filieri, R., Acikgoz, F., Zollo, L., Rialti, R.: The effect of utilitarian and hedonic motivations on mobile shopping outcomes. A cross-cultural analysis. Int. J. Consum. Stud. **47**(2), 751–766 (2023)

Japutra, A., Song, Z.: Mindsets, shopping motivations and compulsive buying: insights from China. J. Consum. Behav. **19**(5), 423–437 (2020)

Jay, M.: Songs of Experience: Modern American and European Variations on a Universal Theme. University of California Press, Berkeley (2005)

Kahneman, D., Diener, E., Schwarz, N.: Well-Being: Foundations of Hedonic Psychology. Russell Sage Foundation, New York (1999)

Kane, S.K., Jayant, C., Wobbrock, J.O., Ladner, R.E.: Freedom to roam: a study of mobile device adoption and accessibility for people with visual and motor disabilities. In: Proceedings of the 11th International ACM SIGACCESS Conference on Computers and Accessibility, pp. 115–122 (2009)

Khan, I., et al.: Mobile app vs. desktop browser platforms: the relationships among customer engagement, experience, relationship quality and loyalty intention. J. Mark. Manag. **39**(3–4), 275–297 (2023)

Kim, S.C., Yoon, D., Han, E.K.: Antecedents of mobile app usage among smartphone users. J. Mark. Commun. **22**(6), 653–670 (2016)

Krause, A.E., North, A.C., Hewitt, L.Y.: Music-listening in everyday life: devices and choice. Psychol. Music **43**(2), 155–170 (2015)

Law, E.L.-C., Roto, V., Hassenzahl, M., Vermeeren, A.P., Kort, J.: Understanding, scoping and defining user experience: a survey approach. In: Proceedings of the SIGCHI Conference on Human Factors in Computing Systems, pp. 719–728 (2009)

Linnhoff, S., Smith, K.T.: An examination of mobile app usage and the user's life satisfaction. J. Strateg. Mark. **25**(7), 581–617 (2017)

Meena, R., Sarabhai, S.: Extrinsic and intrinsic motivators for usage continuance of hedonic mobile apps. J. Retail. Consum. Serv. **71**, 103228 (2023)

Miltenberger, R.G., et al.: Direct and retrospective assessment of factors contributing to compulsive buying. J. Behav. Ther. Exp. Psychiatry **34**(1), 1–9 (2003)

Qi, C.: A double-edged sword? Exploring the impact of students' academic usage of mobile devices on technostress and academic performance. Behav. Inf. Technol. **38**(12), 1337–1354 (2019)

Qin, H., Peak, D.A., Prybutok, V.: A virtual market in your pocket: how does mobile augmented reality (MAR) influence consumer decision making? J. Retail. Consum. Serv. **58**, 102337 (2021)

Ramírez-Correa, P., Rondán-Cataluña, F.J., Arenas-Gaitán, J., Martín-Velicia, F.: Analysing the acceptation of online games in mobile devices: an application of UTAUT2. J. Retail. Consum. Serv. **50**, 85–93 (2019)

Rodríguez-Ardura, I., Meseguer-Artola, A., Fu, Q.: The utilitarian and hedonic value of immersive experiences on WeChat: examining a dual mediation path leading to users' stickiness and the role of social norms. Online Inf. Rev. (2023)

Ryu, S., Cheng, K., Schreieck, M.: User value perception of native apps versus mini programs: a means-end theory approach. SMR-J. Serv. Manag. Res. **6**(3), 167–180 (2022)

Souppaya, M., Scarfone, K.: Guidelines for managing the security of mobile devices in the enterprise. NIST Spec. Publ. **800**, 124 (2013)

Staykova, K.S., Damsgaard, J.: Platform expansion design as strategic choice: the case of WeChat and KakaoTalk. In: 24th European Conference on Information Systems, ECIS 2016, p. 78 (2016)

Tilson, D., Sorensen, C., Lyytinen, K.: Change and control paradoxes in mobile infrastructure innovation: the Android and iOS mobile operating systems cases. In: 2012 45th Hawaii International Conference on System Sciences, pp. 1324–1333 (2012)

Tiwana, A.: Evolutionary competition in platform ecosystems. Inf. Syst. Res. **26**(2), 266–281 (2015)

Varshney, U., Vetter, R.: Emerging mobile and wireless networks. Commun. ACM **43**(6), 73–81 (2000)

Vrhovec, S.L.: Challenges of mobile device use in healthcare. In: 2016 39th International Convention on Information and Communication Technology, Electronics and Microelectronics (MIPRO), pp. 1393–1396 (2016)

Wakefield, R.L., Whitten, D.: Mobile computing: a user study on hedonic/utilitarian mobile device usage. Eur. J. Inf. Syst. **15**(3), 292–300 (2006)

Wan, F., Xu, B., Chang, N.: Discussion on the application of WeChat mini program in the lifelong education of basic computer knowledge in the age of mobile learning. In: E-Learning, e-Education, and Online Training: 5th EAI International Conference, eLEOT 2019, Kunming, China, 18–19 August 2019, Proceedings 5, pp. 48–55 (2019)

Wright, P., McCarthy, J., Meekison, L.: Making sense of experience. In: Blythe, M.A., Overbeeke, K., Monk, A.F., Wright, P.C. (eds.) Funology: From usability to enjoyment, vol. 3, pp. 43–53. Springer, Dordrecht (2003). https://doi.org/10.1007/1-4020-2967-5_5

Yang, X., Sun, S.L., Lee, R.P.: Micro-innovation strategy: the case of WeChat. Asian Case Res. J. **20**(02), 401–427 (2016)

Zhang, Y., Turkistani, B., Yang, A.Y., Zuo, C., Lin, Z.: A measurement study of WeChat mini-apps. Proc. ACM Meas. Anal. Comput. Syst. **5**(2), 1–25 (2021)

金铭. 基于用户体验的职业教育类APP评价研究. 北京交通大学 (2022)

Study on User Experience Evaluation and Enhancement of Library Mobile Information Services

Jiangyue Dong[✉]

College of Art and Design, Wuhan University of Technology, Wuhan, China
845027100@qq.com

Abstract. With the rapid development of mobile communication technology, library information services have evolved towards greater intelligence, offering readers more extensive and smarter services. However, ensuring the quality and performance of these services necessitates scientific evaluation. This study aims to delve into the dimensions of user experience in library mobile information services, using Wuhan University of Technology Library's WeChat public platform as a case study. We defined six key dimensions of user experience, including sensory experience, content experience, interaction experience, functionality experience, service experience, and emotional experience, along with corresponding observation items. Through the use of a questionnaire survey method, we successfully collected 94 valid questionnaires and performed reliability and validity analyses. The research findings reveal differences in the importance of various dimensions of user experience. Furthermore, the utilization of factor analysis identified nine key indicators with higher significance. Additionally, the analysis employing statistical methods provided valuable insights into eight indicators that were associated with user dissatisfaction, contributing to the guidance of future improvement measures. In conclusion, this study summarizes ten key improvement indicators and implements corresponding improvements. These indicators cover critical aspects of user experience, such as content experience, interaction experience, functionality experience, and emotional experience. The research results offer concrete recommendations for enhancing library mobile information services, better meeting user needs, improving service quality, and serving as a reference for other higher education institutions offering similar services. This study emphasizes the significance of scientific user experience evaluation in the context of rapid technological advancement and how it can enhance service quality and performance.

Keywords: Digital Library · Mobile Information Services · User Experience · Factor Analysis · Evaluation

1 Introduction

With the ongoing advancement of social informatization, the need for intelligent online service among readers is increasing daily. Libraries, as pivotal hubs for knowledge dissemination, have undergone innovations in service models. In this context, mobile

J. Wei and G. Margetis (Eds.): HCII 2024, LNCS 14738, pp. 205–216, 2024.
https://doi.org/10.1007/978-3-031-60487-4_16

information services have become an integral component of library services. This surge in research on library online services, particularly in the exploration and innovation of mobile services, has been notable [1].

Nevertheless, current research in this domain primarily concentrates on general library mobile services in a broad context. Wang Jingyun and colleagues [2] conducted a meta-quantitative analysis of diverse research findings concerning factors influencing user experience in mobile libraries, deriving several overarching conclusions with guiding significance. However, perspectives from M. Hassenzahl and N. Tractinsky [3], as well as JJ Garrett [4], posit that user experience is not solely linked to the user's internal perceptions but is also influenced by the interaction between the product and the specific external environment. In other words, the impact of specific scenarios needs to be taken into consideration.

Therefore, considering the distinctiveness of platforms across different library systems, encompassing functionalities and usage habits of user groups, it is imperative to concentrate research on specific platforms and delve deeply into their user experience. Regarding platform selection, insights from Qin Yanmei and team offer valuable guidance. They gathered usage data from major libraries in Guangdong Province and, through statistical analysis, found that the "WeChat public platform" has the highest usage ratio, exceeding 70% in the realm of library mobile information services [5]. This indicates widespread usage of WeChat public accounts among users. Consequently, I have chosen the WeChat public platform of Wuhan University of Technology Library, with which I am familiar, as the subject for further research.

In the following sections, we will gain an in-depth understanding of the platform's characteristics, service positioning, and target user groups to uncover specific challenges related to user experience. Through thorough examination of a particular platform, a more comprehensive comprehension of the platform's service model and user needs can be obtained. This, in turn, enables the provision of practical suggestions for enhancing the quality and effectiveness of library mobile services.

2 Construction of Evaluation Model Based on User Experience

2.1 Overview

Upon reviewing the information architecture of the WeChat public platform of Wuhan University of Technology Library, the author observed a predominant focus on the "Service" column, which encompasses sections such as "My Library - Micro Service Hall" and "My Library - Online Selection." The platform further integrates four major sections, namely the "seat system," "cloud reading," and "common services." Through these sections, users can access a multifaceted, fundamental, and convenient service experience within this comprehensive information service system. This structure aligns with the description of the library WeChat public platform service provided by Zhang Xian, encompassing information push release, reading promotion platform, and consultation and inquiry services [6].

2.2 Concept Definition

Donald Norman first introduced the term "user experience" in the late 1980s and early 1990s, providing a more detailed explanation in his subsequent book "Emotional Design." In this book, he divided the user experience into three layers: the instinctive layer, behavioral layer, and reflective layer. Norman emphasized the importance of designers considering both the practicality of the product and the emotional needs of users [7].

In the context of library mobile information services, how do we define user experience? Drawing on relevant definitions from ISO [8] and applying them to library mobile information services, user experience can be succinctly summarized as follows: it encompasses the user's perception, emotion, interaction, and evaluation during the utilization of library mobile information services. This comprehensive experience extends to various aspects, including user search, browsing, reading, as well as the entire process and end-to-end experience of service engagement and feedback. Cui Jingfeng and colleagues [9] conducted a comprehensive review of prior research findings, revealing that existing evaluation systems are predominantly structured around the dimensions of user experience in library mobile information services. These dimensions are based on the senses, emotions, thinking, actions, and connections proposed by Dr. Schmitt, unfolded through five distinct processes [10].

The definition of user experience and the research findings of other scholars highlight a crucial aspect: the user experience of library mobile information services is not solely confined to users themselves but involves the intricate interaction among users, products, and the environment. Library mobile information services, through sensory experiences, evoke emotional responses from users, shape their perceptions of the service, and ultimately drive them to take action throughout the experience. These interconnected processes contribute to the creation of a profound and comprehensive service experience, effectively enhancing user engagement and fostering loyalty.

2.3 Model Construction

After researching and analyzing user experience-related theories and considering the information service characteristics of the Wuhan University of Technology Library WeChat public platform, this article adopts the three-level division method proposed by Zhang Mingxia, which includes sensory experience, interactive experience, and emotional experience [11]. In essence, it is suggested that the user experience of the WeChat public platform of Wuhan University of Technology Library should be analyzed through the following six dimensions:

1. Sensory Experience: The process of perceiving and cognizing the visual organizational form of the library's WeChat public platform.
2. Content Experience: The extent to which users understand and interpret the text, pictures, and other content provided by the library's WeChat public platform.
3. Interactive Experience: User interaction experience with the library's WeChat public platform in terms of performance and efficiency.
4. Functional Experience: The experience and evaluation of the degree of realization of its own functions on the library's WeChat public platform.

Table 1. Evaluation model of library WeChat public platform based on user experience

Evaluation dimension	Evaluation index
Sensory experience (SO)	SO1: I think the functional division of the platform interface is clear and reasonable
	SO2: I think the platform column names are easy to understand and unambiguous
	SO3: I think the platform color combination is comfortable
	SO4: I think the platform interface design is beautiful
Content experience (CE)	CE1: I think the platform information resources are updated in a timely manner
	CE2: I think the resources provided by the platform are rich and comprehensive
	CE3: I think the accuracy of retrieving literature resources through the platform is high
	CE4: I think the message content pushed by the platform is of more interest to me
Interactive experience (IE)	IE1: I can complete query and reading related operations by myself when using the platform
	IE2: I think the platform provides a variety of communication channels with librarians
	IE3: I think the platform provides a way for users to share information with each other
	IE4: I think that except for network reasons, the platform operation is very responsive
Functional experience (FE)	FE1: I think the functions provided by the platform are diverse
	FE2: The platform has prompts for errors or accidents during use
	FE3: Through the platform, I can recommend books to librarians
	FE4: Through the platform, I can check announcements, new book announcements, contact librarians, etc
Service experience (SE)	SE1: I think the platform can conduct real-time consultation and respond promptly
	SE2: I think you can quickly find the information resources you need at any time and anywhere through the platform
	SE3: I think the platform provides a variety of personalized services
Emotional experience (EE)	EE1: I am generally satisfied with the platform
	EE2: I think the platform has brought convenience to my study or scientific research

(*continued*)

Table 1. (*continued*)

Evaluation dimension	Evaluation index
	EE3: I think the platform can stimulate motivation for learning
	EE4: I think using the platform does not pose a threat to personal privacy and makes people feel trustworthy

5. Service Experience: The perception and cognitive impact of the library's WeChat public platform and its services on the user's psychological level.
6. Emotional Experience: The user's emotional experience and perception at the psychological level during the use of the mobile library platform.

The six dimensions mentioned above progress layer by layer, starting from the basic sensory and content levels that users can directly feel, then delving into deeper interaction and functional levels that require users to mobilize their cognition to understand, and finally settling into providing services and emotional experiences that complement users' basic mobile information services.

Subsequently, we conducted a cognitive test on user experience, inviting 10 library users from different majors in our school to participate. The aim of this test was to gain an in-depth understanding of users' perceptions and cognitions when using the library's WeChat public platform on a daily basis and to collect feedback on their experiences at all levels. Combining the results from user feedback, we meticulously constructed 3–4 evaluation indicators in each dimension to fully explain the dimension in a way that is easily understandable for users. Finally, we established the evaluation scale as shown in Table 1. The pre-systematic and detailed test design is intended to ensure that the evaluation of the user experience of the library's WeChat public platform is comprehensive and targeted, thereby enhancing the credibility of the established evaluation indicators.

2.4 Questionnaire Survey

This study employs the empirical research method of a questionnaire survey, with the WeChat public platform of Wuhan University of Technology Library as the research object and teachers and students of Wuhan University of Technology as the investigation subjects. To ensure the reliability and validity of the questionnaire, a pre-test involving 15 familiar teachers and classmates was conducted before issuing the formal questionnaire. During the pre-test, interviews were also conducted with some users to gather their suggestions. Based on the feedback received, we made necessary modifications to the questionnaire items. Through desktop research, which involved assessing the current status of the platform and defining user experience evaluation indicators for the library's WeChat public platform, a finalized questionnaire was ultimately developed.

The first section of the questionnaire comprises non-scale questions designed to collect users' basic information, including user identity, gender, whether they have used the library's WeChat public platform, and the duration and frequency of use.The second section of the questionnaire is structured in the form of a 5-point Likert scale, facilitating statistical analysis of the survey results. To ensure respondents accurately comprehend each indicator, additional explanations were provided in parentheses after some of the questions. Participants are required to make a unique choice from the five options: "completely disagree," "somewhat disagree," "neutral," "somewhat agree," to "completely agree," corresponding to the points 1, 2, 3, 4, and 5, based on their actual usage experience.

3 Date Analysis

The dataset underwent a thorough screening process to ensure data quality. Irrelevant responses, illogical inconsistencies before and after answers, outliers in the time taken to fill in the questionnaire, and duplicated answers were all removed. After screening for gender and abnormal values, it was confirmed that 94 valid questionnaires were obtained.

In the subsequent analysis, the sample data will be examined for background and characteristics, reliability, validity, and weight analysis. This comprehensive analysis will help us gain a deeper understanding of the relationship between variables, ensuring that the data is reliable and valid. This, in turn, provides robust support for the ongoing evaluation and improvement process.

3.1 Background Analysis

The analysis of valid sample data reveals that the surveyed users are primarily under-graduates, comprising 65 individuals, accounting for 69.15% of the total sample. The remaining sample users are distributed as follows: 14 graduate students (14.89%), 11 faculty members (11.70%), 2 doctoral students (2.13%), and 2 graduates (2.13%). There is a basic gender balance, with women slightly outnumbering men. The number of female samples is 52, making up 55.32%, while the number of male samples is 42, accounting for 44.68%.

Regarding the experience of using the Wuhan University of Technology Library WeChat platform, users who have utilized it for one to three years or more are defined as senior users. A total of 64 users fall into this category, representing 68.09%. This indicates that the majority of platform users are experienced, providing highly convincing results for this survey. Additionally, 36 users use the platform frequently or almost every day, constituting 38.30%.

3.2 Reliability Analysis

Reliability analysis is employed to assess the stability and consistency of scale samples in questionnaires, typically using methods such as test-retest or internal consistency analysis, such as Cronbach's alpha. According to scholarly consensus, a Cronbach's alpha coefficient above 0.9 suggests excellent reliability, between 0.8–0.9 indicates good reliability, between 0.7–0.8 signifies acceptable reliability, and between 0.6–0.7 suggests average reliability. A range between 0.5–0.6 indicates less-than-ideal reliability, and if below 0.5, reconsideration of the questionnaire structure may be necessary.

Calculated using SPSS, the Cronbach's alpha coefficient value for the model is 0.978, signifying that the questionnaire exhibits very good reliability. This indicates that, in this survey, the scale's measurement results demonstrated high consistency and stability within the sample, attesting to its overall reliability. Therefore, maintaining the settings of the six evaluation dimensions as established earlier without making any changes, the analysis process can proceed (Table 2).

Table 2. Scale sample internal consistency analysis measurement results

Cronbach's alpha coefficient	Standardized Cronbach's alpha coefficient	Number of items	Number of samples
0.978	0.979	23	94

3.3 Validity Analysis

Validity analysis assesses the accuracy and correctness of the questionnaire scale, examining whether the design of the questionnaire questions is reasonable. In this study, validity analysis serves two purposes: to evaluate whether the questionnaire accurately measures the concepts of each dimension of the desired user experience, and to determine if the item setting successfully distinguishes different concepts, ensuring that the six dimensions, such as sensory experience and content experience, are effectively captured.

The KMO test and Bartlett test were initially employed to measure and judge the correlation and significance between variables, assessing the applicability and validity of factor analysis. The factor loading coefficient table was then calculated to confirm whether the factor structure aligns with the hypothesis and if each indicator effectively expresses its corresponding dimension.

The KMO test yielded a value of 0.908, significantly higher than the standard of 0.9, indicating a high degree of correlation between the item variables. This aligns with the requirements for factor analysis. Additionally, Bartlett's sphericity test resulted in a significant P-value of 0.000***, below the significance level of 0.05, leading to the rejection of the null hypothesis. This outcome signifies a significant correlation between variables, supporting the conduct of factor analysis (Table 3).

Table 3. KMO test and Bartlett's test

KMO value		0.908
Bartlett's test of sphericity	Approximate chi-square	2754.656
	df	253
	P	0.000***

Note: ***, **, and * represent the significance levels of 1%, 5%, and 10% respectively

In factor analysis, common factor variance is typically expressed as the extent to which each variable can be explained by a common factor. This measure is known as communality or common factor variance. The larger the value of "extraction," the better the variable can be expressed by common factors. Generally, a communality greater than 0.5 indicates that most of the variance of the variable can be explained by common factors, and a value greater than 0.7 suggests that the variables can be reasonably expressed by common factors.

From Table 4, it is evident that the common factor variances corresponding to the evaluation indicators set in the questionnaire are all higher than 0.7. This indicates that these indicators can reliably reflect the multi-dimensional experience of users when using library mobile information services.

Table 4. Factor loading coefficient table

	Factor loading coefficients after rotation						Common degree (common factor variance)
	Factor 1	Factor 2	Factor 3	Factor 4	Factor 5	Factor 6	
SO1	0.748	0.378	0.222	0.324	0.055	0.164	0.887
SO2	0.755	0.368	0.242	0.216	0.031	0.25	0.874
SO3	0.804	0.137	0.227	0.339	0.172	0.104	0.872
SO4	0.842	0.18	0.252	0.242	0.231	0.016	0.916
CE1	0.308	0.294	0.439	0.261	0.278	0.627	0.913
CE2	0.33	0.345	0.661	0.284	0.014	0.341	0.862
CE3	0.387	0.37	0.47	0.538	−0.07	0.081	0.809
CE4	0.437	0.399	0.669	0.243	0.201	−0.006	0.897
IE1	0.568	0.48	0.266	0.332	0.018	0.298	0.822
IE2	0.248	0.195	0.819	0.155	0.219	0.196	0.88
IE3	0.22	0.571	0.547	0.096	0.41	0.092	0.859
IE4	0.276	0.325	0.359	0.331	0.653	0.252	0.909
FE1	0.276	0.775	0.373	0.203	0.091	0.084	0.873
FE2	0.292	0.759	0.238	0.195	0.053	0.284	0.839
FE3	0.179	0.379	0.792	0.251	0.071	0.091	0.879
FE4	0.21	0.69	0.417	0.381	0.185	0.015	0.873
SE1	0.333	0.671	0.258	0.369	0.36	0.051	0.896
SE2	0.306	0.587	0.341	0.464	0.227	0.121	0.837
SE3	0.374	0.338	0.172	0.708	0.085	0.278	0.87
EE1	0.536	0.327	0.356	0.547	0.144	0.041	0.843
EE2	0.376	0.156	0.317	0.714	0.095	0.286	0.866
EE3	0.511	0.366	0.495	0.364	0.271	−0.046	0.849
EE4	0.34	0.292	0.148	0.717	0.34	−0.076	0.858

3.4 Weight Analysis

In this study, the author conducted an indicator deduplication operation, aiming to consider the advantages of two analysis methods, the entropy weight method and the classification statistics method. This ensures that the final indicator list is both comprehensive and non-duplicate. The rationality of this operation lies in the integration of indicators from different analysis methods to gain a more comprehensive insight into the key factors of users' comprehensive evaluation. The entropy weight method emphasizes the overall impact of indicators, while the classification statistics method focuses on specific dissatisfaction points in user feedback. By combining the two, we can identify indicators that are both important and have room for improvement.

The core logic of the merger is to fully integrate the different perspectives of the two analysis methods to make the final result more credible. During this process, a reintegration check was performed on the indicator lists of the entropy weight method and the classification statistics method to ensure no duplicate items between them. Through this deduplication process, a final list of indicators covering the importance obtained by the entropy weight method and the classification statistics method was obtained.

Next, the entropy weight method was used to output the importance weight of the questionnaire survey indicators. The definition of information entropy was employed to evaluate the degree of dispersion of each indicator. A smaller information entropy value indicates a greater degree of dispersion of the indicator and a more significant impact (i.e., weight) on the comprehensive evaluation. Conversely, if the values of an indicator are all equal, the indicator does not play a significant role in the comprehensive evaluation.

Considering a total of 23 indicators, if the weight of each indicator is the same, the weight calculation result of each indicator will be 4.348%. Therefore, nine indicators with weights greater than 4.348% were screened out: IE3 (8.500%), IE2 (6.900%), FE3 (5.800%), IE4 (5.600%), FE2 (5.000%), FE4 (5.000%), CE4 (4.900%), EE3 (4.800%), FE1 (4.700%).

Through classification statistics, the top 8 items that most resonate with users' positive/negative emotions among the 23 evaluation indicators were screened and made into the following Table 5.

Table 5. The top 8 items of users' selected content as "disagree/strongly disagree"

Index	Option content	Proportion
IE3	I think WeChat library provides a way for users to share information with each other	20.213%
IE2	I think WeChat library provides a variety of channels for communication with librarians	14.894%
CE4	I think the message content pushed by the platform is more interesting to me	11.702%

(continued)

Table 5. (*continued*)

Index	Option content	Proportion
IE4	I think except for network reasons, the platform operation is very responsive	11.702%
FE3	Through the WeChat platform, I can recommend books to librarians	11.702%
IE1	I can complete query and reading related operations by myself when using the platform	9.574%
FE1	I think the functions provided by WeChat library are diverse	9.574%
FE4	Through the WeChat library, I can check announcements, new book announcements, etc	9.574%

3.5 Classification of Experience Dimensions

The weight analysis in the previous section using the entropy weight method identified 9 indicators that have a significant impact on the comprehensive evaluation. The classification statistical method analysis identified 8 indicators where the user group expresses dissatisfaction. After deduplication, a total of 10 key improvement indicators were obtained: IE3, IE2, FE3, IE4, FE2, FE4, CE4, EE3, FE1, IE1.

It is evident that these 10 indicators pertain to content experience, interactive experience, functional experience, and emotional experience. Among them, interactive experience and functional experience are categorized as important experience dimensions, while content experience and emotional experience are classified as secondary experience dimensions. Sensory experience and service experience, which are not reflected in the above 10 indicators, are grouped into general experience dimensions (Fig. 1).

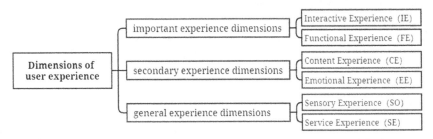

Fig. 1. Classification of library mobile information service experience dimensions

4   Improved Design

By analyzing the data, the importance weights of the questionnaire indicators have been determined. The focus is on addressing pain points within important user experience dimensions and secondary user experience dimensions. Targeted improvement designs have been developed to enhance the overall user experience based on the identified areas of importance and user dissatisfaction.

4.1 Interactive Experience Improvement Design

Improved Operational Convenience: Enhance the ease of operation by refining the transition between different modules, incorporating a welcome text guide, optimizing keyword search efficiency, and providing a more detailed help page.

Additional Channels for Contacting Librarians: On the "Contact Librarian" interface, include telephone contact information. Also, on the "Feedback" interface, enable users to choose various feedback types and upload text and pictures for detailed explanations.

Launch of User Sharing Platform: Introduce a new "Book Friends Communication" function, enabling users to freely share their reading experiences and fostering interaction among users.

4.2 Functional Experience Improvement Design

Increased Functional Diversification: Introduce functions such as book collection, book borrowing navigation, and personalized seat selection to enhance flexibility and convenience for platform users.

Prompt Information Enhancement: Add user account and password prompt information above the login interface to boost the engagement of new users.

Book Recommendation Function: Implement a new "recommended book purchase" function, allowing users to actively suggest books for acquisition by the library.

4.3 Content Experience Improvement Design

Platform Message Push Optimization: Enhance the relevance of content and user interest by regularly pushing personalized information, such as the number of times users visited the library last month and the status of borrowed books.

4.4 Emotional Experience Improvement Design

Improving Learning Motivation: Introduce a learning time ranking curve chart in the "Personal Center" interface to stimulate users' learning motivation through data visualization.

5 Conclusion and Future Work

This study conducted an in-depth analysis of the user experience of the WeChat public platform of Wuhan University of Technology Library by establishing a detailed evaluation scale. The research results not only propose a series of practical guidance strategies to optimize content, interaction, functionality and emotional experience, but also demonstrate its uniqueness in the specific platform context. This targeted research not only provides practical guidance for the further development of the platform, but also provides useful experience for improving user experience on similar platforms.

Future research can conduct in-depth discussions on improving the accuracy of model building. By using the factor loading matrix heat map, indicators with potential design confounds were verified and reordered to optimize the questionnaire structure. At the same time, considering the problem of low sample size, the scope of the study can be expanded and sample collection increased to improve the statistical significance of the study. In addition, research should not be limited to a single school platform. Platform samples with similar characteristics can be collected to conduct more general research and broaden the research perspective.

References

1. Shen, J., Ni, F., Zheng, D.: User experience evaluation of mobile library platforms. Libr. Inf. Work **58**(23), 54–60 (2014)
2. Wang, J., Qunyi, W.: Meta-analysis of factors influencing mobile library user experience. Natl. Libr. J. **27**(05), 44–53 (2018)
3. Hassenzahl, M., Tractinsky, N.: User experience - a research agenda. Behav. Inf. Technol. **25**(2), 91–97 (2006)
4. Garrett, J.: Elements of User Experience – User-Centered Web Design, vol. 4. Machinery Industry Press, South Norwalk (2007)
5. Qin, Y., Wang. C.: Research on library mobile information service evaluation based on UX (user experience) evaluation model. J. Guangdong Tech. Normal Univ. **42**(06), 90–95 (2021)
6. Zhang, X.: Library business reconstruction—research on mobile information services based on WeChat public accounts. Inner Mongolia Sci. Technol. Econ. (07), 77–78+86 (2020)
7. Norman, D.: Emotional Design: Why We Love (or Hate) Everyday Things. Basic Books, New York (2007)
8. ISO 9241-210: 2010, Ergonomics of human-system Interaction-Part 210: Human-centered design for interactive systems. International Organization for Standardization, Geneva (2010)
9. Cui, J., Zheng, D., Sun, Y., et al.: Research on satisfaction of library WeChat public platform from the perspective of user experience. Libr. Forum **38**(03), 133–140 (2018)
10. Schmitt, B.: Experiential marketing. J. Mark. Manag. **15**(1–3), 53–67 (1999)
11. Zhang, M., Qi, Y., Li, L., et al.: The connotation and improvement strategies of library user experience. New Century Libr. **7**, 10–13 (2015)

Design Research of User-Driven Mobile Sleep Aid Audio App Based on User Needs

Chang Guo[✉] and Anglu Li

Arts College of Sichuan University, Chengdu 610207, Sichuan, China
guoagcchang@gmail.com

Abstract. With the development of society and the accelerated pace of life, insomnia has become a problem that affects people's physical and mental health. How to alleviate the problem of insomnia and improve the quality of sleep has become the focus of people's attention. Therefore, it is meaningful to design a suitable mobile sleep aid audio APP product for insomnia people. This paper proposes a method for designing a mobile sleep aid audio APP based on Kano-AHP-QFD theoretical model. Firstly, the study used a questionnaire to obtain insomnia patients' opinions on the 16 requirements of mobile sleep aid audio APP and use Kano model to categorize the requirements by attributes. Secondly, Analytic Hierarchy Process (AHP) was used to analyze the weights of the requirements, and then sort the weights of the requirements for the design of mobile sleep aid audio APP. Lastly, by using Quality Function Deployment (QFD), the customer's requirements and expectations were changed into product design features and ensure that these design features are met. In this paper, by uniting three classic quality management tools, we conduct a design study on mobile sleep aid audio app and verify the possibility of its method in solving similar design problems. This paper can not only provide a practical mobile sleep aid audio design for people with insomnia, but also provide methodological references for other mobile app designs.

Keywords: Mobile Sleep Aid Audio App · Kano-AHP-QFD · User requirements · Interaction design

1 Introduction

According to the World Health Organization (WHO), insomnia is a global health problem. About 50% of the world's adult population suffers from insomnia to some degree, and the number is increasing (Burgdorf et al., 2018). One of the reasons could be the modern lifestyle and increased stress in life (Kim et al., 2011). It is worth noting that the problem of insomnia can have a negative impact on human health (Palagini et al., 2015). This is why people need to take timely steps to alleviate and treat insomnia (Nguyen et al., 2022). In modern society, mobile devices have become an indispensable part of people's daily lives (Exelmans and Van Den Bulck, 2016). Providing convenient and effective insomnia solutions on mobile has become an increasingly popular way of managing health (Baron et al., 2018). Designing a mobile sleep aid audio app is a promising

© The Author(s), under exclusive license to Springer Nature Switzerland AG 2024
J. Wei and G. Margetis (Eds.): HCII 2024, LNCS 14738, pp. 217–236, 2024.
https://doi.org/10.1007/978-3-031-60487-4_17

solution (Krause et al., 2014), and it has attracted the attention of many scholars. Carpi, Matteo etc. (Carpi et al., 2022). In their paper, the researchers analyzed the extent of insomnia widespread on Italian students based on measures of sleep quality and utilized a latent profile analysis to explore insomnia subtypes. Lund, Helle Nystrup etc. (Lund et al., 2022). In the paper, the researchers used the mobile app MusicStar and utilized phenomenological methods for qualitative research analysis. They use audio as an adjunctive therapy for patients with depression-related insomnia and explore the multiple effects of audio in depression-related insomnia. Harmat, Laszlo etc. (Harmat et al., 2008). In the paper, the researchers investigated the effect of audio on sleep quality in young participants with poor sleep. The conclusion proves that relaxing classical audio is an effective intervention to reduce sleep problems. Humphreys, T. etc. (Humphreys et al., 2008). They embed expert users in the interaction design process, to turn having a group of expert users as clients into a participatory interaction design project. Trischler, J. etc. (Trischler et al., 2019). They move public service design from an expert-driven process to one in which users actively and equally contribute ideas. Xuenan Li etc. (Xuenan and Jianghong, 2017). In the paper, the researchers analyzed the interaction design methodology and output forms of sound modeling by using random sampling methodology and user participation in design. In the current research on mobile interaction design for audio for insomniacs, there is a lack of rigorous user needs analysis in the process of solving the actual problem, and there is limited analysis of user needs weighting and functional importance. They do not alleviate the problem of insomnia by way of design. Meanwhile, few previous studies have investigated the design and development of a mobile sleep aid audio APP to alleviate insomnia. For this reason, this paper proposes a design solution for a mobile sleep aid APP based on the Kano-AHP-AD theoretical model, to provide a solution that better fits the needs of insomnia populations, while exploring how to use modern design theories and technologies to better meet user needs.

2   Research Model and Design Process Construction

2.1   Building a Kano-AHP-QFD Design Methodology for a Mobile-Based Sleep Aid Audio App

The combination of multiple design theory models can help designers develop design solutions more scientifically and efficiently (Kubler et al., 2016). Kano model classifies user needs attributes into five types by means of questionnaires and evaluation forms, and it clearly presents the connection between user needs and product satisfaction. It can help researchers to identify and categorize customer needs effectively. According to the different characteristics and priorities of the needs, researchers can make effective resource allocation and product design (Madzik, 2018). However, the Kano model does not accurately evaluate the importance of user requirements and does not provide clear user requirement weights (Xu et al., 2009). User requirement weights are a key basis for designers to prioritize their designs. Highly accurate user requirement weights can have a significant impact on focused design. And the AHP methodology can help prioritize the relationship between customer needs and product features, and how to maximize the satisfaction of customer needs given limited resources (Liu et al., 2020). Using AHP it is possible to determine the user requirement weighting coefficients in the Kano model and to rank them (Xiang et al., 2022). However, neither the Kano nor the AHP model suggests a solution for how the final user requirements are converted into specific design parameters. Therefore, QFD methodology is introduced in this study, which is a combination of qualitative and quantitative methods that can convert customer requirements into product design guidelines and ensure that these guidelines are realized to maximize customer satisfaction (Fang et al., 2022; Wei, 2022).

After analyzing and organizing the above models, this study proposes a design development process that integrates Kano, AHP and QFD models to balance the advantages and disadvantages of each model. By organically combining these models, the design process can be effectively guided, and the efficiency and quality of product design can be improved. The product development process constructed by integrating the three methods of Kano model, AHP model and QFD theory can not only avoid the design limitations of a single model, but also combine qualitative and quantitative design research (Lin et al., 2008; Neira-Rodado et al., 2020). Using Kano-AHP-QFD joint research method can organically combine all aspects of customer demand, product design, product characteristics, and resource allocation to form a complete product design process, making product design systematic and controllable. Researchers and enterprises can effectively manage the product design process, accurately grasp the key aspects and decision points of product design and improve the efficiency and quality of product design through the combined Kano-AHP-QFD research method. Figure 1 shows the design process schematic of the method. Therefore, this study applies the Kano-AHP-QFD product development process to the design of a mobile sleep aid APP (Nilsson, 2009).

2.2 User Requirements Acquisition

At this stage, existing mobile sleep aid APPs were analyzed, and relevant literature was reviewed. To further understand the needs of the target users, the researchers randomly selected 50 mobile audio APP users as survey subjects through field research and extracted basic information such as age, gender, frequency of use, and occupation of 30 sample users for cross-statistical analysis. The research study found that the largest percentage of users who use audio software are school students. They have a high demand for audio and 62.5% of them suffer from insomnia. The researchers conducted semi-structured in-depth interviews with insomniacs and acquired users' explicit and implicit needs through on-site observation, and then screened and merged the preliminary acquired needs with the KJ Affinity Diagram method to obtain a total of three levels of needs, namely, appearance, function, and personalization, with a total of 16 design needs. They took the three demand levels as the standard layers (F1–F3) and summarized the demands of the target population to get 16 specific indicators (r1–r16) for the design of mobile sleep aid APP, as shown in Table 1.

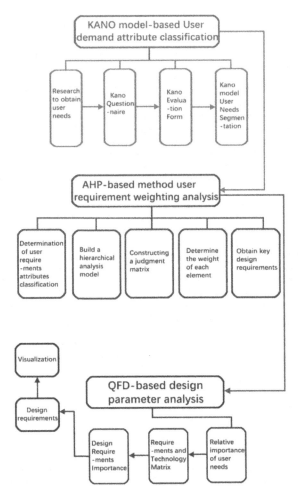

Fig. 1. Design flow of Kano-AHP-QFD

Table 1. Survey on User Requirements of Sleeping Aid Audio APP.

Classification of needs	Tickers	Needs	Tickers
Appearance	F1	Customized theme appearance	R1
		Toggle the appearance of the player	R2
		Warm and cozy visual experience	R3
Function	F2	Audio recommendations based on user preferences	R4
		Suggests audio based on user's mood	R5
		Suggests audio based on the user's psychological condition	R6
		Diverse audio categorization	R7

(continued)

Table 1. (*continued*)

Classification of needs	Tickers	Needs	Tickers
		Provide sheet music for users	R8
		Playing songs on different instruments	R9
		Setting the run time and slowly reducing the volume until it turns off	R10
		Patterned buttons	R11
		Gentle touch effects	R12
		Soft light mode	R13
Personalization	F3	Simple mode and customized function boards	R14
		Customized sorting of audio within the song list	R15
		Replacing the covers of singles and song lists	R16

3   The Use of Kano-AHP-QFD Based Design Methodology in the Design of a Mobile Sleep Aid App

3.1   Kano Model Based User Requirements Classification for Mobile Sleeping Aid Audio Apps

The Kano Model is a quality management tool, proposed by Japanese quality scientist Noriaki Kano, which is why it is called the "Kano Model". The model is used to analyze and categorize user needs and expectations for products or services, and to obtain comprehensive attributes of user needs (Ullah and Tamaki, 2011).

In the design and development process of the mobile sleep aid app, Kano model is utilized to conduct comprehensive qualitative analysis and quantitative calculation of user requirements. Through in-depth evaluation of user requirements, Kano model can identify the importance of different types of requirements and help designers prioritize product functions and features. Using the Kano model, design teams can better meet user expectations to improve user experience and satisfaction (Hong-yu and Jia-lun, 2023). The researchers designed Kano questionnaire with the indicators of 16 mobile sleep aid APP designs obtained from the preliminary research and conducted questionnaire surveys on different insomnia user groups. According to the Kano evaluation criteria, shown in Table 2, the user needs are classified into five categories: Must-have (M), One-dimensional (O), Attractive (A), Indifferent (I), and Reverse (R), and an additional category of Questionable (Q). A detailed explanation of the types of user requirements for mobile sleep aid APP design is shown in Table 3.

Subsequently, based on the design principles of the Kano questionnaire, a two-way questionnaire based on the Kano model was created in this study to analyze the level of satisfaction of this type of needs in both positive and negative dimensions based

Table 2. KANO evaluation table

Forward-looking question	Reverse questions				
	Satisfied	Should be	Not matter	Accepted	Dissatisfied
Satisfied	Q	A	A	A	O
Should be	R	I	I	I	M
Not matter	R	I	I	I	M
Accepted	R	I	I	I	M
Dissatisfied	R	R	R	R	Q

Table 3. Explanation of types of user requirements

Type of needs	Explanation
Must-have (M)	These are basic requirements that are taken for granted by users. Users will not be satisfied if these requirements are not met but meeting them does not necessarily lead to increased users' satisfaction
One-dimensional (O)	These are requirements that are directly proportional to users' satisfaction. Users are more satisfied when these requirements are met to a higher level
Attractive (A)	These are unexpected features that delight users when present, but their absence does not necessarily lead to dissatisfaction
Indifferent (I)	These are features that do not significantly affect users' satisfaction
Reverse®	These are features that, if present, decrease customer satisfaction
Questionable (Q)	Refers to a question that the respondent did not understand or answered incorrectly

on the user needs obtained from the Kano questionnaire. The researchers designed the questionnaire to consider the limitations of users' knowledge of insomnia and differences in the frequency of use of music software. To ensure the validity and accuracy of the results, the subjects invited to complete the questionnaire in this study covered long-term insomniacs, short-term insomniacs, and music lovers. Such diverse choices help to solve the problems of ambiguity of needs and limited level of cognition, thus improving the reliability of the research results. The detailed questionnaire content and structure are shown in Table 4. A total of 40 questionnaires were distributed in the study and 40 valid questionnaires were collected. The researchers integrated the results of the questionnaires and calculated the DA, DO, DM, DI, and DR for each demand indicator.

$$D_A = \frac{A}{A+O+M+I+R} \quad D_O = \frac{O}{A+O+M+I+R} \quad D_M = \frac{M}{A+O+M+I+R} \quad D_I = \frac{I}{A+O+M+I+R}$$
$$D_R = \frac{R}{A+O+M+I+R}.$$

In the above formula, A is the percentage of charismatic, O is the percentage of expected, M is the percentage of essential, I is the percentage of undifferentiated, and R is the percentage of reversed. By calculating individual values of DA, DO, DM, DI, DR, researchers derive maximum values to determine Kano attributes of demand metrics. For example, if DA is maximal, this demand attribute is charismatic. Using Kano evaluation system with user satisfaction coefficients, the types of user requirements are categorized as shown in Table 5.

Table 4. KANO Two-Way Questionnaire

If yes, your attitude is (positive question)					Sleep aid audio app interaction requirements	If not, your attitude is (negative question)				
Satisfied	Should be	Not matter	Accepted	Dissatisfied	Customized theme appearance	Satisfied	Should be	Not matter	Accepted	Dissatisfied
					Toggle the appearance of the player					
					Warm and cozy visual experience					
					Audio recommendations based on user preferences					
					Suggests audio based on user's mood					
					Suggests audio based on the user's psychological condition					
					...					

Table 5. Types of Interaction Requirements for Sleep Aid Audio Apps (%)

Tickers	A	O	M	I	Q	R	Causality
R1	82.500	7.500	0.000	7.500	0.000	2.500	A
R2	10.000	7.500	0.000	80.000	0.000	2.500	I
R3	7.500	80.000	5.000	7.500	0.000	0.000	O
R4	10.000	17.500	67.500	5.000	0.000	0.000	M
R5	45.000	47.500	2.500	5.000	0.000	0.000	O
R6	12.500	80.000	2.500	5.000	0.000	0.000	O
R7	12.500	15.500	65.500	7.500	0.000	0.000	M
R8	30.000	7.500	0.000	62.500	0.000	0.000	I
R9	75.000	2.500	0.000	22.500	0.000	0.000	A
R10	2.500	25.000	65.000	7.500	0.000	0.000	M
R11	7.500	7.500	2.500	82.500	0.000	0.000	I
R12	37.500	5.000	7.500	50.000	0.000	0.000	I
R13	10.000	10.000	75.000	5.000	0.000	0.000	M
R14	47.500	37.500	10.000	5.000	0.000	0.000	A
R15	35.000	22.500	7.500	35.000	0.000	0.000	A
R16	17.500	7.500	0.000	75.500	0.000	0.000	I

By organizing the Kano attributes of the 16 user requirements in Table 5, there are five Indifferent requirements (I), four must-have requirements (M), three One-dimensional requirements (O), and four Attractive requirements (A), and the reverse requirements (R) and questionable results (Q) did not occur. Indifferent (I) include switchable player appearance, provision of sheet music for songs, patterned buttons, mild touch effects, and replacement covers for singles and song lists. Among the effects of user satisfaction, undifferentiated demand does not have a direct improvement effect and therefore does not require optimization measures. This type of requirement does not significantly impact user satisfaction, so attention can be focused on other types of requirements during the design process to improve overall user satisfaction and quality of experience. Must-have requirements includes audio recommendation based on user preferences, diverse audio categorization, set runtime to slowly reduce the volume over a defined period until it turns off, and soft light mode. Must-have requirements refer to basic needs that must be met. Failure to fulfill these needs will significantly reduce user satisfaction. Therefore, must-have requirements should be prioritized and satisfied during the design process. These types of requirements usually relate to the basic functionality and core features of the product, which are essential to the user. By prioritizing must-have requirements, the design team can ensure the basic usability and functionality of the product, providing a reliable experience that meets basic expectations. It is essential for improving user satisfaction and enhancing product acceptability and reliability. Therefore, the prioritization of must-have requirements should be given high priority in design decisions. One-dimensional requirements include warm and welcoming visuals, audio recommendations based on the user's mood, and audio recommendations based on the user's mental state. In the design process of mobile sleep aid app, meeting One-dimensional requirements will directly enhance user satisfaction. Therefore, to enhance user satisfaction, it is necessary for designers to fulfill such needs as much as possible. By meeting users' One-dimensional requirements, products can exceed their expectations and create a satisfying and enjoyable experience. In the design of a mobile sleep aid app, focusing on meeting One-dimensional requirements can help build a positive user experience and increase product competitiveness and user loyalty. Therefore, the design team should pay full attention to and fulfill the One-dimensional requirements of users as much as possible during the product design process to increase the level of user satisfaction. Attractive requirements include a customizable theme appearance, the ability to select different instruments to play the user's favorite music, a clean mode and customizable feature panel, and customizable sorting of audio within the song list. Optimizing the above requirements in the design of a mobile sleep aid app can bring a surprising experience to users. Once these needs are met, it will significantly increase the level of user satisfaction. Through the Kano model of the mobile sleep aid APP design requirements screening, the final focus on the importance of meeting M, O, A.

3.2   Analyzing User Requirement Weights for Mobile Sleep Aid App Design with AHP

Building an AHP Hierarchical Analysis Model for Mobile Sleep Aid App Design. Although the Kano model can categorize the user needs of the mobile sleep aid app, it does not explicitly show the relative importance of each need, nor can it rank these needs. In order to meet the requirements of key user requirements in subsequent product design and to accurately obtain relatively important user requirement information, this study adopts an approach that combines the Kano model and the AHP model in order to realize the calculation and evaluation of user requirement weights (Li et al., 2009). Analysis of Hierarchy (AHP) is a multi-criteria decision analysis method proposed by American mathematician Thomas Saaty in the early 1970s (Kwong and Bai, 2002). This research method is based on the idea of hierarchical structure, which decomposes the complex decision-making problem into several levels to simplify the analysis of the problem and the decision-making process. AHP decomposes the decision-making problem into a hierarchy, including the objective layer, criterion layer and sub-criterion layer, and then uses methods such as expert questionnaires or fuzzy mathematics to quantitatively evaluate the decision-making factors. It ranks the user requirements divided by the Kano model in terms of weights and sizes, obtains the relative importance of each factor in the whole hierarchy, compares different design factors to determine which factors are most important for satisfying different needs, and helps decision makers to make trade-offs among multiple available options to realize rational decision making.

According to the results of the Kano questionnaire, the analysis will not be focused due to the lack of direct correlation between I and improved user satisfaction. On this basis, the study analyzes the requirements M, O and A by generalizing them as the 11 design requirements of the mobile sleep aid audio APP, which are used as the evaluation indexes, and builds a hierarchical model by using AHP, as shown in Fig. 2. According to the user requirements and design objectives of the mobile sleep aid APP, the structural model is divided into the following three levels. (1) The goal layer is the general goal of the design and the design program of the mobile sleep aid audio APP. (2) The guideline layer is divided into M, O, and A. (3) The content of the sub-criteria layer is divided into 11 aspects: recommending audio according to the user's preference, diversified audio classification, Set the run time and slowly reduce the volume until it shuts off, soft-lighting mode, warm and cozy visual experience, recommending audio according to the user's mood, recommending audio according to the user's psychological condition, customizing the theme appearance, different instruments play music, simple mode and customizing the functionality of the boards and customizing the sorting of audio in the song list.

Research and Weighting of Mobile Sleep Aid APP Design Based on AHP Method. To scientifically rank the weights of user requirements and quantitatively analyze the qualitative issues, this study adopts the 1–9 scale of proportionality proposed by Saaty to assess the importance of each design element, thus constructing a judgment matrix. (1) The study used AHP questionnaire and invited 10 respondents to participate. The respondents included three professional interaction designers (with more than 5 years of experience), three associate professors in the interaction design field and two professors in the interaction design field. Respondents compared and rated the importance of each level of need on a two-by-two basis, based on a rating scale of 1–9. We used the average of these ratings as the basis for weighting calculations to derive judgment matrices for each tier. (2) The researchers used the geometric mean method to calculate the weight coefficients of each tier to derive the weight value of the user needs in the guideline tier of the mobile sleep aid APP, and the arithmetic process is as follows.

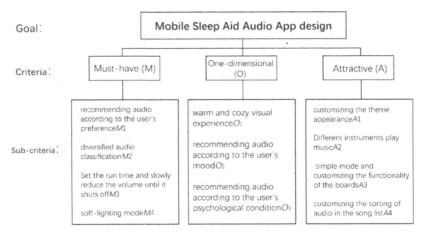

Fig. 2. AHP Hierarchical Analysis Model for Mobile Sleep Aid App Design

1) Create a judgment matrix:

$$X = \left(X_{ij}\right)_{n \times n} = \begin{bmatrix} X_{11} & X_{12} & \cdots & X_{1n} \\ X_{21} & X_{22} & \cdots & X_{2n} \\ \vdots & \vdots & \ddots & \vdots \\ X_{n1} & X_{n2} & \cdots & X_{nm} \end{bmatrix} \tag{1}$$

2) Calculate the product of the scales of each layer:

$$M_i = \prod_{j=1}^{m} b_{ij} (i = 1, 2, ..., 3) \tag{2}$$

3) Determining the geometric mean of the product of the scales of each layer:

$$a_i = \sqrt[m]{M_i} \ (i = 1, 2, ..., 3) \tag{3}$$

4) Calculating relative weights:

$$W_i = \frac{a_i}{\sum\limits_{i=1}^{m} a_i} \tag{4}$$

5) Calculate the maximum characteristic root:

$$\lambda_{\max} = \frac{1}{n} \sum_{i=1}^{n} \frac{B_{W_i}}{W_i} \tag{5}$$

6) Consistency of test results:

$$CI = \frac{\lambda_{\max} - n}{n - 1} \tag{6}$$

$$CR = \frac{CI}{RI} \tag{7}$$

To ensure the scientific validity of the calculations, it is necessary for the researcher to conduct a consistency test of the calculations. When CR ≤ 0.1, the consistency test passes; if CR > 0.1, it fails. It is important to note that in the AHP analysis method, when there are only two indicators, it is not necessary to calculate the consistency ratio (CR) to verify the consistency results. At this point, it is only necessary to calculate the CI value and determine whether it is less than or equal to 0.1, so that the results of the judgment can be consistent. However, when the number of indicators is greater than 2, the consistency results need to be verified by calculating the CR value even if the CI value is less than or equal to 0.1. This is because when the number of indicators increases, the size of the CI does not fully reflect the consistency of the judgments. However, for analyses of three or more indicators, in addition to calculating CI values, researchers need to calculate CR values to ensure the reliability of the analysis results.

The CI values of sub-criteria layers M, O, and A are less than 0.1, and their CR values are all less than 0.1, so the judgments can be considered consistent (Tables 6, 7, 8 and 9).

Table 6. Criteria indicator weights

	M	O	A	weights	CR
M	1	2	3	0.540	0.009
O	1/2	1	2	0.297	
A	1/3	1/2	1	0.163	

Table 7. AHP sub-criteria layer M of requirements weights table

must-have (M)	Judgment matrix				Weights	Relative weights	CI	CR
M1	1	3	1/3	5	0.291	0.157	0.066	0.075
M2	1/3	1	1/3	3	0.151	0.082		
M3	3	3	1	5	0.491	0.265		
M4	1/5	1/3	1/5	1	0.067	0.036		

According to the results of the relative weight ordering of user requirements in Table 10, it is known that the design of mobile sleep aid audio APP should prioritize M requirements. The sequencing in the M requirements are setting the run time and slowly reducing the volume until it turns off during the specified time period, recommending audio based on the user's preferences, diverse audio categorization, and soft light mode. Secondly, the design team should consider O needs. The ordering in the O requirements is warm and cozy visuals, audio recommendation based on the user's current mood, and

Table 8. AHP sub-criteria layer O of requirements weights table

One-dimensional (O)	Judgment matrix			Weights	Relative weights	CI	CR
O1	1	3	5	0.633	0.188	0.019	0.037
O2	1/3	1	3	0.261	0.078		
O3	1/5	1/3	1	0.106	0.031		

Table 9. AHP sub-criteria layer A of requirements weights table

Attractive (A)	Judgment matrix				Weights	Relative weights	CI	CR
A1	1	1/4	3/5	3/8	0.099	0.016	0.039	0.044
A2	4	1	15/4	3	0.514	0.084		
A3	5/3	4/15	1	1/3	0.128	0.021		
A4	8/3	1/3	3	1	0.259	0.042		

Table 10. AHP weighting ranking.

Criteria	Criteria ranking	sub-criteria	Relative weights	sub-criteria ranking
Must-have (M)	1	M1	0.157	2
		M2	0.082	3
		M3	0.265	1
		M4	0.036	4
One-dimensional (O)	2	O1	0.188	1
		O2	0.078	2
		O3	0.031	3
Attractive (A)	3	A1	0.016	4
		A2	0.084	1
		A3	0.021	3
		A4	0.042	2

audio recommendation based on the user's psychological condition. The design team should then consider A requirement. Sorting in Requirement A is selecting different instruments to play the song, customized sorting of audio within the song list, clean mode and customized function boards, and customized theme appearance. Designers can prioritize top-ranked requirements and increase user satisfaction with limited resources by referring to the relative weighting. (Isaai et al., 2011).

3.3 Transformation of Design Parameters of Mobile Sleep Aid APP Based on QFD Theory

Neither the Kano nor the AHP model suggests a solution for how the final user requirements can be converted into specific design parameters (Kwong and Bai, 2002). Therefore, QFD methods are introduced in this study to help in design parameter transformation. QFD (Quality Function Deployment) QFD is a quality management methodology first introduced in the 1970s by Dr. Yoji Akao, a Japanese quality management expert. (Kahraman et al., 2006). The core idea of QFD is to translate customer needs and expectations into design features of a product or service and to ensure that these features are met. QFD systematically organizes and analyzes customer requirements, translates them into design guidelines for products or services, and ensures that these principles are implemented (Bhattacharya et al., 2005; Yu-xuan et al., 2022).

By reviewing the information about the mobile APP design, and according to the user needs ranking obtained by Kano-AHP method, the researchers determined the following 10 design elements after many rounds of opinion consultation to reach theoretical saturation: User habit analysis, audio data classification (Livingstone and Russo, 2018), Editing Features, Concise Mode, Feature Extensions, Mood Testing (Marchewka et al., 2014), Emoji buttons (Barrett et al., 2019), Graffiti Board (Marchewka et al., 2014), Psychological Tests (Seabra-Santos et al., 2019), The timekeeping function. Using the weighted values of target user needs obtained by the AHP method, the researcher can build a QFD quality house for the design of suitable mobile sleep aid APP, as shown in Table 11. In the QFD quality house, the weights f represented by the different symbols are default values ○ = 1, ▲ = 1.2, ◉ = 1.5. The sum of the product of all the requirements under the function and the corresponding weights is the final score for the function.

Table 11. QFD Quality House

needs		Weights	User habits analysis	Audio data classification	Editing function	Simple mode	Functionality expansion	Emotional testing	Emoji buttons	Scrawl board	Psychological test	Timekeeping
M	M1	0.157	◉	▲				○				
	M2	0.082		◉		○						
	M3	0.265	▲		○	○	○				○	◉
	M4	0.036			○		▲					▲
O	O1	0.188				○		▲			▲	
	O2	0.078	▲	◉				◉	▲	▲	○	
	O3	0.031	▲	◉				○	○	◉	◉	
A	A1	0.016			▲	▲	○					
	A2	0.084	▲	▲	○		◉					
	A3	0.021			◉	◉	▲				○	
	A4	0.042		○	▲		○					
Weights			0.785	1.525	0.486	0.586	0.517	0.453	0.125	0.140	0.615	0.462
Weights ranking			2	1	6	4	5	8	10	9	3	7

The researchers ranked the calculated importance of the design elements after normalization, as shown in Table 11. According to the prioritization of the design elements of the mobile sleep aid APP, it can be learned that its main design elements are audio data classification, user habit analysis, psychological testing, etc., which can be focused and prioritized.

4   Interface Design for Mobile Sleep Aid App

Second, this study proposes an interface design that recommends audio based on the user's mood and psychological condition, aiming to meet the individual differences of different users. We take individual needs as the starting point and tailor the song list to help users relax while falling asleep or reduce the impact of negative emotions through music in daily life. The interface was designed to include four core elements: brief information about the recommended audio, a pictorial representation of the current mood (Elliot and Maier, 2014), a psychometric test report, and a recommended song list based on the psychological profile. Based on the previous research on user needs and combined with visual images to guide the user's perceptual experience, a cozy visual effect was produced (Palmer et al., 2013), as shown in Fig. 4. The visual elements are designed to guide users through appropriate font sizes, color temperatures (O'Connor, 2011), and clear and concise function icons. In the recommendation interface based on personal preferences, the system uses the user habit analysis function and diversified audio classification function to summarize the user's listening habits. APP pushes song lists with different themes at different times according to users' personal preferences and

Fig. 3. Timer Interface

behavior. In addition, to avoid the problem of a single type of recommended audio and the creation of aesthetic fatigue, the system will randomly recommend niche audio to the user with a low probability, and at the same time, the user can also try out new styles in the audio categorization. In the interface based on mood recommendation, users can draw pictures to express their current mood state through patterned buttons and a doodle pad. If the user favorites the audio during the audition process, the system will further analyze the user's habits through the user's attention behavior in that mood to better identify the user's complex emotional state. In the interface based on psychological situation recommendation, users can learn about their psychological situation through simple and interesting psychological tests and utilize the graffiti board and short story collection to express their personal psychological situation and life experience. The system will analyze the user's psychological state based on the user's assessment report and calculate a comfortable environment for the user to feel at ease. The system also utilizes a combination of image therapy and sound therapy in psychology to recommend a psychological healing audio that suits the user's individual needs (Burgdorf et al., 2018; Harmat et al., 2008). In this interface, users could save or share their psychometric test reports and record the process of psychological changes after using the software in their personal homepage. If the results of the user's psychological tests are not promising, the system will encourage the user to actively participate in the psychotherapeutic services provided by the hospital (Fig. 3).

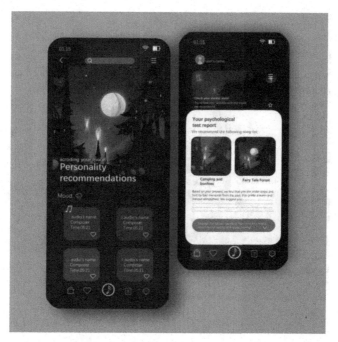

Fig. 4. Personal Recommendation

Finally, there are the song list interface design, the customized function option interface design, the playback interface design, and the clean mode playback interface design (Lee et al., 2015), as shown in Figs. 5 and 6. Based on previous data calculations, the design of these interfaces focused on meeting user customization needs. In the song list interface, users can intuitively obtain relevant information such as song name, song list author, song list theme and song playing time. At the same time, users can also perform batch editing operations, such as sorting, adding, or subtracting, sharing, and favoriting the audio within the song list. To meet the needs of different user groups, the Customize Function Options screen allows users to keep desired functions, hide unwanted functions, or add extensions and plug-ins according to their personal preferences. Users also have the option to use the Concise Mode, which is like a player that plays audio in a concise manner or share their favorite features or plug-ins with their friends on social media as if they were sharing audio. In the design of the playback interface, the user can use the interface to understand the background of the creation of the audio or the situational story related to the audio. Users can also choose from a variety of different instruments to play their favorite songs. In addition, to help users relax and fall asleep, the playback interface is designed with a tone scale mode that visualizes the currently playing audio in the center of the screen in the form of a regular, slow-moving image. This is designed to provide a combined audio-visual experience that simultaneously meets the user's visual and auditory needs and produces a certain sleep-aiding effect.

Fig. 5. Player interfaces

Fig. 6. Song list interface and customized function

5 Conclusions

To help insomniacs improve their sleeping experience, this paper proposes a mobile audio sleep aid APP design and development process that gathers KANO-AHP-QFD theory. In this study, the researchers use Kano model to analyze user requirements and use AHP model to rank the requirements in terms of weights. We then combine this with QFD quality house to quantify the requirements and transform them into design elements, to help designers better develop a mobile sleep-assisting audio app that can optimize the sleeping experience of insomniacs and improve design efficiency. This product development process helps to make up for the shortcomings of single-method design, helping designers accurately identify user needs in ambiguous scenarios and make scientific and rational design decisions. At the same time, this process also provides new research ideas for other user requirement-oriented product development.

References

Baron, K.G., Duffecy, J., Berendsen, M.A., Mason, I.C., Lattie, E.G., Manalo, N.C.: Feeling validated yet? A scoping review of the use of consumer-targeted wearable and mobile technology to measure and improve sleep. Sleep Med. Rev. **40**, 151–159 (2018). https://doi.org/10.1016/j.smrv.2017.12.002

Barrett, L.F., Adolphs, R., Marsella, S., Martinez, A.M., Pollak, S.D.: Emotional expressions reconsidered: challenges to inferring emotion from human facial movements. Psychological Science in the Public Interest **20**(1), 1–68 (2019). https://doi.org/10.1177/1529100619832930

Bhattacharya, A., Sarkar, B., Mukherjee, S.K.: Integrating AHP with QFD for robot selection under requirement perspective. Int. J. Prod. Res. **43**(17), 3671–3685 (2005). https://doi.org/10.1080/00207540500137217

Burgdorf, A., et al.: The mobile sleep lab app: an open-source framework for mobile sleep assessment based on consumer-grade wearable devices. Comput. Biol. Med. **103**, 8–16 (2018). https://doi.org/10.1016/j.compbiomed.2018.09.025

Carpi, M., Marques, D.R., Milanese, A., Vestri, A.: Sleep quality and insomnia severity among Italian university students: a latent profile analysis. J. Clin. Med. **11**(14), 15, Article ID 4069 (2022). https://doi.org/10.3390/jcm11144069

Elliot, A.J., Maier, M.A.: Color psychology: effects of perceiving color on psychological functioning in humans. In: Elliot, A.J., Maier, M.A. (eds.) Annual Review of Psychology, vol. 65, pp. 95–120 (2014). https://doi.org/10.1146/annurev-psych-010213-115035

Exelmans, L., Van Den Bulck, J.: Bedtime mobile phone use and sleep in adults. Soc. Sci. Med. **148**, 93–101 (2016). https://doi.org/10.1016/j.socscimed.2015.11.037

Fang, H., Li, J., Song, W.Y.: A new method for quality function deployment based on rough cloud model theory. IEEE Trans. Eng. Manag. **69**(6), 2842–2856 (2022). https://doi.org/10.1109/tem.2020.3020339

Harmat, L., Takacs, J., Bodizs, R.: Music improves sleep quality in students. J. Adv. Nurs. **62**(3), 327–335 (2008). https://doi.org/10.1111/j.1365-2648.2008.04602.x

Hong-yu, Z., Jia-lun, W.: 基于Kano-QFD的适老化卫浴产品设计研究 In: 周红宇 & 王嘉伦 (Eds.), 包装工程, vol. 44, pp. 150–157. Design of elderly-oriented bathroom products based on Kano-QFD: Packaging Engineering (2023)

Humphreys, T., Leung, L., Weakley, A.: Embedding expert users in the interaction design process: a case study. Des. Stud. **29**(6), 603-U602 (2008). https://doi.org/10.1016/j.destud.2008.07.006

Isaai, M.T., Kanani, A., Tootoonchi, M., Afzali, H.R.: Intelligent timetable evaluation using fuzzy AHP. Expert Syst. Appl. **38**(4), 3718–3723 (2011). https://doi.org/10.1016/j.eswa.2010.09.030

Kahraman, C., Ertay, T., Buyukozkan, G.: A fuzzy optimization model for QFD planning process using analytic network approach. Eur. J. Oper. Res. **171**(2), 390–411 (2006). https://doi.org/10.1016/j.ejor.2004.09.016

Kim, H.C., Kim, B.K., Min, K.B., Min, J.Y., Hwang, S.H., Park, S.G.: Association between job stress and insomnia in Korean workers. J. Occup. Health **53**(3), 164–174 (2011). https://doi.org/10.1539/joh.10-0032-OA

Krause, A.E., North, A.C., Heritage, B.: The uses and gratifications of using Facebook music listening applications. Comput. Hum. Behav. **39**, 71–77 (2014). https://doi.org/10.1016/j.chb.2014.07.001

Kubler, S., Robert, J., Derigent, W., Voisin, A., Le Traon, Y.: A state-of the-art survey & testbed of fuzzy AHP (FAHP) applications. Expert Syst. Appl. **65**, 398–422 (2016). https://doi.org/10.1016/j.eswa.2016.08.064

Kwong, C.K., Bai, H.: A fuzzy AHP approach to the determination of importance weights of customer requirements in quality function deployment. J. Intell. Manuf. **13**(5), 367–377 (2002). https://doi.org/10.1023/a:1019984626631

Lee, D., Moon, J., Kim, Y.J., Yi, M.Y.: Antecedents and consequences of mobile phone usability: linking simplicity and interactivity to satisfaction, trust, and brand loyalty. Inf. Manag. **52**(3), 295–304 (2015). https://doi.org/10.1016/j.im.2014.12.001

Li, Y.L., Tang, J.F., Luo, X.G., Xu, J.: An integrated method of rough set, Kano's model and AHP for rating customer requirements' final importance. Expert Syst. Appl. **36**(3), 7045–7053 (2009). https://doi.org/10.1016/j.eswa.2008.08.036

Lin, M.C., Wang, C.C., Chen, M.S., Chang, C.A.: Using AHP and TOPSIS approaches in customer-driven product design process. Comput. Ind. **59**(1), 17–31 (2008). https://doi.org/10.1016/j.compind.2007.05.013

Liu, Y., Eckert, C.M., Earl, C.: A review of fuzzy AHP methods for decision-making with subjective judgements. Expert Syst. Appl. **161**, 30, Article 113738(2020). https://doi.org/10.1016/j.eswa. 2020.113738

Livingstone, S.R., Russo, F.A.: The Ryerson audio-visual database of emotional speech and song (RAVDESS): a dynamic, multimodal set of facial and vocal expressions in North American English. Plos ONE **13**(5), 35, Article e0196391 (2018). https://doi.org/10.1371/journal.pone. 0196391

Lund, H.N., Hannibal, N., Mainz, J., Macdonald, R., Pedersen, I.N.: Music, sleep, and depression: an interview study. Psychol. Music **50**(3), 830–848, Article ID 03057356211024350 (2022). https://doi.org/10.1177/03057356211024350

Madzik, P.: Increasing accuracy of the Kano model - a case study. Total Qual. Manag. Bus. Excell. **29**(3–4), 387–409 (2018). https://doi.org/10.1080/14783363.2016.1194197

Marchewka, A., Zurawski, L., Jednorog, K., Grabowska, A.: The Nencki affective picture system (NAPS): introduction to a novel, standardized, wide-range, high-quality, realistic picture database. Behav. Res. Methods **46**(2), 596–610 (2014). https://doi.org/10.3758/s13428-013-0379-1

Neira-Rodado, D., Ortiz-Barrios, M., De La Hoz-Escorcia, S., Paggetti, C., Noffrini, L., Fratea, N.: Smart product design process through the implementation of a fuzzy Kano-AHP-DEMATEL-QFD approach. Appl. Sci.-Basel **10**(5), 28, Article ID 1792 (2020). https://doi.org/10.3390/app10051792

Nguyen, V.V., Zainal, N.H., Newman, M.G.: Why sleep is key: poor sleep quality is a mechanism for the bidirectional relationship between major depressive disorder and generalized anxiety disorder across 18 years. J. Anxiety Disord. **90**, 10, Article ID 102601 (2022). https://doi.org/10.1016/j.janxdis.2022.102601

Nilsson, E.G.: Design patterns for user interface for mobile applications. Adv. Eng. Softw. **40**(12), 1318–1328 (2009). https://doi.org/10.1016/j.advengsoft.2009.01.017

O'Connor, Z.: Colour psychology and colour therapy: caveat emptor. Color. Res. Appl. **36**(3), 229–234 (2011). https://doi.org/10.1002/col.20597

Palagini, L., Drake, C.L., Gehrman, P., Meerlo, P., Riemann, D.: Early-life origin of adult insomnia: does prenatal-early-life stress play a role? Sleep Med. **16**(4), 446–456 (2015). https://doi.org/10.1016/j.sleep.2014.10.013

Palmer, S.E., Schloss, K.B., Sammartino, J.: Visual aesthetics and human preference. In: Palmer, S.E., Schloss, K.B., Sammartino, J. (eds.) Annual Review of Psychology, vol. 64, pp. 77–107 (2013). https://doi.org/10.1146/annurev-psych-120710-100504

Seabra-Santos, M.J., Almiro, P.A., Simoes, M.R., Almeida, L.S.: Psychological tests in portugal: attitudes, problems and user profiles. Revista Iberoamericana De Diagnostico Y Evaluacion-E Avaliacao Psicologica **4**(53), 101–112 (2019). https://doi.org/10.21865/ridep53.4.08

Trischler, J., Dietrich, T., Rundle-Thiele, S.: Co-design: from expert- to user-driven ideas in public service design. Publ. Manag. Rev. **21**(11), 1595–1619 (2019). https://doi.org/10.1080/147 19037.2019.1619810

Ullah, A., Tamaki, J.: Analysis of Kano-model-based customer needs for product development. Syst. Eng. **14**(2), 154–172 (2011). https://doi.org/10.1002/sys.20168

Wei, Q.: 基于Kano-QFD的新能源汽车移动端交互设计 In: 强威 (ed.), 包装工程, vol. 43, pp. 212–219. Interaction design on mobile terminal of NEVs based on Kano-QFD: Packaging Engineering (2022)

Xiang, Z., Feng, W., Yuan, M.: 用户需求驱动下的家具产品设计方法 In 赵项, 魏峰, & 缪远 (eds.) 林业工程学报, vol. 7, pp. 194–200. Research on design methods of furniture products driven by user demands: Packaging Engineering (2022)

Xu, Q.L., Jiao, R.J., Yang, X., Helander, M., Khalidk, H.M., Opperud, A.: An analytical Kano model for customer need analysis. Des. Stud. **30**(1), 87–110 (2009). https://doi.org/10.1016/j.destud.2008.07.001

Xuenan, L., Jianghong, Z.: 基于智能制造的声音建模交互设计 In: 李雪楠 & 赵江洪 (eds.), 包装工程, vol. 38, pp. 103–107. Voice modeling interaction design based on intelligent manufacturing: Packaging Engineering (2017)

Yu-Xuan, D., Zhang, Z., Ning-Feng, C., Ling, T.: 基于AHP, QFD与AD的居家适老座椅设计研究 In: 戴宇轩, 章彰, 陈宁峰, & 唐琳 (eds.), 包装工程, vol. 43, pp. 228–236. Design of home-suitable seat for the elderly on AHP, QFD and AD: Packaging Engineering (2022)

The Effects of Pop-Up Window Position and Gender Difference on the Visual Search of Mobile Applications

Jiwei He and Chien-Hsiung Chen[✉]

Department of Design, National Taiwan University of Science and Technology, Taipei 10607, Taiwan
{D11010802,cchen}@mail.ntust.edu.tw

Abstract. In user interface design, pop-up windows are widely used to help direct user attention effectively. The reasonable use of the characteristics of pop-up windows can accurately guide users' attention, emphasize the importance of crucial information, and thus improve users' efficiency in visual-searching and decision-making. This study aims to investigate the effects of the pop-up window position and gender difference on the users' visual search process pertinent to mobile applications. The research variables were the locations of the pop-up window (i.e., at the center and bottom of the screen) and gender difference (i.e., male and female). A total of 40 participants were invited to take part in the experiment via convenience sampling methods. The experiment was a 2 × 2 between-subjects design. The data generated in the experiment were obtained from participants' task performance, questionnaire of System Usability Scale (SUS), participants' subjective evaluations, and post-experiment semi-structured interviews. The results of the study showed that: (1) The main effect of gender difference revealed significant difference in task performance, with males were more likely to find task goals than females. (2) The main effect of the pop-up window position made a significant difference on the System Usability Scale (SUS), with participants' perceived ease-of-use being higher when the window was located in the center of the screen. (3) There were also significant gender difference in users' subjective evaluation pertinent to the pop-up windows. (4) There was a significant interaction effect between the pop-up window position and gender difference on the search task, i.e., when the window was located in the center of the screen, the female performed better than the males. When the pop-up window was at the bottom of the screen, males performed better than females. The research findings can be good design references for the interaction designers in the near future.

Keywords: Pop-up Windows · Gender Difference · Visual Search · Interaction Design

1 Introduction

Government healthcare systems are under cost pressure as the number of people with chronic diseases increases globally (Wootton, 2012). As a result, there has been a gradual shift in care models to home and community-based settings and an increase in the

© The Author(s), under exclusive license to Springer Nature Switzerland AG 2024
J. Wei and G. Margetis (Eds.): HCII 2024, LNCS 14738, pp. 237–247, 2024.
https://doi.org/10.1007/978-3-031-60487-4_18

number of telecare models where patients are involved in self-management (National Association for Home Care & Hospoce, 2010). Telecare enables online communication through the Internet and mobile devices, breaking through the limitations of traditional care and enhancing patient consultation flexibility (Qiu et al., 2018). With the popularity of mobile applications, more and more patients use mobile devices for online consultation (McGowan, 2008). Mobile devices have become an indispensable part of people's lives as communication tools and for handling application tasks (LavidBen Lulu & Kuflik, 2016). Touch interfaces reduce user anxiety and improve efficiency and performance compared to traditional methods (Umemuro, 2004; Iwase & Murata, 2002). However, system usability issues with telecare applications mainly arise during the online consultation interaction phase (Agnisarman et al., 2017). Thus, user decision-making is directly governed by interactive interface usability issues, which have a direct and far-reaching impact on information search.

However, the fundamental goal of information search is to provide support for decision-making in terms of reducing risk and uncertainty and enhancing the decision and selection process in terms of content information selection. At this point, providing information for decision-making is essential by directing the user's attention through pop-up windows. A small pop-up window appears suddenly on a display and attracts the user's attention by popping up unexpectedly (Chou et al., 2008). These windows can be used to draw the user's attention to a specific location on the screen in a targeted manner to achieve an attention-getting effect (Constantin, 2007). More specifically, pop-up windows can increase the visual presentation by emphasizing the information presented in the window to elicit a higher level of attention from the user (Bétrancourt & Bisseret, 1998). Therefore, in this study, window presentation position was used as an independent variable, and two levels of comparative evaluation were conducted with on-screen pop-ups at the middle and bottom to explore users' visually-guided performance in a telecare application.

It has been shown that gender differences in user interface design are considered to be essential factors (Hubona & Shirah, 2006). With the development of digital information technology, effective management of information overload on mobile devices, including searching, selecting, organizing, and synthesizing information from multiple sources, has become important (Moore, 1995). The popularity of mainstream platforms such as Internet social media, e-commerce, and search engines has raised widespread concern about how different user groups interact (Bloch et al, 1986; Fodness & Murray, 1997). Recent studies have shown that age, education level, and gender are the main factors influencing online information search behavior (Maghferat & Stock, 2010; Singer et al, 2012; Steinerová & Šušol, 2007). Therefore, it is essential to consider these human factors while we study the usability of pop-up window interfaces.

2   Method

2.1   Research Methodology and Participants

In this study, the task performance measure and the subjective evaluation questionnaire were used to collect the experimental data and a 2×2 between-subjects design was adopted. The first independent variable is the pop-up window position (i.e., middle position, bottom position); The second independent variable is the participants' gender (i.e., male, female). Through analysis of variance (ANOVA) on task performance and subjective evaluation of the experimental samples, the aim is to summarize and generalize the actual effects of pop-up window position and gender difference in user interface of applications and, ultimately, present conclusions and recommendations. The study invited 40 participants through convenience sampling method. These participants were all university students, mainly in the age range of 18–30 years old, including 20 males and 20 females, 17 of whom had experience in using applications related to telecare online booking. All participants had no visual impairment, and were accustomed to using their right hand to operate mobile apps. They also had no barriers to using mobile apps. Before the start of the study, participants were informed of their right to stop the experiment at any time. After the experiment, their data would be collected and analyzed confidentially and anonymously.

2.2 Research Samples and Tools

This study took the references of the user interfaces from the top three downloaded telemedicine applications (apps) in Taiwan. Experiment prototypes were created in this study. That is, the process included graphic design and drawing via Illustrator, and high fidelity interface layout and editing graphics with Figma. Eventually, these user interfaces were imported into the mobile app in order to be rendered on the mobile handset as shown in Fig. 1 and to ensure that the task instructions were completed properly between the components. The following tools and devices were used in this study; (1) an Apple 13 Pro mobile phone equipped with a touch-sensitive screen; (2) System Usability Scale (SUS) and Subjective Evaluation Scale; (3) on-screen recording software.

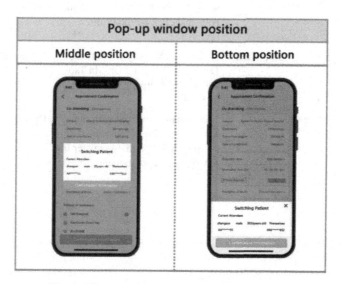

Fig. 1. The two prototypes used in this experiment

2.3 Experimental Task Design and Flow

In this study, the participants were randomly divided into four groups according to the experimental requirements. The experiment lasted for 15 min in a noise-free environment and the procedure is shown in Table 1. After the participants signed the informed consent form, they were informed about the experimental procedure, and then the task manipulation was officially started. The experiment contained three appointments in the front-end of the telemedicine application. The experiment recorded the time spent on each task from the start of the task instruction to the time the participant successfully identified the target. The manipulation time was recorded by the on-screen software for subsequent quantitative analysis. In addition, at the end of the experiment, participants were asked to complete a subjective evaluation questionnaire about the task of operating telemedicine applications (apps). The questionnaire used a 7-point Likert scale with a minimum score of 1 (very dissatisfied) and a maximum score of 7 (very satisfied) for each item. The results of these data helped analyze the subjective feelings of the participants towards the application. All participants had not used the prototypes created in this experiment before performing the task operations to avoid participants having a learning effect on performance. In addition, the researcher observed the participants' task operations in the field, followed by semi-structured interviews with a representative sample of participants. The research framework of this study is shown in Fig. 2.

Table 1. Experimental task designs of this study

Task	Mission Theme	Descriptions	Mission Difficulty
1	Find Personal Information	Locate the My Member Info section at the bottom of the home page and click on the Profile option	Easy
2	Comparison of Outpatient Doctors	Enquiry on Surgery Outpatient, Dr. Wang Hong and Dr. Ma Tao Remaining Outpatient on 13 May at 14:00	Moderate
3	Find a Doctor	Make an appointment with the Gastroenterology Department on 13 May at 9:30 a.m. to register for any doctor's appointment	Difficult

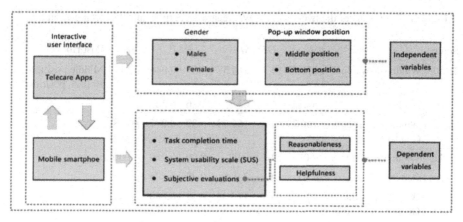

Fig. 2. The research framework of this study

3   Results and Discussions

The data collected in this study were analyzed using SPSS statistical software. The process of analyzing the data was carried out through a two-way ANOVA, which aimed to compare the differences between the pop-up window positions (middle position, bottom position), as well as a comparison of the gender of the participants (i.e. male, female).

3.1   The Analysis of Task Performance

Task performance, defined as the combined time taken from the start of a participant's task instruction to the participant's successful identification of the target in each task, was generated from an intergroup experimental comparison between the two pop-up window positions and the genders, to analyze the differences between the main effect and the interaction effect. The experimental results were illustrated in Table 2.

The find personal information feature option in Task 1 through the Telecare mobile app. The result of the two-way ANOVA regarding task completion time was revealed in Table 4. It showed a significant main effect of pop-up window position ($F = 4.29$, $P = 0.046 < 0.05$; $\eta^2 = 0.11$). Specifically, participants took less time to find personal data under the pop-up window in the middle position ($M = 15.16$, $SD = 5.79$) relative to the pop-up window in the bottom position ($M = 19.81$, $SD = 8.59$). The reason may be that it was related to participants' visual search habit, when participants only needed to complete the confirmation information in the window, the pop-up window in the middle position is more in line with their needs for simple task visual search. That is, participants performed faster in searching and confirming information when the pop-up window was in the middle of the window. This result is consistent with earlier research that the center of the screen has a higher sensitivity in visual perception, relative to the perception of information in surrounding areas (Vitu et al., 2004). There was no significant main effect between participants' gender ($F = 1.26$, $P > 0.269$; $\eta^2 = 0.03$). In addition, there was

Table 2. The results of the two-way ANOVA regarding participants' task completion time

Source		SS	DF	MS	F	P	η^2	Post Hoc
Task1	Window position	215.57	1	215.57	4.29	0.046*	0.11	Middle position < Bottom position
	Gender	63.35	1	63.35	1.26	0.269	0.03	
	Window position × Gender	166.79	1	166.79	3.32	0.077	0.08	
Task2	Window position	0.07	1	0.07	0.00	0.959	0.00	
	Gender	7.91	1	7.91	0.32	0.578	0.01	
	Window position × Gender	113.33	1	113.33	4.53	0.040*	0.11	
Task3	Window position	29.38	1	29.38	2.70	0.109	0.07	
	Gender	0.14	1	0.14	0.01	0.909	0.00	
	Window position × Gender	60.22	1	60.22	5.54	0.024*	0.13	

*Significantly different at the $\alpha = 0.05$ level (*p < 0.05).

no significant interaction between the location of the pop-up window and participants' gender ($F = 3.32$, $P < 0.077$; $\eta^2 = 0.08$).

In Task 2, we compared the telecare app's outpatient registration time using the two-way ANOVA. The results showed no significant difference in the main effect of pop-up window position ($F = 0.00$, $P > 0.959$; $\eta^2 = 0.00$). In addition, there was no significant difference in the main effect of participants' gender ($F = 0.32$, $P > 0.578$; $\eta^2 = 0.01$). However, it was found that a significant interaction between pop-up window position and the participants' gender ($F = 4.53$, $P = 0.040 < 0.05$; $\eta^2 = 0.11$), as shown in Fig. 3. Specifically, males searched for information more efficiently than females when the window was located at the bottom; on the contrary, females searched more efficiently when the visual window was located in the middle. This may be because females are more likely to focus on local information during task manipulation. When the pop-up window is located in the middle, it can direct visual attention to focus on local information processing within the window. On the contrary, the viewport window at the bottom may lead to overlapping information, distracting females' attention. In contrast, although males' visual search was not as focused on local information as females, their problem-solving efficiency was relatively faster in the face of potentially distracting information. This finding is consistent with studies by Halpern (2013) and Rohr (2006), suggesting that females are more likely to focus on local information when solving a problem or performing a task. In contrast, males are more speed-orientated and are more efficient as problem solvers in tasks with complex information.

Task 3 is the completion of the gastroenterology department's May 13th, 9:30 a.m. Arbitrary physician clinic registration. After a two-way ANOVA of task completion time, the findings indicated no significant main effect in the pop-up window position ($F = 2.70$, $P > 0.109$; $\eta^2 = 0.07$). There was also no significant difference in the main effect of the

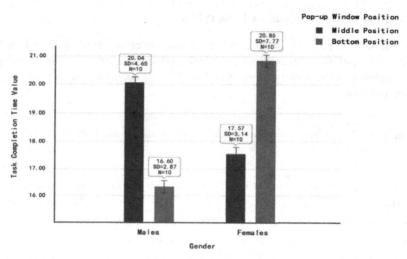

Fig. 3. Interaction between pop-up window position and gender of Task 2

participants' gender ($F = 0.01$, $P > 0.909$; $\eta^2 = 0.00$). However, there was a significant interaction effect between the pop-up window position and participants' gender ($F = 5.54$, $P < 0.024$; $\eta^2 = 0.13$), as shown in Fig. 4. Unlike Task 2, Task 3 attempted to explore the differences by adding the Confirmation of Outpatient Registration pop-up window, but the interaction plot showed results is consistent with Task 2. This means that the confirmation session did not present results that differed from Task 2.

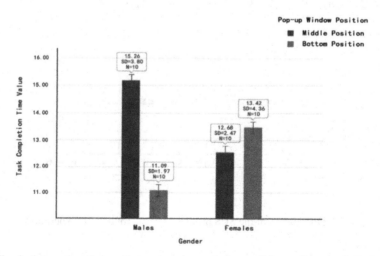

Fig. 4. Interaction diagram between pop-up window position and gender in Task 3

3.2 Analysis of System Usability Scale (SUS)

At the end of the experiment, participants were asked to complete the System Usability Scale (SUS) questionnaire containing a 5-point Likert scale assessment of the prototype's system usability. Subsequently, a two-way ANOVA was conducted, and the results was presented in Table 3.

Table 3. The results of the two-way ANOVA regarding the System Usability Scale (SUS)

Source	SS	DF	MS	F	P	η^2	Post Hoc
Window position	975.16	1	975.16	5.28	0.028*	0.13	Bottom position < Middle position
Gender	472.66	1	472.66	2.56	0.118	0.07	
Window position × Gender	237.66	1	237.66	1.29	0.264	0.03	

*Significantly different at the $\alpha = 0.05$ level (*p < 0.05).

The results of the two-way ANOVA regarding the System Usability Scale (SUS) was shown in Table 3. There was a significant difference in the main effect of pop-up window position ($F = 5.28$, p < 0.028; $\eta^2 = 0.13$). There was no significant difference in the main effect of participants' gender ($F = 2.56$, $P > 0.118$; $\eta^2 = 0.07$). In addition, there was no significant interaction effect between pop-up window position and the participants' gender ($F = 1.29$, $P < 0.264$; $\eta^2 = 0.03$) (Fig. 5).

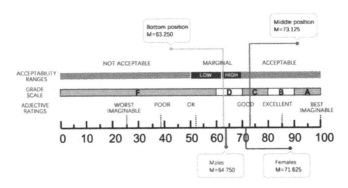

Fig. 5. Distribution of the SUS profiles of each group in the experiment

In summary, with the pop-up window in the middle position, the participant demonstrated a significant increase in system usability ($M = 73.125$, $SD = 14.00$). This result exceeded the participant's required score (i.e., 68). It further emphasizes the importance of a middle-positioned pop-up window for improving system usability.

3.3 Analysis of Subjective Evaluations

The subjective evaluation questionnaire was based on a 7-point Likert scale, with the highest value of 7 indicating a strong preference and the lowest value of 1 indicating a strong dislike. The subjective evaluation questionnaires were completed by the participants after they finished the required task. The collected data were analyzed by a two-way ANOVA, and the results were presented in Table 4.

Table 4. The two-way ANOVA of participants' subjective evaluations.

Source		SS	DF	MS	F	P	η^2	Post Hoc
Degree of reasonableness	Window position	6.40	1	6.40	4.10	0.050	0.10	
	Gender	16.90	1	16.90	10.83	0.002*	0.23	Males < Females
	Window position × Gender	0.90	1	0.90	0.58	0.453	0.02	
Helpfulness	Window position	7.23	1	7.23	5.07	0.031*	0.12	Bottom position < Middle position
	Gender	4.23	1	4.23	2.97	0.094	0.08	
	Window position × Gender	0.23	1	0.23	0.16	0.693	0.00	

*Significantly different at the $\alpha = 0.05$ level (*p < 0.05).

The results of analyzing the subjective evaluations of the degree of reasonableness was shown in Table 4. There was no significant difference in the main effect of the pop-up window position (F = 4.10, P = 0.050 > 0.05; $\eta^2 = 0.10$). There was a significant difference in the main effect of participants' gender (F = 10.83, P = 0.002 < 0.05; $\eta^2 = 0.23$). Specifically, females (M = 4.30, SD = 1.42) rated the reasonableness of the pop-up window higher comparing to males (M = 5.15, SD = 1.09). In addition, there was no significant interaction effect between the pop-up window position and participants' gender (F = 0.58, P = 0.453 > 0.05; $\eta^2 = 0.02$).

The results of the analysis of the subjective evaluations pertinent to helpfulness was shown in Table 4. There was a significant difference in the main effect of the pop-up window position (F = 5.07, P = 0.031 < 0.05; $\eta^2 = 0.12$). Specifically, participants perceived a higher degree of help interacting with the pop-up window in the middle position (M = 5.45, SD = 1.19) relative to the pop-up window in the bottom position (M = 4.60, SD = 1.23). There was no significant difference in the main effect of participants' gender (F = 2.97, P = 0.094 > 0.05; $\eta^2 = 0.08$). In addition, there was no significant interaction effect between the pop-up window position and the participant's gender (F = 0.16, P = 0.693 > 0.05; $\eta^2 = 0.00$).

In summary, the perceived usability of subjective evaluations was all better when the pop-up window was in the middle position of the screen than when the window was in the bottom position. This may be because the pop-up window is a very effective attention-getting design, which can quickly draw users' attention and response (Tasse et al., 2016). The middle position of window is likelier to direct the user's visual attention during information reading habitually (Lee et al., 2003). This habitual focus on specific areas can help users reduce the visual span of searching for information (Kwon, Legge, & Dubbels, 2007). Moreover, the semi-structured interviews yielded more consistent results. Interestingly, females were generally more sensitive to the presentation of the visual window in the middle position of the screen, which increased the evaluation of overall reasonableness.

4   Conclusions

The main focus of this study was to explore the impact of pop-up window position in the user interface of a telemedicine application regarding the effect of visual guidance for users. The summarized results are as follows: (1) The main effect of gender difference revealed significant difference in task performance. Males were more likely to find task goals than females. (2) The main effect of the pop-up window position made a significant difference in the System Usability Scale (SUS), with participants' perceived ease-of-use being higher when the window was located in the center of the screen. (3) There were also significant gender difference in users' subjective evaluations pertinent to the pop-up window position. (4) There was a significant interaction effect between the pop-up window position and gender difference on the search tasks, i.e., when the pop-up window was located in the center of the screen, the females performed better than the males. These findings provide valuable design references for interaction designers.

Acknowledgements. Financial support of this research study by National Science and Technology Council under the grant MOST 111-2410-H-011-031-MY3 is gratefully acknowledged.

References

Agnisarman, S.O., Chalil Madathil, K., Smith, K., Ashok, A., Welch, B., McElligott, J.T.: Lessons learned from the usability assessment of home-based telemedicine systems. Appl. Ergon. **58**, 424–434 (2017)

Bétrancourt, M., Bisseret, A.: Integrating textual and pictorial information via pop-up windows: an experimental study. Behav. Inf. Technol. **17**(5), 263–273 (1998)

Bloch, P.H., Sherrell, D.L., Ridgway, N.M.: Consumer search: an extended framework. J. Consum. Res. **13**(1), 119–126 (1986)

Chou, Y.P., Horng, S.J., Gu, H.Y., Lee, C.L., Chen, Y.H., Pan, Y.: Detecting pop-up advertisement browser windows using support vector machines. J. Chin. Inst. Eng. **31**(7), 1189–1198 (2008)

Constantin, C.D.: The psychological significance of pop-up windows in online information processing. Unpublished doctoral dissertation. The Pennsylvania State University, State College, PA (2007)

Fodness, D., Murray, B.: Tourist information search. Ann. Tour. Res. **24**(3), 503–523 (1997)

Halpern, D.F.: Sex Differences in Cognitive Abilities, 4th edn. Psychology Press, New York, NY (2013)

Hubona, G.S., Shirah, G.W.: The paleolithic stone age effect? Gender differences performing specific computer-generated spatial tasks. Int. J. Technol. Hum. Interact. (IJTHI) 2(2), 24–48 (2006)

Iwase, H., Murata, A.: Empirical study on improvement of usability -for touch-panel for elderly - comparison of usability between touch-panel and mouse. In: Proceedings of the IEEE International Conference on Systems, Man and Cybernetics, pp. 252–257. IEEE, Piscataway, NJ (2002)

Kwon, M., Legge, G.E., Dubbels, B.R.: Developmental changes in the visual span for reading. Vis. Res. 47(22), 2889–2900 (2007)

Lavid-Ben Lulu, D., Kuflik, T.: Wise mobile icons organization: apps taxonomy classification using functionality mining to ease apps finding. Mob. Inf. Syst. 2016, 3083450 (2016)

Lee, H.W., Legge, G.E., Ortiz, A.: Is word recognition different in central and peripheral vision? Vision. Res. 43(26), 2837–2846 (2003)

Maghferat, P., Stock, W.G.: Gender-specific information search behavior. Webology 7(3) (2010)

McGowan, J.J.: The pervasiveness of telemedicine: adoption with or without a research base. J. Gen. Intern. Med. 23(4), 505–507 (2008)

Moore, P.: Information problem solving: a wider view of library skills. Contemp. Educ. Psychol. 20(1), 1–31 (1995)

National Association for Home Care & Hospice: Basic Statistics About Home Care. National Association for Home Care & Hospice, Washington, DC (2010)

Qiu, Y., Liu, Y., Ren, W., Qiu, Y., Ren, J.: Internet-based and mobile-based general practice: cross-sectional survey. J. Med. Internet Res. 20(9), e266, 1–6 (2018)

Rohr, L.E.: Gender-specific movement strategies using a computer-pointing task. J. Mot. Behav. 38(6), 431–437 (2006)

Singer, G., Norbisrath, U., Lewandowski, D.: Impact of gender and age on performing search tasks online (2012). arXiv preprint arXiv:1206.1494

Steinerová, J., Šušol, J.: Users' information behaviour-a gender perspective. Inf. Res. Int. Electron. J. 12(3) (2007)

Tasse, D., Ankolekar, A., Hailpern, J.: Getting users' attention in web apps in likable, minimally annoying ways. In: Proceedings of the 2016 CHI Conference on Human Factors in Computing Systems, pp. 3324–3334. Association for Computing Machinery, New York, NY (2016)

Umemuro, H.: Lowering elderly Japanese users' resistance towards computers by using touch-screen technology. Univ. Access Inf. Soc. 3(3), 276–288 (2004)

Vitu, F., Kapoula, Z., Lancelin, D., Lavigne, F.: Eye movements in reading isolated words: evidence for strong biases towards the center of the screen. Vision. Res. 44(3), 321–338 (2004)

Wootton, R.: Twenty years of telemedicine in chronic disease management-an evidence synthesis. J. Telemed. Telecare 18(4), 211–220 (2012)

Effects of Social Media Usage on Sojourners' Sense of Belonging in Cross-Cultural Environments: The Combination of Environmental and Personal Factors

Fengle Ji[1] and Shangui Hu[2(✉)]

[1] Beijing Foreign Studies University, Beijing, People's Republic of China
fengle@bfsu.edu.cn
[2] Ningbo University of Finance and Economics, Ningbo, Zhejiang, People's Republic of China
stanleyhu@nbufe.edu.cn

Abstract. The development of international sojourners' sense of belonging in a cross-cultural environment has been research focus for long. However, with the development of information technology, how social media usage (SMU), as an indispensable tool in people's lives, affects the enhancement of individuals' sense of belonging, especially for international sojourners, has not received sufficient attention. This study aims to explore how different dimensions of SMU affects sense of belonging by taking the sample of international students in two separate studies, and unveil the underlying mechanism (fit to the university as a mediating variable) and boundary condition (personality of extroversion as a moderating variable). Data from two studies found that SMU (information and socializing) positively influenced sense of belonging and fit to the university mediated the positive relationship between SMU (information and socializing) and sense of belonging. In addition, personality of extroversion not only negatively mediated the positive relationship between SMU (information and socializing) and fit to the university, but also indirectly moderated the positive relationships between SMU (information and socializing) and sense of belonging.

Keywords: Sense of belonging · Social media usage · Fit to the university · Personality of extroversion · Cross-cultural environments

1 Introduction

Economic development has facilitated the transnational mobility of talent (Zhang and Zeng 2023). And research on how to facilitate their cross-cultural psychological adaptation in a foreign culture is of great value, for example, the formation of a sense of belonging (Wells and Horn 2015; Chen et al. 2022). The development of individuals' sense of belonging is of great significance to their work, study and life in a foreign culture (Hu et al. 2020b; Gopalan et al. 2022). And research has pointed to the important impact of social support on the establishment of a sense of belonging in cross-cultural environment (Wegemer and Sarsour 2023; Wang et al. 2022). Accordingly, with the development of technology, social media is used extensively among cross-cultural individuals and has been identified as an important avenue for them to access information and emotional support (Hu et al. 2023b; Hu et al. 2023a). Through the literature review, we found that existing studies have been conducted to touch upon how social media usage (SMU) enhances sense of belonging (Pang 2020; Eren and Vardarlier 2013; Smith 2022), but the research findings were against a monocultural context, ignoring the complexity of cross-cultural environments. Moreover, the mechanisms and boundary conditions under which different dimensions of SMU (information and socializing) affect the sense of belonging in cross-cultural environments need to be further explored.

2 Research Model and Theoretical Development

Sense of belonging refers to "a pervasive drive to form and maintain at least a minimum quantity of lasting, positive, and significant interpersonal relationships" (Baumeister and Sommer 1997, p.497). In a heterogeneous cultural environment, cultural differences hinder the establishment of good interpersonal relationships between cross-cultural individuals (Hu et al. 2021). Therefore, individuals can use social media to satisfy their knowledge of foreign cultures and remove the barriers caused by cultural distance (Hu et al. 2021). For example, studies have pointed out that SMU can enhance an individuals' intercultural competence, cultural intelligence, helping individuals to exhibit appropriate behavior in different intercultural situations at the metacognitive and cognitive levels to avoid misunderstandings and conflicts (Hu and Zhu 2022; Hu et al. 2020b).

SMU not only fulfills an individual's cognitive needs, but also helps to create good emotional connections between individuals (Hu and Zhu 2022; Hu et al. 2023a). Research suggests that SMU can be used to enhance cross-cultural individuals' ability to communicate with the local community and build good peer relationships (Hu et al. 2021). Moreover, adequate interaction with locals can also facilitate cross-cultural individuals' identity with the host country's culture to build a stronger emotional bond (Hu et al. 2020a).

H1a: SMU for information enhances individuals' sense of belonging in a cross-cultural environment.

H1b: SMU for socializing enhances individuals' sense of belonging in a cross-cultural environment.

Research has shown that personal and organizational fit enhances an individual's sense of psychological safety and demonstrates more safe behaviors. (Wang et al. 2021). In a cross-cultural environment, international students may not be familiar with the rules, regulations and cultural and social environments of their host universities (Yu et al. 2019). Moreover, the differences between Western and Chinese teaching and management styles may make international students feel uncomfortable and difficult to integrate into their university environment (Zhang and Zeng 2023). But, SMU can provide international students with sufficient information to understand their schools and overcome the fear of the unknown in preparing themselves for their university (Yu et al. 2019). On the other hand, SMU can also create an emotional connection between international students and their teachers and classmates at their schools (Hu et al. 2021). Through social media, international students can find classmates who share same interests in order to engage in deeper emotional interactions, and online communication without face-to-face interaction can help students who have offline social difficulties (Chen et al. 2022). In addition, interacting with teachers can help international students understand the meaning of classroom activities, and it can also help teachers understand their students and optimize classroom content (Xu et al. 2022). These behaviors above also lay the foundation for good and lasting relationships and ultimately international students' sense of belonging to their host universities.

H2a: Fit to the university mediates the relationship between SMU for information and sense of belonging.

H2b: Fit to the university mediates the relationship between SMU for socializing and sense of belonging.

Based on the resource conservation theory (Xiang et al. 2023), this study posits that individuals possess finite resources. The study contends that individuals with personality of extraversion will utilize social media proactively to socialize and search for information. On one hand, during the process of gathering information, individuals with personality of extraversion may glean overloaded information that exceeds their cognitive capacity, which in turn creates anxiety and discomfort of missing out on important information (Cao and Yu 2019; Zhang et al. 2021). On the other hand, individuals with personality of extraversion also engage in a wide range of social activities through social media, which may cause social overload (Hu et al. 2020b). Moreover, larger social networks consume lots of individuals' resources and cause social fatigue (Guo et al. 2020). Therefore, individuals with personality of extraversion can overuse social media and cause failure to fit to the university.

H3a: The positive relationship between SMU for information and fit to the university is weakened when the level of personality of extraversion is high.

H3b: The positive relationship between SMU for socializing and fit to the university is weakened when the level of personality of extraversion is high.

Furthermore, the present study further suggests that personality of extraversion further moderates the indirect relationship between SMU and sense of belonging through fit to the university. When personality of extraversion is high, individuals may overuse social media resulting in cognitive and affective overloads that diminish their ability to fit to the university, resulting in barriers to campus inclusion for international students and preventing them from developing a sense of belonging.

H4a: Personality of extroversion negatively moderates the indirect relationship between SMU for information and sense of belonging through fit to the university.

H4b: Personality of extroversion negatively moderates the indirect relationship between SMU for socializing and sense of belonging through fit to the university (Fig. 1).

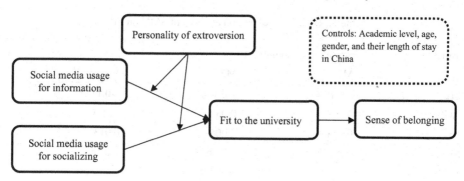

Fig. 1. Proposed research model

3   Research Methodology

The study regarded international students studying in China as good samples and data were collected through two separate questionnaires. A total of 332 questionnaires were collected in the first to confirm whether SMU (information and socializing) has a significant effect on sense of belonging in cross-cultural environment. The second questionnaire was used to collect data from a large sample (N = 2058) to explore how SMU (information and socializing) affects sense of belonging and its boundary effects.

The current study adopted a six-item scale from Hughes et al. (2012) to assess the two dimensions of social media usage. Personality of extroversion was tested with a 4-item scale from Tsang (2001). Sense of belonging included 4-item scale from Glass and Westmo (2014). And the measurement of fit to the university was adopted from Cable and Judge (1996).

4   Results

4.1   Study 1

Table 1 demonstrates the impact of different dimensions of SMU on sense of belonging. From Model 1 we know that the SMU for information (SMUI) has a significant positive impact on the sense of belonging (r = 0.204, p < 0.01); and the SMU for socializing (SMUS) also has a significant positive impact on the sense of belonging (r = 0.222, p < 0.01). Therefore, H1a and H1b were verified.

4.2   Study 2

Based on the research conclusions drawn from Study 1, this study conducted a further Study 2 to explore the mediating mechanisms by which SMU has an impact on sense of belonging, as well as its boundary effects. And, Table 2 demonstrates that there is a good convergent and discriminant validity between the variables of this study.

What's more, fit to the university not only positively mediated the relationship between SMUI and sense of belonging (r = 0.102, 95% CI [0.057, 0.148]), but also

Table 1. Results of regression analysis of SMU on SB

Variable	Sense of belonging		
	M1	M2	M3
SEX	−0.109	−0.124*	−0.115*
AGE	0.061	0.080	0.080
HD	0.034	0.005	0.013
SL	−0.177**	−0.161**	−0.156
SMUI		0.204**	
SMUS			0.222**
R^2	0.048	0.088	0.096
ΔR^2		0.040	0.048
ΔF		14.185**	17.111**

SB = Sense of belonging; SMUI = social media usage for information; SMUS = social media usage for socializing;

Table 2. Measurement of constructs

Constructs	Dimensions	Items	Loadings	CR	AVE	Cronbach alphas
SMU	Socializing	3	0.853–0.885	0.766	0.908	0.843
	Information	3	0.791–0.873	0.869	0.689	0.763
FTU		3	0.933–0.940	0.956	0.877	0.930
PE		4	0.737–0.883	0.910	0.718	0.861
SB		4	0.876–0.910	0.943	0.807	0.920

Notes: SMU = social media usage; PE = Personality of extroversion; FTU = Fit to the university; SB = sense of belonging.

positively mediated the relationship between SMUS and sense of belonging (r = 0.204, 95% CI [0.160, 0.248]). So, H2a and H2b were both supported.

Finally, we test the conditional indirect effect of SMUI (SMUS) on sense of belonging through fit to the university at different levels of personality of extroversion with Mplus8.3 (see Table 4). This study found that personality of extroversion also moderated the indirect effect between SMUI (SMUS) and sense of belonging. Hence H4a and H4b were supported as well.

4.3 Hypothesis Testing

Based on the structural equation model analysis, Fig. 2 and Table 3 present the results of the large sample data analysis. From Fig. 2, we know that the SMUI (r = 0.050, p < 0.01) and SMUS (r = 0.082, p < 0.01) have a significant positive impact on the sense of belonging. Therefore, H1a and H1b were verified in study 2. Besides, personality

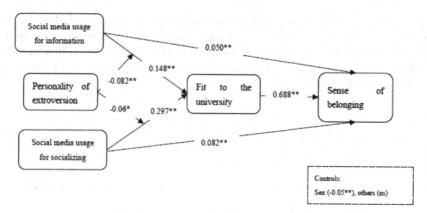

Fig. 2. Results of the hypothesized model

Table 3. Results of the mediating effect

Mediating effect	estimate	SE	P	BC 95% CI	
				lower	upper
SMUI-FTU-SB	0.102	0.023	0.000	0.057	0.148
SMUS-FTU-SB	0.204	0.022	0.000	0.160	0.248

Notes: SMUI = social media usage for information; SMUS = social media usage for socializing; FTU = fit to the university; SB = sense of belonging.

Table 4. Indirect effects of SMUI (SMUS) on sense of belonging

Moderator	Level	Indirect Effect	SE	95% CI
personality of extroversion (SMUI-FTU-SB)	high	0.145	0.000	[0.108, 0.184]
	low	0.046	0.012	[0.011, 0.082]
	The index of moderated mediation	−0.099	0.000	[−0.139, −0.053]
personality of extroversion (SMUS-FTU-SB)	high	0.166	0.000	[0.125, 0.204]
	low	0.095	0.000	[0.055, 0.135]
	The index of moderated mediation	−0.070	0.004	[−0.116, −0.019]

Notes: SMUI = social media usage for information; SMUS = social media usage for socializing; FTU = fit to the university; SB = sense of belonging.

of extroversion negatively moderated the positive relationship between SMUI and fit to university (r = −0.082, p < 0.01), and also negatively moderated the positive relationship between SMUS and fit to university (r = −0.06, p < 0.01). So, H3a and H3b were tested. And, the negative moderating effect personality of extroversion was tested in the simple slope analysis (Fig. 3 and Fig. 4).

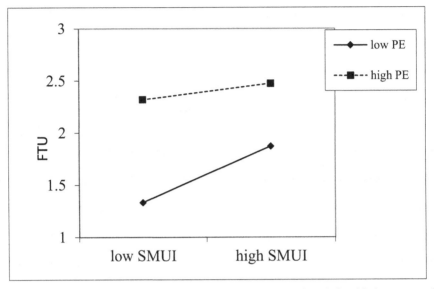

Fig. 3. Moderating effect of Personality of extroversion (PE) on the relationship between social media usage for information (SMUI) and Fit to the university (FTU)

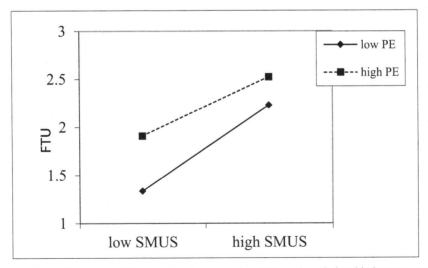

Fig. 4. Moderating effect of Personality of extroversion (PE) on the relationship between social media usage for socializing (SMUS) and Fit to the university (FTU)

5 Discussion

This study, grounded on P-E fit theory, illuminates how social media usage in conjunction with individual factors (personality of extroversion) influence sense of belonging through fit to the university. The results of the study indicated that both SMUI and SMUS positively influenced the enhancement of sense of belonging; fit to the university played a positive mediating role between two dimensions of SMU (SMUI, SMUS) and sense of belonging; and personality of extroversion negatively moderated not only the direct relationship between two dimensions of SMU and fit to the university, but also the indirect relationship between two dimensions of SMU and sense of belonging. The current study makes significant contributions both theoretically and practically.

This study expands research in the area related to sense of belonging in a cross-cultural context. Most of the previous studies about SMU and sense of belonging have been conducted in a monocultural context (Pang 2020; Eren and Vardarlıer 2013), and this study considers how the informational and social dimensions of SMU affect sense of belonging through fit to the university in a cross-cultural context, using international students in China as the study subject. It enriches our understanding of how SMUI (SMUS) affects international students' sense of belonging through fit to the university. In addition, this study takes into account a combination of how individual and environmental factors impact on fit to the university and sense of belonging in a cross-cultural context. The present study found that personality of extroversion plays a negative moderating role between SMU, fit to the university, and sense of belonging. It enriches the literature related to exploring boundary conditions in the formation of sense of belonging in a cross-cultural setting.

This study found that fit to the university is an important channel for SMU to influence international students' sense of belonging. Therefore, school administrators should stress the use of social media to provide international students with relevant information and emotional interactions so that they can better integrate into the campus and the classroom, thus laying the foundation for the establishment of a sense of belonging. Moreover, this study also found the negative impact of personality of extroversion. Accordingly, it's important for school administrators to emphasize students' personality tests for the purpose of facilitating timely guidance for international students with high levels of personality of extroversion to avoid over-utilization of social media and to reduce the negative impact of personality of extroversion on fit to the university and sense of belonging.

6 Limitations and Future Research Avenues

This study also has the following limitations. Firstly, due to the limitations imposed by cross-sectional data, this study's conclusions are correlational, rather than causal. Specifically, the study suggests that SMU can contribute to an individual's sense of belonging through its affective and information exchange functions. However, the research also found that individuals with a sense of belonging have a greater intrinsic motivation to be socially active and are therefore more dependent on SMU (Miranda et al. 2023). Therefore, longitudinal data can be used in the future to further substantiate the causal relationship between variables. Secondly, the findings of this study are based on international students in China. However, due to the differences between Chinese and Western cultures, future research could be conducted in Western individualistic countries to further substantiate the findings of this study. Thirdly, this study only investigated the role of international students' fit to the university as a mechanism to enhance their sense of belonging. Due to the complexity of cross-cultural environments, future research could consider other important factors to enrich this area of study.

Acknowledgement. This research was supported by Zhejiang Philosophy and Social Sciences Foundation (grant no. 22LLXC05Z) and 2019' National Education Sciences Planning Project of China (BBA190019).

References

Baumeister, R.F., Sommer, K.L.: What do men want? Gender differences and two spheres of belongingness: comment on Cross and Madson. Psychol. Bull. **122**(1), 38–44 (1997)

Cable, D.M., Judge, T.A.: Person–organization fit, job choice decisions, and organizational entry. Organ. Behav. Hum. Decis. Process. **67**(3), 294–311 (1996)

Cao, X., Yu, L.: Exploring the influence of excessive social media use at work: a three-dimension usage perspective. Int. J. Inform. Manage. **46**, 83–92 (2019)

Chen, Y.A., Fan, T., Toma, C.L., Scherr, S.: International students' psychosocial well-being and social media use at the onset of the COVID-19 pandemic: a latent profile analysis. Comput. Hum. Behav. **137**, 107409 (2022)

Eren, E., Vardarlıer, P.: Social media's role in developing an employees sense of belonging in the work place as an HRM strategy. Procedia Soc. Behav. Sci. **99**, 852–860 (2013)

Glass, C.R., Westmont, C.M.: Comparative effects of belongingness on the academic success and cross-cultural interactions of domestic and international students. Int. J. Intercult. Rel. **38**, 106–119 (2014)

Gopalan, M., Linden-Carmichael, A., Lanza, S.: College students' sense of belonging and mental health amidst the COVID-19 pandemic. J. Adolesc. Health. **70**(2), 228–233 (2022)

Guo, Y., Lu, Z., Kuang, H., Wang, C.: Information avoidance behavior on social network sites: information irrelevance, overload, and the moderating role of time pressure. Int. J. Account. Inf. **52**, 102067 (2020)

Hu, S., Akram, U., Ji, F., Zhao, Y., Song, J.: Does social media usage contribute to cross-border social commerce? An empirical evidence from SEM and fsQCA analysis. Acta Psychol. **241**, 104083 (2023)

Hu, S., Hu, L., Wang, G.: Moderating role of addiction to social media usage in managing cultural intelligence and cultural identity change. Inform. Technol. People **34**(2), 704–730 (2020)

Hu, S., Hu, L., Wu, J., Wang, G.: Social media usage and international expatriate's creativity: an empirical research in cross-cultural context. Hum. Syst. Manage. **40**(2), 197–209 (2021)

Hu, S., Ji, F., Liu, H., Chi, M.: Exploring the impacts of mobile devices usage on individual's creativity: a cross-cultural perspective. Int. J. Mob. Commun. **22**(4), 449–475 (2023)

Hu, S., Liu, H., Zhang, S., Wang, G.: Proactive personality and cross-cultural adjustment: roles of social media usage and cultural intelligence. Int. J. Intercult. Rel. **74**, 42–57 (2020)

Hu, S., Zhu, Z.: Effects of social media usage on consumers' purchase intention in social commerce: a cross-cultural empirical analysis. Front. Psychol. **13**, 837752 (2022)

Hughes, D.J., Rowe, M., Batey, M., Lee, A.: A tale of two sites: twitter vs. Facebook and the personality predictors of social media usage. Comput. Hum. Behav. **28**(2), 561–569 (2012)

Miranda, S., Trigo, I., Rodrigues, R., Duarte, M.: Addiction to social networking sites: motivations, flow, and sense of belonging at the root of addiction. Technol. Forecast Soc. **188** (2023)

Pang, H.: Examining associations between university students' mobile social media use, online self-presentation, social support and sense of belonging. Aslib J. Inform. Manag. **72**(3), 321–338 (2020)

Smith, C.: #iBelong: the stories of sense of belonging and social media from black college students. University of Georgia (2022)

Tsang, E.W.: Adjustment of mainland Chinese academics and students to Singapore. Int. J. Intercult. Rel. **25**(4), 347–372 (2001)

Wang, D., Zong, Z., Mao, W., Wang, L., Maguire, P., Hu, Y.: Investigating the relationship between person–environment fit and safety behavior: a social cognition perspective. J. Safety Res. **79**, 100–109 (2021)

Wang, H., Kodzo, L.D., Wang, Y., Zhao, J., Yang, X., Wang, Y.: The benefits of career adaptability on African international students' perception of social support and quality of life in China during the COVID-19 pandemic. Int. J. Intercult. Rel. **90**, 1–10 (2022)

Wegemer, C.M., Sarsour, N.: College services, sense of belonging, and friendships: the enduring importance of the high school context. J. Lat. Educ. **22**(3), 1046–1064 (2023)

Wells, A.V., Horn, C.: The Asian American college experience at a diverse institution: campus climate as a predictor of sense of belonging. J. Stud. Aff. Res. Pract. **52**(2), 149–163 (2015)

Xiang, K., Liu, J., Qiao, G., Gao, F., Zhang, H.: Does bullying reduce occupational commitment in hospitality employees? Mixed empirical evidence from resource conservation theory and embodied cognition perspectives. Int. J. Hosp. Manag. **108**, 103365 (2023)

Xu, X., Schönrock-Adema, J., Jaarsma, A., Duvivier, R., Bos, N.: A conducive learning environment in international higher education: a systematic review of research on students' perspectives. Educ. Res. Rev. **37**, 100474 (2022)

Yu, Q., Foroudi, P., Gupta, S.: Far apart yet close by: social media and acculturation among international students in the UK. Technol. Forecast Soc. **145**, 493–502 (2019)

Zhang, Y., Li, S., Yu, G.: The relationship between social media use and fear of missing out: a meta-analysis. Acta Psychol. Sin. **53**(3), 273 (2021)

Zhang, Y., Zeng, H.: Acculturation of international students in a non–first-tier city in China. Int. J. Intercult. Rel. **97**, 101873 (2023)

Enhancing User Experience of WeChat Mini-programs on Mobile Devices: A Comprehensive Analysis

Guoying Lu[✉] and Siyuan Qu

Department of Art and Design, Shanghai Dianji University, Shanghai 200240, People's Republic of China

lugy@sdju.edu.cn

Abstract. WeChat mini-programs have over 120 million monthly active users as of 2021, making it a widely used platform. The application scenarios of WeChat mini-programs have penetrated every aspect of people's lives, making user experience a crucial aspect. The focus of user experience is user research. User research enables the construction of user experience by considering the user's perspective. This study aims to optimize the user experience of WeChat mini-programs from a user research perspective. This study employed a scientific bibliometric method to select relevant journal articles from 2016 to 2023 in the Chinese National Knowledge Infrastructure (CNKI) using 'WeChat mini-program' as the keyword and 'user' as the theme. Two software tools, VOSviewer and CiteSpace, were used for analysis. A visual knowledge mapping analysis of the literature exported from the CNKI library search was conducted. In recent years, research on WeChat Mini-program from a user perspective has focused on several areas, including WeChat, CloudBase, Management Systems, System Design, and User Experience. In the future, research on WeChat mini-programs may focus on interdisciplinary aspects such as technology development, application scenarios, and user experience interaction. This study focuses on the hot issues of WeChat mini-program user research in China, understands the current demand for WeChat mini-program user aspects in the Chinese market, explores the optimisation of WeChat mini-program user experience from user research, and guides the future research direction for subsequent researchers.

Keywords: WeChat mini-program · User research · User experience · Users · Bibliometric analysis · Technology development

1 Introduction

1.1 Background to the WeChat Mini-program

Figure 1 shows the evolution of WeChat mini-program since its launch in 2016, from conception to online availability, rapid development to ecological perfection, and finally to the deepening of industry applications. WeChat mini-program is a lightweight application that can run directly within WeChat without the need for downloading and installing.

J. Wei and G. Margetis (Eds.): HCII 2024, LNCS 14738, pp. 258–277, 2024.
https://doi.org/10.1007/978-3-031-60487-4_20

Its primary purpose is to meet the diverse needs of users in various scenarios [1, 2]. The development of WeChat mini-programs involves various technical aspects. Its development technology is characterised by being short, flat, and fast, resulting in a high-quality user experience [3]. As of the third quarter of 2019, the number of active WeChat accounts had reached 1.151 billion [4]. WeChat mini-programs are a new type of application that leverage WeChat's large user base [4]. They can be easily shared through WeChat's social features and have been proven effective for promotion. According to the Aladdin Research Institute, the number of WeChat mini-programs surpassed 3.8 million in 2020, with an average daily usage time of 20 min per person [5]. Mini-programs were developed to cater to the segmented light living application scene in the Web3.0 era, aligning with the fragmented and diversified needs of users in this era[6]. WeChat mini-programs have successfully covered various contents, including games, tools, e-commerce, and information, serving as an entrance to these scenes. WeChat mini-programs have become a popular tool for constructing O2O scenes [1]. Due to the continuous advancement of technology and evolving user needs, it is believed that they will have even greater development potential in the future.

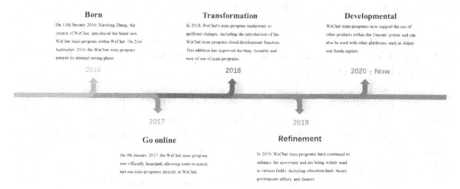

Fig. 1. The evolution of WeChat mini-programs.

1.2 Technology Development of WeChat Mini-program

In terms of technology development, WeChat mini-programs offer cost advantages over the development of general Android and iOS platform applications [4]. This is due to the fact that they do not require complex system architecture design. In 2018, the introduction of the CloudBase function brought significant changes to WeChat mini-programs, further improving their functionality and ease of use. The Tencent Cloud's basic applications and service system architectures form the foundation of its underlying design, resulting in reduced costs for constructing the basic system structure [4]. The ease of use and spatial flexibility of mini-programs have contributed to the rise of the 'wave of mobility' [7]. The WeChat mini-program architecture is similar to an application, classified as a client/server architecture. The server side is responsible for basic data provision and complex processing, using HTTPS for secure data transmission, while user interaction is handled by the client side. When using any mini-program, WeChat assigns a permanent and unique OpenID to each user. Once authenticated, users do not need to re-login every time they access the mini-programs. The WeChat mini-program is based on XML, CSS, and JS. It provides relatively closed WXML, WXSS, and JS and does not support third-party JavaScript frameworks such as DOM, WINDOW, and JQUERY. This distinguishes it from HTML5 [8]. The direct flow of data and information for complex multi-device interfaces, such as APP and WeChat mini-programs [9], is now possible with the development of 5G technology.

1.3 User Research on WeChat Mini-programs

Based on Aladdin's survey data, it appears that WeChat mini-program users are predominantly young, with 46% of users aged 18 to 29. WeChat is developing a super APP ecosystem to meet users' needs for social interaction, e-commerce, information, and services. The functions of WeChat mini-programs, such as QR codes, group chats, search, promotion, and association with WeChat official accounts, are continuously improving. Mini-programs are scene sensors that WeChat uses to construct its super APP ecosystem [1]. They simplify information architecture and provide users with a more direct path to services [3]. For example, mini-programs and QR codes can optimize library services in offline settings [11]. In new retail environments, mini-programs can offer personalized services [7]. Additionally, a second-hand book trading platform based on the circular economy has been developed [12].

WeChat mini-programs can perform the same functions as traditional web technology, but with a superior user experience. This includes faster loading speeds, smoother operation and greater responsiveness [7]. The user experience of a mini application is similar to that of a native mobile application, and the usability of the mini application is equivalent to that of a native application. The mini-program can adapt to different mobile platforms and systems, eliminating the need for repeated page reloads. It loads faster than the website and provides a high-quality user experience [3].

User research typically involves analysing user behaviour, assessing user satisfaction, exploring user participation, designing user experiences and protecting user privacy. By analysing users' behaviour, it is possible to understand their preferences and needs, which provides a basis for optimising and improving the WeChat mini-program [13]. User satisfaction evaluation involves collecting user opinions and feedback on the WeChat mini-program through questionnaires or other means. Users' engagement with WeChat mini-programs, including their activity, frequency of use, retention rate and other relevant indicators. User experience design refers to the study of WeChat mini-program's interface design, interaction design, information architecture, and other aspects. User privacy protection refers to protecting the privacy of users who have concerns about the collection and use of personal information, data security, and other related aspects when using WeChat mini-programs [14].

1.4 User Research and User Experience

User experience design (UXD) is a field that utilises human-computer interaction and user-centred design methods. It encompasses elements from interaction design, visual design, information architecture, and other related disciplines [15]. User research is crucial in providing users with personalised services, optimising the user experience, and enhancing user acceptance [16]. The focus of user experience design should be on user research from the user's perspective. The design object encompasses not only the personalised service but also the entire user experience process within the service [17]. For example, Deng Shengli (2008) [18] highlights the importance of prioritising user experience design in the development and improvement of information service platforms based on network development. This involves focusing on user research and adopting a user-centred approach. Similarly, Li Xiaoqing (2010) [19] notes that since the 1970s, researchers have proposed the use of cognitive research as a theoretical basis for user research, demonstrating the significant impact of users' cognitive and emotional characteristics on their network search behaviour. In her 2019 study, Lan Yuqi [20] proposed an emotional design method for interactive products based on user experience. In order to design effective activities, the study emphasised the importance of focusing on users and analysing their requirements through research. Similarly, Chen Yuehong [21] highlighted the importance of user research in UI design, especially in relation to visual psychological cognition and emotional design. The need for such research is further emphasised by the design industry's increasing focus on user experience. In order to optimise the user experience, this study examines WeChat mini-programs from a user research perspective. The main focus is on how user research can be used to support the construction of the user experience for WeChat mini-programs.

2 Sources and Methods

2.1 Data Sources

As WeChat mini-programs are mainly used in China, this study analyses research data on WeChat mini-program users by Chinese scholars. The data retrieval platform used was CNKI on China Knowledge Network. As WeChat mini-programs were introduced in 2016, the literature review was conducted from 2016 to 2023.

2.2 Research Method

Using the China Knowledge Network CNKI as a data retrieval platform, research data from Chinese scholars on WeChat mini-programs and users were analysed. The analysis tools used were VOSviewer (version 1.6.20) and CiteSpace (version 6.4.R7). The literature exported from CNKI library searches was analysed using visual knowledge mapping. The study examines user research on WeChat mini-programs, with a focus on optimising the user experience. A total of 1,066 articles were identified using a keyword search for 'WeChat mini-programs' and a subject search for 'users'. After de-emphasising and cleaning the data, 1,066 valid articles remained.

CiteSpace and VOSviewer can be used to perform diverse, dynamic and time-shifted visual analyses of literature samples. This can help researchers discover the historical research paths and future development trends of academic research sites from a large amount of sample literature [22].

3   Results and Analysis

3.1   Bibliometric Analysis

Analysis of Document Quantity Distribution Based on Time Axis. The analysis of paper distribution based on timeline is a criterion for evaluating the level of research activity in an academic field [22]. In this research, 1066 documents retrieved from CNKI journals are analysed for their distribution by year. The analysis shows that China published 8 and 31 papers in 2016 and 2017, respectively. From 2018 onwards, the number of published documents exceeded 100 per year, and in 2021, the number of published documents exceeded 200, indicating a sharp increase in research on WeChat mini-programs and user-related research over the past seven years. Figure 2 illustrates this trend.

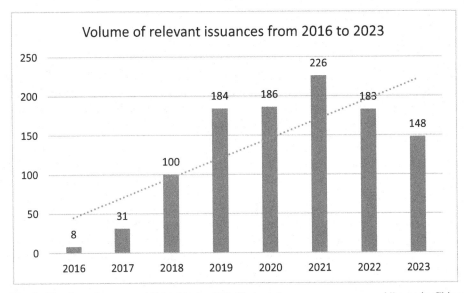

Fig. 2. Number of papers published in the "WeChat mini-program user research" area in China (2016–2023) in China

Distribution and Research Topics of Documentation Discipline Analysis in China. Figure 3 shows that the field with the highest number of published academic papers is 'Computer software and computer applications' with 63.26%. Higher education' follows with 8.49%. The third category is 'Library intelligence and digital libraries', with 4.62%. The fourth category is 'News and media', with 4.47%, and the fifth is 'Commerce', with 4.32%.

The correlation between rows and columns was determined by cross-analysing the 1066 valid search results from CNKI using Co-Occurrence Matrix analysis data. Figure 4a shows the major theme cross-research areas of related fields, including design and research based on APPs, research on WeChat mini-programs based on APPs, development research based on APPs, and research on related functional platforms based on APPs. Figure 4b shows the secondary theme research areas include mobile application development based on APPs, technology used in APP development, research on WeChat mini-programs based on APPs, research on mobile applications based on APPs, and research on related development technologies, functional modules and user experience.

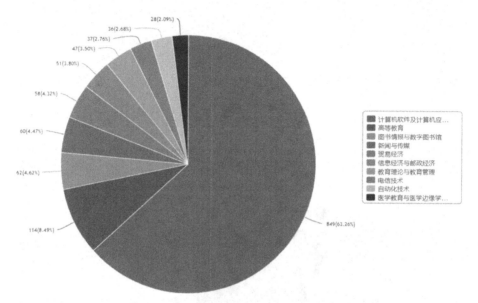

Fig. 3. Distribution of subject areas of WeChat mini-program user research in China (2016–2023)

Statistical Analysis of Literature Periodicals. By analysing the journal articles published in the field of 'WeChat mini-programs', as shown in Fig. 5, it can be seen that Chinese journals pay attention to the topic of WeChat mini-programs research. This research analyses selected key journal articles through the CNKI database. By graphically visualising and analysing the distribution of academic articles in journals in China in the field of "WeChat mini-programs" from 2016–2023, the research articles were mainly published in journals such as Computer and Networks, New Media Research, Technology and Markets, Young Journalists, and Surveying, Mapping and Geographic Information.

Overall, the distribution of academic journals for the study of WeChat users is mainly concentrated in a few major fields, such as Computer, Higher Education, Book Intelligence and Digital Libraries, News and Media, but did not focus on specific journals. The distribution of the research field to which the journal belongs is more consistent with the distribution of the percentage of the number of articles published in the field of research disciplines, as shown in Fig. 3.

Core Author Analysis. The analysis of 1,066 articles in CNKI shows that from 2016 to 2023, in CNKI database, Zhu Yuqiang, Chen Zhengming, Guo Canjie and other authors in the field of WeChat mini-programs published a slightly higher number of articles

Fig. 4. Theme co-occurrence matrix analysis(a) and Secondary theme co-occurrence analysis(b)

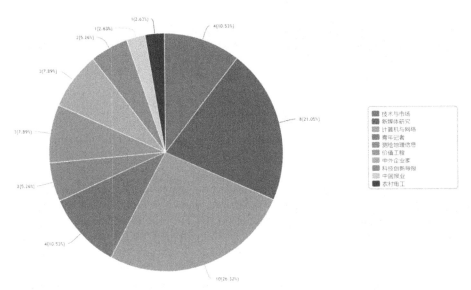

Fig. 5. Distribution of journals in the field of WeChat mini-program user research in China (2016–2023)

than other authors. According to the statistics of the author authentication page of CNKI database, it is found that most of the authors' research fields are related to computer software and computer applications, which is consistent with the results of distribution of subject areas (Fig. 3). Table 1 shows that there are no authors with more prominent publications in the field of WeChat mini-programs.

The author cooperation network analysis of Citespace shows that the connecting line between nodes represents the existence of cooperation between authors, and the width of the connecting line represents the intensity of cooperation [23]. Figure 6 indicates that most WeChat mini-program researchers in China are scattered. Tianlun Zeng, who has published numerous research papers on WeChat applets, has collaborated with Jianzhe Li, Qing Shen, and Ziyan Shu. Their research focuses on WeChat mini-programs that

Table 1. Summary of authors' information

Author name	Paper numbers	Institutions	Research Directions
Zhu Yuqiang	4	Shandong Normal University	Computer software and computer applications; Library information and digital libraries; Light industrial crafts
Guo Canjie	4	Quanzhou Trade Vocational and Technical College	Computer software and computer applications; Sociology and statistics
Chen Zhengming	4	Shaoguan University	Computer software and computer applications; Telecommunications technology; Internet technology
Zhu Ming	3	Suzhou vocational University	Computer software and computer applications; Educational theory and management; Vocational education
Yu Yanbo	3	Hainan Medical University	Computer software and computer applications; Light industrial crafts; Computer hardware technology
Shen Qing	3	Wuhan Business University	Computer software and computer applications; Automotive industry; Higher education
Luo Yaguo	3	Xi'an University	Computer software and computer applications; Computer hardware technology; Internet technology
Ju Hongjun	3	North China Institute of Science and Technology	Computer software and computer applications; Internet technology; Telecommunications technology

(*continued*)

Table 1. (*continued*)

Author name	Paper numbers	Institutions	Research Directions
Zen Tianlun	3	Wuhan Business University	Computer software and computer applications; Biomedical engineering; Higher education
Wu Jingnan	2	Shanghai Bosten Network Technology Co., Ltd. Brain Science Research Center	Computer software and computer applications; Telecommunications technology; Clinical medicine

utilize facial recognition technology. Jingnan Wu has formed a collaborative team with Nan Chen, Yatian Li, and Huanhuan Xia. Their research focuses on cognitive impairment and its relation to WeChat mini-programs. The remaining authors in the top 10 did not appear to have formed a cohesive research team. In general, collaboration among domestic researchers in the field of WeChat mini-program users is relatively sparse, typically involving only two or three individuals, and the level of collaboration is not particularly close.

Fig. 6. Collaboration map of core authors of WeChat mini-program user research in China.

Visualisation Analysis of Research Institutions. The co-occurrence analysis of research institutions was conducted using CiteSpace on 1066 papers in the CNKI database from 2016 to 2023, as illustrated in Fig. 7. The thickness of the connection between nodes indicates the intensity of cooperation between institutions. The analysis of the figure reveals that there is less cooperation between research WeChat mini-program organisations, and the cooperation between organisations is not strong. The analysis of institutional co-occurrence also shows that the types of organisations that co-operate are mainly based on agriculture, medical care, economic management and information intelligence.

4 Research Hot Spots and Frontier Analysis

4.1 Analysis of Research Hotspots

Keyword Co-occurrence Map Analysis. The distribution of keyword co-occurrences is an indication of the focus of the research topic and the direction of the hotspot that researchers are exploring [24]. Figure 8 displays the distribution graph of key-word co-occurrences, which was analysed using CiteSpace on 1066 relevant papers. The keywords that appear more frequently include mini-program, WeChat, CloudBase, Libraries, Internet of Things, Management Systems, System Design, QR codes, Internet+, and User Experience. The presented keywords are mostly in network form with fewer isolated nodes, indicating a stronger correlation between them. The research hotspots for the users of the WeChat mini-program in China include cloud base, management systems, system design and user experience. These areas are highlighted in warmer colours in Fig. 9, which shows the density view of VOSviewer. It is important to note that this information is based on recent years' data and is presented objectively. The shade closer to yellow indicates a higher volume of literature. The areas of focus for published articles include WeChat, CloudBase, Management System, System Design, User Experience, and other related aspects.

Keyword Frequency and Centrality Analysis. Through analysis of the frequency and centrality of keywords in the CiteSpace keyword co-occurrence graph, a better understanding of the hotspots and frontiers of WeChat mini-program user research development in China can be gained. Table 2 displays the top ten high-frequency keywords, including mini-programs, CloudBase, WeChat, Management System, Library, System Design, Internet of Things (IoT), QR code, Big Data, Internet+, Design, User Experience, Facial Recognition, Cloud Server and Service Platform. The top ten keywords for centrality are mini-programs, CloudBase, Management Systems, WeChat official accounts, New Retail, QR codes, Libraries, IoT, WeChat, Big Data, System Design, Cloud Servers, Design, Internet+ and User Experience.

Analysis of Hot Research Topics. The keyword co-occurrence network was obtained through keyword co-occurrence analysis in CiteSpace. This research focuses on the top 9 clusters, as shown in Fig. 10. Among them, Q = 0.7233, which generally indicates a significant cluster structure when Q > 0.3. Additionally, s = 0.9096, which is considered reasonable for classifying clusters when s > 0.5, and s > 0.7 indicates that the clusters

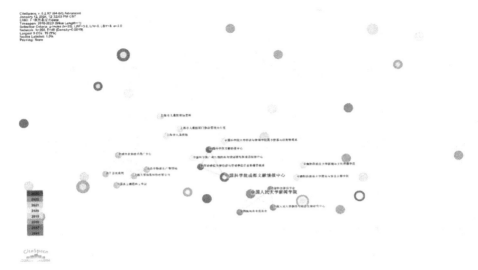

Fig. 7. Map of WeChat mini-program user research cooperation among institutions in China

are persuasive [25]. From 2016 to 2023, the top 9 areas of research in the field of WeChat mini-program users in China are WeChat, CloudBase, QR code, Face Recognition, User Experience, Big Data, System Design, Library and Cloud Platform.

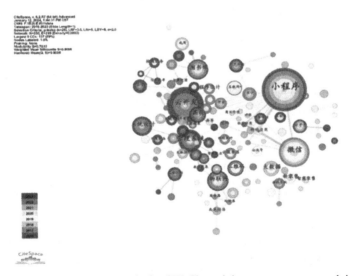

Fig. 8. Keyword co-occurrence analysis of WeChat mini program user research in China.

Time-zone Map Analysis of Keyword Clustering. This research describes how clustering analysis can be used to identify changes and trends in research priorities over time [26]. It follows a conventional structure and format, with uniform citation and footnote

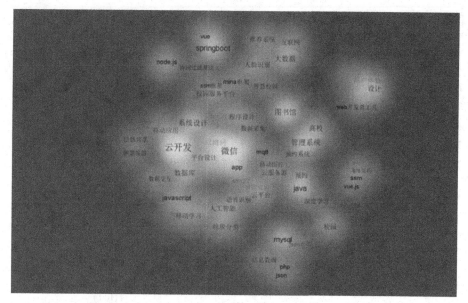

Fig. 9. Keyword density view of WeChat mini-program user research in China.

styles. It grammatically, spell and punctuate correctly. The clustered time zone view generated by CiteSpace is shown in Fig. 11, with Cluster 0 focusing on Mobile Application, mHealth, Service Platform, and Online Appointment. Cluster 1, 'CloudBase', focuses on Campus Services, Interface Design, Mobile Learning, Platform Design, and Smart Tourism. Cluster 2, 'QR Code', focuses on Sharing Economy, Internet of Things (IoT), QR code, Artificial Intelligence, Refuse Classification, and more. Cluster 3, 'Internet of Things', focuses on Management Systems, WeChat Platform, Face Recognition, Smart Healthcare, and more. Cluster 4, 'Big Data', primarily focuses on User Experience, Development, Design, and Trading Platforms. Cluster 5, also focused on 'Big Data', primarily focuses on Big Data and Machine Learning. Cluster 6, 'System Design', mainly revolves around Database, System Implementation, System Design, and Student Management. Cluster 7, 'Library', mainly focuses on Library Management, Application Development, Seat Management, and Mobile Services. Cluster 8, 'Cloud Platform', mainly focuses on 3D printing and Cloud Platforms.

Keyword Burstiness Analysis. The research focuses on the use of CiteSpace burstiness to identify frequently occurring keywords over time and analyse hot spots and trends in research [27]. Figure 12 displays the keyword highlighting map generated by the visual analysis, ranked according to the intensity of the burstiness. The popular research keywords include Seat Management, Platform Design, Artificial Intelligence, Recommender Systems, and Second-hand Transactions. The research field concerning WeChat mini-program users has 20 key terms. Research on the impact factor related to this topic began to gain attention in 2016, with a maximum intensity of 4.55. The second highest ranking keyword is 'New Retail', which emerged in 2018 with a burst intensity as high as 2.13. The third keyword is 'Monolithic', which gained attention in 2020 with an intensity

Table 2. Statistics of high frequency keywords, word frequency and centrality of WeChat mini-program user research in China.

Keyword frequency				Keyword centrality			
Freq	Degree	Centrality	Label	Freq	Degree	Centrality	Label
72	39	0.38	Mini-program	72	39	0.38	Mini-program
48	18	0.14	CloudBase	48	18	0.14	CloudBase
38	17	0.04	WeChat	19	14	0.11	ManagementSystems
19	14	0.11	Management-Systems	4	3	0.09	WeChat official accounts
19	8	0.06	Libraries	5	6	0.08	New Retail
17	8	0.03	System Design	12	7	0.07	QR codes
16	10	0.06	Internet of Things (IoT)	19	8	0.06	Libraries
12	7	0.07	QR codes	16	10	0.06	Internet of Things (IoT)
10	8	0.04	Big Data	38	17	0.04	WeChat
9	3	0.02	Internet+	10	8	0.04	Big Data
8	3	0.03	Design	17	8	0.03	System Design
7	3	0.02	User Experience	8	3	0.03	Design
7	3	0.02	Facial Recognition	6	4	0.03	Cloud Servers
6	4	0.03	Cloud Servers	9	3	0.02	Internet+

as high as 1.82. The term 'Internet+ ' gained attention in 2018 with an intensity as high as 1.73. From 2018 to 2020, field research primarily focused on Service-related topics such as WeChat, New Retail, Internet+, Scenes, WeChat Official Accounts, QR codes, and Big Data. In 2020–2021, the focus shifted to Interface Design, WeChat platform, Lost And Found, Take-away, College Students, and Booking Systems.

5 Discussion

5.1 Hotspots of WeChat Mini-program User Research in China

This Study sorts academic research papers on WeChat mini-program user research in China by topic and keywords. The hotspots of research on China's WeChat mini-program users from 2016 to 2023 are grouped into three areas using analyses of keyword co-occurrence maps, frequency and centrality of high-frequency keywords, clustering timeline maps, and keyword burstiness analysis.

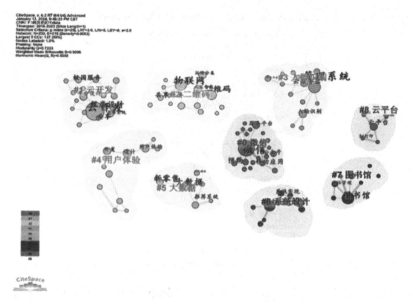

Fig. 10. Keyword clustering map of "WeChat mini-program" user research via CiteSpace.

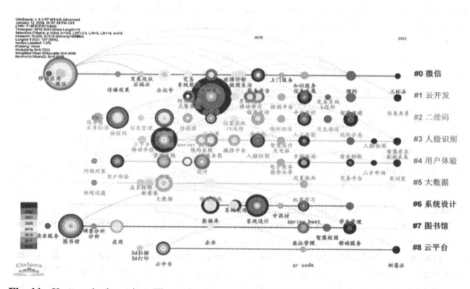

Fig. 11. Keyword clustering Timezone map of "WeChat mini-program" user research via CiteSpace.

Research on Technical Performance of WeChat Mini-program Development. The focus of developers' attention is applet performance optimization [28]. Previous scholars have mainly discussed how to optimise the performance of applets, such as reducing the number of requests and optimising rendering performance. It is important to use clear and

Top 20 Keywords with the Strongest Citation Bursts

Keywords	Year	Strength	Begin	End	2016 - 2023
微信	2016	4.55	2018	2019	
新零售	2018	2.13	2018	2019	
单片机	2020	1.82	2020	2021	
互联网+	2018	1.73	2018	2020	
场景	2018	1.7	2018	2019	
公众号	2018	1.7	2018	2019	
大数据	2018	1.47	2018	2019	
界面设计	2020	1.45	2020	2021	
微信平台	2020	1.45	2020	2021	
失物招领	2020	1.45	2020	2021	
外卖	2020	1.45	2020	2021	
座位管理	2021	1.23	2021	2023	
平台设计	2021	1.14	2021	2023	
设计	2019	1.06	2021	2023	
人工智能	2021	0.98	2021	2023	
二维码	2018	0.92	2018	2019	
推荐系统	2017	0.84	2021	2023	
二手交易	2019	0.84	2021	2023	
大学生	2019	0.81	2019	2021	
预约系统	2019	0.81	2019	2021	

Fig. 12. Keywords burstness analysis map of WeChat mini-program user research via CiteSpace.

concise language when discussing technical topics like this. Secondly, when choosing an applet framework, it is important to consider the various options available on the market, each with its own advantages and disadvantages [29]. Previous experts and scholars have primarily focused on comparing the performance and optimization methods of different applet frameworks. Thirdly, improving mini-program development tools is crucial for developers to carry out efficient development [30]. Studies have been conducted to enhance the efficiency of code editing and optimize the speed of compilation. Fourthly, the security of mini-program is becoming increasingly important with the rising number of applet applications [31]. Several studies have investigated methods to enhance applet security, including preventing XSS attacks and data leakage. Additionally, there have been studies on cross-platform development of small programs, such as through H5 technology and React Native [32].

Research on WeChat Mini-program Application Scenarios. Firstly, WeChat mini-program can be combined with IoT technology to achieve smart home control functions, such as controlling lights, temperature, security and other devices through mini-program [33]. Some studies have explored the use of mini-program and IoT technology for smart home applications. Secondly, smart health applications can be combined with IoT technology to achieve smart health monitoring functions. This includes monitoring heart rate, blood pressure, body temperature and other data through mini-program [34]. Previous studies have explored how to use mini-program and IoT technology to achieve intelligent health applications. Thirdly, intelligent transport applications can be achieved by combining WeChat mini-programs with IoT technology [35]. These applications allow users to query transport information, such as buses, subways, and shared bicycles, through the mini-programs. Some studies have explored the use of mini-programs and IoT technology for intelligent transport applications. Intelligent agriculture applications can be combined with IoT technology to achieve monitoring and control functions. For example, soil humidity and temperature can be monitored through mini-programs, and irrigation and fertiliser operations can be controlled [36]. The main purpose of small programs and IoT technology is to achieve the application of smart agriculture. Fifth, smart city applications can be achieved by combining WeChat mini-programs with IoT technology [37]. For instance, the applet can be used to access information on the city's public facilities, traffic conditions, and meteorological data.

Research on User Research and User Experience of We Chat Mini-programs. Firstly, the design of the user interface has a significant impact on the user experience. Several studies have explored how to create a more aesthetically pleasing and user-friendly interface that aligns with user habits [38]. Secondly, personalised recommendations can improve the user experience. Previous scholars have explored how to use user behavioural data, interest labels, and other information to achieve this function [39]. Thirdly, the interaction design of mini-programs has a great impact on the user experience. Previous research has explored how to design interactions that are more natural, smooth, and consistent with the user's expectations [40]. Fourthly, the use of multimedia technology can enhance the user experience of the mini-program. Several studies have explored the use of audio, video, pictures, and other multimedia technologies to improve the visual and auditory effects of the mini-program [41]. Fifth, the use of speech recognition technology can enhance the user experience of the mini-program. The main focus of research is on achieving voice search, voice input, and other functions through speech recognition technology [42].

5.2   Research Trend of WeChat Mini-program User Experience in China

From 2016 to 2023, research on WeChat mini-program user research in China has taken an interdisciplinary, policy-oriented, and market-driven approach. The number of published papers has steadily increased, reflecting the growing research interest in this area. Future research on WeChat mini-program user experience through user research in China is likely to focus on the following areas.

Regarding Technical Support for WeChat Mini-program. Firstly, the application of CloudBase Technology can assist developers in creating applets more efficiently and conveniently. Future research could explore ways to further optimize CloudBase technology to improve the development efficiency and performance of mini-programs [43]. Secondly, with the increasing popularity of Intelligent Hardware, WeChat mini-programs may become more integrated with such hardware to offer users more intelligent and convenient services. For instance, by integrating with devices like smart bracelets and smart homes, they can provide more personalized and scenario-based services [44]. Thirdly, the application of Artificial Intelligence technology can assist WeChat mini-programs in better understanding user needs and providing more intelligent and personalised services. Future research could explore the use of AI technology to enhance the mini-program's voice recognition, image recognition, natural language processing, and other functions [3, 45]. Fourthly, the application of Blockchain Technology can assist WeChat mini-programs in achieving decentralised, secure, and reliable transactions and data storage.

Future research could explore the implementation of Blockchain Technology to enhance the security and credibility of mini-programs [46]. Fifth, Cross-platform Development Technology can aid developers in achieving compatibility of mini-programs across different platforms. Future research can explore ways to optimize this technology to improve cross-platform compatibility and performance of mini-programs [47].

Regarding WeChat Mini-program User Experience. Firstly, the potential integration of Augmented Reality (AR) and Virtual Reality (VR) technologies with the user interaction experience of WeChat mini-programs. Future research may explore how to combine these technologies to provide a more immersive experience for users [48]. Secondly, the application of Natural Language Processing (NLP) can assist WeChat mini-programs in comprehending user input and providing a personalised interaction experience. Future research could investigate how NLP technology can enhance applet functions such as speech recognition, semantic understanding, and intelligent recommendations [49]. Thirdly, researchers can use Affective Computing and User Sentiment Analysis to understand the emotional state of users when using WeChat mini-program. This can help to optimize the user interaction experience by adjusting the mini-program interface, content, or recommendation strategy based on the user's emotional state [50]. Fourth, future research can explore the use of Machine Learning and Data Mining technologies to provide Personalised Recommendation Content and Intelligent Interaction based on users' interests, preferences and behavioural patterns, in order to enhance User Experience [51]. Fifth, with the development of intelligent devices, future WeChat mini-programs may support Multiple Interaction Modes such as voice, gesture, and eye movement. Future research can explore how to design mini-program interfaces and interactions that support Multimodal Interactions to improve User Experience [52].

6   Conclusion

This study examines user research on WeChat mini-programs and aims to optimize the user experience. Literature analysis was conducted using CiteSpace (version 6.4.R7) and VOSviewer (version 1.6.20). The literature was analysed using the China Knowledge Network database with "user" as the theme and "WeChat mini-program" as the keyword. 1066 relevant documents were analysed for multilevel visual knowledge mapping analysis.

Research on the user research of WeChat mini-programs began to appear in relevant academic literature in 2016 and has since developed. The number of articles published and the time frame are noteworthy. From the perspective of the growth rate of published articles, researches have experienced rapid development since 2018. In 2018, 100 research documents in related disciplines were retrieved, and this number has increased every year since. In 2019, 184 articles were published, followed by 186 in 2020, 226 in 2021, and 186 in 2022. Finally, 148 articles were published. It is clear that research on the user of mini-program is an emerging field that will continue to grow in the future.

From view of the research subject areas, papers published on the topic of 'users' and the keyword 'WeChat mini-program' exhibit clear interdisciplinary characteristics, involving a variety of fields such as Computer Science, Education, Library Science, Media Studies, Economics, Information Technology, Electronics, and Automation.

In terms of research hotspots, technical performance, User Experience and Functional Scenarios have been the main focus of studies on WeChat mini-programs from the user research perspective. With the advancement of innovative technologies such as Artificial Intelligence, future research on WeChat mini-programs may focus on technical support and User Interaction Experience. The integration of CloudBase, Intelligent Hardware, Artificial Intelligence, Blockchain Technology, and Cross-platform Development technologies in technical support is a potential area of research and future trends. In the field of User Interaction Experience, Augmented and Virtual Reality, Natural Language Processing, Affective Computing, User Sentiment Analysis, Personalised Recommendation, Intelligent Interaction, and Multimodal Interaction are potential research focuses and future trends.

References

1. Yu, G., Cheng, S.: From "connection" to "scene": an important step in the development of the internet: examining the value logic and market territory of wechat applet. J. Res. **01**, 121–127+146+153–154 (2015)
2. Guo, B.: The progression of internet communication from a scene perspective: an analysis of wechat small programs' scene embedding and ecological layout. View Publish. **21**, 66–68 (2020). https://doi.org/10.16491/j.cnki.cn45-1216/g2.2020.21.019
3. Xu, Y., Hu, Z., Song, Y.: research and practice on wechat mini programs for subject knowledge service. Libr. Inform. Serv. **64**(14), 54–62 (2020). https://doi.org/10.13266/j.issn.0252-3116. 2020.14.006
4. Yu, L.: Practice and prospect of applying wechat mini-programs in higher education libraries. View Publish. **12**, 73–75 (2018). https://doi.org/10.16491/j.cnki.cn45-1216/g2.2018.12.021
5. Zhang, S., Zhao, Y., Zhang, P.: Research and practice of using wechat mini program to carry out electronic resource service during the pandemic: taking the welibrary mini program of Tsinghua university library as an example library J. **41**(11), 49–54 (2022). https://doi.org/10. 13663/j.cnki.lj.2022.11.006
6. Yu, G.: Mini Programs: A big expansion of wechat's eco-level apps. J. Educ. Media Stud. **05**, 95–96 (2017). https://doi.org/10.19400/j.cnki.cn10-1407/g2.2017.05.027
7. Chen, J., Wu, M., Zhang, X.: The new possibilities and practical focus of library internal office automation empowered by wechat applets--taking Xiamen university as an example. Res. Libr. Sci. (04), 30–39 (2018). https://doi.org/10.15941/j.cnki.issn1001-0424.2018.04.005
8. Zhu, Y.: The use of wechat applets in mobile library services: an example of the shelving game. Library Tribune **37**(07), 132–138 (2017)
9. Li, W.: The reform and development strategy of library in the 5G Era. Libr. Inform. **05**, 94–97 (2018). https://doi.org/10.11968/tsyqb.1003-6938.2018089
10. Zhao, X. Wang, S.: Research of Customers'Continuance Intention on WeChat Mini Program. J. Mod. Inform. **39**(06), 70–80+90 (2019). https://doi.org/10.3969/j.issn.1008-0821. 2019.06.008
11. Lu, X.: The application of wechat applets in libraries: current situation and outlook. Res. Libr. Sci. **11**, 19–25 (2018). https://doi.org/10.15941/j.cnki.issn1001-0424.2018.11.004
12. Wang, S.: Exploring and practicing online second-hand book platforms in the context of the circular economy: a case study of 'roaming whale'. View on Publishing **03**, 52–54 (2021). https://doi.org/10.16491/j.cnki.cn45-1216/g2.2021.03.012
13. Yi, M., Zhang, L., Zhou, T.: Development and application of university o2o book sharing platform based on wechat mini-apps. Libr. Theor. Pract. **03**, 94–97 (2019). https://doi.org/10. 14064/j.cnki.issn1005-8214.2019.03.021

14. Chen, H., Zhou, S., Lin, J.: Application practice and analysis of wechat mini program in institutional repository service: a case study of xiamen university institutional repository. Inform. Stud.: Theor. Appl. **42**(09), 123–127 (2019). https://doi.org/10.16353/j.cnki.1000-7490.2019.09.021

15. Tu, Y., Zhang, L., Zhai, Z.: Understanding the metaverse: culture, society and the future of mankind. Explor. Free Views **04**, 65–94+178 (2022)

16. Lin, L., Ma, X.: The theme discovery and evolution analysis of domestic library and information science research based on LDA. Inform. Sci. **37**(12), 87–92 (2019). https://doi.org/10.13833/j.issn.1007-7634.2019.12.013

17. Li, Y., Wu, H., Lai, Q.: The relationship between user's experience and personalized service in digital libraries. Libr. Inform. Serv. **53**(11), 88–91 (2009)

18. Deng, S., Zhang, M.: User experience: a new perspective for research on information service. Libr. Inform. **04**, 18–23 (2008)

19. Li, X.: User experience design based on user mental research. Inform. Sci. **28**(05), 763–767 (2010)

20. Lan, Y., Liu, P.: Emotionalization of interactive products based on user experience. Packag. Eng. **40**(12), 23–28. https://doi.org/10.19554/j.cnki.1001-3563.2019.12.005

21. Chen, Y., Wang, S.: Analysis of visual psychological cognition and emotional design in UI design. Art Design Res. **02**, 74–79 (2021)

22. Chen, C., Chen, Y., Hou, J.: CiteSpace II: identification and visualization of new trends and trends in scientific literature. J. China Soc. Sci. Tech. Inf. **28**(3), 401–421 (2009)

23. Xie, L., Dong, Y., Wu, D.: Analysis of scientific collaboration network based on Pajek. Library **7**, 62–65 (2016)

24. Xiao, J., Yu, M., Liu, Y.: Research status of university wisdom library during the 13th five-year plan period based on CNKI bibliometric analysis. Stat. Appl. **11**(6), 1372 (2022). https://doi.org/10.12677/SA.2022.116143

25. Li, B., Qin, Y., Xu, Z.: Dynamic tracking of research status and frontiers in the field of management science. Chinese J. Manage. Sci. **31**(7), 276–286 (2023). https://doi.org/10.16381/j.cnki.issn1003-207x.2021.1830

26. Hu, Z., Sun, J., Wu, Y.: Research review on application of knowledge mapping in China. Libr. Inform. Serv. **57**(03), 131 (2013)

27. Zhao, T.: CiteSpace-based bibliometric analyses on input-output. China J. Comm. (6). 3 (2021). https://doi.org/10.19699/j.cnki.issn2096-0298.2021.06.103

28. Tian, L., Zhang, H.: A review of new media development in 2018. Youth J. (36) 20–22 (2018). https://doi.org/10.15997/j.cnki.qnjz.2018.36.006

29. Ni, H., Li, X., Zhou, Q.: Construction of university laboratory safety education platform based on wechat mini-program. Res. Explor. Laboratory **39**(12), 280–284 (2020)

30. Shu, K.: The media materiality approach of social media research——a case study of WeChat API open and use project. J. Mass Commun. **05**, 80–90 (2020)

31. Wang, D., Han, J., Cai, P.: A research on the continuous usage of WeChat applets from the lightweight perspective. Sci. Res. Manage. **41**(05), 191–201 (2020)

32. Wu, S., Xie, Q., Zhang, Y.: Study on the development of WeChat applets. Wireless Internet Sci. Technol. **15**(11), 52–54 (2018)

33. Xian, J., Bi, S.: Research on embedded system teaching based on innovative comprehensive experimental project. Exper. Sci. Technol. **20**(4), 82–85 (2022)

34. Wang, R., Yu, Q., Ai, C.: A systematic evaluation of the impact of mobile healthcare management on medication adherence in patients with hypertension. Eval. Anal. Drug-Use in Hospitals **21**(12), 1504–1509. https://doi.org/10.14009/j.issn.1672-2124.2021.12.019

35. Wei, Y.: Research on the application of internet of things technology in intelligent transportation. China Manage. Informa. **25**(18), 197–199 (2022). https://doi.org/10.3969/j.issn.1673-0194.2022.18.063

36. Wang, W., Zhu, X.: Research on the status quo and countermeasures of green development of intelligent agriculture in Henan province. Hebei Agricult. Mach. **10**, 101–102 (2021). https://doi.org/10.15989/j.cnki.hbnjzzs.2021.10.052

37. Zhou, L., Cui, R.: Research on the mechanism of opening and sharing government data from the perspective of smart city. J. Modern Inform. **41**(08), 147–159 (2021). https://doi.org/10.3969/j.issn.1008-0821.2021.08.015

38. Zhang, M.: Continuous use intention of social reading APPs of college students—mediation effect of flow experience. J. Acad. Libr. **39**(01), 100–109. https://doi.org/10.16603/j.issn1002-1027.2021.01.018

39. Lin, Y., Xie, X.: User portrait of diversified groups in micro-blog based on social identity theory. Inform. Stud.: Theor. Appl. **41**(03), 142–148 (2018). https://doi.org/10.16353/j.cnki.1000-7490.2018.03.027

40. He, S., Qin, Y.: From VR/AR to metaverse: immersive interaction design of children's picture books for generation alpha. Libr. Develop. **05**, 66–72 (2022). https://doi.org/10.19764/j.cnki.tsgjs.20220169

41. Chen, C.: Metacosmos: the practice of deep mediatisation. Modern Publishing **02**, 19–30 (2022). https://doi.org/10.3969/j.issn.2095-0330.2022.02.004

42. Lan, Y., Liu, S.: Overview of product user experience research under artificial intelligence technology. Packag. Eng. **41**(24):22–29(2020). https://doi.org/10.19554/j.cnki.1001-3563.2020.24.004

43. Liu, Y., Yang, Q., Li, Z.: Cloud computing development environment: from code logic to dataflow diagram. Scientia Sinica(Informationis) **49**(09), 1119−1137 (2019) https://doi.org/10.1360/N112018-00264

44. Wu, J., Li, W., Cao, J.: AIoT: a taxonomy, review and future directions. Telecommun. Sci. **37**(08), 1–17 (2021). https://doi.org/10.11959/j.issn.1000-0801.2021204

45. Bie, J., Shi, X., Zhou, L.: Man-computer collaboration, cross-media perception and life service under the guidance of artificial intelligence and supercomputing technology. Future Commun. **26**(04), 8–14+110–111 (2019)

46. Zhang, W., Li, Y.: Survey of block chain. Chinese J. Netw. Inform. Secur. **10**, 51–52 (2020). https://doi.org/10.11959/j.issn.2096-109x.2016.00107

47. Xu, S., Liu, Y.: Construction and practice of interactive live streaming service platform for integrated business under media convergence development. Radio TV Broadcast Eng. **48**(12), 24–28 (2021). https://doi.org/10.16171/j.cnki.rtbe.20210012002

48. Yang, Q., Zhong, S.: A review of foreign countries on the development and evolution trends of virtual reality technology. J. Dialectics Nature **43**(03), 97–106 (2021). https://doi.org/10.15994/j.1000-0763.2021.03.013

49. Wu, D., Li, H., Chen, X.: Analysis on the influence of artificial intelligence generic large model on education application. Open Educ. Res. **29**(02), 19–25+45 (2023). https://doi.org/10.15994/j.1000-0763.2021.03.013

50. Xu, R., Chen, W., Zheng, S., et al.: Integration of environment and body:the connotation construction, realization mechanism and educational application of immersive experience: also discuss the new form of AI + immersive Learning. J. Dist. Educ. **39**(01), 28–40 (2021). https://doi.org/10.15881/j.cnki.cn33-1304/g4.2021.01.003

51. Gu, L.: Review of personalized interaction design. Data Anal. Knowl. Disc. **11**, 10–16 (2010)

52. Xue, Y., Zhu, F., Wang, K.: Metaverse: learning space for the next generation. J. School. Stud. **19**(02), 23–32 (2022). https://doi.org/10.3969/j.issn.1005-2232.2022.02.003

A Study of Older People's Attitudes Towards Digital Banking

Martin Maguire[✉]

School of Design and Creative Arts, Loughborough University, Leicestershire LE11 3TU, UK
m.c.maguire@lboro.ac.uk

Abstract. This study explored older people's opinions of digital banking (online and mobile) and the risks they perceived in relation to these services. A total of 20 older users were recruited for a short interview to explore their views on different banking services. While most of the participants were interested in digital banking services, they expressed concerns about the security risks of using them. However, the involvement of friends or relatives were found could mitigate these negative perceptions.

Following this, prototype user interfaces for a mobile banking app and an online web-based banking service were developed to explore whether experience of digital banking affected their feelings towards them. Each prototype was tested by 6 older users under two conditions, one using the service on their own and the other with simulated online help from another person.

The experience of the participants with the prototypes raised interest in adopting digital banking services. It was found that when assisted by a friend or relative, the perceived risks were reduced.

Keywords: Older people · Digital banking · Online baking · Mobile banking · Perception of risk · Safety online

1 Introduction

Online banking has been in existence for a long time. However, take up has been gradual until recent years. In the UK, it has increased from 30% of account holders in 2007 to 73% in 2019. Reasons for the increase are:

- It is offered free as part of the banking service.
- The increase in internet speeds has made it more effective.
- The greater range of services available can be presented conveniently online.
- The growth of smart phone use so banking can be carried out from anywhere.

Yet many older people remain sceptical of online banking. As discovered by Age UK [1], fear of fraud, not trusting online banking services, and not having the IT skills (tech-savviness) required are the top 3 reasons why older people are uncomfortable with online banking. Due to these barriers, physical banking services remain very important

© The Author(s), under exclusive license to Springer Nature Switzerland AG 2024
J. Wei and G. Margetis (Eds.): HCII 2024, LNCS 14738, pp. 278–289, 2024.
https://doi.org/10.1007/978-3-031-60487-4_21

to older people who also worry that their local bank branch will close leaving them cut adrift, particularly if they live in a rural area.

It was found by [2] that barriers that influence the adoption of mobile banking by the elderly include: a lack of information and understanding, security and trust issues, demographic factors, language, the complexity of mobile banking applications, and resistance to change. Some studies have found that the reasons for not using mobile banking are security issues. It is also reported that performance risk (connection breakdown) and financial risk (losing money) discourage older people from using digital banking services [3].

Mobile banking takes digital banking further by allowing customers to access information on the move while the convenience of an app style interface and its interactivity can make it a convenient flexible way of carrying out banking transaction [4]. The ongoing COVID-19 crisis has also reinforced the need for increased digital financial inclusion. Since the pandemic, banks and non-banking institutions have moved towards providing appropriate services for the financially excluded and underserved, such as easy money transfers [5]. However, while smartphones may play a big part in helping advance older people's uptake of digital banking services, they also come with concerns about trust - the perception that there is a high level of insecurity and perceived risk related to mobile phones, fearing the theft or loss of crucial information if they lose their mobile device [6]. There is also concern about the instability of mobile banking, such as problems with software, system errors and connectivity problems; and it is because older consumers are more likely to be aware of possible web-based fraud and abuse and therefore more sceptical about online purchases [7] so that older people are prone to mistrusting it and therefore have low usage of mobile banking.

Many older people now use contactless card payments since customers do not need to worry about remembering a PIN, or don't need to get their glasses out to use the card machine keypad [1]. Yet this customer group remain sceptical of contactless payments and feel that it can affect their ability to budget effectively as they may carry out numerous small, and forgettable, transactions which soon mount up. It has also been reported that because of using contactless payments, nearly one in five people in Great Britain have trouble remembering their PIN which can make older users feel vulnerable and leave them open to fraud in relying on contactless payments.

Mobile banking does face more complex security issues, and the security policies of online banking cannot easily be applied to mobile banking as mobile devices are more susceptible to hacking or malware infection and therefore require more robust security measures to protect users' account information. As mobile devices often have different operating systems, applications, and hardware configurations compared to desktop computers, this also affects security. Yet techniques exist that can effectively protect mobile banking security, such as: implementing encryption techniques to protect data privacy; ensuring system and data integrity; and using authentication and digital signatures [8, 9].

This research aimed to explore ways to increase the use of digital banking by older people that can positively influence the design of banking applications. Note: The term 'digital banking' in the paper refers to both 'online banking', used via a laptop or desktop, and 'mobile banking', used via a mobile phone.

2 Perceived Risks and Digital Banking

Perceived risk is 'a subjectively determined expectation of loss by an online banking user when considering a particular online transaction' [10]. The same idea can be applied to mobile banking. The higher the amount of money involved in a transaction, the higher the risk is generally perceived by the customer. So, in this case, higher perceived risk reduces trust in mobile banking, so becomes a significant barrier to customer acceptance of electronic services. One study classified perceived risks related to internet delivered e-services into six components: performance, financial, time, psychological, social, privacy [11]. Table 1 provides a definition of each risk type.

Table 1. Featherman and Pavlou's perceived risk scale.

Could a family member or relative help you better understand and use a digital bank?

Facet	Description - Definition
1. Performance risk	The possibility of the product malfunctioning and not performing as it was designed and advertised therefore failing to deliver the desired benefits
2. Financial risk	The potential monetary outlay associated with the initial purchase practice as well as the subsequent maintenance cost of the product. This can include the potential for financial loss due to fraud
3. Time risk	Consumers may lose time when making a bad purchasing decision by wasting time research and making the purchase, learning how to use a product or service only to have to replace it if it does not perform to expectations
4. Psychological risk	The risk that the selection or performance of the producer will have a negative effect on the consumer's peace of mind or self-perception. Potential loss of self-esteem from the frustration of not achieving a buying goal
5. Social risk	Potential loss of status in one's social group as a result of adopting a product or service, looking foolish or untrendy
6. Privacy risk	Potential loss of control over personal information, such as when information about you is used without your knowledge or permission. The extreme case is where a consumer is "spoofed" meaning a criminal uses their identity to perform fraudulent transactions
7. Overall risk	A general measure of perceived risk when all criteria are evaluated together

Ways to reduce these perceived risks to customers include building secure firewalls to avoid intrusion, performing authentication, and developing enhanced encryption methods [12]. Because older people may not have used the service before, they do not feel that they can trust mobile banking services. Although mobile banking security is enhanced, if customers do not use it for subjective reasons, they cannot feel that the security of mobile banking is relieved of their perceived risks.

Older people need to develop trust in mobile banking, and developing trust in technology has been identified as a critical predictor of mobile service acceptance [6]. For older users to develop trust, they may need to rely on support from close relationships (e.g., family or friends) around them. Because of their inexperience and low frequency of use, older people often rely on the help of family or friends when they need to use digital banking. In this regard, an interesting question is whether social connections can help older customers to reduce their perceived risk or increase their use of mobile banking. It has also been noted that older adults were concerned about information disclosure, even though they had delegated assistance to family members [13].

3 Study Aim

This study aimed to gain an understanding of the perceived risk of using digital banking amongst older people, and to consider the effect of family members being involved in use of these services. For example, whether their involvement in an online bank transaction would be effective in helping them to reduce their perceived risks.

4 Questionnaire Survey

A face-to-face survey was conducted with a sample of participants aged 60 and over while visiting a local social and community centre. 20 participants were recruited including 18 females and 2 males. They had different levels of experience with different kinds of banking services. Some participants indicated that, while they mainly use local banks, they would choose to use online banking in different situations, implying that online banking is attractive for some specific needs or scenarios.

4.1 Reasons for Choosing to Use Local Bank Branches

Participants were asked to indicate the reasons why they preferred to use local bank branches for their banking needs. They could select one or more options from: 'high security', 'better protection of privacy', 'simple operation' and 'prefer face-to-face'. Figure 1 shows the frequency with which the different options were chosen.

As shown in Fig. 1, the main reasons why the participants chose local banks were: simplicity of use (n = 12), and the perception that they offered a high security (n = 11).

Participants were also asked to indicate the reasons why they preferred to use online banking for their banking needs. They were given a series of options to select from. Figure 2 shows that of the 4 users responding the reasons selected were: convenience of transacting from home (n = 3) and online banking being relatively easy to use (n = 1).

4.2 Reasons for not Using Mobile Banking

The survey explored the types of perceived risk that prevented participants from using mobile banking, by choosing from the options: 'worried about accidents' (breaking or losing phone), 'difficulty in operation', 'fear of making wrong choices', 'privacy issues',

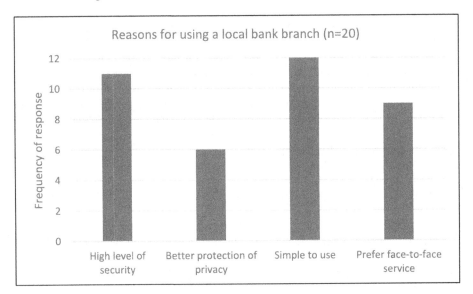

Fig. 1. Reasons for using a local bank branch.

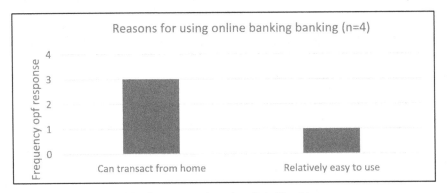

Fig. 2. Reasons for using digital banking.

'security issues', 'forgetting your password'. Figure 3 shows that the main reasons were security fears (n = 11), worries about accidents (losing or damaging mobile phone), and privacy loss (n = 8).

Figures 2 and 3 indicate that security plays an important role in the choice of banking service used by older customers.

When asked whether participants were willing to try digital banking (online or mobile), Table 2 shows that the majority were unwilling.

One aspect of the study was to investigate whether friends or family members can help older people reduce perceived risk. Participants were asked, 'Do you think a family member or relative could help you better understand and use a digital bank?'.

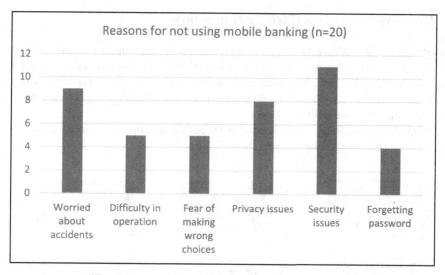

Fig. 3. Reasons for not using mobile banking services.

Table 2. Participants' interest in using digital banking (online or mobile).

Are you interested in using digital banking?	
Yes	2
No	13
Not sure	5

Table 3. Whether friends or family help you use digital banking.

Could a family member or relative help you better understand and use a digital bank?	
Yes	6
No	9
Not sure	5

Six participants stated that friends or family would be a positive influence on their potential use of a digital banking service. The potential support that adult children or friends could give in learning and using online banking services was discussed with participants. Some said that their children were willing to assist them in using digital and online banking services, while others said their children were more concerned about their online safety and were less willing to support their access to online services. Some participants did not want to share personal financial information with friends and family members.

5 Prototype User Interface Testing Study

Based on the results of this study, two prototype user interfaces, one for a mobile banking app and one for an online web-based service were developed. Two versions of each were also developed, one in which the user used the application or website on their own, and the other where they could request help from a relative, who could provide help remotely without seeing the user's financial details.

Example screens from the app version of the prototype where assistance can be given by a relative (the user's daughter) are shown in Fig. 4.

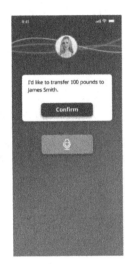

Fig. 4. Screens from assisted version of mobile banking prototype.

The first screen shows the user being asked if they would like help with the task (transferring £100 from their account to the account of another person) from a family member. The second screen shows the participant describing the task they want to carry out verbally. The third screen shows the relative (simulated in the study) providing guidance by indicating what the participant needs to do.

The aim of the study was to compare the different prototypes to see which were quicker to use and whether perceptions of privacy or security varied between them.

Six participants participated in the study. The order of presentation of prototypes for each participant was randomised. The test completion time of each set of prototypes of the participants was recorded (Table 3). After using each prototype, each participant gave ratings of ease of operation and different kinds of risk when using digital banking alone (mobile or online) and with the assistance of someone (mobile or online). They used a Likert scale where 1 represents little or no concern, and 5 represents high concern.

The mode values shown in Fig. 5 indicate that both forms of digital prototype (use alone and assisted) were relatively easy to operate. The risk levels for different risk categories when using the prototypes alone were rated as moderate to high (3 or 4) while when using the prototypes that provided assistance, they were rated lower (1 to 3).

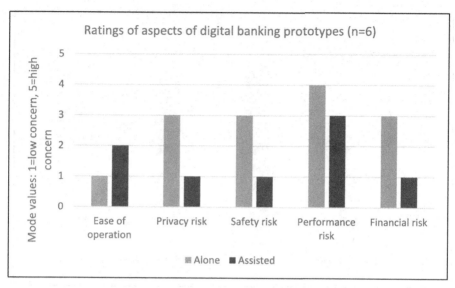

Fig. 5. Ratings of aspects of digital banking protypes.

The average task completion times (to transfer £100 into another person's account) for each prototype are shown in Table 4.

Table 4. Task time for each test condition.

Participant	Mobile-alone	Mobile-assisted	Online-alone	Online-assisted
P1	60 s	150 s	120 s	135 s
P2	95 s	140 s	120 s	140 s
P3	85 s	179 s	180 s	200 s
P4	75 s	134 s	121 s	143 s
P5	60 s	180 s	150 s	129 s
P6	118 s	130 s	166 s	143 s
Average time	**82 s**	**152 s**	**142 s**	**148 s**

The lowest average completion time of 82 s is for using mobile banking alone, while the average completion times for the other three prototypes are similar: 142 s being recorded for online alone, 148 s for online assisted, and 152 s for mobile assisted. These results perhaps indicate that users could proceed more quickly when interacting on their own, compared to when being assisted by a family member, even though being assisted decreased levels of risk concern (Fig. 6).

After testing the four prototypes, the participants completed a questionnaire to find out whether their preferences for digital banking services. It was found that 4 would like to use mobile banking while 2 preferred online banking (Table 5).

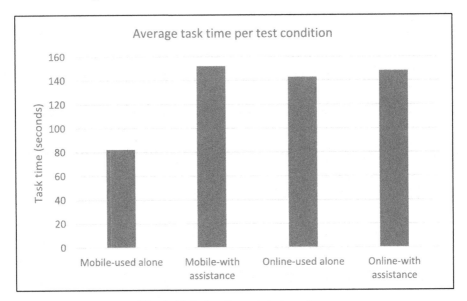

Fig. 6. Task time for each test condition

Table 5. Participants' preferences for digital banking after the prototype test.

Having used the prototypes which type of digital banking would you like to use?	
Mobile banking	4
Online banking	2
Neither	1

The participants were also asked which type of digital banking they thought was most secure (Table 6).

Table 6. Participants' opinions on which type of digital banking was most secure.

Having used the prototypes which do you think is (1) More secure, (2) More private?	More secure	More private
Mobile banking	1	1
Online banking	3	3
Both equally	2	2

Among the 6 participants, online banking was thought by 3 people to be to be more secure and more private than mobile banking, while one felt that mobile banking was the superior, and two felt that both were equally secure and private. Illustrative comments from the participants about their experiences are shown below (Table 7).

Table 7. Participants' comments on of mobile and online banking experiences.

Participant	Comment
P1	"I've used digital banking before, just not often because I only use it on weekends when the banks are closed. Throughout the testing process, I felt that it was quite friendly to me, and the security was well done, significantly when relatives helped with a double security system protection."
P2	"The process steps of *mobile banking* are relatively simple, but the information you see is not as much as online banking and not detailed enough. And I think *online banking* is more secure because it has security tips."
P3	"I think having someone to help use it would give me more peace of mind, especially seeing that you're showing the interface that family members use, and they can't see how much money I have. And an extra person to help me ensure the information is correct during the transfer process [would help]. I prefer to use *mobile banking* because *online banking* requires too many steps and is not very convenient for me."
P4	"I prefer online to *mobile banking* because the screen is big enough to see."
P5	"I don't need [to use] *digital banking* because my home is close to the bank. I think older people will be more security conscious than younger people. I have a few friends around me who have experienced mobile phone scams, which leads me to trust digital banking less."
P6	"I do think a *mobile phone* looks more convenient and easier to carry. Still, I am worried about losing my mobile phone. Because of this reason, I am reluctant to use *digital banking. Online banking* is too much information for me. I am worried about the operation process and whether I will make any mistakes."

The comments show that some participants appreciated the convenience and simplicity of the mobile format. However, with online banking, the user can sit and think through the interaction steps more clearly and respond to any advice offered by the bank about reducing security risks more comfortably.

6 Summary

The aim of the studies report here was to investigate the attitudes (ease of use and perceived risks) of older adults to digital banking services. There was a general feeling among the 20 participants survey that local branches were more secure, more private, and simpler to use.

Following this, prototype user interfaces for a mobile banking app and an online web-based banking service were developed to explore whether experience of digital banking affected their feelings towards them. Each prototype was tested by 6 older users under two conditions, one using the service on their own and the other with simulated online help from another person.

After the participants tested the prototype, it was found that most preferred mobile banking over digital banking because of their apparently simpler interfaces. However, online banking was said to offer a broader view of the customer's banking data. There was a balance of views about whether mobile and online banking offered more security and privacy.

This study also explored whether the involvement of friends and relatives could help to reduce the perceived risk and complexity of digital banking use by older people. After testing the different user interface prototypes. It was found that perception of risks was lower when simulated assistance by a family member was lower. When designing the prototype, enhanced security was emphasised by hiding important information so that family members could not view it when assisting. This helped to provide assistance while maintaining privacy.

7 Conclusion

This paper has explored the attitudes and concerns about digital banking among older people. While these services were underused by participants generally reasons of lack of trust, the benefits of convenience and control over their banking that digital banking offered were appreciated.

Questions arose that would benefit from further investigation. Firstly, how can bank services offer clearer information about the risks of using banking services, and whether the needs of older people are being fully met when a simplified service with high security are priorities for them? Also, how can customers be given confidence that they will be provided with adequate support when a problem occurs such as losing their mobile device.

Banking in different cultural and national contexts and understanding whether there are differences in these contexts would also provide a more comprehensive understanding of older people's usability and security needs with digital banking.

Acknowledgement. Grateful thanks to Haishan Huang. Her Ergonomics Master's project, entitled 'A study into the reduction of perceived risk in using digital banking for older people', was completed at Loughborough University in 2023.

References

1. Age UK: 'You can't bank on it anymore' - The impact of the risk of online banking on older people. Banking Policy Report, May 2023. https://www.ageuk.org.uk/globalassets/age-uk/documents/reports-and-publications/reports-and-briefings/money-matters/the-impact-of-the-rise-of-online-banking-on-older-people-may-2023.pdf. Accessed 21 Mar 2024
2. Msweli, N.T., Mawela, T.: Financial inclusion of the elderly: exploring the role of mobile banking adoption. Acta Informatica Pragensia **10**(1), 1–21 (2021). https://doi.org/10.18267/j.aip.143

3. Thomas, D., Chowdhury, G., Ruthven, L.: Exploring older people's challenges on online banking/finance systems: early findings. In: CHIIR '23: Proceedings of the 2023 Conference on Human Information Interaction and Retrieval, pp. 333–337 (2023). https://doi.org/10.1145/3576840.3578324

4. Malaquias, R.F., Hwang, Y.: An empirical study on trust in mobile banking: a developing country perspective. Comput. Human Behav. **2016**(54), 453–461 (2016)

5. The World Bank: Financial inclusion is a key enabler to reducing poverty and boosting prosperity. June 2021. https://www.worldbank.org/en/topic/financialinclusion/overview. Accessed 21 Mar 2024

6. Almarashdeh, I., Aldhmour, K., Aljamaeen, R., Alsmadi, M., Jaradat, G.: The effect of perceived trust in technology, trust in the bank and perceived risk on customer adoption of mobile banking. In: 2019 International Conference on Internet of Things, Embedded Systems and Communications (IINTEC), Tunis, Tunisia, pp. 118–123 (2019)

7. Rajaobelina, L., Brun, I., Line, R., Cloutier-Bilodeau, C.: Not all elderly are the same: fostering trust through mobile banking service experience. Int. J. Bank Market. **39**(1), 85–106 (2021). https://doi.org/10.1108/IJBM-05-2020-0288

8. Nie, J., Hu, X.: Mobile banking information security and protection methods. In: International Conference on Computer Science and Software Engineering, Wuhan, China, pp. 587–590 (2008). https://doi.org/10.1109/CSSE.2008.1422

9. Panja, B., Fattaleh, D., Mercado, M., Robinson, A., Meharia, P.: Cybersecurity in banking and financial sector: Security analysis of a mobile banking application. In: 2013 International Conference on Collaboration Technologies and Systems (CTS), San Diego, CA, USA, pp. 397–403 (2013). https://doi.org/10.1109/CTS.2013.6567261

10. Aboobucker, I., Bao, Y.: What obstruct customer acceptance of internet banking? Security and privacy, risk, trust and website usability and the role of moderators. J. High Technol. Manage. Res. **29**(1), 109–123 (2018)

11. Featherman, M.S., Pavlou, P.A.: Predicting e-services adoption: a perceived risk facets perspective. Int. J. Human Comput. Stud. **59**(4), 451–474 (2003)

12. Yaghoubi, N.M., Bahmani, E.: Behavioral approach to policy making of the internet banking industry: the evaluation of factors influenced on the customers' adoption of internet banking services. Afr. J. Bus. Manage. **5**(16), 6785–6792 (2011)

13. Latulipe, C., Dsouza, R., Cumbers, M..: Unofficial proxies: How close others help older adults with banking. In: Proceedings of the 2022 CHI Conference on Human Factors in Compu-ting Systems (CHI 2022). Association for Computing Machinery, New York, NY, USA, Article 601, pp. 1–13 (2022). https://doi.org/10.1145/3491102.3501845

The Device Effect on Visitor Critique: A Study of Mobile and Desktop Museum Reviews on TripAdvisor

Evangelia Palla[1]([⊠]), Nikolaos Korfiatis[2], Leonidas Hatzithomas[1], Polyxeni Palla[3], and George Lekakos[3]

[1] Department of Business Administration, University of Macedonia, Thessaloniki, Greece
{evapalla,hatzithomas}@uom.edu.gr
[2] Norwich Business School, University of East Anglia, Norwich, Norfolk, UK
n.korfiatis@uea.ac.uk
[3] Department of Management Science and Technology, Athens University of Economics and Business, Athens, Greece
{palla,glekakos}@aueb.gr

Abstract. This paper investigates the influence of device choice on the critique visitors leave on TripAdvisor for museum experiences. Utilizing a dataset of 286,379 reviews, we examine whether mobile reviews differ in promptness, negativity, and length compared to those submitted via non-mobile devices. Our findings reveal that mobile reviewer post more promptly after their visit, indicating a closer psychological proximity to the experience. These reviews are typically shorter and more negative, reflecting the constraints and immediacy of mobile interactions. The paper introduces novel insights into the role of device context in shaping visitor feedback and employs interaction effects to understand the complex dynamics between visit recency, sentiment, and review length. This research provides museums with actionable data to strategically tailor digital engagement and manage visitor relations in the evolving landscape of online reviews.

Keywords: TripAdvisor · Online Reviews · Museums

1 Introduction

The recent digital revolution has created significant challenges for tourism, and in particular the museum sector (Alexander, et al., 2018). There is a proliferation of travel review websites (Taecharungroj and Mathayomchan 2019), with valuable feedback for attractions, hotels, restaurants, and museums. Online reviews generated by users (UGC), reflect visitors' estimations, describe their experience, and express their emotions (Taecharungroj and Mathayomchan 2019). In that capacity the literature has identified the significant influence that online review aggregators such as TripAdvisor exert on travelers and tourists in selecting destinations to visit (Súa and Teng 2018) as well as in planning their journey before arrival (Antón et al., 2018).

© The Author(s), under exclusive license to Springer Nature Switzerland AG 2024
J. Wei and G. Margetis (Eds.): HCII 2024, LNCS 14738, pp. 290–300, 2024.
https://doi.org/10.1007/978-3-031-60487-4_22

A significant body of research has already pointed to the influential power of online review aggregators in guiding tourists' choices and expectations. Studies have meticulously documented the elements that contribute to a museum's appeal, including the quality of service, cost considerations, and available activities, all through the lens of visitor reviews. Alexander et al. (2018) in their analysis of the frequent topics in comments from TripAdvisor underline that visitor observe all characteristics and details of their museum experience; staff, service, restaurant, cost, queues, and activities for children. Several studies further indicate that online reviews significantly affect traveler behavior and trust toward the website and the destination (Ayeh and Law, 2014; Antón et al., 2018). Focusing on visitor dissatisfaction Sú and Tend (2018), classified the negative reviews in TripAdvisor provided significant insight the recognition and recovery of museum service failures.

The advent of mobile technology has introduced a new dimension to this dynamic, altering the nature and quality of feedback. The focus of this study is the impact of this channel on the way museum visitors will choose to evaluate his experience and more specifically this study looks at the mobile channel. In terms of channel selection, 62,2% of TripAdvisor traffic is generated through mobile[1]. Mobile-generated reviews often exhibit distinct characteristics in terms of emotionality and detail, suggesting a nuanced interplay between the review medium and the content it produces. According to Ransbotham et al. (2018), the textual content of reviews posted via mobile devices differs significantly from that of reviews posted via non-mobile devices. Mobile reviews have differences in affection, concreteness, and extremity in content. The textual content of mobile reviews appears to be more concrete and emotional (Burtch and Hong, 2014). Drawing from.

The ongoing digital transformation has profoundly affected the tourism industry, particularly museums, by altering how visitors share and reflect on their experiences. Travel review websites have burgeoned, becoming a vital source of user-generated content that shapes public perception. This paper explores the nuanced relationship between this mode of digital engagement—mobile versus desktop—and how it affects museum visitor ratings on TripAdvisor. We investigate the temporal proximity of reviews post-visit, the sentiment expressed, and the length of reviews, hypothesizing that mobile reviews manifest distinct immediacy, conciseness, and emotional candor. The advent of mobile technology has not only augmented the quantity but also the character of feedback, potentially affecting visitor behavior and institutional response strategies. This study aims to unravel the interplay between device choice and review characteristics, providing insights into visitor behavior and informing museum professionals on optimizing digital engagement to enhance visitor satisfaction and manage online reputation.

2 Theoretical Framework and Hypotheses Development

2.1 Device Mode and Construal Level Theory

Research within the field of social psychology suggests that there is often a disparity between how people remember events and how they perceived those events when they actually occurred (Wirtz et al., 2003). Construal Level Theory (CLT), a conceptual

---

[1] Tripadvisor channel report. Tripadvisor.com.

model, offers an explanation for these discrepancies. It posits that as individuals' psychological distance from objects, events, or people increases, the nature of their mental representations—or construal's—of those experiences' changes (Trope and Liberman, 2010). A central pillar of CLT is grounded on the fluidity of memory and perception, highlighting how distance can shape the way experiences are recalled and understood.

In the context of online reviews, especially those posted on online platform, the temporal dimension is associated with access to the digital platform. Following the theoretical anchor of CLT, reviews written immediately after a museum visit experience might focus on concrete details of the service or visit because the experience is psychologically close (in terms of the time experienced). In contrast, reviews written after some time has passed might reflect a more abstract reflection on the experience, focusing on the overall impression rather than specific details.

Mobile devices have been long studied in the context of enabling direct access to the digital channels where a visitor may choose to express its review as a direct result of his/her experience. These affordances manifest in the following three categories:

(a) Immediacy and Convenience: Mobile devices offer the immediacy and convenience of posting reviews in real-time or shortly after the experience, potentially capturing more emotional and spontaneous reactions. This immediacy can lead to more vivid and detailed accounts of an experience, reflecting a low-level construal perspective. *(b) Length and Detail*: Reviews written on desktop computers tend to be longer and more detailed, possibly due to the ease of typing and the ability to review and edit content more effectively. This might lead to a more considered and reflective review, possibly incorporating higher-level construal and finally *(c) Contextual Influences*: Where the context in which a device is used (e.g., on-the-go with a mobile vs. at home with a desktop) can also affect the content of a review.

Mobile reviews might be influenced by immediate environmental factors and emotions, while desktop reviews might reflect a distanced, more reflective perspective.

To this end we can hypothesize the following:

H1 (Review Promptness). Reviews written in a mobile device will appear faster in the review aggregator than the reviews in a non-mobile device.

2.2   Reviewer Negativity and Length of Feedback

Negative experiences are typically more salient in a reviewer's memory and can lead to more extensive narrative feedback. When a visitor has a less-than-satisfactory experience, the motivation to elaborate is heightened by the desire to warn others or to prompt service improvement. This is consistent with the notion of a 'negativity bias,' where individuals give more weight to negative aspects of an experience than to positive ones. The Construal Level Theory (CLT) adds a layer of complexity to this, suggesting that the proximity of the event in memory influences the level of detail provided. Reviews written soon after the experience tend to be detailed and specific, reflecting the vividness of recent events in the reviewer's mind.

Additionally, the medium through which feedback is provided plays a critical role in the length and tone of reviews. Mobile devices, which facilitate immediate reaction, often see shorter and more emotionally charged reviews due to the ease of use and context of mobility. In contrast, desktop environments, which encourage reflection and elaboration, are conducive to longer, more comprehensive accounts. This disparity is crucial for businesses to understand, as it affects the way they interpret and respond to feedback. For instance, a brief, negative comment left via a mobile device might not carry the same weight as a longer, more thoughtful critique composed on a desktop, even if the sentiment is the same.

The length of feedback is also an important indicator of a reviewer's engagement and investment in the sharing process. Longer reviews not only provide more detailed information but also signal a deeper cognitive and emotional investment by the reviewer. This suggests a complex interaction between the reviewer's psychological state, the device used, and the resulting feedback. As CLT would predict, more abstract and generalized feedback often comes from a place of psychological distance, whereas immediate, detailed responses may arise from a sense of proximity to the event. Understanding these nuances can empower businesses to tailor their customer service strategies, accordingly, addressing the underlying concerns of their visitors in a manner that aligns with the nature of the feedback received. Thus, we have:

H2 (Review Negativity). Reviews written in a mobile device will be on average more negative towards the museum than reviews provided in a non-mobile device.

In addition, and considering the impact and influence of the device on the expressiveness of the review we have:

H3 (Length of Feedback). Reviews written in a mobile device will be on average shorter than reviews provided in a non-mobile device.

3 Data and Methods

3.1 Dataset

We programmed a web crawler to crawl the profile pages of museums that appear in the Art Newspaper Annual Museum survey. For each museum page we extracted the review characteristics as to the device type that the review was pasted, the date of the visit, the review content and the type of the reviewer posting the review.

The platform categorizes devices that the user has used to post the review in mobile, desktop and tablet. For the purpose of this study, we considered mobile and desktop devices only. Table 1. offers a quantitative foundation for understanding the dichotomy in user engagement across mobile and non-mobile devices within the context of museum reviews. The subtle yet statistically significant difference in ratings, with mobile devices showing a slightly lower mean, may hint at a differential evaluative approach or the influence of contextual factors inherent to mobile usage. The brevity of mobile reviews, with a mean word count approximately 10% less than non-mobile entries, likely reflects the immediacy and potential situational constraints of mobile interactions.

The expedited timeframe in which mobile reviews are posted suggests a closer psychological proximity to the experience, potentially leading to a more emotive and less contemplative critique. The demographical data depicting a higher incidence of mobile reviews among couples and families can be attributed to the social and spontaneous

Table 1. Descriptive Characteristics of the sample

	OTHER (N = 184833)	MOBILE (N = 101546)	All (N = 286379)
Rating			
Mean (SD)	4.62 (0.709)	4.57 (0.790)	4.61 (0.739)
Median [Min, Max]	5.00 [1.00, 5.00]	5.00 [1.00, 5.00]	5.00 [1.00, 5.00]
Review Word Count			
Mean (SD)	60.4 (56.4)	54.4 (44.2)	58.3 (52.5)
Median [Min, Max]	44.0 [1.00, 2150]	42.0 [1.00, 1500]	43.0 [1.00, 2150]
Days Since Visit			
Mean (SD)	64.4 (87.6)	37.4 (66.2)	54.8 (81.7)
Median [Min, Max]	29.0 [0, 1170]	20.0 [0, 1230]	25.0 [0, 1230]
Reviewer Type			
SOLO	17554 (9.5%)	10754 (10.6%)	28308 (9.9%)
BUSINESS	4291 (2.3%)	1107 (1.1%)	5398 (1.9%)
COUPLES	58547 (31.7%)	38683 (38.1%)	97230 (34.0%)
FAMILY	36688 (19.8%)	24976 (24.6%)	61664 (21.5%)
FRIENDS	27920 (15.1%)	17952 (17.7%)	45872 (16.0%)
NONE	39833 (21.6%)	8074 (8.0%)	47907 (16.7%)

nature of mobile device usage, accentuating the relevance of such devices in collective experiences (Fig. 1).

We take this time frame further evaluating graphically the relationship between rating and time here are plenty of reviews that are posted at later intervals. As can be seen there is a reversal of the relationship on the top panel at approximately 100 days since the review suggesting that after a particular period, mobile ratings become more positive.

3.2 Estimation Approach

In estimating the influence of the review characteristics on the likelihood of the review to be posted for a mobile device we define the following estimation approach.

For a visitor i visiting a museum j assigning a rating r_{ij} we model the propensity of this review to be from a mobile device as follows:

$$\hat{y} = \log\left(\frac{P(Mobile_{ij} = 1)}{1 - P(Mobile_{ij} = 1)}\right)$$

Therefore, the following model logistic regression model can be defined:

Table 2. Results from the logistic regression model

	Model 1		Model 2	
	(S)	(FE)	(S)	(FE)
H1: Time from Experience	-0.005^{***} (0.000)	-0.003^{***} (0.000)	-0.008^{***} (0.001)	-0.004^{***} (0.001)
H2: Rating (r_{ij})	-0.087^{***} (0.006)	-0.072^{***} (0.007)	-0.078^{***} (0.009)	-0.096^{***} (0.011)
H3: Length	-0.003^{***} (0.000)	-0.003^{***} (0.000)	-0.0002 (0.000)	-0.003^{***} (0.000)
Visitor Type	Yes	Yes	Yes	Yes
Interaction Effects				
Time from Experience × Rating (r_{ij})			0.001^{***} (0.000)	0.000^{***} (0.000)
Time from Experience × Length			-0.000^{***} (0.000)	-0.000^{***} (0.000)
Rating (r_{ij}) × Length			-0.001^{***} (0.000)	0.0001 (0.0001)
Museum Fixed Effects	No	Yes	No	Yes
Time Fixed Effects	No	Yes	No	Yes
Observations	238,472	238,472	238,472	238,472
Log Likelihood	$-155,766.800$	$-126,040.100$	$-155,690.400$	$-126,014.200$
Akaike Inf. Crit	311,549.600	252,470.300	311,402.800	252,424.400

Note: $^{*}p < 0.05$; $^{**}p < 0.01$; $^{***}p < 0.001$, S: Standard Model, FE: Fixed Effects model

$$\hat{y} = \beta_0 + \beta_1 timefrom_{ij} + \beta_2 r_{ij} + \beta_2 length_{ij} + \gamma_1 \sum_{\iota=Solo}^{Friends} ReviewerType_i + \gamma_2 m_j + \delta publishtime_j \tag{1}$$

where coefficients $\beta1$, $\beta2$ and $\beta3$ correspond to hypotheses H1, H2 and H3 respectively and coefficients $\gamma1$, and δ to controls for visitor type as well as museum and publish time fixed effects. In addition to this we will also consider interaction effects which will be estimated as follows:

$$\hat{y} = \beta_0 + \beta_1 timefrom_{ij} + \beta_2 r_{ij} + \beta_2 length_{ij} + \gamma_1 \sum_{\iota=Solo}^{Friends} ReviewerType_i + \gamma_2 m_j$$
$$+ \gamma_3 publishtime_j + \delta_1 timefrom_{ij} \times r_{ij} + \delta_2 timefrom_{ij} \times length_{ij}$$
$$+ \delta_3 r_{ij} \times length_{ij} \tag{2}$$

where coefficients $\delta1$, $\delta2$ and $\delta3$ represent the interaction effects between the rating of the visitor i visiting a museum j and the time elapsed from the experience as well as the

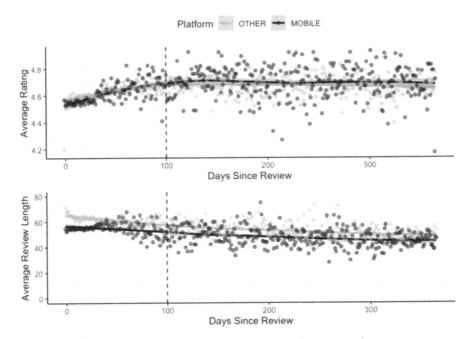

Fig. 1. Time effects on Review Length and Average rating.

length of the review with the time elapsed and the rating. Models (1) and (2) will be estimated as nested models in order to compare the influence of the interaction effects on the model fit.

For the interaction term between the time from the review and the rating we expect this to be negative owning to the effect of the temporal construal providing more concrete foundation on negative experiences to be more salient and lead to quicker reviews from mobile devices. As time passes, the salience of negative experiences may fade, potentially reducing the urgency to leave a negative review or shifting the platform preference for leaving such reviews.

For the interaction term between the time from visit and review length we also expect this to be negative. If reviews are written soon after the experience, when memories are fresh, they may be more detailed and hence longer, but as time passes, the details might not be as easily recalled, leading to shorter reviews which are also dependent on the fact that museum collections are seen as part of a larger visit, and they may not warrant a concrete effect to detail in a review. Since mobile devices are often used for more immediate and possibly shorter feedback due to their convenience, we might expect this effect to be stronger with immediate reviews. Finally, the last interaction term could be positive in suggestion that reviews that are both negative and longer might be less likely to be written on mobile devices due to the difficulty of typing longer texts on mobile keyboards. Conversely, positive reviews, which may require less cognitive effort and detail, could be more commonly associated with mobile device usage, regardless of length.

4 Results

4.1 Estimation of the Logistic Regression Model

Having defined the specification of the model we now proceed with the estimation using maximum likelihood estimation. We considered two model variations for each model specification, one standard model (without fixed effects) and one robust model with fixed effects. All models were estimated on the original corpus of N = 238,472 observations, and the robustness of the findings is evident through the consistency of the results across different model specifications.

For Hypothesis 1, which posited that reviews would be posted more promptly following the museum experience on mobile devices, the coefficient for Time from Experience was negative and significant across all models. In the non-Fixed-effects model, a one-day increase in time from experience is associated with a decrease in the likelihood of a mobile device review by 0.005 (p < 0.001) in Model 1 and 0.008 (p < 0.001) in Model 2. In the Fixed Effects models, the coefficients were −0.003 (p < 0.001) in Model 1 and −0.004 (p < 0.001) in Model 2, indicating a slightly smaller effect when controlling for museum and time fixed effects.

Hypothesis 2 suggested that reviews on mobile devices would be more negative. The Rating (r_{ij}) coefficients were also negative and significant, indicating that higher ratings (less negative) were associated with a lower probability of a review being posted from a mobile device. Specifically, in the non-Fixed-effects model, each one-point increase in rating decreased the likelihood of a mobile review by 0.087 (p < 0.001) in Model 1 and 0.078 (p < 0.001) in Model 2. The Fixed Effects models showed a decrease of 0.072 (p < 0.001) in Model 1 and a more pronounced effect of 0.096 (p < 0.001) in Model 2. For Hypothesis 3, concerning the Length of feedback, the Standard model indicated a significant decrease in the likelihood of a mobile review by 0.003 (p < 0.001) for each additional word in Model 1, with a non-significant effect in Model 2. The Fixed Effects model showed a consistent decrease of 0.003 (p < 0.001) in both Model 1 and Model 2.

Additionally, the inclusion of Interaction Effects in Model 2 revealed that the interaction between Time from Experience and Rating was positively associated with mobile device review likelihood (0.001, p < 0.001), suggesting that the promptness of reviews interacts with their sentiment. In contrast, the interaction between Time from Experience and Length showed a negative association (−0.000, p < 0.001), indicating that longer reviews tend to be less immediate. The interaction between Rating and Length was negatively associated in the Standard model (−0.001, p < 0.001) and not significant in the Fixed Effects model, suggesting that the relationship may be contingent upon the inclusion of fixed effects.

Museum Fixed Effects and Time Fixed Effects were included in the FE models, which showed improved model fit as indicated by the lower Akaike Information Criterion (AIC) values. The Log Likelihood also improved in the FE models, affirming better model specification when controlling for unobserved heterogeneity. In addition, and following the findings from the descriptive analysis we also evaluated the model with reviews that have been posted within the first 100 days from the visitor experience in the museum and results were similar with the ones for the whole cohort.

4.2   Marginal and Interaction Effects Analysis

Having provided the estimation, we proceed with an evaluation of the marginal effects on the individual covariates. Figure 2 provides an estimation of the relationship between the likelihood of using a mobile device and time from the experience of the museum visit.

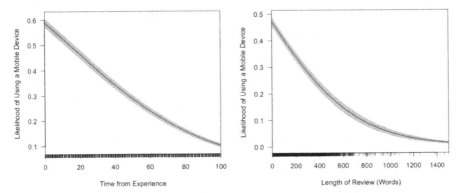

Fig. 2. Marginal effects on the likelihood of using a mobile device for the first 100 days from the experience.

As seen in the graph, there is a clear negative relationship: as the time from the experience increases, the probability of a mobile device review decreases. This effect diminishes slightly over time but remains consistently negative, suggesting that the immediacy of the mobile platform is a significant factor immediately following the visit. The shaded area represents the 95% confidence interval, indicating the precision of the estimated marginal effects.

The same can also be seen in the negative relationship is also observed in the panel on the right; longer reviews are associated with a lower likelihood of mobile device use. The effect is more pronounced for shorter reviews and gradually flattens as review length increases. This pattern reflects the constraints of mobile device usage for extensive writing tasks and suggests that users prefer desktop platforms for longer narratives. The confidence interval in this figure also indicates that the estimated effect is statistically significant across the range of review lengths.

We also evaluated the likelihood on the interaction terms that we included in the regression model 2. As can be seen in Fig. 3.

The surface plot shows how the probability of mobile device usage changes across different combinations of time from experience and rating levels. It is evident that the likelihood decreases as the time from the experience increases, and this effect is further modulated by the rating given. Higher ratings, which indicate more positive experiences, appear to lessen the decline in mobile device usage probability over time. This suggests that positive experiences may have a longer-lasting influence on the propensity to use mobile devices for reviews.

On the contrary the second panel regarding the length of the review The second graph presents the interaction between the time from experience and the length of the

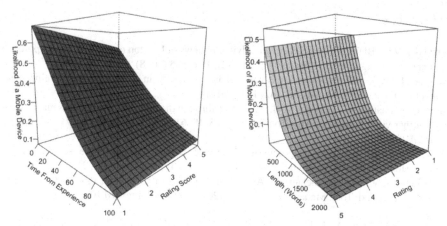

Fig. 3. Interaction Effect of Time from Experience and Rating on Mobile Device Review Likelihood

review on the probability of posting from a mobile device. The three-dimensional surface indicates that both longer times from the experience and longer review lengths contribute to a lower probability of using a mobile device for posting reviews. The steepness of the surface suggests a stronger combined effect when both the time from experience is long and the reviews are extensive, highlighting that immediate experiences and shorter reviews are more conducive to mobile device usage.

5   Discussion and Conclusions

This dichotomy in visitor engagement and medium expression is pivotal for museums aiming to harness visitor feedback effectively. The immediacy and accessibility of mobile devices allow for real-time engagement, capturing visitors' emotions and reactions with heightened specificity. Such concrete feedback can be invaluable for museum professionals seeking to address visitor needs promptly and enhance the overall museum experience. Conversely, the reflective and abstracted feedback from desktop interfaces offers museums insights into visitors' broader perceptions and longer-term impacts of their experiences.

Understanding these dynamics, grounded in Construal Level Theory, enables museums to tailor their communication strategies, engagement practices, and exhibit designs to cater to the nuanced preferences and feedback patterns of their diverse visitor segments. By acknowledging the construal levels induced by different devices, museums can more adeptly manage visitor relations, fostering an environment that encourages positive reviews, repeat visits, and deeper engagement with the cultural and educational offerings of the museum. The findings provide also significant insights to museum professionals, wishing to understand the motivations and desires of their visitors. Museum professionals can use specific extrinsic emotion regulation strategies to alter visitors' negative emotions and reviews and pursue service recovery with precision.

References

Alexander, V.D., Blank, G., Hale, S.A: Tripadvisor reviews of London museums: α new approach to understanding visitors. Museum Int. **70**(1–2), 154–165 (2018)

Ayeh, A., Law, R.: Investigating cross-national heterogeneity in the adoption of online hotel reviews. Int. J. Hosp. Manag. **55**, 142–153 (2014)

Antón, C., Camarero, C., Garrido, M.-J.: A journey through the museum: visit factors that prevent or further visitor satiation. Ann. Tourism Res. **73**, 48–61 (2018). https://doi.org/10.1016/j.annals.2018.08.002

Sú, Y., Teng, W.: Contemplating museums' service failure: extracting the service quality dimensions of museums from negative on-line reviews. Tour. Manage. **69**, 214–222 (2018)

Taecharungroj, V., Mathayomchan, B.: Analysing TripAdvisor reviews of tourist attractions in Phuket, Thailand. Tour. Manage. **75**, 550–568 (2019). https://doi.org/10.1016/j.tourman.2019.06.020

Ransbotham, S., Lurie, N.H., Liu, H.: Creation and consumption of mobile word-of-mouth: how are mobile reviews different? Mark. Sci. **38**, 5 (2018)

Burtch, G., Hong, Y.: What happens when word of mouth goes mobile? In: In 35th International Conference on Information Systems: Building a Better World through Information Systems, ICIS 2014. Association for Information Systems (2014)

Robert, P.: Emotion: Theory, research, and experience, Theories of emotion, vol. 1. Academic, New York (1980)

Roberts, M.E., et al.: Structural topic models for open-ended survey responses. Am. J. Polit. Sci. **58**(4), 1064–1082 (2014)

Cunnell, D., Prentice, R.: Tourists' recollections of quality in museums: a servicescape without people? Museum Manage. Curatorsh. **18**(4), 369–390 (2000). https://doi.org/10.1080/09647770000401804

Zeelenberg, M., Pieters, R.: Beyond valence in customer dissatisfaction. J. Bus. Res. **57**(4), 445–455 (2004). https://doi.org/10.1016/S0148-2963(02)00278-3

Wirtz, D., Kruger, J., Scollon, C.N., Diener, E.: What to do on spring break? The role of predicted, on-line, and remembered experience in future choice. Psychol. Sci. **14**(5), 520–524 (2003)

Trope, Y., Liberman, N.: Construal-level theory of psychological distance. Psychol. Rev. **117**(2), 440 (2010)

Capturing the Details Around Me: Exploring the Innovation of Multimodal Conference Headphones and User Satisfaction

Jing Xu and Guanghui Huang[(⊠)]

Faculty of Humanities and Arts, Macau University of Science and Technology, Avenida Wai Long, Taipa, Macau, China
ghhuang1@must.edu.mo

Abstract. This research delves into examining the correlation between channels for spreading information and the behaviour of users. The objective is to revamp the design of headphones that are suitable for use in office settings, to enhance the communication experience while on the move, and to enrich methods for presenting the information. The design process was informed by interviews with experts and observations of users. Before investing in the user experience, the system's usability was evaluated by experts in smart design and industrial design. The system facilitates information transmission through touch and visual methods, enabling real-time camera-based remote display. The results of the ANOVA single-factor analysis and Likert scale indicate that the combination of visual and tactile interaction modes enhances user satisfaction and the allure of expression. The article concludes that maintaining consistency between user expression and communication methods, as well as reducing the learning curve for new features, is crucial for enhancing user satisfaction. The research findings offer valuable insights for future innovative applications in new scenarios that involve multiple modes of interaction.

Keywords: human-computer interaction · Multimodal interaction channels · Mobile office · Conference headset design · User satisfaction

1 Introduction

The advancement of multimodal interaction has expanded into the design field, bringing about interdisciplinary innovation. Traditional human-computer interaction has evolved into a "perceive-learn-feedback" format, based on research on user behavior in various environments. This discussion will explore multimodal interaction in new office scenarios, aiming to address people's information transmission needs from a first-person perspective. The design of intelligent headphone systems for conferences starts by understanding user perception in information dissemination, identifying communication behaviours in office settings, and matching them with intelligent interaction methods. We will examine how different modalities complement each other in mobile office settings, where multiple senses are used for information exchange. Our design exploration will focus on "environment adaptability," "feedback format," and "multimodality," aiming to optimize the interaction channels of current conference intelligent headphones by incorporating tactile, olfactory, and haptic functionalities. This will inspire product innovation in other scenarios.

This study focuses on optimizing headphones for mobile scenarios by enhancing the visualization of information and expanding the forms of information transmission. The goal is to design and evaluate an intelligent headphone system. As office products are essential tools, the development of multimodal technology can efficiently serve users more naturally and provide effective solutions for multidimensional information transmission in mobile office settings. The study aims to answer the following questions:

1. How can multimodal interaction be designed based on user behaviour?
2. What do users value the most in the mobile office process?
3. Does the use of smart headphones in mobile office settings meet expectations?

The design innovation of this study includes:

1. Optimizing the design of smart products by focusing on the mapping relationship between device communication channels and user behaviour.
2. Expanding the forms of information transmission by combining visual and tactile information delivery channels in hardware products.
3. Broadening the application of the product in new scenarios by focusing on showcasing on-site details from the user's perspective in mobile office settings.

2 Related Works

2.1 Development of Multimodal Interaction Theory and Practice

The term "modality" was first proposed by German physiologist Helmholtz, which refers to the channels through which organisms receive information from shared sensory perception and experience, commonly known as "sensory". In the late 20th century, there were many achievements in multimodal research in the Western world. Nowadays, multimodal technology has made different advancements in the fields of biology, linguistics, computer science, and education. Professor R. [1] Barthes explored the interaction between "image" and meaning in language in his book "Image Rhetoric" (1977). Currently, scholars realize that communication between humans and devices requires a combination of speech and tactile signals, which highlights the importance of multimodality in human-computer interaction [2]. However, not all instructions in current interactions are explicit; many hidden commands exist. Therefore, it is necessary to broaden the channels of perceptual communication between humans and devices. In recent years, there has been an increase in the use of different modal channels between smart devices and user experience. These channels aim to simulate communication between people and improve the quality of human-computer interaction [3]. Examples of such modal channels include kitchen robots, smart butlers, and medical care systems. Currently, research on multimodal interaction focuses on areas such as emotion recognition, intent perception, and collaborative development [4]. There is also a focus on addressing the reduced efficiency caused by user distraction in motion environments. The application of multimodal interaction in multi-window work scenarios is progressing rapidly [5], and efforts are being made to present a more human-like emotional interaction to users [6]. In the industrial field, haptic communication has been found to have a strong potential to improve interaction and enhance the user experience of devices [7]. In smart homes, it can create a seamless living environment [8] and extend haptic interaction to the living experiences of special populations [9]. In 2019, the multimodal and sensory products received strong attention from domestic and international teams, opening up new possibilities for hardware interaction innovation.

In addition, in McDanie's study [10], it was found that enhancing communication through the tactile channel is valuable. Researchers have designed a tactile rhythm guidance product and found that using touch instead of hearing in special populations leads to higher satisfaction. In summary, when choosing a mode, it is important to consider the sensory elements that the human body can access in a mobile environment. Touch and hearing are good options. Applying multimodal interaction to the interaction between hardware products and humans has the potential for research in terms of naturalness, quality, and closeness.

2.2 Problems and Trends in the Office Scene

The global pandemic has sparked new office formats, leading to a reassessment of office supplies for different scenarios. VITRA introduced the Club Office concept at the 2020 industrial design summit, allowing employees to engage in communication, presentations, debates, and online video interactions. With over 72% of people favouring hybrid office formats in 2022, the realization that flexible workspaces can increase productivity by 43% has brought about renewed demand for office environments, breaking the constraints of traditional spaces. Small and medium-sized enterprises are embracing coworking, driving the transformation of user-device interactions through different channels. In the initial stage of this study, I conducted a quick survey to verify the trends. There have been significant changes in the office scenarios over the past year (Fig. 1). 55.15% of people frequently go out and need to communicate online multiple times while on the go. This means that more than half of the people have had the experience of working in public places. Additionally, 45.15% of people have been working from home due to the pandemic and have had remote reporting situations. Currently, there is a greater need for collaboration in modern office environments. With an increasing number of variables in the office space, most people face communication discrepancies between online and offline interactions. This indicates that there will be a new round of exploration in optimizing office equipment.

2.3 Application of Multimodal Interaction Technology in Office Products

Human perception is influenced by the senses of hearing, sight, touch, and taste, resulting in a user experience that is based on sensory input. "Multimodal" interaction takes advantage of sensor technology to expand the ways in which people receive information, allowing for multi-dimensional information transmission [11]. Compared to traditional methods, "multimodal interaction" engages users in a more immersive way, utilizing various forms to stimulate their perception [12]. Many scholars have recognized the

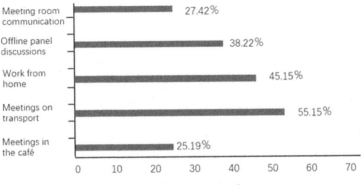

Fig. 1. Online survey results.

need for a combination of signals between humans and devices in order to enhance the user experience. This involves transforming everyday human behaviors into signal patterns that machines can recognize. This key aspect guides future interaction designers in effectively translating user behavior into everyday interactive patterns. By observing how users receive information in workplaces, human-to-human interaction can be transformed into human-machine interaction. For example, a handshake can be transformed into a "tap" and lifting something can be transformed into an "awakening" in an interactive form. By using human instinctive behavior to guide interactive forms, an inherent cognitive pattern is formed in human-machine interaction. This reflective layer ultimately assists in conveying emotions, which is a crucial way to enhance user satisfaction in future interactions [13]. It also provides a guiding framework for extracting human behavior and transforming it into patterns that promote satisfactory human-machine interaction".

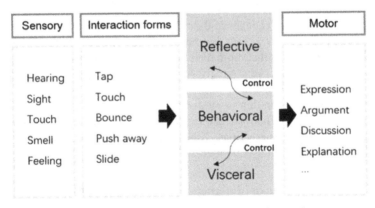

Fig. 2. A framework for translating behaviour into interaction patterns.

Currently, creating an interactive process that aligns with user perception has practical value in various future scenarios. Although there is a foundation for multimodal interaction development in China, few teams have focused on exploring the "product-user" perception aspect of multimodal interaction. Therefore, this study uses user behavior observation and the optimized guidance framework shown in Fig. 2 to transform human behavior patterns into interactive functions that combine visual and tactile senses, thereby expanding the information transmission channel. This is an attempt to innovate headphone functionality.

3   Multimodal Conference Headset Design

3.1   Visual-Tactile Sensory Modes Introduced into the Headset

In this design, our goal is to utilize tactile vibration and visual lighting as the primary mechanisms for transmitting information through the headphones. Additionally, the headphones are designed to be multitasking, portable, and adaptable to different environments, to facilitate clear expression across various scenarios. Since most interactive expressions involve both sound and visuals, the contextual description of visual elements tends to be static, which significantly limits information transmission when people are in motion [14].

In summary, there are three design objectives specifically for the mobile office environment:

- A. Immediate feedback should be provided, particularly in a mobile office setting. By carefully observing the audience's body language and distinguishing between positive and negative expressions, specific behavioral cues can be identified. For example, frequent leg shaking may indicate impatience. These body language cues can be reflected through visual indications such as different frequencies of light flashes, varying intensities of vibration, and changes in the brightness of light in interactive mode. This combined immediate feedback can prevent information from being overlooked and assist the presenter in understanding the interactive impact of the presentation (Fig. 3).

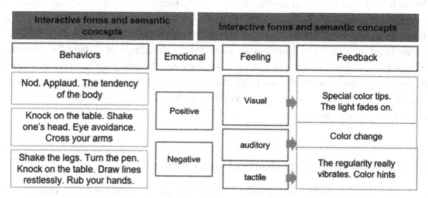

Fig. 3. A guiding framework for translating behaviour into interaction patterns.

- B. This point highlights the importance of visually representing the presenter's actions to effectively communicate various information. Given the constraints of virtual meetings, it is essential to offer more intuitive feedback through visual, auditory, and tactile methods. This alerts the presenter to the audience's responses selectively. Furthermore, as illustrated in Fig. 4, creating tactile vibrations of different frequencies on the hands can reduce speaker overload from excessive information.

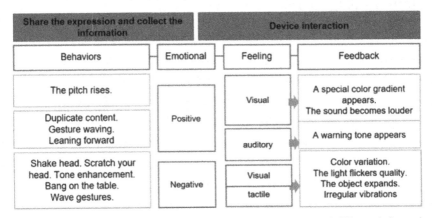

Fig. 4. Behavioural and functional transformation of the perception of different information.

- C. In the mobile context, it is crucial to consider the appropriate mode of interaction aligned with the user's intent. Mobile devices excel in receiving real-time and dynamic information. Different forms of interaction convey distinct messages, influencing various user behaviors. This research project gathered diverse insights on user behavior through focus group discussions, as illustrated in Fig. 5. The objective is to integrate natural interactive behaviors into the design of intelligent devices. Whether through visual, auditory, or tactile changes in frequency, these interactions effectively convey meanings such as "warning" or "prompt". Some interactive forms follow traditional conventions (depicted in the left image), while others deliberately reconstruct symbols (shown in the right image). For instance, the action of "lifting" traditionally signifies checking the time, but now it symbolizes "waking up" in product design. Additionally, user feedback was used to extract different frequency patterns that signify the level of urgency, and the brightness of light was utilized to represent the amount of information.

3.2 Multimodal Conference Headset Using Process

The prototype smart earphone product for multimodal conferences was connected to the conference software using a simulated connection cable and was technically constructed using Arduino accessories (see Fig. 6). The online software's message area

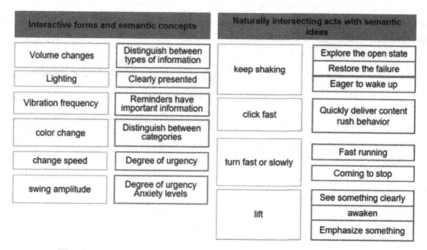

Interactive forms and semantic concepts		Naturally intersecting acts with semantic ideas	
Volume changes	Distinguish between types of information	keep shaking	Explore the open state
Lighting	Clearly presented		Restore the failure
			Eager to wake up
Vibration frequency	Reminders have important information	click fast	Quickly deliver content rush behavior
color change	Distinguish between categories		
change speed	Degree of urgency	turn fast or slowly	Fast running
			Coming to stop
swing amplitude	Degree of urgency Anxiety levels	lift	See something clearly
			awaken
			Emphasize something

Fig. 5. Natural interactions and interpretation of human behavior.

conveys information to the first speaker through the earphones' visual changes and tactile vibrations. When the discussion involves ten or more users ($\geq$10 people), the device starts "vibrating" to draw the speaker's attention to online "questions". At this time, the "lights" on the outside of the earphones gradually illuminate, encouraging others to join the discussion (see Fig. 7). In the future, the earphone system will smoothly convey online listeners' questions to the presenter in a complete, low-interference manner that is comfortable and does not interrupt the presentation.

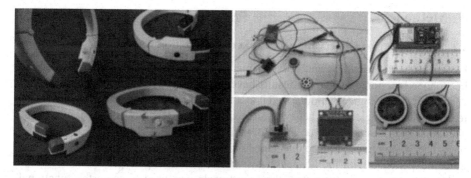

Fig. 6. Details.

When giving a presentation, the speaker can enable the high-intensity discussion mode by long-pressing the button on the left earphone. In this mode, the speaker's focus is not on the online discussion area. The earphone will vibrate continuously and the light will gradually brighten when there is a high volume of discussion on a specific question. This notifies the speaker about the intensity of the ongoing discussion. Moreover, the speaker can activate the earphone camera to live stream the details of their surroundings from a first-person perspective. This innovative feature of the earphones enables remote presentation from varied and unique viewpoints. The specific instructions for using this feature are detailed in the diagram below.

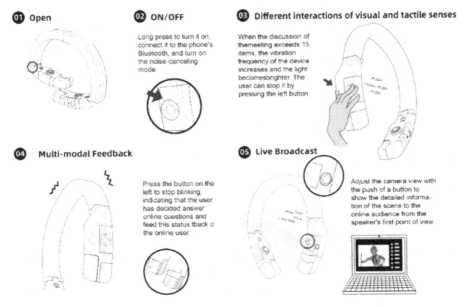

Fig. 7. Using progress.

4   Method

4.1   User Behavior Observation and Likert Satisfaction Analysis

Expert evaluation is a fast and efficient method. A professional group will score the headphone functionality, and the results have practical and practical evaluative significance [15]. The designers summarized it as a scenario observation method, which is key to observing the logic behind behavior and exploring the usability of natural interaction. This time, real feelings were obtained in unfamiliar scenarios for the users. 28 participants had 30 min to experience the headphone system, allowing 10 participants to have a deep experience with the headphones (with a focus on "prompt form", "comfort", and "operation time"). After that, the Likert scale was used to score the functionality innovation [16], environmental compatibility, comfort, and multimodal coordination dimensions. This scale aims to confirm participants' satisfaction with the use of smart headphones and their views on the product [17].

4.2   Participants and Procedure

The experiment was conducted in an office setting. Before the start of the experiment, participants were informed about the purpose of the data (Table 1). A total of 28 participants, consisting of 12 females and 16 males, were invited from the Haizhu, Tianhe, and Yuexiu districts of Guangzhou city (12F, 16M, Average = 32.45). All participants had prior experience with issues related to office product usage, online meeting communication, and perception of interactive modes. To analyze the different behaviors of the 28 participants, three observation factors were constructed using the obtained data: Participants were informed in detail about the methods for using the prototype, including the office experience in mobile scenes, the user experience of new products, and the communication frequency in mobile scenes. They had 40 min to use and record their observations. After that, the Likert scale questionnaire was collected and user feedback was organized. Among the participants, 10 of them continued to have an in-depth experience for 2 days, totalling 23 days. After the experience, ten Likert scale satisfaction scores were collected, focusing on four aspects: human-machine consistency, environmental compatibility, user comfort, and multimodal interaction coordination. The emphasis was on the new ways of visual and tactile prompts and the coordination between the product and the environment, and whether they affected people's satisfaction with receiving online information.

Table 1. Descriptive statistics for the sample of participants.

Type	Options	Frequency	Percentage(%)
Gender	Female	16	57.14
	Male	12	42.86
i. The experience of having a meeting in an out-of-office scenario is bad	Yes	25	70.00
	No	3	30.00
ii. Poor interaction with online users	Yes	27	96.42
	No	1	3.58
iii. Smart products are often used in the office to interact with others	Yes	23	82.14
	No	5	17.86
Total	/	28	100

5 Result and Data Analysis

5.1 Expert Evaluation Results

In this evaluation, 4 experts and practitioners in industrial design were invited to assess the following elements (Fig. 8):

1. Function innovation: Addressing noise challenges in complex mobile office settings, particular emphasis was placed on the speaker's perception function, with a focus on utilizing light gradients and varying frequency vibrations.
2. Environmental compatibility: The color scheme is in line with everyday headphones, while the structure emphasizes the professional image of office headphones.

3. User comfort: The product prides itself on a simple design, moderate size, and easy storage.
4. Multi-modal coordination: For younger users, learning is facilitated through familiar light prompts and vibration frequency, engaging visual and tactile senses to transform the behavior of disregarding irrelevant information into interactive operations.

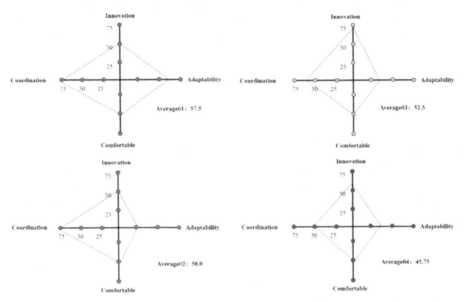

Fig. 8. Expert assessment of radar charts

5.2 Likert Satisfaction Scale Data Evaluation

According to the Likert scale, the participants' attitudes towards interaction innovation, environmental adaptability, and usability/interaction consistency were divided into 8 experience questions, ranging from "strongly disagree" to "strongly agree" and marked as 1 to 5, as shown in Table 2. Questions 1 (Mode = 4, Average = 4.25) and question 2 (Mode = 5, Average = 4.46) determine the usability and practicality of this product. Questions 7 and 8 determine the level of mastery of the combination of visual and tactile information transmission. Although most participants indicated that they needed some time to adapt (question 5, Mode = 3, Average = 3.93), they were able to quickly understand the specific meaning of online information transmission from the new pattern combination (question 2, Mode = 3, Average = 3.93).

In this research, we utilized a one-way analysis of variance (ANOVA) to investigate the association between various levels of satisfaction. Upon assessing for variance homogeneity, we observed that certain variables did not meet the criteria for significant analysis. Table 3 demonstrates a noteworthy correlation ($P < 0.05$) between "comfort of wearing" and "environmental compatibility", which can influence user satisfaction.

Table 2. Statistics table of questions related to user attitudes.

Questions	Q1	Q2	Q3	Q4	Q5	Q6	Q7	Q8
Average	4.25	4.36	4.11	4.46	3.93	4.39	4.32	4.04
variance	.752	.678	.832	.508	.979	.629	.612	.838
Mode	4.00	4.00	5.00	5.00	4.00	4.00	4.00	3.00

This is because headphones are frequently utilized as work tools and are essential for outdoor use, as they can be adapted to diverse environments. Furthermore, the interactive mode was deliberately designed to not draw excessive attention from others, thereby ultimately enhancing user integration into their work environment.

Table 3. Descriptive statistics for environmental comfort.

Title		The sum of squares	Degrees of freedom	Mean	F	P
Q3. Using equipment outside with a lot of people watching me. (1:uncomfortable-5:comfortable)	between groups	6.287	3	2.096	4.059	.018

No correlation was found between participants' perception of innovation in the appearance of this product and innovation in the modal combination, as indicated in Table 4. However, a definite relationship was observed between the addition of vibration mode and user satisfaction ($P < 0.05$). This is attributed to people's heightened sensitivity to vibrations, with different frequencies of vibrations being able to quickly capture their attention, making it more noticeable and quicker than traditional sound prompts.

Table 4. Descriptive statistics of experiences.

Title		The sum of squares	Degrees of freedom	Mean	F	P
Q2. I can feel the vibration of the headphones and need to adjust the reporting effect. (1:no-5yes)	between groups	4.268	2	1.134	3.275	.062

5.3 Descriptive Statistics and User's Participation Behavior

In addition, the experiment invited 10 participants (F = 5, M = 5) and collected 42 suggestions after a 21-day experience. After categorizing the keyword distribution using Excel2022, two directions of suggestions emerged: "function combination efficiency" and "learning cost". U5 and U6 participants expressed the need for more feedback to validate the efficiency of communication during use. When asked about suggestions for the operation process of using the conference smart earphones, U10 mentioned that the conference smart earphones are an interesting new thing, especially being able to have meetings outside and share more details with others from their own perspective, like live streaming. At the same time, U7 mentioned that the innovative use of touch to indicate the intensity of discussions is exciting, and they are looking forward to the product being launched in the market. However, U4 is concerned that they might not be able to focus enough on the meeting during use, and the combination of photography and video functions might increase the learning curve for older individuals. On the other hand, U1, U2, U3, and U9 users all agreed that the timely reminders for discussions are helpful, and U7 and U8 users suggested optimizing the ergonomics of wearing the earphones, considering future use for people with cervical spine problems.

Overall, all participants were willing to use the headphone system for office use. During the testing period, the smart headphone system met users' expectations well (Fig. 9). The results indicate that the conference smart headphone system effectively facilitates users in obtaining key information and enabling real-time interaction in a mobile environment.

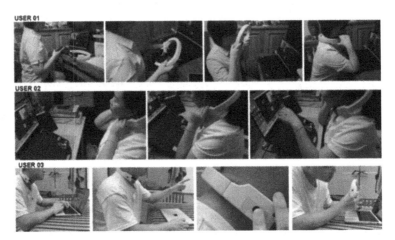

Fig. 9. Participants experience the process of smart headsets

Based on the feedback from 10 users with deep experience, they expressed a high level of curiosity and provided some suggestions. For example, users u1, u2, u3, u4, u6, and u10 mentioned that more feedback from users is needed to effectively evaluate the new product for iteration. In question 2 (Min = 4; Max = 5; SD = 0.502), the lowest score was 4. Two participants believed that the vibration of the smart earphone during meetings can quickly and intuitively inform users about what they need to pay attention to. However, there is a higher initial learning cost for using vibration compared to regular volume prompts. Lastly, in question 4, four participants highlighted the value of real-time feedback in practical applications (Min $= 3$; Max $= 5$; $\mu = 4.00$). Users perceived the product to have strong portability ($\mu = 4.20$).

6 Discussion

The findings suggest that translating user actions into tactile rhythms and using light patterns to convey information is effective. Participants were able to perceive information through sound and tactile vibrations, understand the importance of information, and engage with online content without text prompts. Different light patterns effectively indicated the popularity of online discussions without disturbing others in the same space. The introduction of a camera aided participants in quickly displaying current details during movement. However, the difficulty of perceiving new interaction forms may vary with age groups. The new interaction method of smart headphones compensates for this deficiency and enhances user satisfaction in mobile scenarios.

In summary, this design innovation offers a unique way of displaying information in daily life, leisure activities, and work. The focus on core office needs in mobile computing takes a multimodal interactive approach, combining multiple channels for receiving information and enhancing user satisfaction with conference headphones.

By incorporating user feedback, intelligent headphones have transitioned from entertainment and office tools to interactive devices. They establish emotional connections among remote workers, enhance social interactions, and expand information display beyond traditional headphones. Tactile interaction and camera technology address the limitations of traditional office social interactions, allowing for more natural expression. Due to the pandemic, we couldn't conduct extensive validation activities and interviews, resulting in a limited participant number. As a first-generation prototype, integration with multiple online meeting software was not possible, leading to some missing evaluation data. Prototype testing with core users is planned for the future to gather feedback.

Despite pandemic challenges, on-site observations and scale analysis show that the smart conference earphones are suitable for various scenarios and effectively assist users in mobile office settings, with valuable implications for multimodal interaction in smart products for mobile office use.

Disclosure of Interests. It is Now Necessary to Declare Any Competing Interests or to Specifically State that the Authors Have no Competing Interests. Please Place the Statement with a Third-Level Heading in 9-point Font Size Beneath the (Optional) Acknowledgements (If EquinOCS, our proceedings submission system, is used, then the disclaimer can be provided directly in the system.)

References

1. Fu, X.: Research on the optimization of English teaching mode in multimodal universities. China Electr. Power Educ. **2014**(08), 247–248 (2014)
2. Steinicke, F., Lehmann-Willenbrock, N., Meinecke, A.L.: A first pilot study to compare virtual group meetings using video conferences and (immersive) virtual reality. In: Proceedings of the 2020 ACM Symposium on Spatial User Interaction (SUI 2020), pp. 1–2. Association for Computing Machinery, New York, NY, USA (2020). Article 19. https://doi.org/10.1145/338 5959.3422699
3. Hao, T., He, R., Yin, L., Ma, K.: Fault expression of the household sweeping robot based on emotional interaction. Packag. Eng. (02), 98–105+115 (2022). https://doi.org/10.19554/j. cnki.1001-3563.2022.02.013
4. Sears, A., Lin, M., Jacko, J.: When computers fade: pervasive computing and situationally induced impairments and disabilities (2003)
5. Lin, S., Huang, R.: Research on product sound perception based on multimodal sensory user experience. Ornament (08),102–105 (2019). https://doi.org/10.16272/j.cnki.cn11-1392/ j.2019.08.023
6. Xu, J., Xi, T.: Research on interactive digital art based on multimodal sensory theory. Ind. Des. (03), 97–99 (2018)
7. Kuber, R., Sear, A.: Towards developing perceivable tactile feedback for mobile devices (2011)
8. Yuan, F.: Research on the interaction design of small household appliances suitable for aging based on multi-channel behavior characteristics. Nanjing University of Science and Technology (2017)
9. Berrett, J.: Augmented assistive technology: the importance of tailoring technology solutions for people living with dementia at home (2022)
10. McDaniel, T.L., Krishna, D.S.: Using tactile rhythm to convey interpersonal distances to individuals who are blind (2009)
11. Moss, J., Scisco, J., Muth, E.: Simulator sickness during head mounted display (HMD) of real world video captured scenes. Proc. Hum. Factors Ergon. Soc. Ann. Meet. **52**(19), 1631–1634 (2008). https://doi.org/10.1177/154193120805201969
12. Hu, H., Zhou, Z., Jin, Y.: Research on the design of teaching aids for school-age children from the perspective of multimodal interaction. Design **11**, 88–91 (2021)
13. Yang, D., Zhang, C., Zhang, J.: Multi-channel perception and behavior of the elderly based on embodied cognition. Packag. Eng. **43**(14), 122–128 (2022). https://doi.org/10.19554/j.cnki. 1001-3563.2022.14.014
14. Maćkowski, M., Brzoza, P., Spinczyk, D.: An alternative method of audio-tactile presentation of graphical information in mathematics adapted to the needs of blind (2023)
15. Yao, Y., Lou, J., Huang, G., Li, X., Li, Y.: Digital-Pen: an interactive system for correcting writing posture of primary school students. In: Göbl, B., van der Spek, E., Baalsrud Hauge, J., McCall, R. (eds.) Entertainment Computing – ICEC 2022. ICEC 2022. LNCS, vol. 13477, pp. 342–353. Springer, Cham (2022). https://doi.org/10.1007/978-3-031-20212-4_28
16. Lewis, J.R.: Measuring perceived usability the CSUQ, SUS, and UMUX (2018)
17. Qi, L.: Statistical analysis and fuzzy comprehensive evaluation of Likert scale. Shandong Sci. **19**(2), 7 (2006). https://doi.org/10.3969/j.issn.1002-4026.2006.02.006

Author Index

J. Wei and G. Margetis (Eds.): HCII 2024, LNCS 14738, pp. 315–316, 2024.
https://doi.org/10.1007/978-3-031-60487-4